02
DEEPEST
KNOWLEDGE.

Only Veritas Prep offers dedicated specialists for every top school in your admissions package.

03
PERSONAL
ATTENTION.

With the industry-leading 4:1 client-to-consultant ratio, you know your consultant is focused on you.

04
PROVEN
RESULTS.

Our success has led applicants to rate Veritas Prep the highest of any MBA admissions consultancy.

★★★★★

Managing Editor: Travis Morgan
Editor: Lindsay Haselton
Copy Editor: Jodi Brandon
Design: George Renfro, Emily Bailey
Printing: Vision Web Press

Co-founders: Markus Moberg, Chad Troutwine

Thank you for choosing Veritas Prep to assist in your journey to business school! We know that the application process can be a daunting and life-changing decision, so we've designed this Guide with you in mind.

Many applicants may be looking only for essay tips and tricks, but success in business school admissions is not driven merely by a flashy essay. Conducting deep due diligence on each of your target schools and demonstrating academic, professional, and cultural fit with each program will be critical to crafting the kind of personal and genuine application that admissions officers are looking for.

The *2016 Essential Guide to Top Business Schools* offers insights you cannot find anywhere else:

> Insider perspectives from current students and recent alumni

> Expert insights focused on program features that students care most about

> Data-driven analysis and comparisons to peer schools

> Easily scanned headings so you can focus your attention on what matters to you

> Admissions advice from the world's leading MBA admissions experts

This Guide wouldn't be possible without the unparalleled insight of the largest and most experienced MBA admissions consulting team in the world. As you start to think about your own applications, we encourage you to take advantage of this industry-leading expertise through our personalized admissions consulting services.

For a free consultation about your individual profile and chances of admission, please reach out at **1-800-925-7737** or **www.veritasprep.com/mba-eval.**

We hope this Guide will become an essential tool in your business school pursuit.

2016
ESSENTIAL GUIDE TO TOP BUSINESS SCHOOLS

Travis Morgan
Director of Admissions Consulting

TABLE OF CONTENTS

178
Duke (Fuqua)

234
NYU (Stern)

288
Yale School of Management

206
MIT (Sloan)

260
Dartmouth (Tuck)

318
Berkeley (Haas)

GETTING THE MOST OUT OF THIS GUIDE

Deciding Where to Apply

As you determine where you want to apply, you can use the Academics, Employment & Careers, and Culture & Campus Life sections for each school. When you find aspects of a program that are particularly appealing, be sure to check out the similar programs listed at the end of each section.

Maximizing Your Campus Visits and Info Sessions

Although you'll gain many insiders' perspectives on the top schools throughout this Guide, there's no substitute for visiting campus if you have the means to do so. A campus visit will open your eyes to just how different each business school can be. Use this Guide to ask more insightful questions in your campus visit or information session. While you're there, we recommend speaking one-on-one with current students in an informal setting in addition to the formal tours and classroom visits.

Discussing with Your Recommenders

We suggest that you look closely at each school's Snapshot and other sections, determine your strengths and weaknesses compared to their admitted class, and have a frank discussion with each of your recommenders about why you're applying to each school. This way, your recommenders can emphasize stories and examples that will clearly make your case to the admissions committee.

Writing the Essays

Once you've decided which schools are the right fit for you, use the Admissions sections to find our suggestions for tackling each of the application components, particularly the essays. Applying for an MBA is not an essay-writing contest; making a compelling argument for admission based on your unique background is much more important than using fancy language.

Preparing for Your Interview

If you have received an interview invitation, congratulations! Expect to field questions about why you want to get your MBA and how the school will enable you to achieve your goals. Show how you'll contribute to campus by highlighting the student clubs and organizations in which you will get involved. Use this Guide to see how interviewing styles and questions differ from school to school.

Getting Ready for Campus Life

Were you one of the lucky few applicants to be admitted to your target school? You've made it! Now it's time to prepare for your new life on campus. Check out the Culture & Campus Life sections to learn where most students decide to live and what to expect at school. The Academics section will help you step into class with confidence on day one. Good luck!

WHAT SHOULD I LOOK FOR IN AN MBA PROGRAM?

Many candidates simply look at one or two of the business school rankings and decide where to apply to school. While the rankings can be a good start, you should dive in much deeper to determine where you will ultimately thrive. We recommend that you ask the following questions as you research your target schools:

1

Do the school's academic offerings match my goals?

Review the Academics section to determine whether the school's teaching methods match your learning style. Dive into the course offerings to see what interests you most.

2

Am I qualified to be there?

Look at class profile statistics to see how you stack up. Be wary of full GMAT ranges; a good rule of thumb is if you are 35 points or more below the school's average, you'll end up in the bottom 10% of the class. You will need a compelling reason for the admissions committee to admit you over similar candidates who are more qualified.

3

Do my target industries/companies recruit at the school? Does this program send many people into my desired field?

This can be one of the key factors in determining whether a particular program is a match for your professional goals, so don't just gloss over the Employment & Careers section. To be honest, you can probably get a job in pretty much any industry coming out of a top-tier MBA program. However, more stress and legwork may be necessary to find a job in particular industries, so you should understand the recruiting strengths and weaknesses of your target schools.

4

I'm going to be living there for two years (at most full-time programs). Am I going to thrive in the school's culture and geography?

Are you looking for a large program or a small one? Urban, suburban, or rural? U.S. or international? East Coast, Midwest, South, or West? A school where almost everyone lives together close to campus or where the student body tends to be more spread out? An academic "meat grinder" or a "two-year vacation"? A buttoned-down or more casual atmosphere? Check out our Culture & Campus Life section to experience the school from the students' perspective.

HARVARD BUSINESS SCHOOL

One of the oldest, largest, and most prestigious programs, there's no doubt HBS develops leaders.

♀ CAMBRIDGE, MA

CLASS SIZE
935

PROGRAM FOUNDED
1908

CHARACTERISTICS
LEADERSHIP, CASE METHOD, PRESTIGE

SECTIONS

HARVARD BUSINESS SCHOOL SNAPSHOT

What HBS Is Known For

Prestige. Harvard Business School (HBS) is obviously one of the most prestigious graduate business programs in the world. It's also one of the largest at around 900 students in each graduating class and—having been founded in 1908—one of the oldest. The moment you step foot on the business school campus, you know you're in a place that's steeped with Ivy League tradition. There's something like a thrill in the air to be there, and leaving the program with a Harvard degree will become part of your identity for the rest of your life. Perhaps it's best explained in terms of sheer scale: While most business schools occupy one or two buildings, the HBS campus has 34, including five on-campus residence halls and five Executive Education buildings! It's both imposing and impressive.

Leadership. Leadership is paramount at HBS, both as a key focus of the educational experience and also in the admissions process. HBS looks for evidence of leadership throughout an applicant's profile, and leadership is embedded in the DNA of the curriculum. Leadership takes many forms, however, and this diversity is reflected in the composition of each HBS section as well as the viewpoints presented during case discussions.

Shedding its elitist image. Particularly under the leadership of Dean Nitin Nohria (2010–present), the school has been seeking to shed its reputation as an exclusive institution for the privileged and entitled, and instead seeks candidates who "make a difference in the world." In speaking with MBA recruiters, we have found that HBS grads and interns still carry a bit of a reputation of entitlement, less willing to roll up their sleeves and dive into any needed task than their counterparts from other MBA programs. In the past few years, several articles have outlined class and gender gaps at the program. However, we think that the school has certainly moved in the right direction, giving it a much more open and friendly vibe. The program has diversified its student body with many more candidates coming from non-traditional backgrounds, and all the students we speak with have found their classmates to be almost unexpectedly friendly and welcoming.

What Makes HBS Different

HBS introduced the interactive case method to business education in 1925 and is one of only two top-tier MBA programs in the U.S. to use nearly 100% case method in the classroom.

The case method. You can't have a two-minute conversation about HBS without mentioning the case method. HBS introduced the interactive case method to business education in 1925 and is one of only two top-tier MBA programs in the U.S. to use nearly 100% case method in the classroom. (The University of Virginia's Darden School is the other.) MBA students will read approximately 500 cases during their two-year program. Learn more in our Academics section.

Impactful research. Harvard Business Publishing publishes hundreds of new business cases each year, used in nearly every business education institution in the world, and the *Harvard Business Review* has been dubbed "the bible of management theory" by *The Wall Street Journal*. In short, the school's impact on business is unparalleled.

Name-brand faculty. Many of today's standard practices and frameworks of business, from the balanced scorecard to Porter's Five Forces to the Innovator's Dilemma, have come from the hallowed halls of Harvard Business School. Faculty members are required to teach, so MBA students have the opportunity to directly engage with some of the greatest minds in business today.

General management education. The first-year HBS curriculum is perhaps the least flexible of any business school, requiring students to receive a broad, general management education (whether they want it or not!). However, the second year is completely open. HBS does not offer any majors, so students are encouraged to experience a wide range of elective courses to round out their MBA experience.

The section experience. Dividing a class into sections (or blocks, or clusters—pick your favorite term) is nothing new for business schools. At HBS, the class is divided into 10 sections of roughly 90 students each. The difference at HBS is that for your first year, you will take every class with your section—in the same classroom and in the same seat. (Okay, you'll get a new seat for your spring semester classes.) This means that you'll get to know every member of your section incredibly well, and much of your social life and professional networking will be section-driven. On the flipside, you may not be quite as close with the other 830 students in your class.

What's New at HBS

More women. In early 2014, Dean Nohria made a widely reported apology to women, acknowledging that at times HBS female students felt "disrespected, left out, and unloved by the school. I'm sorry on behalf of the business school," he said. "The school owed you better, and I promise it will be better." We've seen HBS make great strides in this area, even before the dean's public comments. Forty-one percent of the Class of 2016 is made up of women, leading every other top-tier MBA program except Stanford (42%) and Berkeley-Haas (43%). Harvard is also working to increase the number of women on the faculty and is sponsoring academic research on women in business. The dean vowed that 20% of protagonists in HBS cases will be women within five years, up from just 9% now. Even so, we continue to hear from some female students who do not feel fully welcome in the campus culture.

> **Forty-one percent of the Class of 2016 is made up of women, leading every other top-tier MBA program except Stanford (42%) and Berkeley-Haas (43%).**

Greater professional diversity. Over the past several years, we have seen HBS move away from the traditional consulting and finance candidates and toward a more diverse range of backgrounds. Fifty-four percent of the Class of 2013 came from consulting or finance backgrounds, and that number has been consistently lower since the Class of 2014. This change may be due to Dean Nohria's concern about the bad rap that business schools have gotten in the press and their perceived responsibility in contributing to the economic crisis, although it more likely exemplifies a trend of more young professionals applying from non-traditional industries. Nonetheless, it is likely that this trend will continue in future admissions cycles as HBS strives to diversify its classes beyond the standard business school types.

Dipping a toe into online education. We can't say that HBS's new online offering is particularly bold, but it represents a cautious acknowledgment that online learning is here to stay—even at the world's most prestigious institutions. While other schools such as Stanford, MIT, and Penn have opened up their classrooms for free to anyone through massive open online courses (MOOCs), HBS has taken a much more limited approach. Called HBX, the school's online offering includes CORe (Credential of Readiness); HBX Courses, which is starting with just one available course; and HBX live, which is a live online classroom initially available by invitation only.

CORe consists of a nine-week program for pre-MBA students who wish to take three courses covering business analytics, managerial economics, and financial accounting. We see this foray as Harvard's compromise to extend its offerings to undergraduate students interested in business without diluting its brand. Tuition is just $1,500 for the three-course program, and significant participation is required to take the final exam.

HBS Is a Good Fit for You If...

You are a proven leader. With nearly 10,000 applicants a year, HBS clearly looks for strong undergraduate academics, a good GMAT score, and stand-out professional experience. That's a given. But what sets successful applicants apart is their clear, consistent track record of leadership. Every element of your application will be viewed through this lens, so showcase your leadership skills and experience at every turn!

You aren't easily intimidated. Whether you're a professional athlete or a CPA, every HBS student takes all core classes together. This means that you'll be in accounting, finance, marketing, and other courses with people who have four years of undergraduate education in the field plus a few years more of professional experience. On top of that, classroom participation accounts for 30 to 50 percent of your grade. In the first few days of school, you may find students jockeying for "air time" in class, but after that the section will typically settle into a good rhythm. In the words of HBS professor Jim Heskett, "[HBS] is not an environment that rewards introverts. Most conversations between faculty and failing MBA students are about helping the students overcome their fears of engaging in classroom discussion, to improve the frequency of their classroom contributions." Since classroom time is spent discussing the business case, students must learn basic skills on their own in their individual study, with their learning teams of six to seven students, or with a second-year tutor if needed.

> **Classes begin and end precisely on time, so every student must be in his or her seat, ready to dive into the day's case.**

You thrive in a structured environment. HBS tends to have a much more formal culture than other top-tier business schools such as Stanford, Kellogg, and NYU Stern. The Georgian architecture on campus lends itself to an air of formality, and this extends into the classroom. Classes begin and end precisely on time, so every student must be in their seat, ready to dive into the day's case. Late arrivals, computers, side conversations, and any other distractions are strictly prohibited, creating an environment of engagement and focus that is rarely seen in other graduate schools. Adding to the formality, standing ovations are not uncommon to welcome guests or recognize a particular achievement of a student or professor. Applause also commonly follows student comments that are found to be particularly insightful.

You are a high-achieving college senior. Applications from current undergrads are welcome at Harvard Business School through its unique HBS 2+2 Program. If admitted, you will be offered an automatic deferment and enter the program after two to three years of approved professional experience.

You're coming from venture capital or private equity (PE). Seventeen percent of the HBS admitted Class of 2016 had venture capital or private equity experience prior to starting their MBA program, the highest percentage of any top B-school. Many candidates see HBS as the top school to get into private equity—and it is—but be aware that most PE recruiters are typically looking for two years of investment banking experience plus another two years of pre-MBA private equity experience. It'll be a real challenge to get a PE interview at HBS at without it.

You want to be an entrepreneur. Although people typically see Stanford as the place to be for entrepreneurs, HBS is increasingly becoming a rival in this area. Approximately 50% of HBS graduates become entrepreneurs within 15 years of graduation, with students pursuing more than 60 new ventures immediately upon graduation each year. Students have access to a wide range of resources, including the Rock Center for Entrepreneurship, the vast alumni network, and the more than 35 different professors teaching entrepreneurial management electives.

ACADEMICS AT HBS

What HBS Is Known For

A rigorous curriculum. The HBS academic experience is intense, particularly in the first year. This is no "two-year vacation"! As discussed below, students must read, analyze, and come to conclusions on two to three business cases every day across a wide variety of subjects. However, most HBS students really thrive on the intellectual challenge, and they are more than happy to help one another out when a fellow classmate is struggling.

One program, one degree. Careful not to dilute its brand name, HBS is confident that the two-year, full-time MBA is the only way to receive an immersive HBS experience. Through the years, the school has added a very profitable Executive Education program and the new online CORe curriculum, but neither of these offerings bestows a Harvard University degree. Applicants looking for a reputable one-year, part-time, executive, or online MBA program will have to look elsewhere.

The case method. A large part of being a leader is the ability to make decisions under limited information and take responsibility for one's decisions. This is really difficult! Many people are talented at analyzing situations and weighing the pros and cons, but HBS teaches you how to make decisions under time constraints and with limited information, and then to stand by those decisions.

Structured preparation. The case method puts students in key decision-making roles as they face problems taken from real-life situations. Sometimes characterized by Harvard as "participant-centered learning," the case method is built on identifying, analyzing, and then proposing recommendations for the particular business situation at hand. Students convene in their assigned Learning Team from 8:00 to 8:50 a.m. each day to review and discuss cases. Then students largely drive the classroom discussion, facilitated by the professor with pointed questions and observations.

> **Many people are talented at analyzing situations and weighing the pros and cons, but HBS teaches you how to make decisions under time constraints and with limited information, and then to stand by those decisions.**

HARVARD AT A GLANCE

APPLICANTS BY SCHOOL

With an acceptance rate of 11%, the competition at Harvard is tough.

Harvard 9,543	Stanford 7,355	Wharton 6,111	Columbia 5,799
11%	7.1%	20.7%	18.2%

◄ Percent admitted

AVERAGE GPA

Harvard	3.67	Stanford	3.74
Haas	3.62	Wharton	3.60

WOMEN

41% of the Class of 2016 is made up of women, leading every other top-tier program except Stanford (42%) and Berkeley-Haas (43%). Harvard is also working to increase the number of women on the faculty and is sponsoring academic research on women in business.

Harvard	Haas
41%	43%

Wharton	Ross & Tuck
40%	32%

NATIONALITY

Comprised of 73 nationalities, Harvard has the most internationally diverse class of any top-tier MBA program.

Countries Represented
73

OTHER NORTH AMERICA
3%

U.S. 65%

EUROPE
9%

International Citizens

ASIA
14%

CENTRAL / SOUTH-AMERICA
5%

AFRICA
3%

OCEANA
1%

GMAT SCORES

Average Score

726

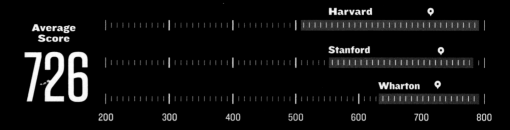

Harvard

Stanford

Wharton

200   300   400   500   600   700   800

CLASS SIZE

Harvard has the largest overall class size of any MBA program. A less intimate MBA experience translates into a huge alumni network of 80,000+ strong.

Harvard	932
Wharton	837
Columbia	749
Kellogg	652
Booth	581
Ross	455
Duke	437
Sloan	406
Stanford	406
Stern	392
Anderson	360
Yale	291
Tuck	277
Haas	252

UNDERGRAD MAJORS

Harvard has the largest percentage of STEM majors next to MIT Sloan. 20% of the Class of 2016 came from a technology/health care/bio-technology background, which is on par with STEM-heavy schools such as Stanford.

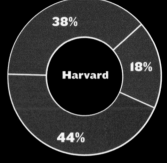

Harvard — 38% / 18% / 44% / 18%

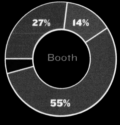

Booth — 27% / 14% / 55%

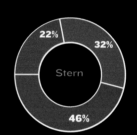

Stern — 22% / 32% / 46%

☐ **STEM**

☐ **Humanities/Social Science**

☐ **Business (Inc. Economics)**

☐ **Other**

FROM CONSULTING/FINANCE SECTOR PRE-MBA

Over the past several years, we have seen HBS move away from the traditional consulting and finance candidates and toward a more diverse range of backgrounds.

	Harvard	Columbia	Wharton
Consulting	18%	25%	20%
Finance	31%	36%	34%

Classroom participation. While different professors may adopt individual approaches, the discussions usually follow a similar format. First, the professor will begin by calling on a student (selected at random, or on the basis of geographic or industry familiarity with the subject matter) to introduce the case, by posing either an open-ended or specific question. After the introduction, the professor calls upon other students to enter the discussion. The professor may challenge anyone's comment with further questions for clarification or argument. The discussion will move in a direction aided by the professor, but ultimately will be driven by the content and conflicts identified by the students. Often at the end of class, the actual protagonist of the case—who may be quietly listening to the entire discussion—will offer his or her perspective on what actually happened. The professor will also offer his or her own thoughts and summarize the discussion. However, don't expect a lecture. The professor's summary is often five minutes or less!

A lifetime of experience. By exposing students to 90 different leadership viewpoints on two to three cases every day (approximately 500 cases over the course of the two-year program), the case method is designed to supplement graduates' personal experiences by equipping them with thousands of perspectives that may be analogous to managerial situations they will confront in their careers. The goal of the case method is to approximate a lifetime of experience, with the advantage of being able to leverage that experience at the beginning of one's career, rather than at the end.

You Oughta Know

Even though the case method gets all the attention when you talk about classes at HBS, there's plenty more "you oughta know" as you consider the program's academic offerings.

The Class of 2013 was the first class to go through the FIELD course, a program that pushes students from knowing to doing to reflecting outside of the classroom.

The field method. All first-year students in the HBS program will become involved in field-based learning that's fairly new to the HBS curriculum. The Class of 2013 was the first class to go through the FIELD course, a program that pushes students from knowing to doing to reflecting outside of the classroom. The course is split into three segments over the first year:

FIELD Foundations: Leadership Intelligence (fall term). This is the classroom component where small teams work in interactive workshops. The goal is to learn more about and reshape one's leadership style, emotional intelligence, and other skills.

FIELD 2: Global Intelligence (January Global Immersion). Just before the winter term begins in January, first-year students travel to international destinations and participate in a one-week consulting project with global companies and nonprofit organizations.

FIELD 3: Integrative Intelligence (winter term). FIELD 3 is a unique opportunity to bring leadership and other business skills together by launching a real microbusiness with your team. Each team is given a few thousand dollars in startup capital and, after 10-minute presentations, their companies begin trading on a mini stock market.

Field studies. Second-year students can opt to participate in field studies, which are typically led by teams of students (three or more) who work with a sponsoring organization. Sponsor organizations have included Disneyland, BMW, Nike, the New England Conservatory of Music, and the Children's Hospital of Boston. While "field-based learning" is just another way of saying experiential learning—or action-based learning, or practical learning, or any other business school buzzword—there is no denying that HBS puts its students in position to work with some very intriguing organizations. Deliverables may include developing a marketing strategy for a product/brand and creating a business development plan for a company. It's not uncommon for job offers to come from students' field-study projects.

Individual Student Research (ISR). Aside from the case method and field research, the other way HBS students typically complete coursework is through an independent study under the supervision of a faculty member. Students work on a wide range of projects, from small, personalized endeavors to larger projects facilitated by HBS. Research projects during the second year can be conducted individually or in groups. Frequently, HBS allows a student or group of students with curiosity (entrepreneurial or otherwise) in a particular company, industry, or market to explore that subject matter. Students can take on up to three independent projects across the two semesters of their second year, and many consider it a useful way to put into practice much of their learning from the first year. In addition, some students go on to start companies at graduation from momentum built during an individual project, sometimes with their professor as ongoing advisor or investor.

Nuts & Bolts

Sections. Your section will encompass much of your HBS experience, from academic to social to professional networking interactions. We'll expand more on the section experience in Culture & Campus Life since the section experience infiltrates nearly every aspect of the HBS culture. Regarding academics, you'll take all of your classes together in the Required Curriculum (RC) year during your first two semesters, and you have your own faculty team dedicated to the section's RC classes.

Required Curriculum (RC). Harvard has the most rigid core curriculum model of any top-tier MBA program where every student takes the full regimen of core courses together with his or her section over an entire year. The Required Curriculum (RC) year includes 10 standard "case method" courses (five per semester), plus FIELD coursework.

Elective Curriculum (EC). HBS has no majors, so students may take any classes they like in the EC year, including field studies or Individual Student Research (ISR) projects. There are 120 elective courses to choose from. For more details, see our section on the school's Popular Professors & Courses. HBS students may also enroll in courses at other Harvard graduate programs, MIT Sloan, and the Fletcher School of Law and Diplomacy at Tufts University. The most popular choices are Sloan's Entrepreneurship Lab (E-Lab) and David Gergen's leadership course at the Harvard Kennedy School (when there's space!).

Course bidding. The Elective Curriculum "bidding" process requires all students to rank their preferences from a list of courses that will be taught during the second year. Students submit a ranking of up to 60 courses, selecting from a list of about 120 offerings from the school's 10 academic units.

> **The Required Curriculum (RC) year includes 10 standard "case method" courses (five per semester), plus FIELD coursework.**

Once everyone has submitted their preferences, a computer program allocates 10 classes per student based on a complex algorithm. Extensive historic data detailing past bidding cycles is made available, and several rounds of preliminary bidding precede the final round, providing students with a fairly accurate picture of the competition for classes. Experience has shown that the top five choices are critical, popular professors are more likely to be oversubscribed than clever-sounding course titles, and the add-drop system is not a reliable fallback option for trying to get into a popular class.

Grading system. There are four possible grades for each course: Category I (best), II (middle), III (poor), and IV (fail). Grades are determined by a curve that generally gives out a "1" to up to 20% of the students in a section, a "2" to 70–80% of the students, and a "3" to 10%. There is also the possibility, though rare, of earning a "4," which is usually a precursor to academic probation. If five or more classes in the Required Curriculum (first year) result in 3s, the student will receive an academic warning and an intervention is offered in the form of coaching and tutoring.

> **Because class participation accounts for up to half of a student's final grade, most of the emphasis is placed on speaking up and "adding value" to class discussions.**

Because class participation accounts for up to half of a student's final grade, most of the emphasis is placed on speaking up and "adding value" to class discussions. In spite of the forced curve, most students are surprised at how little the competition for grades detracts from the collaborative and collegial culture at HBS. However, students must be unafraid to speak up in class. More introverted students may want to attend office hours to dive deeper into a case with their professor to show their true engagement in the course.

Grade disclosure. HBS amended its policy of prohibiting students from disclosing their grades to potential employers, a policy that began in 1998 and ended with the Class of 2007. The administration felt that "non-disclosure was inconsistent with the school's mission of developing outstanding business leaders, as much of what business leaders do is define, measure, and seek ways to enhance performance." The school's return to optional disclosure gives students the choice of letting recruiters see their grades.

Popular Professors & Courses

Professor Clayton Christensen
Building and Sustaining a Successful Enterprise (BSSE)
Author of *The Innovator's Dilemma*, Clay Christensen has been a world-renowned disruptive force himself in management education. Many HBS alums describe his course as an "absolute must." Professor Christensen's course, *Disruptive Strategy*, is the first online class available as a part of HBX Courses.

Senior Associate Dean William Sahlman
Entrepreneurial Finance
More than 8,000 students have taken Bill Sahlman's *Entrepreneurial Finance* course since its introduction at HBS in 1985. He has helped shape HBS's philosophy on entrepreneurism and helped design the RC course *The Entrepreneurial Manager*.

Professor Anita Elberse
Strategic Marketing in Creative Industries
For those interested in the media and entertainment space, Professor Elberse's (pronounced EL-ber-say) course in strategic marketing is critical. One of the youngest female faculty members at HBS, Professor Elberse is best known for her book called *Blockbusters: Hit-making, Risk-taking, and the Big Business of Entertainment*.

Professor Richard Ruback and Senior Lecturer Royce Yudkoff
Financial Management of Smaller Firms

Rick Ruback and Royce Yudkoff teach this popular course in the classroom together, now offered in up to three sections. For MBA candidates who are looking to acquire and/or operate small businesses, this class is a key part of their HBS experience. It emphasizes the fundamentals of entrepreneurship through acquisition and is a prerequisite for a winter field course that focuses on raising a search fund, *Entrepreneurship Through Acquisition.*

Similar Academic Programs

If case study is a particularly appealing part of the HBS offering, then you should also consider the following programs, which have similar academic methods and environments.

Virginia (Darden). Darden is the only other top-tier U.S. MBA program that uses the case method in nearly 100% of classes (outside of a couple of elective courses and experiential learning experiences). The program takes pride in its heavy academic rigor, and its integrated curriculum uses the same or similar cases across different courses to view situations with several different businesses lenses.

MIT (Sloan). MIT Sloan's core curriculum has just five required courses, but it's known to be one of the most rigorous of any MBA program worldwide. Quantitative analysis is emphasized, even in subjects that may seem "softer." Just two subway stops away from HBS, MIT Sloan allows its students to take up to three courses at HBS, Harvard Kennedy School, or other MIT grad schools.

INSEAD. With campuses in Fontainebleau, France (near Paris), Singapore, and Abu Dhabi, INSEAD produces dozens of original case studies each year with emphasis on global business. Its cases are second only to HBS's in popularity at business schools around the globe. Case study is also the school's most popular instructional method, but professors may go beyond the HBS-style classroom discussion by incorporating other activities and teaching techniques. INSEAD's 10- to 12-month MBA program has a strong international focus.

IESE. Ranked #7 in the *Financial Times* Global MBA Ranking 2015, IESE Business School launched the first two-year MBA program in Europe 50 years ago, modeled directly after HBS. To this day, the schools continue to hold annual Harvard-IESE Committee meetings. IESE's case method is virtually identical to that used at HBS, and it comprises about 80% of class time at the Barcelona-based school.

Western (Ivey). Canada's Ivey Business School is also totally committed to the case method, with more than 25,000 cases available on the school's website. Ivey emphasizes the cross-functional nature of its cases, requiring students to consider factors across disciplines such as finance, marketing, accounting, and so forth.

> Darden is the only other top-tier U.S. MBA program that uses the case method in nearly 100% of classes.

EMPLOYMENT & CAREERS AT HBS

What HBS Is Known For

General management. HBS is known for being a strong general management program, requiring all students to go through a full year of Required Curriculum and offering no majors or specialties. This provides every HBS student a strong general management foundation. The school places about 13% of grads into general management roles, which may not sound like much, but it's bested by only Tuck (18%) among top-tier schools.

Graduates entering general management positions

Tuck	18%
HBS & Cornell	**13%**
Yale & Haas	11%
Sloan & Anderson	10%
Kellogg, Haas, & Duke	9%
Stanford	7%

The usual suspects. Like any top MBA program, HBS sends a large percentage of grads into consulting and finance. For example, more than 50 percent of the Class of 2014 went into one of these two industries. (If you include sponsored students returning to their employers, this number may be even higher.) This number may seem awfully high, but Wharton, Columbia, and Booth send about two-thirds of their graduates into these two fields! Before the financial crisis, HBS sent as much as 45% of its class into the finance sector alone, but that number was down to just 27% last year.

Graduates entering the consulting and finance industries

Columbia	68%
Booth	64%
Stern	63%
Wharton	62%
HBS	**56%**
Kellogg	49%

Private equity. HBS is known for being a great school for getting a PE job after graduation. Of those students who were actively seeking employment, about 15% went into PE, which equates to about 100 students. By comparison, 12% of Stanford GSB job-seeking grads become private equity analysts, or just more than 30 people. Wharton sent about 9% of job seekers into PE—54 total students. One thing to note is that even at HBS, transitioning into a PE role directly out of school is incredibly difficult. Most schools will be looking for two years of pre-MBA private equity experience to get a "closed" interview spot (more on that later).

Graduates taking private equity positions

School	%
HBS	15%
Stanford	12%
Wharton	9%
Booth	6%
Tuck	4%

You Oughta Know

Diversified industry placement. At first glance, Harvard Business School's employment report doesn't look much different than those at peer schools. There are schools that send more people into finance, consulting, health care, media, technology, manufacturing, or other specialized industries. However, no other school has as much representation in all of those industries. An HBS degree will serve you well in pretty much any industry, but we've found the following "hidden gems" to be quite interesting if you're looking at your post-graduation options.

Tech is growing fast. Tech companies have been snatching up more and more graduates from top-tier MBA programs, and HBS is no exception. Through much of the past decade, about 7% of HBS grads went into the tech sector. In 2010, this number started to steadily creep up until 2013, when 18% of the Class of 2013 decided to work for a technology company. This has remained somewhat constant with 17% of the Class of 2014 placing into technology. This pales in comparison to more traditional "tech schools" on the West Coast, such as Stanford (24%), Berkeley-Haas (43%), and UCLA Anderson (28%), but it's a trend at HBS that's quite notable.

Graduates entering the technology industry

School	%
Haas	43%
UW Foster	41%
Sloan, Anderson, & Texas	28%
Stanford	24%
Ross	20%
HBS	17%

Nonprofit. At HBS? It's true! Although only about 3% of the HBS Class of 2014 went into nonprofit/government roles, that's triple the percentage of most MBA programs, which often send just 1% of the class into the field. In previous years, the only top MBA program to send a higher portion of grads into nonprofit was Yale School of Management, where one in 10 graduates pursued a nonprofit or government position. This trend is starting to spread, however, with other top-tier schools such as Stanford (6%) and Berkeley-Haas (4%) sending higher percentages of their Class of 2014 into the nonprofit sector. HBS grads who go into government or nonprofit earn $90,000 a year on average, which is lower than other industries. However, that's about $5,000 to $10,000 more per year than graduates of other schools going into similar roles.

Graduates entering nonprofit/government jobs

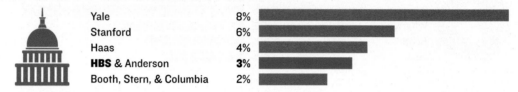

Yale	8%
Stanford	6%
Haas	4%
HBS & Anderson	**3%**
Booth, Stern, & Columbia	2%

Manufacturing. Here's another industry that you might not think of when you think about HBS. At just 5% of graduates going into the field, this certainly wouldn't seem very dominant either. However, HBS leads almost every other top-tier MBA program, including MIT Sloan (1%), and matching Kellogg (5%), both of which have prominent dual-degree programs with their engineering schools. These dual-degree candidates are huge magnets for manufacturing companies.

Graduates entering the manufacturing industry

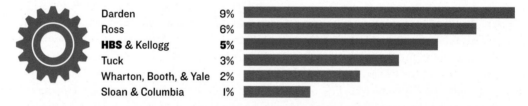

Darden	9%
Ross	6%
HBS & Kellogg	**5%**
Tuck	3%
Wharton, Booth, & Yale	2%
Sloan & Columbia	1%

Media and entertainment. Now hang on a second! Surely this has to be an area dominated by schools in big media hubs like New York and Los Angeles, right? It's true that nearly one in 10 UCLA Anderson students goes into the media/entertainment industry, more than twice the percentage from HBS. We were surprised to discover that, despite a strong media program at Columbia, that school sends just 1.6% of its MBAs into the field, while HBS sends 3% of its (much larger) class. HBS's strong reputation and large class size and the popularity of its Entertainment and Media Club (175 students strong) mean that it can attract many of the biggest names, including Disney, Warner Bros., Sony, Bertelsmann, and others.

Graduates entering media and entertainment jobs

UCLA Anderson	7%
Stern	6%
Yale	5%
Stanford	4%
HBS	**3%**
Wharton & Columbia	2%

Salaries. It's no secret that candidates go to business school to increase their earning potential. The median base salary for HBS grads across all industries is $125,000. Almost three-quarters of candidates receive some kind of signing bonus, and about one in five will receive a guaranteed bonus (with the highest concentration in specialty finance positions such as hedge funds, PE, and investment management). You have to be a bit careful when looking at overall median salary numbers because they can be skewed by high salaries in particular industries. Schools that send fewer students to those industries can be at a disadvantage. Industry-by-industry, HBS grads command slightly lower salaries than Stanford GSB grads, slightly higher salaries than their counterparts at Wharton and Columbia, and—perhaps surprisingly—about the same salaries as those at Kellogg, except in finance, where Kellogg grads make less.

Class of 2014 salaries by sector in thousands

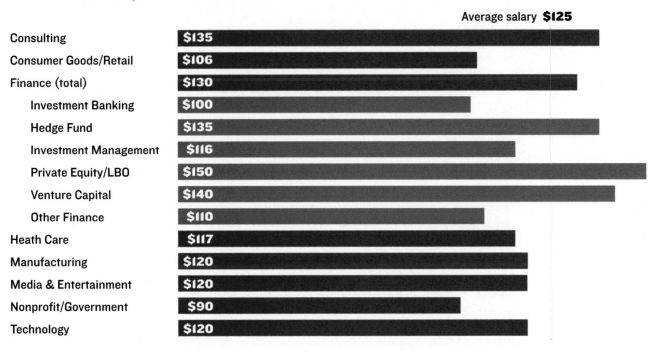

Average salary **$125**

Consulting	$135
Consumer Goods/Retail	$106
Finance (total)	$130
Investment Banking	$100
Hedge Fund	$135
Investment Management	$116
Private Equity/LBO	$150
Venture Capital	$140
Other Finance	$110
Heath Care	$117
Manufacturing	$120
Media & Entertainment	$120
Nonprofit/Government	$90
Technology	$120

Geography and mobility. Even top-rated business schools tend to place the majority of their graduates close to home. While this is often a result of stronger relationships with employers in a school's region, graduates often choose to attend a business school where they ultimately wish to live post-MBA. Most schools have mobility and strong alumni networks across the country and globally, but applicants would be wise to consider placement statistics by location when considering which schools to target.

Class of 2014 who remained in the region after graduation

Similar Programs for Professional Opportunities

Yale School of Management (SOM). Strictly by the numbers, Yale School of Management is the most similar to HBS in terms of the industries its students pursue and the geographies to which they locate after graduation. With each SOM class comprising approximately 300 students, it may be surprising to see that the school has such breadth, but this is a point in which it takes great pride. The one point of departure is that Yale SOM sends more than double the percentage of grads into nonprofit than HBS does, and a surprisingly large percentage (6%) of grads into the energy sector.

Dartmouth (Tuck). Like HBS, Tuck also prides itself on a strong general management curriculum. As such, it sends a relatively large number of students into general management positions upon graduation. Many applicants may not realize that Tuck is quite a "finance school," with 25% of grads headed into the industry each year.

Stanford GSB. As much as these two programs try to differentiate from each other, their recruiting profile is quite similar in a number of ways. Among the top-10 MBA programs, Stanford sends the fewest into consulting and finance, at just 45% of the class. GSB sends 12% of its class into private equity and another 5% into venture capital, which is quite a feat. Despite Stanford's location in Silicon Valley, its distinct advantage in technology recruiting has narrowed in recent years. Stanford sends nearly one-quarter (24%) of its class into the tech sector, while Harvard now sends 17% of its class—which is nearly double the size—into the industry.

> **Among the top-10 MBA programs, Stanford sends the fewest into consulting and finance, at just 45% of the class.**

Virginia (Darden). We've found that Darden often gets left off many applicants' shortlists, likely because of geography, but given its general management case method curriculum, it comes as no surprise that its employment profile is remarkably similar to HBS's. A similar percentage of Darden graduates go into general management roles (10%) as do HBS grads (13%), although fewer students pursue finance careers. Interestingly, Darden also places a comparatively high percentage of its graduates into the manufacturing industry (9%) as does Harvard (5%). Like HBS, about a third of the class pursues consulting or strategy roles. Overall, however, starting salaries at Darden are a bit lower. Consulting salaries are roughly the same, but other industries offer Darden grads about $10,000 less than HBS salaries across the board.

CULTURE & CAMPUS LIFE AT HBS

What HBS Is Known For

An unparalleled campus. As we mentioned at the beginning of this Guide, the Harvard Business School campus is in its own league. No other school even comes close. A 40-acre campus unto itself, HBS is a veritable village of some of the most brilliant minds in business today. With several project rooms, students services, and a well-reviewed food court, the Spangler Center is a major hub of student activity. The three-story, 118,000-square-foot Shad Hall houses the most impressive gym facility dedicated specifically to business school students and faculty that we've seen. Students at most other MBA programs must sweat it out with their undergraduate compatriots in standard university facilities.

Residence campus experience. At most MBA programs, the vast majority of students live in off-campus apartments, trekking to campus for classes, study groups, and events each day. Not so at HBS. Eighty percent of the student body lives on campus in five on-campus, dormitory-style residential buildings or in nearby university-operated apartments. In fact, the dorms are so popular that students must enter a lottery to get a spot. By living and studying on campus, HBS students are perhaps more insulated from their surrounding community than students of many other top programs who live in apartments throughout their community. While the residence halls have some social activities, the sections are a much bigger driver of social life at HBS. Recent students have mentioned that the university apartments are friendly enough to say hi to your neighbors in the halls, but there isn't much in the way of socializing.

Sections. Sections are a driving force at HBS, particularly in the RC year. Each section has a social chair who is in charge of planning official section events, which are typically held at least once a week. There are also lots of informal gatherings arranged over the section e-mail listserv and just by talking to people after class. Second year is a bit more mixed: Some sections are really tight knit and still hang out all the time; others break apart a bit more and people end up hanging out with friends they make in classes. Since 2010, both RC and EC sections compete in the HBS SA (Student Association) Cup, a year-long competition that involves intramural sports, single-day competitions, and the RC Olympics. The competition is fierce, and bragging rights are envied by all!

A formal classroom environment. MBA programs tend to have a certain "vibe" on campus, and HBS's vibe is more formal than most. As we touched on in the HBS Is a Good Fit for You If... section, classes start and end precisely on time, with students expected in their seats and prepared to receive a "cold call" question to kick off the day's case. Sections remain in the same classroom for the entirety of the RC year. Just as HBS students may cross-register for electives in other programs, HBS elective courses also have students from other Harvard graduate programs. Even though they are incredibly accomplished in their own right, these students often find the HBS case method and classroom environment quite intimidating. The difference in culture has been particularly noted by students from the Harvard Graduate School of Education (HGSE, an acronym affectionately pronounced "Hugsy" for its student body's warm and friendly reputation).

> **Eighty percent of the student body lives on campus in five on-campus, dormitory-style residential buildings or in nearby university-operated apartments.**

You Oughta Know

Most students get deeply involved in a leadership position in at least one club, with additional involvement in one or two more.

Student organizations. Per capita, HBS may have fewer clubs and organizations than many MBA programs, but in our opinion, roughly 80 clubs is more than enough for any business school student to choose from. Most students get deeply involved in a leadership position in at least one club, with additional involvement in one or two more. Others may instead get more deeply involved in a leadership position within their section. We'll note that this represents significantly less extracurricular involvement than at MBA programs that are known to be more "student led," such as Kellogg, Stern, Anderson, and Ross, where involvement in clubs, conferences, competitions, student committees, and other activities often overshadows the academic experience. Students at these programs (and others) may easily find themselves overcommitted in eight to 10 different extracurricular organizations or more!

Beyond organizations. At HBS, life outside the classroom is driven far more by the sections and informal groups of students with similar interests. Beyond section activities, aspiring entrepreneurs may grab beers and brainstorm business ideas, the nonprofit folks will organize volunteering opportunities together, the finance people break off to do their thing, and so forth.

Popular hangouts. The most popular hangouts for HBS students tend to be Harvard Square bars and restaurants, followed by Central Square locations. Still the most popular bar for students to meet up late-night in Harvard Square is Hong Kong (known as "The Kong") on the second and third floors. Students are more likely to "cross the river" and go into Boston on the weekends.

Informal excursions. Many HBS students love to get out of town for the weekend. In fact, a number of ECs (second-year students) will travel every weekend of the school year to various exotic locations. As one member of the Class of 2013 mentioned, "In my opinion, coming from a guy who lived in Boston prior to school, I think HBS-ers miss out on a lot of what Boston has to offer by not exploring more into the city. But, I think this has a lot to do with students wanting to hang out with each other and the most convenient way to do so is in Cambridge (Harvard Square). That, and students travel to various places on group trips a lot of the weekends." Considerable press coverage has recently arisen about differences between economic classes at HBS, and extravagant excursions can be part of this apparent divide.

Membership fees are likely a contributing cause of the relatively light extracurricular club involvement at HBS.

Expenses. Beyond tuition and living expenses, travel breaks tend to be the largest driver of additional expenses. Students also pay dues to their section of about $200 per year to cover social events, retreats, uniforms for intramural sports, and other expenses. Most clubs charge a membership fee of $100 or less that includes the cost of various events and conferences. Most other schools use tuition dollars to provide budgets to sections and student clubs, although students typically must pay for attendance at conferences or out-of-town events. These membership fees are a likely contributing cause of the relatively light extracurricular club involvement at HBS compared to some peer schools.

Similar Programs Culturally

Virginia (Darden). Not only does Darden use the case method almost exclusively, but it also has a more formal atmosphere that's similar to HBS's. Darden's vibe has been described as more "blue blazer, gold button" country club, as opposed to some schools that have a much more casual, occasionally even "frat house"–like feel to them.

Penn (Wharton). Wharton's MBA program has a large student body at nearly 1,700 total students, second only to HBS. Add to that another 2,500 undergrads at Wharton, and you have a very large business school. As such, the school tends to attract candidates with assertive personalities who will forge their own path and need minimal hand-holding through the two-year program.

Columbia. Located in the Morningside Heights neighborhood in Manhattan, Columbia's culture is unmistakably "New York." Another large program, at 1,500 MBAs, Columbia tends to foster a culture of students who are not afraid to speak up, question authority, or seek change if they see areas for improvement around them. Once known for its extremely sharp-elbowed and win-at-all-cost culture (not uncommon on Wall Street), the school has focused on developing a more collaborative community over the past few years. Its downtown rival, NYU Stern, is still seen as more collegial, but Columbia simply isn't the same cutthroat community it may have been five or 10 years ago.

Chicago (Booth). The most distinguishing factor of Chicago Booth's culture is intellectual curiosity. Professors are not afraid to ask students to pull out calculators and do some calculus in class, and students are encouraged to question everything, even their professors and one another. So even though the school does not use a 100% case study method, you tend to get more intellectual sparring and debating in the Booth classroom than at its rival to the north, Kellogg, where Booth students assume every class begins and ends with an inspiring rendition of "Kumbaya" (hand-holding required).

Stanford GSB. While these schools differ in many respects, more than half of Stanford's first-year MBA students live together on-campus at the Schwab Residential Center. This provides a residence campus experience similar to HBS's, a dynamic found at few other full-time MBA programs.

ADMISSIONS AT HBS

What HBS Is Looking For

There's no big secret about what HBS looks for in candidates. HBS posts its criteria right on its website, and you should take its word for it. Without clearly demonstrating all three criteria—a habit of leadership, analytical aptitude and appetite, and engaged community citizenship—you'll be climbing up a very steep hill to be admitted. The trick is in how to demonstrate these elements in HBS's short application.

> **Without clearly demonstrating all three criteria—a habit of leadership, analytical aptitude and appetite, and engaged community citizenship—you'll be climbing up a very steep hill to be admitted.**

Habit of leadership. Professional leadership experience is the most common and transferable to the business school experience, but extracurricular, personal, and community leadership accomplishments and qualities are certainly recognized as well.

Analytical aptitude and appetite. While HBS does not state a preferred major or career path, it demands a comfort with and aptitude for quantitative and analytical subjects, and strong communication skills. Intellectual capacity is best demonstrated through academic transcripts and the GMAT or GRE score. Don't be fooled by the wide range of GMAT scores listed in HBS's class profile each year. We estimate that nearly 90% of the admitted class has a GMAT score of 700 or higher. However, lower scores in these categories can be compensated through remarkable professional or community leadership experiences in a few rare circumstances.

Engaged community citizenship. This element is as simple as it sounds: HBS is looking for people who have shown the ability to impact their communities and who will continue to do so both as students and alumni. While this can be demonstrated in a host of settings and ways, paramount is a sincere commitment to helping others, viewed as an integral component of the responsibilities of leadership.

It is often said that HBS looks for the next generation of multinational CEOs, while Stanford looks for the next generation of world-changing entrepreneurs. We think the difference here is overstated, but this is still a good measure for the caliber of candidates both schools are seeking to admit. Most importantly, Harvard Business School is looking to build a class of 900+ students where every member will offer a different perspective to the classroom, contribute richly to the campus community, and make a distinct impact on the world as an alumnus.

Preparing to Apply

Reading this Essential Guide is a great first step in your preparation. Hopefully, this insider's glimpse has been helpful in understanding the most important aspects of the school. However, nothing can replace gaining firsthand knowledge and experience yourself.

 If you are looking for tips on 2016–17 admissions essays, you're in luck! Check out our website at **veritasprep.com/hbs** for our latest advice.

Reach out to current students. Even if you don't have any personal connections to HBS, you can reach out to current students and get their insight and advice. On the school's Activities, Government, and Clubs page, you'll find a list of all campus clubs. Find a few clubs that fit your interests and reach out to the officers. Remember: These are very busy MBA students so you don't want to intrude too much on their time, but you could ask for a 10- to 15-minute conversation or elicit some advice via e-mail. If you're planning to visit campus, perhaps you might even arrange a coffee chat or lunch, if they are available. Officers of major clubs like the Finance or Management Consulting Club have plenty of responsibilities. You might provide a quick background introduction and ask if there's another member of their club who might be able to offer some insights and advice about his or her HBS experience.

Visit campus. If you have the means, we highly recommend you visit the Harvard Business School campus along with a handful of others to understand the significant differences in culture, teaching style, student body, recruiting opportunities, and facilities. A campus visit does not directly impact your admissions chances in any way, but you will be surprised by just how different each school can be. We encourage you to take advantage of the formal campus visit program, including a class visit, campus tour, information session, and student lunch, as available. However, we also encourage you to go to the Spangler Center, grab a bite to eat in the cafeteria, and talk to a few current students informally. The formal program gives a good surface-level experience of HBS, but impromptu conversations can be incredibly enlightening.

Other events. We know that many applicants will not be able to fly to Boston to visit campus, but you should take advantage of other admissions events, such as information sessions, webinars, and specific-audience events. Get to know the school and its culture as well as you can, because your familiarity can shine through your application and essay to help you stand out.

> Get to know the school and its culture as well as you can, because your familiarity can shine through your application and essay to help you stand out.

You Oughta Know

When should I apply? HBS uses a standard three-round system for applications. This means that you may submit your application in any of its three rounds for consideration. However, 90% or more of the class will be filled with the first two rounds of applicants, so we do not encourage you to wait until the final round without compelling circumstances. Round 3 candidates will be considered alongside waitlisted candidates from the first rounds. Waitlisted candidates from Round 1 will be considered with Round 2 applicants, but we've seen a number of R1 waitlistees who were held on the waitlist again and admitted in Round 3.

Traditional applicants. If you are a traditional candidate from the management consulting or finance industry, we encourage you to apply in the first round (assuming you have a strong GMAT score), as you'll be competing against many candidates with very similar profiles. In a later round, it's possible that the school may see you as a viable candidate to the school but may have already admitted several other applicants with similar profiles, so they might pass on you to bring greater professional diversity to the class. Plus, they know you've been planning on an MBA since the day you graduated from undergrad, so there's no reason to delay!

Don't rush! Please note that even though the top schools encourage you to apply in the earliest round possible, this does not mean that you should apply with a rushed application or a mediocre GMAT score. There's no sense in applying early if you're just going to be denied. A GMAT score that's above the school's average will do more for your candidacy than applying in the first round.

2015–16 HBS APPLICATION DEADLINES

All deadlines are noon U.S. Eastern Time on the date indicated.

Round 1:
9 Sep 2015
Notification:
Dec 2015

Round 2:
6 Jan 2016
Notification:
Mar 2016

Round 3:
4 Apr 2016
Notification:
May 2016

Navigating deadlines. For the 2015–16 admissions season, the R1 deadline for HBS is September 9, 2015, an entire year before classes will start for the Class of 2018. To give you an idea of how much this deadline has crept up over the years, back in 2008 HBS's Round 1 deadline came on October 15! This means that you need to really plan on having a great GMAT score under your belt by no later than early August. Why? Because very few applicants are successful when they're writing their essays, managing their recommendation writers, and tracking down transcripts all while also trying to break 700 on the GMAT. And pulling together your applications (and doing it well) will take you at least a few weeks from start to finish.

Planning for backup schools. Many people ask us why the deadlines keep getting earlier. For admissions offices, it helps with logistics so that they can process R1 candidates before looking at R2. For applicants, there's also a big advantage. You'll receive an initial notification of your application by mid-October of whether you're being invited to interview, are being "released" (HBS-speak for being denied), or will be put into a pool for further consideration with Round 2 applicants. By mid-December, you'll receive a final decision from HBS, so you'll still have a couple of weeks to finalize applications to other schools ahead of Round 2 deadlines.

That said, we do not recommend starting your Round 2 applications only after the notifications from your Round 1 schools. Get your applications ready to submit, just in case you get a negative decision. Then, if you are not admitted, you can put final touches on the new apps and submit with confidence!

HBS 2+2. HBS 2+2 is a deferred application for current full-time students in college or graduate school. It's called 2+2 because you receive an automatic two-year deferral before your two-year MBA program. However, many 2+2 candidates are now choosing to defer for three years before starting school. To apply for the 2+2 program this year, you must graduate from your institution between October 1, 2015, and September 30, 2016. The eligibility of graduate students in the 2+2 program is a new addition, but grad students must have gone directly from their undergrad program into graduate school without any work experience in between. HBS 2+2 candidates must apply in the same rounds as all other applicants. However, since 2+2 candidates are applying for the Class of 2020, you aren't competing against the vast majority of applicants aiming to start next fall. As such, there is little advantage to applying in an earlier round, nor a significant disadvantage for applying in Round 3. Instead, you should plan to apply in the round that fits best with your life plans and schedule. You'll still receive your admissions notification on the same time line as all other candidates, so if you apply earlier, you'll be able to plan ahead better.

The Online Application Form

As you're about to see, we've dedicated a lot of space in this Essential Guide to our advice on HBS's online application, and you should view this as an indicator of its importance. As HBS has slimmed down its essays, it has moved some information into the online application instead, so don't treat this lightly. This form contains the most information used by the admissions board member to determine your fate! Much of the online form includes standard biographical information, so we'll comment only on sections where we feel we can add value or provide clarification.

Family. As much as HBS is looking to diversify its class, legacy still matters. HBS has one of the few applications that asks directly whether you have family members who attended the school.

Not to worry: The vast majority of admits have no family legacy, so don't feel an obligation to spin your great-uncle's overnight stay in Cambridge 20 years ago into a family connection. If you have a partner/spouse/significant other who is also applying, be sure to list that person here. To be honest, there's no real advantage to applying with someone else since the applications will be considered separately, based on their individual merits. However, there's a chance that if one of you is admitted and the other waitlisted, the admissions board might be slightly more inclined to admit you off the waitlist because they know your significant other will be headed to Boston.

Resume. Be sure that your resume highlights results and accomplishments rather than job duties. The number-one goal of your resume should be to showcase your leadership experience, so include bullet points such as "Led a team of three engineers to…, resulting in…."

Employment. The field for post-college full-time work experience means just that. Don't try to exaggerate your months of work experience by including work before or during college, or any part-time jobs. This is for accurate reporting of statistics. Note that you should calculate the number of months of expected experience before you start school—not the number of months as of today. You only have the opportunity to list your two most recent employers in this section, so other experience should be listed on your resume. Your key accomplishments will likely repeat some information from your resume, which is perfectly fine. But you have fields here to explain your role and responsibilities, the nature of the company, and your most significant challenge, so you can utilize these fields and save space on your resume for additional results and accomplishments. Salary can be used as a proxy to see your level of responsibility in your given field, but do not exaggerate! Admissions officers know that salaries vary widely based on industry, and admissions decisions are completely need-blind.

HBS used to ask you to write an entire essay about your post-MBA career goals, but it's been reduced to a couple of drop-down menus and a 500-character field. Honestly, that's probably plenty of space to explain what you want to do after graduation and what drives you to want to do it. Columbia only gives you 50 characters!

Education. The admissions board member knows what to look for in transcripts beyond just a GPA. They'll be looking at the quality and reputation of your undergraduate institution, the difficulty of your major, course workload, grades in quantitative courses, and overall trends. (For example, if your grades went up after a "fun" freshman year, that's better than crashing and burning at the end.) Note that you'll need to upload either an official or unofficial copy of your transcript, so plan ahead of time. A high-quality JPEG can be submitted, so you can take a picture of your transcript, as long as it's legible.

Given the nearly 10,000 applicants to HBS each year, the admissions board doesn't need to admit applicants with questionable undergraduate records; you're applying to Harvard, after all! However, if you had extenuating circumstances that led to underperformance in undergrad, we recommend doing three things to improve your chances: 1) Knock the GMAT out of the park and score at or above the school's average of 730 to show that you can thrive at HBS academically; 2) take some additional coursework to shore up your weaknesses (candidates often take calculus, stats, microeconomics, accounting, or finance to hit the ground running at B-school); and 3) mention the circumstances that led to underperformance in in the Additional Information section of your application. Don't try to blame others or offer a bunch of excuses, but concisely and unapologetically explain the circumstances and your reaction to them at the time. You might mention what you learned from the experience as well.

> **The vast majority of admits have no family legacy, so don't feel an obligation to spin your great-uncle's overnight stay in Cambridge 20 years ago into a family connection.**

Deep involvement in a few extracurriculars can show the admissions board how you are an "engaged citizen" (one of their three criteria), where your passions lie, and how you will give back to the community as an alum.

Extracurricular activities. Deep involvement in a few extracurriculars can show the admissions board how you are an "engaged citizen" (one of their three criteria), where your passions lie, and how you will give back to the community as an alum. They may also showcase leadership qualities that may not be apparent from your professional experience. Admissions officers know that certain professions can be extremely demanding with 100-plus-hour weeks at times, allowing for little time for additional commitments. This will be taken into consideration, but even limited involvement in an organization that benefits someone other than yourself can show that you care about more than just next quarter's bonus. If you have been involved in many different organizations, you may want to spread these out among your resume, application, and perhaps your essay, because the online form will allow you to add only three activities.

Awards and recognition. Deciding which awards to list here may say more about you than the awards themselves. Really think about which recognitions are the most important to you and why. You can always use your resume to highlight additional accomplishments.

Test scores. The school says that there's no minimum test score, and that's true. Veritas Prep admissions consulting clients have been admitted with GMAT scores in the 500s, and Harvard's released GMAT score range shows it did admit at least one candidate with a score of 510. However, let's be honest with ourselves: Any application with a GMAT score below a 690 is a significant longshot at HBS! The school says that it has no preference between the GMAT and the GRE, but don't try to hide an application weakness (such as questionable quant skills) behind a GRE score because you think it's an "easier" test. It won't work. HBS started accepting the GRE so that stellar candidates who were considering other graduate programs such as a master's degree in public policy or public health might think about a joint degree or business school instead. If your only goal is to get an MBA, your best strategy is to do whatever it takes to score well on the GMAT. The admissions board will see through other attempts of test score trickery. In the words of Thomas Edison, "There is no substitute for hard work."

Additional information. Use this section as you would an optional essay for other schools. If you have a real sore spot in your application, such as a low undergraduate GPA, then you should expect to devote some words to that here. Don't dwell on it, and don't sound like Mr. or Ms. Excuses, but do address it and move on.

The Essay

In recent years we have made much of the Great Essay Slimdown, in which many business schools cut their number of required essays or reduced word counts. Harvard went down to just one essay two years ago, so there wasn't much more slimming down the school could do, short of eliminating the essay altogether.

For years, Dean of Admissions Dee Leopold has emphasized that applying to business school is not an "essay-writing contest"; it's simply a way for admissions officers to discover and evaluate the candidates who will contribute most as members of the school's student body and ultimately as alums. With essays continuing to slim down over the years, the school is intentionally signaling that what you've accomplished and how you stand out from your peers (as shown in your resume, transcripts, online application, and recommendations) are more important than merely your essay-writing skills or storytelling abilities. However, the essay remains a vital part of the application, as it enables you to direct the admissions officer's attention to areas of your candidacy that really shine.

> **If you come from a very common background (think management consultant, investment banker, or IT consultant from Asia), then you need to stand out even more, and this essay is your chance to do it.**

It's the first day of class at HBS. You are in Aldrich Hall meeting your "section." This is the group of 90 classmates who will become your close companions in the first-year MBA classroom. Our signature case method participant-based learning model ensures that you will get to know each other very well. The bonds you collectively create throughout this shared experience will be lasting. Introduce yourself.

Now it's required. After years of slimming its essays down to the point where it had only one essay and even made it optional, HBS has changed course this year. The school has an all-new essay prompt, and it's no longer optional. The essay becoming mandatory again actually isn't huge news; in a recent blog post, the HBS Admissions Director explained that, not surprisingly, every applicant submitted a response last year. So, no point in making the essay optional and confusing the issue. There's one essay in the application (not counting the Post-Interview Reflection), and you're going to write it if you want to get into HBS.

Your overall goal. We always tell every applicant that they need to do two things to get into HBS or any other top MBA program: 1) Stand out from other applicants (especially those with similar profiles), and 2) show how you fit with the school. If you come from a very common background (think management consultant, investment banker, or IT consultant from Asia), then you need to stand out even more, and this essay is your chance to do it. If your background already makes you unusual compared to the typical HBS class profile (perhaps you have more than the typical amount of work experience or have zero quantitative abilities to point to), then you need to use this essay to demonstrate that you will fit in and thrive at Harvard. Resist the urge to go for a gimmick, but don't be afraid to let your hair down a bit. What brought you to this point in your life? What do you want to do after HBS? (Remember: Write in the voice of someone who's already gotten in.) What do you like to do outside of school and work? What gets you up in the morning? What would you say in your verbal introduction to get a laugh out of your new friends?

Be yourself. By trying to put you in the shoes of students who have already gotten in and are now introducing themselves to their classmates, HBS wants get you to write with as natural a voice as is possible. In fact, in the blog post that introduces this question, Dee Leopold urges you

to imagine "saying it out loud." Of course, you will (and should) put more thought into this essay than you would put into what few words you might say to break the ice in Aldrich Hall. The challenge is that there's a lot that you would normally emphasize in a more traditional essay ("Why an MBA? Why now? Why HBS?") that you probably wouldn't say as you're speaking to your new classmates. While in a traditional essay you might want to go on and on about how your minimal community involvement is actually something you're really passionate about, how much time would you really spend on that in a verbal introduction? So, those things need to come out in your resume, your recommendations, and—should you get that far—your admissions interview.

Choose a theme. One approach we would recommend is to think of a key theme or differentiator that defines you. Recognizing that this kind of self-reflection can be a challenge for many applicants, Veritas Prep entered into a yearlong collaboration with the publishers of the Myers-Briggs personality type assessments to develop our Personalized MBA Game Plan™ assessment tool, available free to all GMAT Prep and Admissions Consulting customers. Using your Myers-Briggs personality type, this assessment helps you analyze your own strengths and weaknesses to determine the unique ways that you may stand out from the crowd. Whether or not you utilize this resource, be very mindful of the key takeaway that you want the admissions board member to remember about you.

Essay length. Notice that they didn't ask, "What *one thing* would you like us to know about yourself?" in the prompt. You should, however, resist the temptation to tell your entire life story here. Overall, we bet that applicants will err on the side of being too formal (and too wordy!) with this essay. One way to combat this is to actually record yourself doing a verbal introduction of yourself, and then, once you have a complete draft of an essay, compare it to see how much it matches it in terms of tone and length (not necessarily in terms of exact content). If your written piece is much longer or much more formal than your verbal sample, you know you have a bit more work to do to get to what the Harvard Business School admissions committee wants to see. Resist the temptation to go beyond 1,000 words. (In fact, we expect that the best essays will be about 500 to 700 words.)

"Show, don't tell." A key strategy for MBA essay writing is "show, don't tell." Don't just tell the admissions board, "I'm a results-oriented leader who communicates a clear vision and then executes it." Anyone can make this unsubstantiated claim in an essay. Instead, use a story from your life that shows how you learned those skills, perhaps by trial and error. Be sure to use some examples that are not necessarily found in other parts of your application. If you decide to expound upon an event or accomplishment found elsewhere, don't simply rehash the same achievements found in your resume bullet points. Instead, help the admissions board see the experience from your own perspective: what was daunting and how you overcame it, what you learned from the experience, which motivations led you to make critical decisions, with whom you consulted, who and what were critical to your success, and so forth.

> **Don't be afraid to take risks such as talking about an abject failure and what you learned from it, as long as you decide it's the best way to help the admissions board see the world through your eyes.**

Taking risks. The biggest weakness we find in MBA essays is that applicants are actually too conservative—both in writing style and in content—resulting in dry, boring treatises that sound more like book reports than honest personal reflections. Don't be afraid to take risks such as talking about an abject failure and what you learned from it, as long as you decide it's the best way to help the admissions board see the world through your eyes. The goals are to help the admissions board see how you've become the person you are today and help them understand the underlying motivations that have driven some key decisions to-date.

Your writing style does not need to be as formal as a college English paper; your personality should show through while maintaining an appropriate level of professionalism. Note the tone of the HBS admissions website and the application itself; it's quite warm, straightforward, and personable. If they can write this way on a boring application form, you're allowed to let your hair down (a little bit), too!

Recommendations

Each applicant is expected to submit two recommendations with their application. Each recommender will fill out a grid to rate you on several personal qualities and skills including: Awareness of Others; Humility; Humor; Imagination, Creativity and Curiosity; Initiative; Integrity, Interpersonal Skills; Maturity; Self-awareness; Self-confidence; Teamwork: Analytical thinking skills; Listening Skills; Quantitative Aptitude; Verbal Communication Skills; and Writing Skills.

Your recommender will also be asked to answer two additional questions:

1. How do the candidate's performance, potential, background, or personal qualities compare to those of other well-qualified individuals in similar roles? Please provide specific examples. (300 words)

2. Please describe the most important piece of constructive feedback you have given the applicant. Please detail the circumstances and the applicant's response. (250 words)

Selecting your recommenders. Harvard suggests that one of your recommendations be your current or recent supervisor. HBS also stresses that it is more important to find recommenders who know you well and can answer the essay questions with depth and detail. As stated directly on the website, "This should take priority over level of seniority or HBS alumni status." They specifically recommend that you find someone who will speak to your leadership abilities, a statement that comes as no surprise given HBS's strong emphasis on finding and building future leaders.

Should I draft it myself? Many applicants to business school are asked by their superiors to draft the recommendation themselves and the recommender will approve it. We strongly recommend that you do not write the recommendation yourself for several reasons. First, your writing style and choice of phrasing are unique, and admissions officers will notice if the recommendations are similar to each other and your essay. Second, you will tend to be too humble or generic. Your supervisor might use language such as "one of the top analysts I've seen in my entire career" that you would not dare include if writing it on his or her behalf. Third, and perhaps most importantly, the admissions officer is looking for a third-party perspective on your candidacy, so writing a recommendation yourself is an unethical breach of trust with the school you are looking to join.

Preparing your recommenders. Instead of writing the recommendation yourself, you should sit down and have candid conversations with your recommenders about the reasons you want to go to business school and why you've selected your target schools, your professional goals, and your experience together. Ask them if they would have the time to write a strong recommendation on your behalf. (This also gives them a nice "out" by telling you that they are too busy rather than saying they don't feel comfortable giving you a positive recommendation.)

> **HBS also stresses that it is more important to find recommenders who know you well and can answer the essay questions with depth and detail.**

Bring a copy of your resume and a bulleted list of projects that you've worked on together and accomplishments they have seen you achieve. Let them know that the admissions committees prefer to see specific, detailed examples in recommendations. Then, let them know that you'll serve as a "project manager" to follow up and ensure that they are able to submit your recommendation ahead of the deadline.

The Interview

Your interview invitation. At Harvard Business School, admissions interviews are by invitation only. An interview is required before an offer is extended, so all accepted students were interviewed at some point during the admissions process. Harvard likes to interview about 1,800 candidates total each year, and they'll admit about 60% of those. So, if you get an invitation, you're in very good shape but not completely home free yet.

If you receive an invitation, you will interview in person, either on campus or in one of the cities the admissions team travels to. Harvard says there is no advantage to interviewing at the school, though if you haven't made it to Cambridge yet (and you're in a position to do so), scheduling your interview at HBS would be a great opportunity to also interact with students and sit in on a class.

Your interviewer. All interviews are conducted by members of the HBS admissions board; alumni do not help with interviews at Harvard. This allows the admissions board to have a more standardized process and a better way to evaluate each person, candidate to candidate. The interviewer will have read your entire application before meeting with you (unlike some other schools, where the interview is "blind" and the interviewer only has your resume).

Anticipated questions. Because the interviewer will already be familiar with your application, he or she will dive into topics that the admissions board wants to explore more deeply. This could include potential weaknesses they see in your candidacy or experiences you didn't have an opportunity to discuss thoroughly in other parts of your application. These behavioral interviews can go in almost any direction, but you should prepare a number of personal and professional stories that exemplify topics of leadership, decision-making, overcoming challenging situations, working on teams, dealing with difficult personalities, and other topics. Be prepared to answer questions about application weaknesses such as academics, test scores, thin work experience, and so forth. Also be advised that Admissions Director Dee Leopold likes to ask students what books they are currently reading to gauge intellectual curiosity. Other members of the admissions board may throw you a question "out of left field" like this to see your response.

The stone-faced response. HBS admissions interviewers notoriously provide almost no verbal or non-verbal feedback during or after the interview. Everyone comes away from the interview feeling like they bombed it! One woman left her on-campus interview, sat on the steps of Dillon House (the building that houses the HBS Admissions Office), and cried. She thought the interview went horribly. Much to her surprise, she received an acceptance letter a few weeks later! As a first-year student, she bumped into the woman who interviewed her. The interviewer said that she not only remembered the candidate, but also how well she performed in the interview. It had been one of the best interviews she conducted all season! Please don't let the interviewer's reaction (or lack thereof) discourage you.

Small talk. In recent years, more applicants have told us about how the interviewer attempted to develop rapport by spending a significant amount of time (sometimes an uncomfortably long amount of time) talking about seemingly irrelevant hobbies listed on the resume or engaged in other small talk. In these circumstances, simply go with the flow and show the admissions officer that you'll be an interesting, intelligent, and enjoyable classmate at HBS.

The Post-Interview Reflection

You just had your HBS interview. Tell us about it. Did we get to know you?

24-hour deadline. Within 24 hours of the interview, candidates are required to submit a written reflection through HBS's online application system. Detailed instructions will be provided to those applicants who are invited to the interview process. The Post-Interview Reflection gives you a chance to include anything you wish you had been able to mention in the interview, and to reframe anything that you discussed but have since thought about a bit more. You will submit this piece within 24 hours of your interview.

Keep it brief. Especially since this letter has no word limit, the temptation will be for you to cram in half a dozen additional things that you wish you had covered in the interview. However, less is always more; keep the note limited to no more than two or three core ideas that you want to highlight. Ideally you covered all of the important things in the interview already, but if not, this is a chance to hit on those. Keep in mind, though, that sharing these ideas in the interview is always going to be more effective than cramming them into this note.

Do not write beforehand. Be realistic about how much this letter will help you. Chances are that it won't turn a dud of an interview into a terrific one in hindsight. Do not go into the interview with this note already drafted; let it truly be a reaction to the discussion, which was hopefully an interesting and provocative one. If your interviewer reads this note and it sounds like a replay of an entirely different discussion from what he or she remembers, that will only serve to hurt you come decision time.

Consistent writing style. When the Post-Interview Reflection was announced in 2012, Admissions Director Dee Leopold described the addition as "a little bit more to what you may be doing in real-life careers. Sometimes you will have months and months to write a report, but more frequently, you'll probably have to write e-mails or memos in real time. So we like to think that this is a preview of not only what you will do in class but what we think you'll be doing throughout your career." She has also been pretty straightforward about her concern that candidates are not writing their own essays. She intends that the Post-Interview Reflection will provide a better picture of a candidate's true thoughts and writing abilities through a slightly less filtered, edited, and crafted forum. Of course, Veritas Prep does not write essays on behalf of our admissions consulting clients, but our consultants will provide personalized insights and feedback for both the HBS essay and Post-Interview Reflection as part of your Comprehensive School Package.

STANFORD GSB

You don't become the tech industry's favorite school without focusing on entrepreneurship.

◉ PALO ALTO, CA

CLASS SIZE	PROGRAM FOUNDED	NICKNAME
410	1925	THE GSB

CHARACTERISTICS

INTIMATE, FORWARD-THINKING, ENTREPRENEURIAL

SECTIONS

STANFORD GSB SNAPSHOT

What Stanford GSB Is Known For

Silicon Valley. Venture capital has its origins on Sand Hill Road, where Kleiner Perkins and Sequoia Capital got their start in the '70s and which runs along the border of the Stanford University campus. Stanford Graduate School of Business (known as "the GSB") is in the heart of Silicon Valley, and this proximity makes the school a natural incubator for great ideas. And, it means that the quality of guest speakers is phenomenal. It is not uncommon to see the likes of Steve Ballmer (the former CEO of Microsoft), Pat House (the founder of Siebel), and Jack Dorsey (the cofounder of Twitter) on campus—in the same week. This close proximity to so many start-ups also means that it's fairly easy for students to set up independent projects and more informal school-year internships than is possible at other schools.

The anti-HBS. We know that Stanford probably doesn't want us to say this, but the school seems to go to great lengths to emphasize that it is everything Harvard Business School (HBS) is not. While HBS boasts the largest full-time MBA program in the world, at more than 900 students per class, Stanford emphasizes that by the end of your two years you'll get to know every member of your graduating class of about 400 students. HBS prides itself in developing the case study method back in 1925, while the GSB emphasizes innovation in the classroom and its wide range of teaching methods. Taking a page from basic business strategy, the school seeks to differentiate itself by laying claim to the "anti-HBS" territory.

A "California culture." GSB students live by the ethos "work hard, play hard." While their schedules are extremely tight—filled with challenging coursework, a ton of recruiting events, study group meetings, class projects, student organizations, and other activities—they enjoy the California lifestyle and the relaxed culture at the GSB, with events such as FOAM, short for Friends of (former dean) Arjay Miller; the informal Tuesday night happy hour; Vegas FOAM, a quick midweek trip some students indulge in toward the end of the term; TALK, a weekly event where two classmates spend 45 minutes each telling the story of their lives to the rest of their class; and the *Take a Professor To Lunch* program, where students host faculty in a more intimate environment.

What Makes the GSB Different

> **The GSB is all about making an impact in the world, and you can't seem to walk more than 50 feet on campus without some kind of discussion about "pursuing your dreams."**

Pursuing one's dreams. GSB admissions officers genuinely want to know what your dreams and aspirations are, as evidenced by the application's largely unchanged first essay. The GSB is all about making an impact in the world, and you can't seem to walk more than 50 feet on campus without some kind of discussion about "pursuing your dreams." As a result, comparatively few GSB grads go into traditional, middle-management positions in industry after school. In fact, a job like this may even seem below many of them since they're pursuing their destiny to change the world, not to clock into a 9-to-5 job.

Sustainability and social innovation. Given its mantra to "change the world" it makes sense that Stanford wants to attract students who will do just that. Stanford is the leader among its business school peers in the areas of sustainable business and social ventures, both for-profit and nonprofit. Putting its money where its mouth is, Stanford ensured the Knight Management Center was certified as LEED Platinum after opening in 2011. The school consistently leads the Aspen Institute's Beyond Grey Pinstripes ranking of business schools that integrate social and environmental stewardship into their programs.

Class size. At just more than 400 students in each graduating class, Stanford is on the smaller end of the top business schools in the world, and this makes for a very different experience for students. While there are advantages of a large class in terms of the vast global alumni network, a smaller class undoubtedly helps students foster closer relationships—not just with one another, but with the faculty, too.

Collaborative community. Everything about Stanford GSB—its small size, the "work hard, play hard" culture, and the fact that more than half of first-years live together in a common residence—encourages the development of Stanford's tight-knit, collaborative culture. Most work at the GSB is done in groups, and there is a strong sense of community that pervades everything that goes on around the GSB campus. This collaboration extends to alumni, as the GSB consistently rates at or near the top of rankings of most helpful alumni in the hiring process.

Focus on self-reflection and change. The GSB's motto is "Change lives. Change organizations. Change the world." The first life it intends to change is yours. As one GSBer put it, "You can't change the world until you change yourself." A key part of the GSB curriculum, particularly in the first year, is to challenge the way students think about themselves and the world around them through a series of seminars, labs, and courses. Students have commented on how much the GSB forces students to reflect and transform themselves. The Stanford MBA application is designed to be the first step in this process of honest self-reflection.

Stanford GSB Is a Good Fit for You If...

You have an interesting backstory. With the lowest admission rate of any MBA program in the world, usually around 6 to 7%, Stanford has the luxury of selecting a class from a huge pool of extremely well-qualified candidates. As a result, the entering class of about 400 students tends to have really interesting backgrounds and stories outside of work in addition to unquestioned academic and professional qualifications. Authenticity, passion, and impact in every aspect of your life will be key. Be sure to flip to our Admissions section for further insight.

You're a techie. While only 13% of the GSB's most recent incoming class came directly from the tech industry (as opposed to 21% of UCLA Anderson's class!), one-quarter of graduates went into the industry immediately upon graduation. Many other members of the incoming class come from consulting and finance jobs that are heavily tech-related as well. As one recent Stanford GSB graduate put it, "This can be a good thing or bad thing. Some students who are less interested in tech probably feel a little alienated or distant at times."

> **Stanford is the leader among its business school peers in the areas of sustainable business and social ventures, both for-profit and nonprofit.**

You want to become an entrepreneur. This probably goes without saying: Stanford is a great place to launch a business. Typically about 60 to 70 students strike out on their own after graduating—about 16% of the overall class, higher than at any other top-tier school. Not all entrepreneurs are launching tech ventures, though clearly those who do are at an advantage, given the Silicon Valley location. Many graduating students with slightly less appetite for risk have the option of cherry-picking and joining early-stage, venture-backed startups and play meaningful roles in the future success of these businesses. For more details on entrepreneurial opportunities at the GSB, see our Employment & Careers section.

Only 5% of Stanford GSB grads went into VC last year, or about 20 members of the entire class. However, that percentage is double or triple most other top programs.

You are interested in a career in venture capital. Let's not oversell this: Only 5% of Stanford GSB grads went into VC last year, or about 20 members of the entire class. However, that percentage is double or triple most other top programs. Venture capital is an extraordinarily competitive field to get into, so if you're planning on pursuing it, you'd better have a Plan B and Plan C ready to go!

You're a well-accomplished college senior. Because Stanford's deferred enrollment program doesn't have a fancy name like HBS 2+2, it may be overlooked by outstanding college seniors who are looking to lock down their MBA future now. With deferred enrollment, you can work for one to three years before starting your MBA program. Stanford has plenty of advice for aspiring seniors on its website, but one thing it doesn't mention is a profile of admitted candidates, or even the number who were successful (which is likely to be in the single digits each year). Because college seniors have limited experience in "the real world," the bar is set even higher to demonstrate leadership potential and articulate a clear vision of how they will impact the world around them.

You are a mid-career manager or executive. The Stanford MSx Program is a one-year, full-time master's of science program for managers with at least eight years of professional experience. Average work experience of Stanford's full-time MBA program participants is just four years, so applicants with more experience may find they are not a great fit. For candidates who prefer a full-time program to a part-time EMBA, the MSx program is a unique opportunity to get the full, on-campus immersive experience of an MBA with a 90-member cohort of "fellows" who are successful mid-career professionals. This Guide focuses primarily on the MBA program, but Veritas Prep has seen great success in helping MSx applicants gain admission to this highly selective program. Interested candidates should also investigate similar programs at MIT Sloan and London Business School.

ACADEMICS AT STANFORD GSB

What Stanford GSB Is Known For

Introspection. As we alluded to in the Stanford GSB Snapshot, the first year and particularly the first quarter encourage GSB students to think in a new way. Called *General Management Perspectives*, the first quarter coursework has the strongest emphasis on self-reflection of any core curricula we've seen, including *Critical Analytical Thinking (CAT)*, *Leadership Labs*, *Managerial Skills Labs*, *Managing Groups and Teams*, *Organizational Behavior*, and *Strategic Leadership*—and that's all in just one quarter!

Personalized curriculum. Although the GSB doesn't offer quite as much flexibility as Chicago Booth, which allows students to dictate their entire academic experience from day one, the Stanford curriculum offers many options. Students are divided into 60-person sections for only the first quarter of their first year. For the next two quarters, students get to know the rest of their class. You can select Beginner, Intermediate, or Advanced options of many core classes such as finance, statistics, marketing, and so forth. This way, you'll gain value from each class in your first-year core curriculum without boring students who have studied and worked for years in a subject or intimidating those with nontraditional backgrounds.

More classes. Because the school year is divided into three quarters rather than two semesters, you have the opportunity to take more classes with a narrower scope. For example, rather than taking a broad marketing strategy course, you could take *Marketing for Startups*. There are no majors at the GSB, so during your second year you can build your own curriculum of electives as you see fit.

Global focus. Today, all top MBA programs emphasize the global nature of business. There's no escaping it! However, Stanford was one of the first graduate business programs to focus on the international aspects of business. With more than 40% of each class coming from overseas, the GSB seems to integrate international perspectives into its DNA perhaps more than any other U.S. school. (Go outside the U.S. to programs like INSEAD and you'll see a whole new definition of international focus, however!) *Global Strategy* is a key part of the *General Management Perspectives* core curriculum in Autumn Quarter, requiring students from the start to think systematically about the challenges and opportunities brought about by globalization.

The vast majority of students complete their Global Experience Requirement (GER) in Winter or Spring Break of the first year, so the entire GSB community benefits when they return to campus and share their experiences with their classmates and professors. About one in five students has such a good time that he or she decides to lead a Global Study Trip in his or her second year, too!

STANFORD AT A GLANCE

APPLICANTS BY SCHOOL

Stanford GSB is the most selective MBA program in the world, with just 7% of applicants receiving a positive result. Competition is tough.

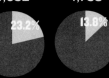

Stanford
7,355
7.1%

Harvard
9,543
11%

Wharton
6,111
20.7%

Columbia
5,799
18.2%

Kellogg
4,652
23.2%

Sloan
4,735
13.8%

Percent admitted

AVERAGE GPA

3.74 Stanford

3.67 Harvard

3.62 Haas

3.60 Wharton

RANGE OF WORK EXPERIENCE IN YEARS

 0-15 Stanford

 0-16 Wharton

 0-13 MIT Sloan

With experience ranging from zero to zero to 15 years, Stanford appears to be quite open to admitting both early career and more experienced candidates.

WOMEN

With women at 42% of the class, Stanford now has one of the highest percentages of women among the top-tier business schools. This is a huge jump from previous years when we saw percentages in the mid-30s range.

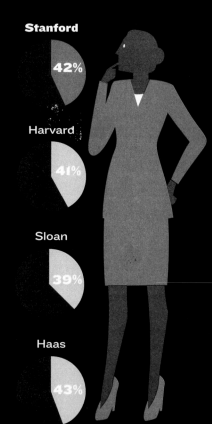

Stanford 42%

Harvard 41%

Sloan 39%

Haas 43%

NATIONALITY

Stanford has the highest percentage (44%) of international students of any top-tier program, creating a very culturally diverse atmosphere. The GSB integrates international perspectives into its DNA perhaps more than any other U.S. school.

56% U.S.

44% International Citizens

62 Countries Represented

GMAT SCORES

Average Score

732

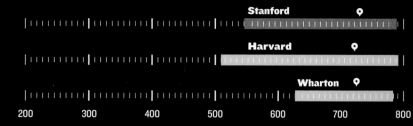

Stanford

Harvard

Wharton

200   300   400   500   600   700   800

STANFORD

UNDERGRAD MAJORS

Not surprisingly, Stanford attracts a large percentage (38%) of students from STEM backgrounds. Interestingly, other schools not traditionally known for technology including Ross (36%) and Harvard (40%) are catching up!

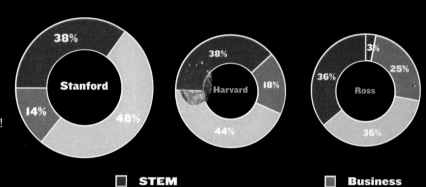

Stanford: 38%, 48%, 14%

Harvard: 38%, 44%, 18%

Ross: 3%, 25%, 36%, 36%

- ■ **STEM**
- ■ **Humanities/Social Science/ Economics**
- ■ **Business**
- □ **OTHER**

FROM CONSULTING/FINANCE SECTOR PRE-MBA

Stanford has one of the lowest percentages of its incoming class coming from traditional pre-MBA industries. Interestingly, 15% of its Class of 2016 came from a government or nonprofit background—the largest percentage of any top-tier program—and higher than those entering the program from technology (13%).

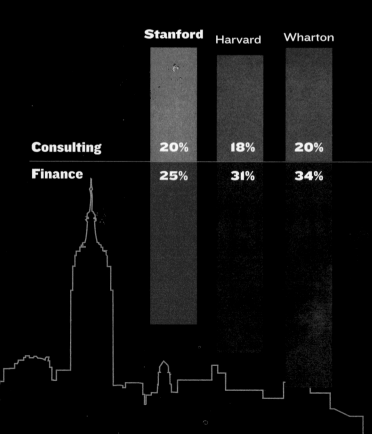

	Stanford	Harvard	Wharton
Consulting	20%	18%	20%
Finance	25%	31%	34%

CLASS SIZE

Despite having the second-highest volume of applications next to Harvard, GSB keeps its class size relatively small and intimate at 410—less than half the size of Harvard's class.

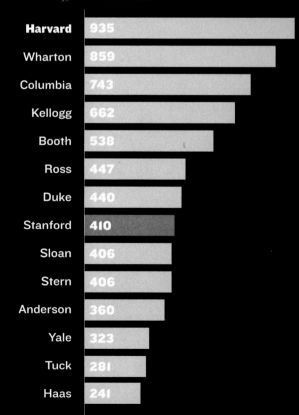

School	Size
Harvard	935
Wharton	859
Columbia	743
Kellogg	662
Booth	538
Ross	447
Duke	440
Stanford	410
Sloan	406
Stern	406
Anderson	360
Yale	323
Tuck	281
Haas	241

You Oughta Know

The admissions committee specifically looks for evidence of humility and teamwork skills in applicants. Those who come off as arrogant or solo performers, particularly those who succeed at the expense of others, will be denied.

Teamwork. The GSB experience is all about reducing competition and building relationships, so very little work at the GSB is done individually. Teamwork and collaboration are key components of the academic philosophy at the school. Understanding this philosophy isn't just "nice to know" as you prepare for school; it will be vital to a successful application. The admissions committee specifically looks for evidence of humility and teamwork skills in applicants. Those who come off as arrogant or solo performers, particularly those who succeed at the expense of others, will be denied.

Interdisciplinary opportunities. The GSB has the fewest number of students who go into "traditional" MBA professional functions and the most joint-degree candidates of any top-tier program. So it comes as no surprise that many Stanford MBA students take advantage of classes outside of the GSB across all university departments. In fact, many of the GSB classes are cross-listed with other schools, including engineering, law, medicine, social sciences, and the design school (d.school). *Biodesign Innovation*, for example, spans two quarters; brings prominent faculty members from the schools of medicine, business, and engineering; and mixes students from every department to work on developing innovative solutions for existing clinical needs. If this is an appealing aspect of the GSB education, then you may want to check out Stanford's course catalog, connect with professors of those interdisciplinary courses that appeal most to you, and talk to them about how the course is structured and some of the impressive accomplishments that students have gone on to achieve with their Stanford GSB education as a foundation.

Variety of teaching methods. Stanford professors are given leeway to teach their courses using the methods they feel will be most effective for the subject at hand. This shakes out to be about 50% case method and 50% lecture or other methods such as group projects, hands-on learning labs, problem-solving sessions, simulations, and so forth. Students really enjoy the variety. As one recent GSB grad put it, "Having done this, I now can't imagine going to a business school that is 100% case study."

About one in every five students at the GSB is a joint-degree candidate, showing the GSB's extensive integration with the broader Stanford community.

Joint-degree programs. About one in every five students at the GSB is a joint-degree candidate, showing the GSB's extensive integration with the broader Stanford community. (This compares to just 5% of students at Harvard Business School, which is more typical.) The MBA program recently started offering two new joint degrees with the Engineering School: a Computer Science MS/MBA program that launched in 2014 and Electrical Engineering MS/MBA in 2015. Honestly, we're surprised these programs haven't been offered for decades, given the deep relationship between the GSB and the tech industry. These new joint-degree programs add to the robust offering of existing joint and dual degrees: JD/MBA, MA Education/MBA, MS Environment and Resources/MBA, MPP/MBA, MD/MBA with the Stanford School of Medicine, and degrees offered from graduate schools at Harvard, Johns Hopkins, Princeton, and Yale.

Nuts & Bolts

How the school year works. The school year starts in mid-September and runs through May, divided into 11-week quarters: Fall, Winter, and Spring. Coursework is split into three parts: *Management Perspectives* and *Management Foundations* in the first year, and up to 18 electives in the second year.

Important grading policies. The most important feature of GSB grading is the non-disclosure policy. Students are not allowed to share their grades and recruiters are not allowed to ask. Because of this, grades are never an issue at Stanford and there is little competition among students. In fact, Stanford MBAs have a long tradition of freely sharing study notes with their section-mates for tough classes such as Corporate Finance and Microeconomics. Students receive the following grades for their coursework: (H) Honors, (HP) High Pass, (P) Pass, (LP) Low Pass, and (U) Unsatisfactory. Students are graded on a curve, but it is important to note that most students are not aware of how they are performing against their peers.

On graduation day, the top 10% of students are designated as "Arjay Miller Scholars." The top-ranked student wins the Henry Ford II award. At the end of the first year, the top five students (based on grades and contribution, as nominated by faculty) are named Siebel Scholars and win a $35,000 fellowship.

Getting the classes you want. Like at many other schools, the GSB uses an algorithm to allocate classes, but the system has a few twists. Students must rank their course preferences and enter into a lottery system. However, there's also a "Super Round," when students can rank up to two high-demand courses regardless of the quarter in which the class meets. To make matters even more complicated, you can trade your two Super Round choices for one "Round Zero" selection to further improve your chances of getting into that top-choice class. Lastly, a few popular electives, such as *Entrepreneurial Design for Extreme Affordability* (jointly offered with the Stanford School of Engineering) and *Interpersonal Dynamics* (known as "Touchy-Feely"), require an application for admission. You won't be able to get into every popular class with the best professors, so you'll need to plan in advance.

> **Students are not allowed to share their grades and recruiters are not allowed to ask. Because of this, grades are never an issue at Stanford and there is little competition among students.**

Popular Professors & Courses

Among GSB students, there are a handful of professors and courses that are considered a "must" in order to have the full GSB experience. Not surprisingly, many of the top courses are related to entrepreneurship and venture capital, although there are a few that fall outside of that scope. The following list identifies a few of the top courses and professors at the GSB.

Professor H. Irving "Irv" Grousbeck
Managing Growing Enterprises
Professor Grousbeck founded Continental Cablevision, where he served as chairman until 1985, has served on nonprofit and corporate boards, and is a principal owner of the Boston Celtics. His course places MBA students in the role of CEO and challenges them to deal with difficult managerial situations through a process assessment, prescription, and execution, including frequent role-playing. He brings a mixture of industry credibility and an engaging teaching style to the class, which sets the tone and brings out the best in his students. Grousbeck is well-known for cold-calling in almost every class. Capped at just 40 students per section, this course is a common "Round Zero" pick.

Scott Bristol, Richard Francisco, Gary Dexter, Andrea Corney, Carole Robin
Interpersonal Dynamics
While its name marks it as one of the "softer" classes at the GSB, *Interpersonal Dynamics* (aka "Touchy-Feely") is a perennial favorite of GSB students. This course has been around for nearly 50 years; for earlier generations of businesspeople, it branded Stanford as a "new age-y" school making the most of its California location. However, many GSB graduates feel that this is the class that gives them the most relevant skills that they carry forward into their careers. Touchy-Feely focuses on improving the way managers and individuals communicate. Almost all MBAs take this course at some point during their second year, with most taking it during the spring. If you have ever heard GSB alumni talking about their "t-group," then you know it is a not-to-be-missed part of the Stanford GSB experience. A shortened version of this course has been offered during the pre-term September cycle to better meet student demand..

Peter Wendell, Peter Ziebelman, John Glynn
Entrepreneurship and Venture Capital
Peter C. Wendell is the founder and a managing director of Sierra Ventures, and has been recognized by *Forbes* magazine as one of the top-100 technology venture investors in the United States. The class is co-taught by Peter Ziebelman and John Glynn, founders of Palo Alto Venture Partners and Glynn Capital, respectively. This is one of the top classes at the GSB and provides an opportunity for second-year MBAs to learn about all aspects of the venture capital business from industry giants. This class is known for its strong guest speakers and engaging discussions. Also, the all-star faculty of *Entrepreneurship and Venture Capital* is often willing to go to lunch with students after class.

Professor Julian Gorodsky, Professor James Patell, Professor David Beach, Professor Stuart Coulson
Entrepreneurial Design for Extreme Affordability
This course, offered in conjunction with the Stanford School of Design (d.school) and the engineering school, has become one of the top offerings at the GSB. It is difficult to get into and requires an application. This collaborative, hands-on experience of creating solutions to

real-world problems has already produced many inspired ideas. Students take ideas all the way from design to prototype, grappling with the real-world problems of production for scale in emerging markets. Professor Jim Patell is one of the seven core founding faculty of the d.school. He also served as the GSB's associate dean for academic affairs from 1985 through 1991, and was director of the MBA program from 1986 through 1988. While the coursework is exceptionally demanding, it is known to be one of the most rewarding classes at the GSB because the work results in a tangible output and students get the experience of working on a project with a multidisciplinary team. Each year, several class projects are taken forward and have real-world impact. In 2007, a team launched its company, d.light designs, delivering affordable solar-rechargeable LED lamps to developing countries.

Professor Baba Shiv
The Frinky Science of the Human Mind

Professor Shiv is one of the most respected and adored professors by GSB students, conducting one-on-one research projects with many students on topics of their choosing. He's known for his research into neuroeconomics, combining biology of the brain with studies of emotion and decision-making. His new course, *The Frinky Science of the Human Mind*, helps students put this knowledge of the "instinctual brain" into practice from business and management perspectives

Similar Academic Programs

If you are particularly interested in Stanford's wide variety of teaching methods and strong emphasis on collaboration, then you're in luck! Many other top MBA programs take a similar approach. However, its unrelenting focus on individual self-reflection and personal development is difficult to find elsewhere. The following programs share a number of academic similarities:

Northwestern (Kellogg). Four decades ago, Kellogg pioneered the collaborative, team-based MBA experience, which has now been widely adopted across MBA programs large and small. However, its level of collaboration—with students often double or triple booked with various group projects, team meetings, club activities, and competitions—remains unmatched. It utilizes a quarter system and allows students to waive core courses or take more accelerated versions to tailor their academic experience to their individual needs.

Yale. With its small class size, varied teaching methods, and close ties to its parent university, Yale School of Management offers a tight-knit, collaborative experience similar to Stanford's. The two programs also put a strong emphasis on leadership in global business, but in very different ways. Stanford emphasizes its diverse student body and global experiences, while Yale highlights its global network of partner business schools. Yale's Leadership Development Program provides an emphasis on personal growth throughout the two-year program.

Chicago (Booth). Booth represents the epitome of academic flexibility, with just one required course in leadership development, so students may fulfill all other core requirements with their choice of a number of basic and advanced courses in 10 different categories. Booth is also highly collaborative in the classroom, although the Booth take on collaboration differs somewhat from the GSB, as direct challenges to other viewpoints and debate among students and faculty are encouraged. Although its Leadership Effectiveness and Development (LEAD) Program offers opportunities for self-awareness and improving personal effectiveness, "soft skills" and reflection receive less emphasis in Booth's core requirements than at Stanford.

> **Booth is also highly collaborative in the classroom, although the Booth take on collaboration differs somewhat from the GSB, as direct challenges to other viewpoints and debate among students and faculty are encouraged.**

EMPLOYMENT & CAREERS AT STANFORD GSB

What Stanford GSB Is Known For

Nearly one-quarter of recent graduates went into the tech industry immediately upon graduation.

Tech. We've already said it several times in this Guide, but Stanford is synonymous with technology and the GSB is no exception. One-quarter (24%) of the Class of 2014 took a position in the tech sector upon graduation, although this number was even higher (32%) for the Class of 2013. Other West Coast schools are now outpacing Stanford's strong placements in technology, with Haas sending a whopping 43% of its Class of 2014 this industry, followed by UCLA Anderson which placed 28% in technology, but this doesn't diminish GSB's long-standing reputation in this industry. A large number of candidates go into product management and marketing functions, although GSBers fill all sorts of roles in the tech industry, including finance, general management, operations/logistics, and strategic planning.

Graduates entering the technology industry

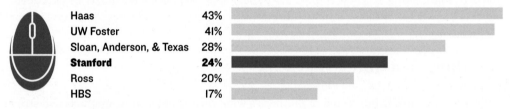

Haas	43%
UW Foster	41%
Sloan, Anderson, & Texas	28%
Stanford	**24%**
Ross	20%
HBS	17%

Seventeen percent of the Class of 2014 went into PE (12%) or VC (5%), outpacing any other business school.

Private equity & venture capital. Stanford isn't necessarily known as a "Finance School" along the lines of Wharton or Columbia, but the highest percentage of its class goes into the finance industry (30%). Seventeen percent of the Class of 2014 went into PE (12%) or VC (5%), outpacing any other business school. Harvard sent 15% of its class to these fields, followed by Wharton at 11%. No other MBA program sent more than 8% of its class into PE/VC, which shows just how selective these industries can be.

Graduates entering the private equity or venture capital industry

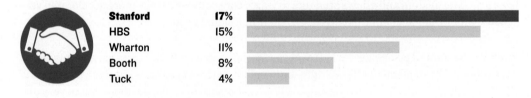

Stanford	**17%**
HBS	15%
Wharton	11%
Booth	8%
Tuck	4%

Entrepreneurship. It's no secret that many students go to the GSB to start up their own ventures. In fact, a key part of the GSB experience is to connect with other students and faculty members to get a business off the ground. Nearly 70 members of the Class of 2014 (16%) chose not to pursue a job at graduation so that they could start their own company or nonprofit. This represents a dramatic departure from many MBA programs that often encourage students to make their mistakes "on another company's dime," and then start their own venture a few years after graduation.

Graduates electing to pursue entrepreneurial opportunities

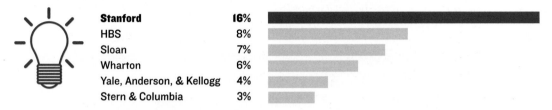

Stanford	16%
HBS	8%
Sloan	7%
Wharton	6%
Yale, Anderson, & Kellogg	4%
Stern & Columbia	3%

You Oughta Know

Staying in the western U.S. Despite Stanford's strong global brand, just 13% of the class takes positions outside of the U.S. at graduation. Nearly 60% of the class stays in the western United States, particularly in California. We hear many applicants criticize lower-ranked MBA programs for being too "regional" in their recruiting opportunities, but it's important to remember that alumni of even the highest-ranked MBA programs tend to take jobs nearby. (Of course, don't read too much into these numbers, because 40% of the class got a job somewhere else, so it's not exactly impossible to escape!)

Nonprofit. With its stated motto to "change the world," it comes as no surprise that Stanford would send a significant number of graduates into the nonprofit or public sector. Six percent of the class won't exactly blow anyone's hair back, but most other schools send just 1 or 2% of their graduates into nonprofit or government jobs, so Stanford's number is quite high compared to peers. Harvard also sends about 3% into the nonprofit field, while Yale School of Management is best known for the intersection of business and society, sending one in 10 grads into nonprofits!

Graduates entering nonprofit/government jobs

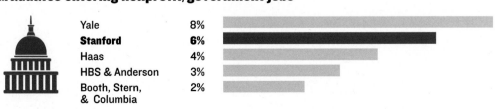

Yale	8%
Stanford	6%
Haas	4%
HBS & Anderson	3%
Booth, Stern, & Columbia	2%

Compensation. Stanford grads have the highest average post-graduation salary, at $125,000, before signing bonuses or other guaranteed compensation. This is about $15,000 more than most other top-tier MBA programs and about $5,000 more than Harvard's average. However, industry-by-industry, Stanford and Harvard grads make almost exactly the same salaries. In the finance sector, Stanford has the biggest edge, with graduates making an average of $10,000 to $15,000 more than HBS graduates. However, these statistics do not include graduates who strike out on their own ventures (where it's not unheard of to sleep on friends' couches while the venture gets up and going!).

Class of 2013 salaries by sector in thousands

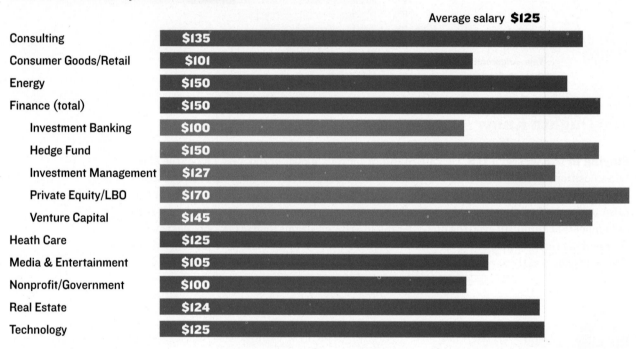

Average salary **$125**

Consulting	$135
Consumer Goods/Retail	$101
Energy	$150
Finance (total)	$150
Investment Banking	$100
Hedge Fund	$150
Investment Management	$127
Private Equity/LBO	$170
Venture Capital	$145
Heath Care	$125
Media & Entertainment	$105
Nonprofit/Government	$100
Real Estate	$124
Technology	$125

GSB encourages students to think about their long-term career goals and explore as many different career tracks as possible. More than 50 percent of GSB students switch function or industry each year.

Career switchers. Nearly half of graduating students accept jobs in finance and management consulting, and an equal number of accepted students come from similar backgrounds. While the relative number of pre- and post-MBA careers are the same, this does not necessarily mean that the same people end up going back to the fields they came from. In fact, the GSB encourages students to think about their long-term career goals and explore as many different career tracks as possible. More than 50% of GSB students switch function or industry each year, although other MBA programs, such as Kellogg, boast that as many as 80% of their graduating classes will make a career switch.

Nuts & Bolts

Academic Adjustment Period (AAP). Stanford wants to ensure its students are able to adjust to campus life before they "release the hounds" of recruiters. Employers may not contact first-year students or hold any recruiting events for first years (on campus or off) until November 1. For second-year students, employers may hold events starting on September 29. Not only can students adjust academically, but it allows them to prepare properly for corporate events and think for a month or two about their career opportunities. However, this transition happens fast, so the admissions office expects applicants to have one or two well-developed plans for their post-MBA prospects by the time they apply.

Open vs. closed list interviews. Similar to many top-tier MBA programs, the GSB requires on-campus recruiters to keep at least 30% of their internship interview spots open so that first-year students can bid points to obtain an interview slot. This allows career switchers to compete with more traditional candidates whose resumes may show a more obvious fit with the employer. However, for full-time (second-year) interview spots, recruiters may now maintain a 100% closed list if they wish, meaning that they select all of the candidates who they want to interview.

Job offers. The GSB has many rules and regulations on employers to protect students. For example, employers cannot offer "exploding offers" that require students to make an immediate decision or risk losing their signing bonus, job offer, desired location, etc. Stanford provides students a set deadline by which they must make a decision among competing offers, although students are welcome to make a decision beforehand.

On-campus vs. off-campus recruiting. About half of GSB grads received the offers they ultimately accepted through on-campus initiatives. All other students received their offers through their own networking and other efforts. This is fairly low compared to other top-tier MBA programs, and it reflects the large number of students who pursue non-traditional paths or more niche industries that do not have massive on-campus recruiting operations. Stanford's strong alumni network is a crucial part of many students' off-campus job searches.

Similar Programs for Professional Opportunities

Stanford has an unusual mix when it comes to the industries its students tend to pursue after graduation. No other top-tier MBA program quite matches. We've listed a number of programs that have similar opportunities in one or two areas.

Harvard. HBS sends quite a few candidates into private equity positions and has a rapidly growing presence in the tech sector. More than 70 students from the HBS Class of 2014 decided to pursue entrepreneurial ventures rather than traditional job recruiting opportunities, which is quite a large number in absolute terms but less than half the percentage of Stanford's entrepreneurs. Harvard also sends about 15% of its class into private equity or venture capital positions, which is higher than any other MBA program.

In absolute terms, Wharton sends more candidates into private equity and venture capital than does Stanford, although 5% of Stanford's class goes into VC compared to just 1.7% of Wharton's.

Penn (Wharton). Wharton and Stanford have very similar employment statistics in the finance sector, except Wharton sends far more candidates into investment banking. In absolute terms, Wharton sends more candidates into private equity and venture capital than does Stanford, although 5% of Stanford's class goes into VC compared to just 1.7% of Wharton's. Outside of finance, the two schools are vastly different, with Wharton producing twice as many consultants, while Stanford leads in general managers, product managers, and marketers (in percentage terms).

Berkeley (Haas). Any discussion of employment in the Bay Area must include Berkeley-Haas. Like Stanford, Haas also sends a large percentage of its class into the tech sector (43%—the largest percentage of any top-tier school), with the majority of its class choosing to stay in California. Haas, however, sends just 13% of its class into finance roles, which is a major departure from Stanford's typical class.

UCLA (Anderson). Anderson is another California school that sends a large number of graduates into the tech sector (28%—outpacing Stanford). Although another 28% of the Anderson Class of 2014 went into finance roles, their median salary was about $100,000, which is considerably lower than Stanford's median. This is primarily due to the fact that Anderson sends far fewer candidates into high-paying jobs in PE, VC, hedge funds, and other specialty finance roles. Over two-thirds of Anderson grads stay in California, with 48% of them remaining in Southern California.

Yale. Like Stanford, the Yale School of Management sends relatively fewer candidates into traditional MBA industries of management consulting and finance compared to peer schools. It is known for nonprofit, sending 8% of its class into the field, but also has a strong showing in the tech sector and in general management roles. Interestingly, even though only 26% of Yale's class describes their industry as consulting, 37% of the class describes their function as a consultant, meaning that many of their graduates serve as consultants in other industries (such as technology or nonprofit consultancies).

Dartmouth (Tuck). Even though Tuck sends only 4% of graduates into private equity, it's known as a "hidden gem" in the PE industry. Applicants interested in private equity should certainly consider this rural campus for their short list. A much larger percentage of the Tuck class goes into investment banking than Stanford's, and the school produces slightly more general managers, many of whom go into management rotational programs.

CULTURE & CAMPUS LIFE AT STANFORD GSB

What the GSB Is Known For

Gorgeous campus setting. Over the past decade, there has been an "arms race" among business schools to build the best and most impressive campuses for management education. Stanford built the Knight Management Center in 2011 to great acclaim. With solar panels visible on every rooftop, the LEED Platinum–certified complex is centrally located within Stanford's beautiful 8,100-acre campus.

On-campus living. With about half of first-year MBA students living in the nearby Schwab Residential Center, Stanford is one of the few MBA programs that offers a truly immersive residential campus experience. This enables first-year GSBers to really bond with their classmates to develop lifelong friends and deep networks. Only Harvard Business School houses more of its student body on-campus in such a "living-learning" atmosphere.

Down-to-earth student body. Although every member of the Stanford GSB student body is incredibly accomplished, it's not uncommon to hear students say, "I don't know why I belong here more than other applicants." The admissions committee specifically looks for outstanding applicants who show humility and a team spirit, and these attributes are clearly seen in the admitted student body. As a result, its alumni are known for being extremely helpful to current students in offering advice to new entrepreneurs and making valuable connections for job seekers.

Numerous speakers. The GSB is known for attracting many high-profile speakers each year to classes and campuswide events. In the course *Leadership Perspectives*, for example, a different CEO speaks to the class in every lecture! The speaker series on campus are very popular and well attended, including View From the Top, the Global Speaker Series, and the Expert Speaker Series. The ability to hear directly from such prominent leaders is a key differentiator in campus life at Stanford.

> The admissions committee specifically looks for outstanding applicants who show humility and a team spirit, and these attributes are clearly seen in the admitted student body.

You Oughta Know

Clubs & activities. Nearly every member of the GSB student body will lead a club, lead a global study trip, or participate in Arbuckle Fellows (the peer leadership training experience). However, clubs, conferences, and school-sponsored extracurricular activities are not nearly as immersive at Stanford as at many peer schools. For example, students at Kellogg say that less than 50% of their learning comes from the classroom, with the majority of their experience coming from the vast array of extracurricular leadership experiences. Rather than club-sponsored activities and conferences, Stanford tends to focus on bringing big-name CEOs to speak in the classroom and to the student body as a whole.

For Vegas FOAM, students fly to Vegas on the Tuesday after Winter Quarter midterms, party all night, and fly home the next day. What happens in Vegas...

FOAM. FOAM is such an integral part of the GSB experience, we decided to give it a separate callout! Short for "Friends of Arjay Miller" (former dean of the GSB), FOAM is a weekly party sponsored by the student government. Because there are no classes on Wednesdays, the FOAM committee rents out a local bar every Tuesday night and throws a party attended by about half the student body. FOAM often hosts themed parties, which are perennial favorites. For Vegas FOAM, students from both classes dress up in their finest '70s attire, fly to Vegas on the Tuesday after Winter Quarter midterms, party all night, and fly home the next day. This is just one example of the active social scene at the GSB!

Popular hangouts. You'll often find first-year students hanging out at Schwab or on the main plaza at the Knight Management Center. Many second-year students live in nearby towns in houses that are handed down each year. They enjoy hosting many parties throughout the year. Off campus, you may find GSB students gathering at a number of local bars, including Dutch Goose, the Nut House, the Old Pro, Nola's, and Rudy's.

Similar Programs Culturally

Berkeley (Haas). With an even smaller student body and its Bay Area location, Haas is known for its friendly vibe and tight-knit community. Both programs belong to elite parent universities, although Stanford is a private university and Berkeley is the crown jewel of the University of California system.

Yale. Stanford is in the heart of Silicon Valley and is a short drive from San Francisco, while Yale is a two-and-a-half-hour train ride from New Haven to New York City, its nearest hub. Nonetheless, the two schools boast small class sizes, close ties to elite parent universities, and friendly and welcoming environments.

Dartmouth (Tuck). Tuckies are an extremely tight-knit group, largely thanks to Dartmouth's rural setting in Hanover, New Hampshire. The physical climates couldn't be more different at these schools, with long Hanover winters compared to Palo Alto's moderate temperatures, but the social environments of these two schools are strikingly similar.

Northwestern (Kellogg). Kellogg has a much larger student body than the GSB, but the school is widely known for its friendly students, numerous formal and informal events, and active social life. Although it has just one campus residence filled primarily by international students, nearly 80% of Kellogg students live within just a few minutes' walk from campus (very important during Chicago winters!). The majority live as roommates together in a small handful of apartment complexes around Evanston, Illinois.

Michigan (Ross). Perhaps it's the cold weather, but there's something about these Midwest and Northeastern schools that instills a culture of unity, humility, and fun. Ross is no exception. Located in idyllic Ann Arbor, Michigan, the Ross School has a greater connection to its undergraduate traditions than many business schools, largely thanks to its large bachelor's of business administration program and the University of Michigan's dominant sports programs.

ADMISSIONS AT STANFORD GSB

What the GSB Is Looking For

Stanford GSB lists intellectual vitality, demonstrated leadership potential, and personal qualities and contributions as its key evaluation criteria. These sound virtually identical to criteria found at pretty much any other top-tier MBA program, but we've found that successful GSB applicants have something about them that's intangible—a kind of "sparkle" that others candidates don't bring. Let us explain.

Selective. Stanford GSB is the most selective MBA program in the world, with just 6 to 7% of applicants receiving a positive result. About 20% of the class is pursuing a joint degree with another Stanford graduate program. Many of those students started their programs in Stanford Law School or School of Medicine and applied to the GSB after their first year. Having already been admitted to an extremely selective graduate program at Stanford University, these candidates tend to have a higher rate of admission than the overall population. As a result, there are even fewer spots available to outside applicants.

World changers. The Graduate School of Business was not created merely to screen candidates for the management consulting industry; its mission is to change lives, change organizations, and quite literally change the world. There are two things you can do to fit this mission: First, show that you have dreams and ambitions for your future; and second, demonstrate that you've already had an impact on the lives and organizations around you. The first essay is a fantastic opportunity to express your dreams and ambitions, and why they matter most to you. Demonstrating impact is a little trickier. This will happen in every element of your application, from the online application form to your resume, essays, letters of recommendation, and interview. When the admissions committee uses the terms *demonstrated leadership potential* and *personal contributions*, they anticipate that your application will be absolutely oozing with lifelong impact in your professional life and beyond. They are constantly looking for the future leaders who will change the world!

Humble. One critical element that is not included in the three evaluation criteria on Stanford's website is humility. While your resume can and should be chock full of quantifiable accomplishments, those achievements should stand for themselves. The rest of your communication with the admissions committee should showcase your outstanding teamwork skills and give proper credit to those who have helped you along life's path. Many applicants look outstanding on paper but are ultimately denied after the interview because they come off as pompous or too cutthroat.

> When the admissions committee uses the terms "demonstrated leadership potential" and "personal contributions," they anticipate that your application will be absolutely oozing with lifelong impact in your professional life and beyond.

 If you are looking for tips on 2016–17 admissions essays, you're in luck! Check out our website at **veritasprep.com/gsb** for our latest advice.

Interesting. When the Stanford website uses the phrase *personal qualities and contributions*, it means that they like to admit interesting people—and who can blame them? If you have the pick of the litter, would you choose to stock your MBA class full of GMAT-obliterating drones, or would you find people who bring something unique to the classroom? This isn't to say that you have to be a standup comedian or the next Barbara Walters, but the admissions committee will be looking for personality in your applications. Be sure not to drown out your personal voice and passions by submitting essays that are dry, stilted, cookie-cutter, or overly edited by too many people. Including a little personal flair is what we mean by applications that "sparkle."

Intellectually vibrant. With input from Dean Saloner, the GSB admissions committee is currently looking a bit more closely these days at past academic history. Keep in mind that this means more than just grade point average; it means the overall experience you had in college as reflected through the classes you took, the activities you engaged in, and how you challenged yourself. With an average GMAT score higher than any other school, Stanford also values your ability to test well. Yet at the same time, Stanford has always searched across all elements of the application for evidence of intellectual curiosity, passion, and demonstrated leadership ability in its candidates, so a low GPA or GMAT isn't an automatic disqualification, though it will be quite difficult to overcome a weakness in one or both areas.

Accomplished. Above all, the GSB is looking for candidates who are the best-of-the-best in whatever they do. This is often evidenced by the letters of reference. Application readers will spend significant time looking at the references to see if they are table-pounding enthusiastic, or whether they are conspicuously faint in their praise. Not to worry, our Japanese and Scandinavian applicants! These admissions officers have enough experience to know that international recommenders, particularly from Europe and Asia, tend to be more circumspect in their praise than Americans. Nonetheless, from start to finish your application must show that you absolutely shine among your peers. Simply going to work and checking off all the boxes on your job description isn't going to cut it.

Preparing to Apply

Reading this Essential Guide is a great first step in your preparation. Hopefully, this insider's glimpse has been helpful in understanding the most important aspects of the school. However, nothing can replace gaining firsthand knowledge and experience yourself.

Reach out to current students. Even if you don't have any personal connections to the GSB, you can reach out to current students and get their insight and advice. On the school's Activities and Organizations page, you'll find a list of all campus clubs. Find a few clubs that fit your interests and use the e-mail link to reach out to club officers. Remember: These are very busy MBA students so you don't want to intrude too much on their time, but you could ask for a 10- to 15-minute conversation or elicit some advice via e-mail. If you're planning to visit campus, perhaps you might even arrange a coffee chat or lunch, if they are available. Officers of major clubs like the Finance or Management Consulting Club have plenty of responsibilities. You might provide a quick background introduction and ask if there's another member of their club who might be able to offer some insights and advice about his or her Stanford experience.

Visit campus. If you have the means, we highly recommend you visit the Stanford campus along with a handful of others to understand the significant differences in culture, teaching style, student body, recruiting opportunities, facilities, and so forth. A campus visit does not directly impact your admissions chances in any way, but you will be surprised at just how different each school can be. We encourage you to take advantage of the formal on-campus events, including a class visit, tour of the Knight Management Center, information session, and university campus tour, as available. However, we also encourage you to go to the Arbuckle Dining Pavilion in the middle of campus to grab a bite to eat and talk to a few current students. The formal program gives a good surface-level experience of the GSB, but impromptu conversations can be incredibly enlightening.

Other events. We know that many applicants will not be able to fly to the Bay Area to visit campus, but the GSB offers many other admissions events around the globe, including information sessions, forums, and other audience-specific events. Get to know the school and its culture as well as you can, because your familiarity can shine through your application and essay to help you stand out.

> **Get to know the school and its culture as well as you can, because your familiarity can shine through your application and essays to help you stand out.**

APPLICATION DEADLINES

All deadlines are 5PM U.S. Pacific Time on the date indicated.

Round 1
22 Sep 2015
Notification:
9 Dec 2015

Round 2
12 Jan 2016
Notification:
30 Mar 2016

Round 3
5 Apr 2016
Notification:
11 May 2016

You Oughta Know

Application rounds. The GSB uses a standard three-round system for applications. This means that you may submit your application in any of its three rounds in the fall, winter, or spring for admission in the following Fall Quarter. However, 90% or more of the class will be filled with the first two rounds of applicants, so we encourage you to apply in Round 1 or Round 2 unless you have compelling circumstances. Round 3 candidates will be considered alongside waitlisted candidates from the first two rounds.

Finance and management consulting candidates. If you are a traditional candidate from management consulting or finance, we encourage you to apply in the first round (assuming you have a strong GMAT score), as you'll be competing against many candidates with very similar profiles. In a later round, it's possible that the school may see you as a viable candidate to the school but may have already admitted several other applicants with similar profiles, so it might pass on you to bring greater professional diversity to the class. Plus, the admissions committee knows you've been planning on an MBA since the day you graduated from undergrad, so there's no reason to delay!

Avoid rushed applications. Please note that even though the Stanford website encourages you to apply in the earliest round possible, this does not mean that you should apply with a rushed application or a mediocre GMAT score. There's no sense in applying early if you're just going to be denied. A GMAT score that's above the school's average will do more for most applicants than applying in the first round. If you are wondering whether you should hurry an application or Round 1 or wait to apply in Round 2, please give us a call at Veritas Prep, and we'll be happy to discuss your unique circumstances.

Navigating deadlines. As other schools' Round 1 deadlines continued to march earlier in previous years, Stanford's remained essentially unchanged. This year, however, the Round 1 deadline for Stanford GSB is September 22, 2015, nearly two weeks earlier than last year's deadline. The admissions committee looks for true introspection and thoughtfulness, which take time. Because very few applicants are successful when they're writing their essays, managing their recommendation writers, and tracking down transcripts all while also trying to break 730 on the GMAT, be sure to plan out your application tasks and start early! Pulling together your applications (and doing it well) will take you at least a few weeks from start to finish.

College seniors. Stanford GSB has a web page dedicated to encouraging college seniors to apply, and they may apply for direct or deferred enrollment. A few words of caution: First, please don't be overly encouraged by the years of work experience posted on the GSB website. Each year, there are a couple of people admitted who have zero years of work experience, but there's a high likelihood that these are primarily joint-degree candidates who already have a year or two of grad school under their belts at another Stanford program. Being admitted for direct enrollment as a college senior would require an astounding candidate. One example might be an undergraduate who launched, operated, and sold an extremely successful business with several employees while in college, an experience that would provide the level of insight and professional maturity the admissions office is looking for.

For most college seniors, deferred enrollment will be a better route. This means that you apply as a senior, but defer your enrollment in the GSB for two to three years to gain the necessary work experience to be a powerful, contributing member of the class. Stanford does not break out separate statistics for successful deferred admission candidates, but we know the bar is extremely high. The total number of successful deferred enrollment candidates is likely in the single digits each year. The themes discussed above, including impact, world-changing vision, humility, and accomplishment, all still apply to college senior applicants.

The Online Application Form

Many applicants put little thought into the school's online application form, but this is a vital element of your overall profile, so don't blow it off! We'll comment on only the sections where we can provide some actionable insight. Others are pretty straightforward.

Background. There are no "wrong" answers in this section; just be honest! If you're the first member of your family to attend college, the admissions committee may be a bit more forgiving when it comes to the prestige of your undergraduate institution or even your early undergraduate performance. However, applicants aren't judged based on who tells the biggest sob story about their background; they are evaluated based on their own impact and accomplishments. If you have a relative or significant other who is also applying to the GSB this year, please feel free to list him or her. There's no distinct advantage or disadvantage, but it's possible that if one of you is waitlisted and the other is admitted, there's a slightly higher chance that you could be chosen off the waitlist. Actually have some fun with the "just for fun" section! It's a chance to give the admissions committee a little glimmer of your personality.

Application Information. If you're a re-applicant, the key will be to show what has changed about your candidacy since your previous application. In general, re-applicants are admitted at slightly higher rates than first-time applicants simply because they have had an extra year to improve their candidacy. A criminal record will not necessarily preclude you from admission to the GSB. The admissions office outsources background checks on random members of the incoming class, so don't leave off any records here. You may put your admission in jeopardy and risk being expelled if misrepresenting information here. If inconsistencies are discovered later on, you may have your degree stripped from you, as happened to a Stanford MBA graduate in 2014.

> In general, re-applicants are admitted at slightly higher rates than first-time applicants simply because they have had an extra year to improve their candidacy.

Education. If you worked to help support yourself through school, the admissions committee will take this information into consideration with your academic performance, but there's no disadvantage to you if you were primarily funded by family, loans, or scholarships. There's no "preferred" way to make your way through school! If you have some concerns about your undergraduate performance, taking relevant coursework such as calculus, microeconomics, statistics, finance, or other courses at a local community college, extension program, or accredited online university can help showcase your true academic abilities. You can report such additional coursework in this section.

Test Scores. Notice that even if you have taken the GMAT or GRE multiple times, you report only your best score. (However, you cannot mix and match the best sections of multiple exams—sorry!) The admissions committee will only evaluate the score you report. Many admitted students have taken the GMAT or GRE multiple times, and this does not affect your admission. Eventually, your self-reported score will be compared to the official scores on the GMAC or ETS database, so be accurate.

Professional Experience. Two hundred fifty-five characters doesn't seem like much space to talk about your post-MBA career goals, but it's more than you think! If you can use this space to connect your previous experience to your immediate post-MBA goals and maybe even draw a connection to future ambitions, you'll have said a lot. Here's an example: "I seek to leverage my experience in the media sector to transition into a role in a media-focused management consulting team, gain vital strategic experience, and eventually transform the way we create, consume and share content as a media executive." (Five characters to spare!)

Many people think that your desired industry and function after B-school need to be wildly unique and impressive to get into Stanford GSB. They don't! The school knows that even big dreamers many need to take smaller, intermediate steps to achieve their dreams. Not only is this perfectly fine, but it shows that you have carefully thought out your goals and are willing to do what it takes to achieve them. Be honest about your immediate post-MBA goals.

If your current supervisor does not know that you're applying, you may want to include a line or two about why you have selected another person to write your letter of reference in the Additional Information section. Many, many people are admitted without telling their current supervisor, but it can certainly be seen as a signal for the level of relationship and trust you have with your supervisors.

> **Your one-page resume is often the first thing that an admissions reader will look at, simply to get a quick sense of your overall profile.**

Your one-page resume is often the first thing that an admissions reader will look at, simply to get a quick sense of your overall profile. You have an opportunity to explain the nature of your employer, your position, your greatest accomplishment, and so forth, in the Employment History section of the application. While your resume can reinforce some of the same points, it should be even more focused on accomplishments. This is a key opportunity to highlight the impact you've had throughout your professional career.

Activities & Interests. When combined with the first essay about what matters most to you, this section can help the admissions officer get a sense of what makes you tick, what interests you the most, and how you'll contribute uniquely to the GSB class. Although the admissions website says they do not expect candidates to be involved in outside activities, we've found that the most successful candidates show an impact beyond mere self-aggrandizement.

Awards & Honors. Candidates who have left their fingerprints on an organization may find that they receive honors or awards for this effort. However, some industries or organizations may provide more opportunities for recognition than others. You may enter up to five awards, but there is no specific expectation for a certain number of awards. Listing the runner-up award in your elementary-school speaking competition (we've actually seen it!) is going to do more to highlight your lack of other recognitions than impress the admissions committee.

Additional Information. Just as the instructions say, this section is completely optional and should be used only to explain extenuating circumstances not mentioned elsewhere. Droning on for paragraphs about your circumstances will come off as excuse-making. Instead, explain any circumstances in a sentence or two, and take responsibility for your own performance. Perhaps you could include a line about the additional perspective or skills you gained as a result of unfortunate circumstances, but the shorter the better here.

The Essays

Essay A: What matters most to you, and why? (750 words suggested, out of 1,100 total)

Despite all of the changes that have taken place in the MBA admissions essay landscape over the past few years, this question manages to hang on. Before you start to work on this essay, consider the advice that the Stanford MBA admissions team provides: "Reflect the self-examination process you used to write your response."

This question requires a great deal of introspection, after which you should create an essay that truly answers the question asked, whether or not you feel that it's directly applicable to the job of getting into Stanford GSB. Naturally, telling a random story that has nothing to do with anything of relevance can hurt your chances, but mainly because you will have wasted this valuable space to reveal something about yourself. Where many Stanford applicants go wrong is by writing about their grand plans for the future, rather than providing a real glimpse into who they are as people. The latter is much more powerful and, ultimately, much more effective in helping you get in. With the other essay in this application, you have ample opportunity to cover the exact reasons why you want an MBA from Stanford, including your post-MBA ambitions.

Take to heart a few do's and don'ts when it comes to writing this essay:

Don't:

1. ***Don't try to tell the admissions committee what you think they want to hear.*** This results in a cookie-cutter, "packaged" response that will be a huge turnoff to the admissions reader. They are looking for authenticity and passion in this essay—your true motivations. The best essays will show genuine self-reflection and self-discovery through the essay-writing process.

2. ***Don't try to impress the admissions committee with your many accomplishments.*** There's plenty of room in the online application form and in your resume to let your achievements shine; don't be shy about showing the admissions committee what you've accomplished in those sections! But this essay is not the place for it. There's a quiet confidence in humility that will be expressed by following the instructions and answering the question that has been asked. This is the place where the admissions committee gets to see your values, motivations, and passions—what really makes you tick!

3. ***Don't write your essays in overly formal or academic language.*** Don't get us wrong: This isn't a text message you're sending to a friend or even a blog post you're broadcasting to the world, but it's not an academic paper, either. In the words of Assistant Dean for Admissions Derrick Bolton, "Please think of your Stanford essays as

conversations—when we read files, we feel that we meet people, also known as our 'flat friends'—and tell us your story in a natural, genuine way." Notice the tone that we've written this Essential Guide: It's grammatically correct and remains professional, yet isn't afraid to show a little personality! That's how we encourage you to write your essays.

4. ***Don't be afraid to talk about fantastic failures—and what you learned from them.*** This isn't to say that your admissions essays should become a confessional about everything you've done wrong in life. However, many applicants feel like they need to impress the admissions committee by writing narratives where they play the knight in shining armor who rides in to save the day in every circumstance. Let's get real! It's often in our most difficult circumstances that we learn what matters most to us.

> **Use stories from your life to show how you developed your values, passions, etc. These personal stories will show why this has become such an important thing in your life.**

Do:

You'll notice that a number of do's listed below mirror the instructions provided on Stanford's website. The school is *not* using some sort of reverse psychology; it is telling you exactly what it's looking for in this essay. We provide some additional tips here on how to do it.

1. ***Focus on the "why" rather than the "what."*** You may be able to say what matters most to you in one sentence. Rather than simply trying to tell the admissions committee why this matters to you, show them! How do you show versus tell? Use stories from your life to show how you developed your values, passions, etc. These personal stories will show why this has become such an important thing in your life.

2. ***Reflect the self-examination process you used to write your response.*** This is a self-reflection process with an essay as a deliverable. In your essay, actually write out how you determined what matters most to you. Were you primarily consumed in your own thoughts, or did you reach out to others for input? If you reached out to others, whom did you select and why? (Either process is perfectly fine, by the way. There's no "right" way to decide what matters most to you.) Stanford is as interested in the process you took as it is in the resulting essay.

3. ***Share the insights, experiences, and lessons that shaped your perspectives, rather than focusing merely on what you've done or accomplished.*** We like to call this the "Slumdog Millionaire" strategy. In the movie *Slumdog Millionaire*, we get tiny glimpses into a seemingly ordinary boy's life that help us see the world through his eyes and understand how he came to this point. Your essay may weave together "mini stories" that together tell a compelling narrative about yourself. Each story should focus more on what you've learned and how it shaped your perspective rather than what you've accomplished. If you can, find stories that are memorable but make a very specific point about yourself. *Slumdog Millionaire* isn't quite laser-focused enough on "what matters most" to make an outstanding Stanford essay, but you get the idea!

4. ***Write from the heart, and illustrate how a person, situation, or event has influenced you.*** Don't be afraid to get personal and to focus on others. So many applicants are so focused on themselves that they forget their life is often a series of external influences (either positive or negative). Essays that focus on what the applicant has learned from others often showcase the reflection and humility that the GSB is looking for.

Essay B: Why Stanford? (350 words suggested)

Stanford is giving applicants 50 more words than it did last year! Otherwise, this essay prompt carries over unchanged from last year.

Do your homework. Just like HBS, Stanford has the luxury of not having to spend too much time sleuthing out your genuine level of interest in the program. The vast majority of people who are admitted to Stanford end up going there. However, the guidance that the admissions team provides with this question ("Explain the distinctive opportunities you will pursue at Stanford.") shows that they really are paying attention to see if you've done your homework and if you have given any real thought to making the most of your time at Stanford (beyond "plan to be insanely rich one day").

Get beyond a list of classes or professors. Resist the urge to do a few web searches and then simply drop the names of some programs or professors into this essay. An effective response will provide specific details about aspects of the academics, activities, events, professional opportunities, or culture that tie back to you, your past experience, and your future goals. Many applicants will read that "distinctive opportunities" advice and think, "The scavenger hunt is on! Let me find something no one else will write about!" but that misses the point. Stanford simply wants to know that you're applying for reasons other than the fact that it's such a platinum name in education. This Guide is a great place to start in looking for elements of the program about which you'll be most passionate. However, we recommend you also speak to current students or recent alumni about their experience at the GSB so that you can speak passionately about the elements of the program that you're looking forward to the most.

Don't be afraid to dream big, but be ready to back it up. We see a lot of people for whom Stanford is their top-choice school because it will enable them to get a better job upon graduation. This is true for literally every applicant; they'll do better with Stanford on their resume than without it. Remember that Stanford is looking for world changers, and this is your opportunity to show how far you'll be able to go with your Stanford education and experience. Don't be afraid to dream, but realistically show how your past experience sets you up for success in your future endeavors. Spell out how You + Stanford = A World-Changing Business Leader.

> The guidance that the admissions team provides with this question ("Explain the distinctive opportunities you will pursue at Stanford.") shows that they really are paying attention to see if you've done your homework.

Letters of Reference

Don't write them yourself. Former admissions readers for the GSB have told us that the letters of reference are perhaps the most important elements of your entire application. It's the one opportunity that they get to hear about you from a third-party perspective, and they read these letters carefully. If they simply parrot back exactly what you've already mentioned in your application or are written in the same writing style, they will add nothing to what you've already painstakingly crafted. Many recommenders will ask you to write the letter and then they will approve and submit it. We have a three-part series on the Veritas Prep blog about how to get recommenders to write enthusiastic letters.

Instructions. Stanford is a bit more open about its recommender process than a lot of other top business schools. Detailed instructions about selecting your recommenders, advice regarding effective letters of reference, and the recommender questions themselves can be found on the website. Because such ample information is supplied, it's important to follow the guidelines around who should write your recommendations, and how they should do so. The biggest takeaway from these materials is that the admissions committee is looking for recommendations that are so personal that you "jump off the page." This means that selecting people who know you, your work, leadership style, and individual strengths and weaknesses is much more important than an alum of the school or someone with a fancy title.

Whom to select. Stanford used to require three recommenders, but has significantly streamlined the process, now asking for just two references with a much simpler form to fill out. If at all possible, one recommendation should come from your direct supervisor. There are a number of circumstances in which this will be impossible, such as not wanting to tell your current supervisor that you may be leaving the company!

While we still encourage you to bring your direct supervisor into this decision, we understand that it will not be advisable in some circumstances. In that case, you need the next-best substitute—someone who has supervised your work or at least seen your professional life up close and personal. He or she will need to be able to use specific examples of how you have stood out from your peers and how you have responded to constructive feedback. A generic recommendation from your CEO will do far less for you than an enthusiastic, personal, example-ridden recommendation from a lower-level manager or professional mentor.

The other recommendation can come from another supervisor or a peer. This reference can come from your professional, community, or extracurricular experiences. The key here will be to select someone who will give a strong reference regarding the impact you've had on the organization. If you're concerned that your extensive efforts outside of work may not be well represented in other parts of the application, you may decide to choose a supervisor from your extensive extracurricular involvement. However, if your extracurricular involvement is actually quite thin, don't make that fact even more obvious by choosing someone who hardly knows you from "that one time" you volunteered at Habitat for Humanity.

It's perfectly fine to have two professional references, particularly if your two references will be able to speak to different strengths and experiences with you. The references are used by the admissions committee to evaluate both your achievements and the interpersonal, leadership, and other skills you utilized to get there.

What they'll be asked. Your recommenders will be asked to answer the following questions:

- *How long have you known the applicant?*

- *During which period of time have you had the most frequent contact with the applicant? From (mm/yyyy) To (mm/yyyy)*

- *Are/were you the applicant's direct supervisor?*

- *Please comment briefly on the context of your interaction with the applicant. If applicable, describe the applicant's role in your organization. (Limit 500 characters.)*

- *Did you use a translator?*

- *If you are a Stanford MBA alumna/alumnus, please enter your MBA class year.*

- *How many candidates are you recommending to the Stanford MBA Program this year?*

- *Leadership Assessment. [This is a multiple-choice assessment on the following categories: Results Orientation, Strategic Orientation, Team Leadership, Influence and Collaboration, Communicating, Information Seeking, Developing Others, Change Leadership, Respect for Others, and Trustworthiness.]*

- *Summary. Based on your professional experience, how would you rate this candidate compared to her/his peer group? [Multiple-choice: Below Average; Average; Very good (well above average); Excellent (top 10%); Outstanding (top 5%); The best encountered in my career.]*

- *Overall, I [Do not recommend this candidate to Stanford; Recommend this candidate to Stanford, with reservations; Recommend this candidate to Stanford].*

- *Reference questions. The most useful recommendations provide detailed descriptions, candid anecdotes, and specific evidence that highlight the candidate's behavior and impact on those around her or him. This kind of information helps distinguish the very best individuals from a pool of many well-qualified candidates. Please write your answers to the following questions in a separate document and upload that document into the online application.*

Questions:
1. How do the candidate's performance, potential, or personal qualities compare to those of other well-qualified individuals in similar roles? Please provide specific examples.
2. Describe the most important piece of constructive feedback you have given the applicant. Please detail the circumstances and the applicant's response.

Tips:
- Please do not exceed 3 pages, double-spaced, using 12-point font.
- Please do not include graphics or icons such as company letterhead.

We provide this information so that you can select the recommenders who would be able to answer each questions with personal insight and experience.

> **The references are used by the admissions committee to evaluate both your achievements and the interpersonal, leadership, and other skills you utilized to get there.**

In the 2014–15 admissions cycle, the GSB issued interview invitations within a four-week period starting about a month after the Round 1 and Round 2 deadlines. Most candidates who were not invited to interview during this period were denied, providing them an earlier decision so they could make other plans.

The Interview

Your interview invitation. As is the case with many top-tier business schools, the admissions interview is an important part of the Stanford GSB application process. With only about 900 applicants to be interviewed this year (about 14% of expected applications), merely receiving an invitation is a great accomplishment. You'll have about a 50/50 chance of receiving an offer. In the 2014–15 admissions cycle, the GSB issued interview invitations within a four-week period starting about a month after the Round 1 and Round 2 deadlines. Most candidates who were not invited to interview during this period were denied, providing them an earlier decision so they could make other plans. You should expect the same process in the 2015–16 admissions cycle. The interviewers are all members of the GSB alumni network and are selected based on their geographical proximity to the applicant.

What is the interviewer looking for? GSB interviews are "blind," so alumni interviewers do not have access to any application material aside from the applicant's resume. Only a few interviews are conducted by admissions representatives each year.

The interview tends to focus on past actions rather than on hypothetical situations. The primary questions revolve around attitudes, behaviors, and skills that the GSB believes are key to good citizenship in the Stanford community and vital to high-impact leadership post-MBA.

During the interview, the interviewer will be looking for how you demonstrate leadership in your life, so take advantage of this opportunity to think about the people, situations, and events that have shaped you. You will also benefit from relating your past experience and training to your future career goals. The GSB encourages applicants to dig deep into their stories and be able to explain the reasons behind their particular decisions.

The interview is important; you might even say it's a test of whether you fit in at the school. You should have a real appreciation for the culture and what Stanford is about before going for your interview. If the interview report is negative on these aspects, it is unlikely you will get an offer in your inbox.

Applicants are encouraged to maintain their humility during the interview. Avoid dropping names, or coming off as arrogant or pompous. Instead, try to highlight your intellectual curiosity and creativity at every opportunity.

What will I be asked? Some of the typical questions asked during the interview are as follows:

- *Why Stanford?*

- *Why an MBA now? What do you hope to get out of it?*

- *What did you like about your undergrad? Why don't you want to go there for your MBA?*

- *Tell me about a time when you dealt with a problematic person. What was the situation and how did you react? What was the result?*

- *Tell me about a time when you worked on a really analytical project. What was the result and how was it used in your organization?*

- *Tell me about a time when you went beyond the realm of your authority on a project. What was the result?*

- *Tell me about a time when you really led a team. How did you lead the team?*

- *How do you think you've made an impact on your organization?*

- *Tell me about a time when you took the initiative. What was the result?*

- *Do you have any questions for me?*

THE WHARTON SCHOOL

Wharton has invested millions to expand beyond finance and analytics.

📍 PHILADELPHIA, PA

CLASS SIZE

859

PROGRAM FOUNDED

1925

CHARACTERISTICS

ANALYTICAL, EXPERIENTIAL, RIGOROUS

SECTIONS

WHARTON SNAPSHOT

What Wharton Is Known For

Analytics. It's no secret that Wharton is a quant school; for better or worse, that's probably why you're considering it! But that well-deserved reputation doesn't mean that Wharton is just a finance school. Quantitative and analytical skills are woven throughout the curriculum, especially in disciplines like marketing. It's a way of thinking as much or more than a discipline.

We like to refer to Wharton as the "Swiss Army knife" of business schools, because nearly every department is among the best in the world.

Broad strengths. We like to refer to Wharton as the "Swiss Army knife" of business schools, because nearly every department is among the best in the world. In *U.S. News & World Report's* 10 reported specialties for business schools in 2015, Wharton ranked among the top-10 programs in all but one specialty: Finance (#1), Marketing (#2), Accounting (#2), International (#2), Management (#4), Production/Operations (#4), Entrepreneurship (#6), Information Systems (#8), and Supply Chain/Logistics (#10). The only specialty in which Wharton was not listed was Nonprofit, and honestly, it's not a bad program for nonprofit management, either! The school is also known for its world-class specialties in health care, real estate, and insurance.

Global outreach. Wharton offers a number of global learning activities, some integrated into the curriculum and some offered as extracurriculars. Highlights are the elective Global Immersion Programs, the Global Consulting Practicum (a marketing elective), and Global Modular Courses (offered simultaneously to undergrads, MBAs, and EMBAs). Wharton also offers a number of internationally focused dual-degree programs and numerous exchange programs.

Impressive campuses. In March 2015, Wharton opened the Penn Wharton China Center in Beijing, which will augment the school's partnerships with Chinese educational institutions. This opening expands Wharton's reach from Philadelphia and its West Coast campus in San Francisco, launched in 2010 to host a full menu of executive education courses and an Executive MBA program. Full-time MBA students based in Philadelphia also have the option of spending a semester at the West Coast campus, which allows for greater networking opportunities with Silicon Valley.

Dual degrees. Wharton leverages resources available across Penn and even across other schools to offer an impressive array of dual-degree programs. The best-known program is The MBA/MA Lauder Joint-Degree in International Studies program, which underwent a significant restructuring in 2015. In addition to the Lauder Program, Wharton students can also pursue joint or dual degrees in conjunction with Penn's other leading graduate schools, including the law school, the design school, the medical school, and even the veterinary school. Wharton also offers partnerships with the School of Advanced International Studies at Johns Hopkins and Harvard's Kennedy School.

What Makes Wharton Different

Student involvement. There's an old joke at Wharton that the school has "just enough clubs for every student to be president of one," and although that statement might be just a teensy bit of an exaggeration, the array of organizations is wide. Inside and outside of the classroom, students play a leading role in defining the Wharton experience for themselves, their classmates, and future students. The expectation is that Wharton students will be active members of the community—a standard that manifests itself in all aspects of the Wharton experience.

Experiential learning. Nearly every elite business school is advertising its "action-based" or "experiential" approach, but Wharton has recently undergone a comprehensive branding and identity initiative, resulting in a new brand platform called "Knowledge for Action." This brand platform emphasizes and communicates Wharton's strengths of rigorous research, dynamic thinking, and thoughtful leadership. Gaining knowledge and putting it into practice is seamlessly integrated into the student experience through initiatives such as the Global Consulting Practicum. In addition, proprietary simulation exercises are woven into the curriculum in both core and elective courses, primarily in marketing and management.

Leadership. Building leadership acumen is a core of the Wharton program. While we'd be hard pressed to say that leadership is more important at Wharton than it is at other top schools, opportunities to build this skill abound at this school. Wharton features a dedicated Center for Leadership and Change Management, which forms the core of its leadership program. Combining experiential learning and global exposure, Leadership Ventures are perhaps Wharton's most popular leadership offering and may include intense mountaineering, glacier trekking, mountain biking, rafting, sailing, rock climbing, or even military combat training.

> **Combining experiential learning and global exposure, Leadership Ventures are perhaps Wharton's most popular leadership offering.**

The dean. In July 2014, Geoffrey Garrett assumed the role of The Wharton School's 13th dean. A former Wharton management department faculty member (he specializes in political economy), he previously served as dean of two business schools in Australia, the University of Sydney and the University of New South Wales. In an interview with the *Daily Pennsylvanian*, Dean Garrett indicated that he would "leverage" the school's financial reputation and pointed to "globalization" and "technology" as two themes of his tenure in in Australia—a clue, perhaps, of the direction Wharton will head under his leadership. Given Wharton's reputation as a finance school, Dean Garrett's focus on globalization and innovation may, on the surface, appear to make him a surprise pick. However, Garrett believes in not resting on the laurels of Wharton's heritage and notes in a recent interview that "[Wharton] need[s] to come to the world" as much as the world came to Wharton in the past. Shaking things up with the opening of the Penn Wharton China Center is one example of how Garrett is putting his words into action.

Wharton Is a Good Fit for You If...

If you're looking to go to Wall Street, Wharton is a natural for you to consider.

You are interested in finance. We haven't even mentioned it much so far because we figure everybody already knows: Wharton is a finance school. The school has spent millions building and touting its highly recognized programs in marketing, real estate, health care, international studies, and more, but the core strength and the interest of the majority of its students remain in the world of finance. It sends large numbers of graduates into investment banking, portfolio management, and corporate finance, and places a decent number into hedge funds, private equity, and even sales and trading—areas that some schools never place anyone. If you're looking to go to Wall Street, Wharton is a natural for you to consider.

You are interested in entrepreneurship. Behind finance, entrepreneurship is the second-most-popular field of study at The Wharton School. About 50–60 graduates start companies coming out of Wharton every year, although schools like Stanford, MIT Sloan, and Harvard might give Wharton a run for its money on the entrepreneurship side. Nonetheless, it's an area that is seeing more attention with Wharton's renewed interest in innovation and social impact.

You're from or want to transition into the healthcare industry. Wharton has one of the strongest Health Care Management programs of any business school, and it deeply integrates academic and professional development. Unlike other majors, students must choose the Health Care Management major when they apply to Wharton, so if this emphasis interests you, be sure to do your due diligence on this program well before applying. Health Care Management majors at Wharton have their own career counselors and recruiting resources focused in healthcare consulting, biotech, pharmaceuticals, hospitals, and insurance and government agencies. The Class of 2016 included 70 healthcare students, who are grouped together in their own cohort. Take note when you're applying, however, that this program is targeted specifically for students who are sure they want to enter the healthcare industry post-MBA. The vast majority of participants (usually more than 90%) enter the industry upon graduation.

You have had, or want to have, internationally diverse work experiences. Wharton loves those multicultural stories in applicant backgrounds. Overseas work experience is definitely not required in order to gain an offer from Wharton, but it never hurts. Just don't be tempted to try to overstate your two-week European vacation into a "multicultural experience"; oftentimes, vacation stories can come across as fairly routine, and that's not the level of cultural exposure the admissions committee values the most. Whether you make your travel a cornerstone of your application depends both on the real nature of your experiences in that country and, even more importantly, whether it adds an international flavor to your stated future career goals. (For Wharton, it's less the international experience itself that is valuable, but rather what it says about you. For example, are you the kind of person who not only enjoys visiting foreign countries, but is also eager to really experience them beyond staying cooped up in fancy hotels and sticking to traditional tourist paths?)

You're a woman. Sorry, guys. In this case, women may have a slight advantage. While Wharton definitely does not have lower standards for its female applicants, it is actively courting high achievers. Strong women will likely be well received in the application process. While women need to have the same high qualifications as far as GPA, GMAT, and quality of work experience, Wharton has acknowledged that its female students tend to be a little younger, having fewer years of work experience than the average males it admits. So, younger female candidates should not hesitate to apply. In our experience at Veritas Prep, female candidates who gain admission to Wharton also are successful at other great schools.

You're changing careers. Wharton is very welcoming to career changers. If you're in this position, be sure to highlight the relevant skills and experience that you bring with you from your previous life, and show how you will apply those strengths to the new undertaking you are interested in pursuing after Wharton.

You have a military background. Wharton is a very military-friendly school: 13% of the incoming class came from the combined military/government/nonprofit sector. If you're applying as a veteran, the school's targeted recruiting events and Veterans Club will be valuable resources for you. As a Yellow Ribbon School, Wharton is also committed to assisting veterans finance their graduate educations.

ACADEMICS AT WHARTON

What Wharton Is Known For

Majors. Lots of majors. Wharton students may select one of 17 different in-depth majors or create one of their own. The idea behind majoring is that it provides students with the opportunity to delve deeper into specific areas of interest, either to cultivate an area of expertise or to assist in facilitating a future career shift. About a third of students can't pick just one major and elect to double major; 5% don't fit neatly into one of the 17 boxes and pick the "design your own" route. Some of the most popular majors include Finance, Marketing, and Entrepreneurial Management.

Hybrid classroom environment. Do you thrive on the case method? Great, you'll get that. Enjoy lectures, with lots of cold calls? Great! Wharton offers that, too. Wharton attempts to strike a balance among pedagogical methods, using a combination of case-based learning, traditional lectures, team-based projects, simulations, and experiential learning across the curriculum. In any given class, a professor is likely to employ any combination of these approaches. Given the faculty's extensive involvement in key industries, a plethora of real-world examples is integrated into the classroom experience.

Flexibility. There was a time in the not-too-distant past when "flexible" would have been the last word anyone used to describe the curriculum. Unless you were granted a precious course waiver, everyone took the same core classes, mostly with the same people. Not anymore. A new curriculum structure, introduced in 2012, empowers students to make more choices. Now, less than half of the core curriculum is taken with your cohort of about 70 students. The obvious benefit is that you can customize your path and focus on the classes you need for your summer internship. The downside is that the tight relationships that used to form with your cohort and your learning team are a little looser.

> **Women make up 40% of the Class of 2016.**

> **Wharton attempts to strike a balance among pedagogical methods, using a combination of case-based learning, traditional lectures, team-based projects, simulations, and experiential learning.**

WHARTON AT A GLANCE

APPLICANTS BY SCHOOL

◀ Percent admitted

Wharton 6,111	Stanford 7,355	Harvard 9,543	Columbia 5,799	Booth 4,175	Sloan 4,735
20.7%	7.1%	11%	18.2%	24%	13.8%

AVERAGE GPA

3.60	3.67	3.62	3.74
Wharton	Harvard	Haas	Stanford

WOMEN

Wharton has one of the highest percentages of women in its class compared to other top-tier schools, with women making up 40% of the Class of 2016. Wharton has acknowledged that its female students tend to be a little younger, having fewer years of work experience than the average males admitted.

RANGE OF WORK EXPERIENCE IN YEARS

0–16 Wharton	0–15 Stanford	0–13 MIT Sloan	2–12.5 Kellogg

Wharton has a wider range of years in work experience compared to other top-tier schools with both early career and more experienced candidates in the class.

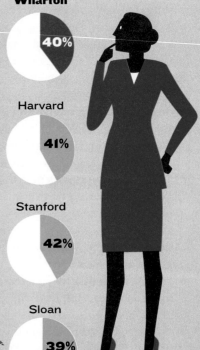

Wharton 40%

Harvard 41%

Stanford 42%

Sloan 39%

NATIONALITY

Bringing in students from 71 different countries, Wharton is the most internationally diverse class next to Harvard.

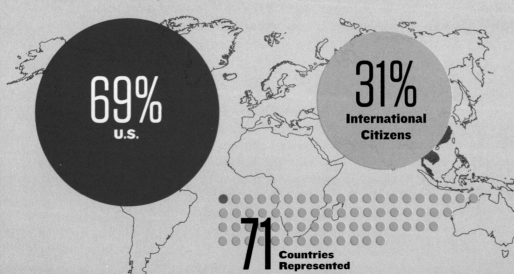

69% U.S.

31% International Citizens

71 Countries Represented

PENN (WHARTON)

GMAT SCORES

Average Score

728

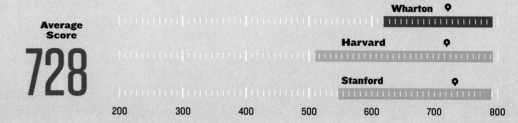

Wharton

Harvard

Stanford

200 300 400 500 600 700 800

UNDERGRAD MAJORS

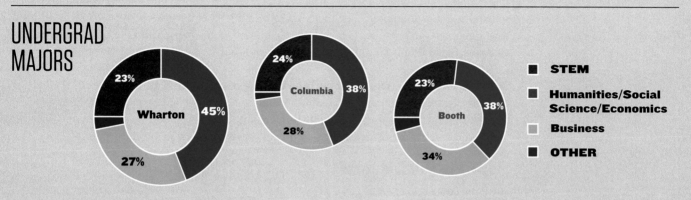

Wharton
- 23%
- 45%
- 27%

Columbia
- 24%
- 38%
- 28%

Booth
- 23%
- 38%
- 34%

- ■ STEM
- ■ Humanities/Social Science/Economics
- ■ Business
- ■ OTHER

FROM CONSULTING/FINANCE SECTOR PRE-MBA

Among top MBA programs, Wharton has one of the highest percentages of its class entering from the "usual suspects" industries of consulting and finance. However, its demographics have been gradually shifting to include more nontraditional candidates. For example, 14% of its Class of 2016 came from technology, up from just 6% in 2015.

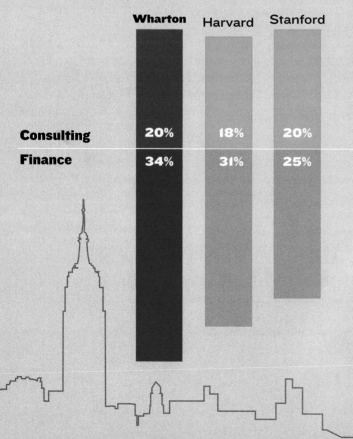

	Wharton	Harvard	Stanford
Consulting	20%	18%	20%
Finance	34%	31%	25%

CLASS SIZE

Of the top-tier business schools, Wharton has one of the largest incoming class sizes. A larger class size translates into a strong alumni network of 93,000 across 153 countries!

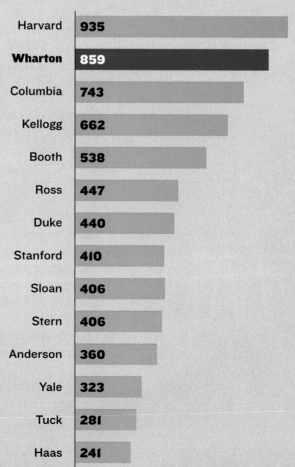

Harvard	935
Wharton	859
Columbia	743
Kellogg	662
Booth	538
Ross	447
Duke	440
Stanford	410
Sloan	406
Stern	406
Anderson	360
Yale	323
Tuck	281
Haas	241

Nuts & Bolts

Class registration. The online bidding system for classes has also gone the way of the fixed core curriculum. (Actually, it was probably more of a simulation exercise for game theory, but that's a moot point now.) Wharton now uses a program in which students input their preferred schedules and a computer does the work, attempting to give everybody as close to an ideal schedule as possible. Students must use this system to get spots in flex core classes as well as electives; they are only automatically enrolled in the fixed core classes.

Submatriculation. (Or, "What's that college senior doing in my cohort?") Chances are, that person has submatriculated into Wharton's 3+2 accelerated program for outstanding undergraduates. There aren't a lot of these "submatrics" around, and you might not even be able to tell who they are, but it's a unique feature of Wharton that some find surprising.

Popular Professors

Wharton's faculty boasts some of the biggest names in the business. It goes without saying that all of the professors are popular, but if you want a coveted spot in one of these professor's classes, you'll be in good company:

Franklin Allen. Professor Allen's approachable and engaging teaching style and ability to make complex corporate finance topics simpler to understand have won over Wharton students year after year. His introductory finance class, which he has taught for 25+ years, has often been referred to as a "well-polished diamond."

Eric Bradlow. Professor Bradlow is well loved by students not just for his teaching prowess and ability to make dry topics such as marketing research dynamic, but also for his affable manner, teaching enthusiasm, approachability, and genuine interest in getting to know students.

Brian Bushee. It's Wharton, so it's no surprise that accounting is popular, and Professor Bushee, who joined Wharton from HBS, is a student favorite. Bushee received the Excellence in Teaching Award in 2007, 2009, 2010, and 2014, the Teaching Commitment & Innovation Award in 2014, and the Award for Distinguished Teaching at the University of Pennsylvania in 2015—proof that tenured professors can and do care about just as much about teaching as about their research.

Stuart Diamond. The recipient of top student ratings every year, Professor Diamond's *Negotiations* course is a tough one in which to gain a seat. Influenced very much by his own experiences versus just negotiation theory, Professor Diamond uses and refines his negotiating methods every day in his own strategic consulting practice, where he advises and trains Fortune 500 companies, veteran executives, and even heads of state. Negotiation courses are a must-take before embarking on any negotiations with potential employers.

Adam Grant. Known for the book *Give and Take,* Professor Grant is the youngest full professor at Wharton. He teaches courses in leadership and negotiation.

Ethan Mollick. Professor Mollick teaches entrepreneurship; courses include *Entrepreneurship* and *Formation and Implementation of Entrepreneurial Ventures.*

Michael Roberts. Professor Roberts's *Corporate Valuation* course is a must-take for future bankers, venture capitalists, and finance executives.

Jeremy Siegel. In addition to being a world-renowned and very high-profile finance expert whose book *Stocks for the Long Run* is considered one of the top books on investing, Professor Siegel is considered one of the best professors on the Wharton faculty. A Wharton legend, Dr. Siegel's macroeconomics class is known for the opening market summary. Standing room only for the first 20 minutes or so, the unenrolled leave after the market recap.

Karl Ulrich. A 20+ year veteran of the operations department, Professor Ulrich's teaching now focuses on *Product Design & Development.*

Michael Useem. A world-renowned expert on corporate leadership and change management, Professor Useem consistently ranks among the most popular professors at Wharton. His extremely interactive teaching approach and dramatic storytelling ability—featuring examples ranging from the boardrooms of Fortune 500 companies to famous military moments to NGO and nonprofit organizations—captivate his students.

Z. John Zhang. Professor Zhang epitomizes genuine enthusiasm for his area of expertise (pricing). It's clear that pricing problems keep Professor Zhang up at night. Students love Professor Zhang's passion for his subject and his ability to integrate real-world examples into very theoretical course content.

Similar Academic Programs

MIT (Sloan). Sloan has one of the most rigorous core curricula of any MBA program in the world. Leveraging its parent institution's brand in engineering and the sciences, Sloan's academics are very data-driven and analytically focused. Even "softer" subjects such as communications and organizational behavior have a strong analytical bent. However, like at Wharton, the number of required core courses is quite limited, providing greater flexibility through the first year.

Chicago (Booth). Booth's curriculum is even more flexible than Wharton's, with just one required course and multiple options to fulfill all other requirements. Its student body is known for intellectual curiosity, and the school takes great pride in the academic rigor of its program compared to other, "softer" business schools. Also known as a strong finance school, the academics tend to be quite analytical in nature.

NYU (Stern). Stern has just two required courses in its core curriculum, plus the option to choose five additional courses from a "menu" of seven others. This model has become more popular in recent years so that first-year career-changers can tailor their core experience early in their MBA experience to properly prepare for internships in their chosen field. Someone seeking a position in brand management may want to tailor his or her experience differently than a candidate looking to move onto a sales and trading desk.

Duke (Fuqua). You don't see many comparisons between Fuqua and Wharton, which tend to attract very different MBA candidates, but their core curricula are remarkably similar. Each school offers students significant flexibility while focusing on the very traditional MBA subjects of statistics, accounting, finance, economics, marketing, and so forth. With Wharton's increased emphasis on management communications, the two schools' core requirements have become even more similar in recent years.

EMPLOYMENT & CAREERS AT WHARTON

What Wharton Is Known For

Finance, finance, finance. It's no surprise that Wharton sends a large number of graduates into finance. Thirty-six percent of the Class of 2014 went into financial services in some capacity—bested only by Booth, which sent 37% of its Class of 2014 into this industry. The diversity of Wharton grads' choices might be somewhat surprising, though: Although 14% went into banking, a relatively large number of students pursued private equity (9%) and venture capital (2%). Only Stanford and Harvard sent a larger percentage of students into these industries. Since Wharton's class is significantly larger than Stanford's you'll find several Wharton grads at most PE and VC firms.

Graduates entering the finance industry

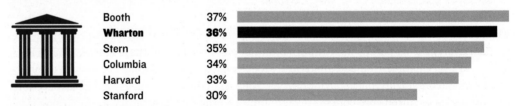

Booth	37%
Wharton	**36%**
Stern	35%
Columbia	34%
Harvard	33%
Stanford	30%

Strength across industries. The sheer number of students going into fields like risk management, insurance, and real estate isn't huge, but if you're interested in one of these specialties, Wharton's strong reputation should make the school one of your top choices. In fact, Wharton's placement statistics indicate that students pursue careers in just about every industry.

Graduates entering the real estate industry

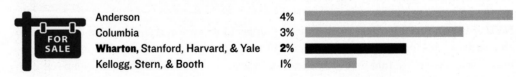

Anderson	4%
Columbia	3%
Wharton, Stanford, Harvard, & Yale	2%
Kellogg, Stern, & Booth	1%

Entrepreneurship. While schools such as Stanford and MIT Sloan may be better for known for the number of their graduates who start up businesses post-MBA, Wharton's employment statistics indicate that they're actually not that far behind. Fifty-five students from the Class of 2014 launched their own business, or 6.4% of the class. This is not as huge as Stanford's nearly 16% of the class, but it's more than double Columbia's 3% and Booth's 1.6%.

Graduates electing to pursue entrepreneurial opportunities

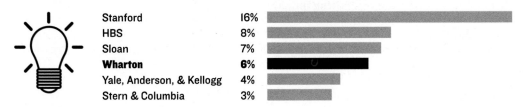

Stanford	16%	
HBS	8%	
Sloan	7%	
Wharton	**6%**	
Yale, Anderson, & Kellogg	4%	
Stern & Columbia	3%	

International opportunities. Wharton places nearly one-fifth of its class outside of the U.S., which is quite a bit higher than other top-tier business schools. In comparison, Stanford placed 13% abroad, as did both Kellogg and Booth. Wharton's incoming international class is only 31% compared to Stanford's 44%, so the ratio of those either returning home or pursuing career opportunities abroad is interestingly higher at Wharton.

Graduates pursuing careers abroad

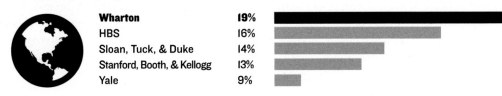

Wharton	**19%**	
HBS	16%	
Sloan, Tuck, & Duke	14%	
Stanford, Booth, & Kellogg	13%	
Yale	9%	

You Oughta Know

Social impact. Despite Wharton's emphasis on social impact and its loan–forgiveness opportunities, only 2% of the Class of 2014 took jobs in nonprofit or the public sector. Nearly 5% of the Class of 2015 accepted internships in that area, so the numbers might increase in future years.

Graduates entering nonprofit/government jobs

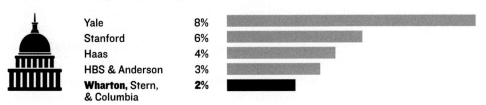

Yale	8%	
Stanford	6%	
Haas	4%	
HBS & Anderson	3%	
Wharton, Stern, & Columbia	**2%**	

Consulting. If you're looking to pursue management consulting post-MBA, Wharton is just as good as other top-tier schools when it comes to placement statistics. Consulting is, after all, highly analytical, so it's always been a popular choice for Wharton grads, although the percentage has decreased as the school has focused on admitting students with broader interests. Twenty-six percent of the Class of 2014 went into the industry, which is a higher percentage of the class than at HBS.

Graduates entering the consulting industry

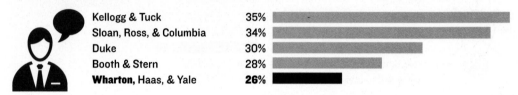

Kellogg & Tuck	35%	
Sloan, Ross, & Columbia	34%	
Duke	30%	
Booth & Stern	28%	
Wharton, Haas, & Yale	**26%**	

Employment statistics. More than 98% of students in the Class of 2014 seeking full-time employment had offers within three months of graduation. That was the highest number in a decade.

Salaries. Not that all you care about is money, but surely you want to make sure your MBA investment is worthwhile. So it should make you happy to learn that the overall median salary for the Class of 2014 was $125,000, with private equity and consulting leading the way. Just remember to be a bit careful when looking at overall average salary numbers because they can be skewed by high salaries in particular industries. Schools that send fewer students to those industries can be at a disadvantage.

Nuts & Bolts

Career development resources. Similar to all the top business schools, Wharton offers a number of resources to its students to assist them in their job-search process. Students are encouraged to take advantage of these resources from the moment they step onto campus and as alumni. However, the career management process is largely in the hands of the students, so they must take the initiative if they want to benefit from Wharton's career management resources. The sheer size of the student body in relation to the relatively small career management staff can make individual career counseling a challenge.

Student resources. In addition to official career management resources, Wharton students themselves are a resource, coming together to help and coach one another in preparation for interviews, etc., as part of professional clubs or as informal groups of students interested in similar career paths. Your fellow students will also tend to be very generous in sharing information about industries and companies, so if you see someone from your target industry or employer, reach out. Buy them coffee. Take them to lunch.

Grade non-disclosure. Since 1994, Wharton has observed a grade non-disclosure policy to separate grades from the recruiting process. Honors, including Director's List, may be disclosed. Although the policy is now voluntary, most students abide by it and, although recruiters may push the envelope, they're accustomed to the policy by now and typically respect it.

Lifelong learning. Through Knowledge for Life, graduates beginning with the Class of 2010 are eligible to take on Executive Education open enrollment course every seven years. Wharton Global Forums bring together alumni from around the world with faculty and staff.

Similar Programs for Professional Opportunities

Chicago (Booth). Not surprisingly, Booth sends a large number of graduates into finance (37% of the Class of 2014). This year, Booth exceeded Wharton's historically high placement numbers in this industry and sent a slightly higher percentage of grads (16%) into investment banking than did Wharton (14%). Booth sends slightly more grads into consulting, but numbers going into technology, consumer goods, and even health care are right in line with Wharton.

Columbia. Columbia (34%) comes very close to Wharton's placement of 36% in the finance industry, and, like Booth, sends a high percentage of graduates (16%) into investment banking compared to other top-tier schools. In fact, by the numbers, Columbia and Wharton are remarkably similar, sending equivalent numbers into consulting, consumer products, and technology.

NYU (Stern). Columbia's downtown rival sends a similar percentage of students into finance (35%) to Wharton. Known as a strong feeder school to Wall Street, Stern placed a much higher percentage of grads (27%) into investment banking than Wharton (14%), Columbia (16%), and Booth (16%). If you're looking to pursue investment banking, Stern is the place to be! Although its consulting numbers are lower than Columbia's, technology numbers are comparable, although overall NYU's range of industry placements is somewhat narrower than either Columbia or Wharton.

Dartmouth (Tuck). If you're looking for a slightly different MBA experience outside of the larger cities but with similar career opportunities, you might want to consider Tuck. Interestingly, Tuck sends a large percentage of grads (25%) into finance, and an impressive number of individuals into consulting (35%). The school is known as a "hidden gem" among private equity recruiters, and it has a strong network of alumni in the field. The tech sector is also well-represented, with 18% of the Class of 2014 pursuing careers in this industry, compared to Wharton's 14% placement in technology.

CULTURE & CAMPUS LIFE AT WHARTON

What Wharton Is Known For

Many consider Wharton to be the best of the six Ivy League graduate business programs, and it is a continual leader among its peers.

Heritage. As the world's first collegiate business school (founded in 1881), Wharton is considered the "birthplace of modern business education." Wharton has for generations been one of the most prestigious MBA programs in the world, consistently appearing at or near the top of most rankings. The Wharton School is Penn's prized program and is positioned at the forefront of the research and business communities. Many consider Wharton to be the best of the six Ivy League graduate business programs, and it is a continual leader among its peers. Wharton was one of the first business schools to change its curriculum in response to the economic crisis, an effort that it continues to this day.

An urban location. Situated in an urban setting, Wharton includes several buildings on the Penn campus just west of downtown Philadelphia. As the campus has expanded west, its neighborhood has undergone something of a transformation in the last 15 years, a trend not totally affectionately termed "Penntrification." The Wharton School is primarily housed in its own state-of-the-art building, Huntsman Hall, essentially isolating the students from the rest of the university. School administration is in Steinberg Hall and Vance Hall, while the Lauder Program is primarily based, appropriately enough, in Lauder-Fisher Hall. Wharton students have access to all the main Penn facilities such Van Pelt Library (and Lippincott Library, the business library housed there) and the David Pottruck Fitness Center.

An innovative building. The 2002 opening of Wharton's Huntsman Hall kicked off a building boom at business schools across the country that is still going strong today. Huntsman was designed to flexibly support the specific needs of an innovative curriculum and changing student body. Wharton undertook the development project the way any smart business would: by conducting research and holding focus groups of its constituents (faculty and students) to incorporate practical needs into the core of the design. At the time of its opening, Huntsman Hall was by far the most advanced and innovative business school facility in the world. Huntsman is still new enough that its technology infrastructure is still relevant; however, technology support for students is a moving target that business schools often struggle to keep up with. Wharton's peers have, of course, studied Huntsman in the quiet quest of top schools to one-up each other, and you will find as good as or better features in the new buildings on other campuses, such as those opened at the University of Chicago in 2004, Stanford in 2011, and Yale in 2013.

You Oughta Know

Social impact. Namesake Joseph Wharton founded the school to produce educated citizens who are "pillars of the state, whether in private or in public life." The emphasis at Wharton is on creating "economic and social good," anchored in the concept now termed "Social Impact." The global economic crisis heightened Wharton's emphasis on the interconnected obligation to both create economic wealth and improve the lives of the world's citizens, and the curriculum features a wide array of related courses. Wharton also offers a loan–forgiveness program for graduates employed in nonprofit or social sectors, and the Nonprofit Board Fellows program offers students the opportunity to advise a local nonprofit.

Surprisingly supportive culture. The culture at some large schools such as Harvard Business School can tend to be more formal. However, alumni have told us that Wharton is actually quite friendly and down-to-earth. While you won't find the tight-knit community of Tuck or Darden or be best friends with every member of your class (partly because Penn's campus is not residential; see below for more on this), you also won't find a lot of sharks, and many students describe the culture as "collaborative." In the words of one former student, "I was surprised at how relaxed students were about schoolwork, and it was very easy to collaborate on school assignments. That also carried over into recruiting; it was a very supportive culture." Although Wharton students enjoy a good party as much as the next MBA student, the partying doesn't tend to reach the frat-house level that might sometimes be associated with schools like NYU Stern or Kellogg.

Expansive community. With a class of 800 people, it could be easy to feel anonymous, or maybe even a little bit lost in the crowd. To foster a sense of community, Wharton uses a cohort system for the first year. Cohorts of about 70 students stay together for core classes; cohorts are combined to make clusters of 210 students. And with such a large class, you can always find friends with similar interests. That being said, due to the larger class size, you can't be afraid to forge your own way to get what you're looking for out of the program by being deliberate in your networking approach.

Interactions outside of the MBA. Although you might find some undergraduates in your classes, outside of academics you'll find very little interaction between the graduate and undergraduate communities at Wharton, or even among grad students in other Penn programs other than Lauder and the occasional joint-degree student. Of course, there are exceptions, including volunteer and extracurricular efforts, such as the Small Business Development Center (SBDC), which combine MBA and undergrad teams, opportunities to take classes outside of Wharton (Penn allows up to four electives to be taken in other graduate schools), and the occasional inter-school social activity. The reality is that if you want to meet anyone outside of Wharton, you'll have to take the initiative.

Variety of study space. Study rooms at Huntsman can be tough to come by given the focus on team-based work at Wharton, and undergraduate and graduate students usually scramble to book them during prime study hours. When rooms are fully booked, students can be found in clusters all over the building. Because most students live off campus, the new Center City study space at 2401 Walnut Street has been extremely popular for team meetings and other events. The large main forum in Huntsman serves as a gathering and meeting place for students. However, graduate students tend to congregate in the MBA Café on the second floor or in one of the building entrances on Locust Walk or Walnut Street.

> **"I was surprised at how relaxed students were about schoolwork, and it was very easy to collaborate on school assignments."**

PENN (WHARTON)

Geographic dispersion. Although not a commuter school in a traditional sense, the vast majority of Wharton students do not live on the Penn campus. Instead, most make the quick trip across the Schuylkill River (typically by foot, bike, trolley, or city bus) to apartments in Center City. Rittenhouse Square is a popular neighborhood, but you can find Wharton students in Society Hill, Queen Village, or the Art Museum area. A few even live in the suburbs and commute in by train (SEPTA has a train station just a few blocks from campus) or car. This geographic dispersion can make organizing team meetings a challenge, but every group finds its own way around it. Most socializing takes place in Center City or Rittenhouse Square—Philadelphia is justifiably very proud of its dining scene—or in nearby neighborhoods like Manayunk.

Family-friendly. It's not uncommon to see children running around on campus, and the school makes every opportunity to integrate families into social activities and even learning opportunities. Wharton Kids have their own club, as do Wharton Partners.

Similar Programs Culturally

Harvard. The world's largest full-time MBA program, at more than 1,850 students, Harvard Business School (HBS) tends to have a much more formal culture than other top-tier business schools such as Stanford, Kellogg, and NYU Stern. Classes at HBS begin and end precisely on time, so every student must be in his or her seat, ready to dive into the day's case. Because class participation accounts for up to half of a student's final grade, most of the emphasis is placed on speaking up and "adding value" to class discussions. Although you won't find Wharton to be quite this formal, class participation is emphasized (and often graded), and you'll experience your fair share of cold calls during your two years on campus.

Columbia, once known for its extremely sharp-elbowed and win-at-all-cost culture (not uncommon on Wall Street), has focused on developing a more collaborative community over the past few years.

Columbia. Located in the Morningside Heights neighborhood in Manhattan, Columbia's culture is unmistakably "New York." Another large program, at 1,500 MBAs, Columbia tends to foster a culture of students who are not afraid to speak up, question authority, or seek change if they see areas for improvement around them. Once known for its extremely sharp-elbowed and win-at-all-cost culture (not uncommon on Wall Street), the school has focused on developing a more collaborative community over the past few years. Columbia's downtown rival, NYU Stern, is still seen as more collegial, but Columbia simply isn't the same cutthroat community it may have been five or 10 years ago. Nevertheless, it maintains a professional, networking-oriented culture similar to Wharton's. In fact, Wharton and Columbia are so similar that they even have partnerships between their social and professional clubs.

Chicago (Booth). The most distinguishing factor of Chicago Booth's culture is intellectual curiosity. Professors are not afraid to ask students to pull out calculators and do some calculus in class, and students are encouraged to question everything, even their professors and one another. So you tend to get more intellectual sparring and debating in the Booth classroom than at its rival to the north, Kellogg, where collegiality is valued above nearly all else.

ADMISSIONS AT WHARTON

What Wharton Is Looking For

Wide range of candidates. Because of its sheer size, Wharton has room for applicants from very diverse backgrounds. Although the school is often seen as a "finance school" or "quant school," its student body has become significantly more diverse in the past few years. As we highlight below, no particular professional background is valued more than another.

Avoid cookie-cutter applications. As with all the top-tier schools, there's no magic formula for admission to Wharton; rather, they say that "a successful application combines substance, presentation, and good timing. It should tell your own story and make each element of your application as strong as possible." What does this mean for you? Don't write what you think they want to hear, because 99% of the time that isn't actually what they want to hear. In this section, we'll provide more tips on how you might approach the Wharton application.

Selection criteria. Applicants are evaluated based on their academic profile, professional experience, personal qualities, and overall presentation of their application. We discuss each area in detail below:

- **Academic profile.** We've established by this point that Wharton is a quant/analytical school, so they'll comb through your transcripts, GMAT scores, and work experience to make sure you can handle the rigorous coursework. Courses like calculus and statistics are especially valuable. If these skills won't be readily apparent from your background, you should take steps to remedy that (extra quant coursework, GMAT tutoring, etc.) prior to applying. Like many top business schools, Wharton will now accept the GRE in addition to the GMAT. In theory, the two tests should be equivalent in the admissions committee's eyes; however, if your quant skills are lacking elsewhere, we would recommend submitting a GMAT score so that you do not give the impression of "hiding" from quantitative rigor.

- **Professional experience.** Wharton's admissions website is pretty transparent when it comes to what it's looking for in professional experience: *The Admissions Committee looks for individuals who exhibit professional maturity. In other words, we evaluate work experience not in terms of years, but the depth and breadth of an individual's position, his or her contributions to the work environment, and level of responsibility and progression. Wharton looks for diversity in the professional backgrounds of its admitted students just as it does in all other parts of our applicants' profiles. No one industry is favored over another, and experience in a Fortune 500 company does not have higher value than experience in a small business or public institution.*

- **Personal qualities.** Two of the key personal qualities that Wharton (and other business schools) will look for are personal introspection and clarity of thought. Your essays are a great place to show that you've spent time to analyze your own strengths and weak-

APPLICATION DEADLINES

All deadlines are 5PM Eastern time on the date indicated.

Round 1
29 Sept 2015
Notification:
17 Dec 2015

Round 2
5 Jan 2016
Notification:
29 Mar 2016

Round 3
30 Mar 2016
Notification:
3 May 2016

nesses, examined your opportunities, and carefully decided that business school is the best path to achieve your unique goals. In particular, the second essay gives you a chance to show the admissions committee what unique qualities or traits you could contribute to your Wharton class. However, don't neglect the other elements of the application including the online form and your resume to showcase your ability to pay attention to details and highlight the most impactful elements of your profile using very limited space.

- **Overall presentation.** Among the largest faux pas that applicants make are careless errors in their application, resume, or essays. The admissions readers will evaluate whether your application appears to be thrown together at the last minute, or carefully crafted. They pay attention to your tone and attitude not only in the team-based discussion, but also throughout your written submissions. Since current students will read your application, it is helpful to have experienced MBA students, alums, and/or consultants review your essays to ensure they demonstrate your genuine attributes that would be most appreciated by your Wharton classmates.

Preparing to Apply

Reading this Essential Guide is a great first step in your preparation. Hopefully, this insider's glimpse has been helpful in understanding the most important aspects of the school. However, nothing can replace gaining firsthand knowledge and experience yourself.

Reach out to current students. Even if you don't have any personal connections to Wharton, you can reach out to current students and get their insight and advice. On the school's Clubs page, you'll find a list of all campus clubs. Find a few clubs that fit your personal and professional interests and reach out to the officers. Remember: These are very busy MBA students so you don't want to intrude too much on their time, but you could ask for a 10- to 15-minute conversation or elicit some advice via e-mail. You might provide a quick background introduction and ask if there's another member of their club, even one with a similar background, who might be able to offer some insights and advice about his or her Wharton experience. Come prepared with specific questions (preferably those that aren't already answered online). If you're planning to visit campus, perhaps you might even arrange a coffee chat or lunch, if they are available.

Because informal and impromptu encounters can be the most informative, don't be afraid to approach students in less-formal settings, such as the legendary Thursday afternoon MBA pub.

Visit campus. The school's website can only tell you so much; by far, a personal visit is the best possible research in the application process. If you have the means, we highly recommend you visit the Wharton campus along with the campuses of your other top choices to understand the significant differences in culture, teaching style, student body, recruiting opportunities, facilities, and so forth. You may be surprised at just how different each school can be and how the reality can differ from the perception. We encourage you to take advantage of the campus visit program, including a class visit, campus tour, information session, and student lunch, as available. Because informal and impromptu encounters can be the most informative, don't be afraid to approach students in less-formal settings, such as the legendary Thursday afternoon MBA pub. (Just make sure not to stand between the pizza delivery guy and the hungry crowd.)

Other events. We know that many applicants will not be able to travel to Philadelphia to visit campus, but you should take advantage of other worldwide admissions events, such as information sessions, webinars, and specific-audience events. In fact, these off-campus events can offer great opportunities for quality time with admissions officers and even other applicants, who can be a great resource and support through the admissions process. Get to know the school and its culture as well as you can, because your familiarity can shine through your application and essay to help you stand out.

You Oughta Know

When should I apply? Wharton uses a standard three-round system for applications. This means that you may submit your application in any of its three rounds for consideration. However, 90% or more of the class will be filled with the first two rounds of applicants, so we do not encourage you to wait until the final round without compelling circumstances. In fact, although many schools maintain that it doesn't matter when you apply, Wharton gives pretty explicit advice on its website: "We strongly encourage you to apply in Round 1 or 2. The first two rounds have no significant difference in the level of rigor; the third round is more competitive, as we will have already selected a good portion of the class." The school does add that there is room "for the strongest applicants" in Round 3, but your mission is clear: Get your application in by January 5!

Traditional applicants. If you are a traditional candidate from management consulting or finance, we encourage you to apply in the first round (assuming you have a strong GMAT score), as you'll be competing against many candidates with very similar profiles. In a later round, it's possible that the school may see you as a viable candidate but may have already admitted several other applicants with similar profiles, so it might pass on you to bring greater professional diversity to the class. (Plus, the school knows you've been planning on an MBA since the day you graduated from undergrad, so there's no reason to delay!)

Timing vs. qualifications. Please note that even though the top schools encourage you to apply in the earliest round possible, this does not mean that you should apply with a rushed application or a mediocre GMAT score. There's no sense in applying early if you're just going to be denied. A GMAT score that's above the school's average will do more for your candidacy than applying in the first round.

Navigating deadlines. Wharton's deadlines are virtually unchanged from last year. The Round 1 deadline for Wharton is September 29, 2015—on par with many of the other top-tier schools. Round 2 follows on January 5, 2016 (there goes your holiday break!), with Round 3 on March 30, 2016. (Note that because of their early start date, Lauder applicants must apply in R1 or R2.) Applications must be received by 5:00 p.m. ET on the deadline, so no procrastinating! Get that app safely submitted before you leave for work in the morning. Decisions are released approximately seven weeks after the deadline.

> **If you are a traditional candidate from the management consulting or finance industry, we encourage you to apply in the first round (assuming you have a strong GMAT score), as you'll be competing against many candidates with very similar profiles.**

The Essays

Wharton requires one essay this year and offers one optional essay.

Essay #1 (Required): What do you hope to gain both personally and professionally from the Wharton MBA? (500 words)

Be introspective. This is the only required essay in Wharton's application and it remains the same as last year's. Note the word "personally" in the question. Wharton isn't only interested in what six-figure job you hope to land after earning your MBA, but also wants to know how you plan on growing as a person from the experience. You definitely still need to nail the professional part—you need to discuss clear, realistic career objectives here—but the admissions committee also wants to see maturity and introspection. How do you see yourself growing during your two years at Wharton? How do you hope the degree and the experience will impact your life 10 years from now? This sort of depth will make the difference between a great response and a merely good one.

Focus on the future. Note that the essay prompt is asking what you want to gain from the Wharton MBA, so the focus is on the future and what you plan on pursuing post-MBA. However, you should still reflect a little on what has brought you to this crossroads in your professional and personal life, and how your past has shaped your what your goals are now. As noted above, the admissions committee will want to see some introspection, so discussing some of your key turning points by using stories and examples could be one way of approaching this question.

Why Wharton? Although the question does not directly ask you to address why you wish to attend Wharton, it is still asking you to address what you will gain from the Wharton MBA. As such, you should tie in specific examples of how this program in particular will help you to achieve your goals. When discussing your professional goals, you may wish to reference professional clubs or specific companies that recruit regularly on campus. Make sure you demonstrate a strong understanding of the wide array of professional opportunities available to you on campus and back up your story with clear example.

Be specific and personal. Resist the urge to do a few web searches and then simply drop the names of some programs or professors into this essay. An effective response will provide specific details about aspects of the academics, activities, events, professional opportunities, or culture that tie back to your future goals. Don't forget to mention your personal goals, as well! As we've mentioned earlier in this guide, Wharton has a student-led culture. A key part of your Wharton experience will be to get involved outside of the classroom and recruiter's interview room through numerous student clubs, activities, and travel opportunities. Reflect upon and communicate what you hope to gain through these personal growth and leadership opportunities, as this essay is another chance to draw attention to ways in which you will be an active member of the Wharton community.

Essay #2 (Optional): Please use the space below to highlight any additional information that you would like the Admissions Committee to know about your candidacy. (400 words)

Beyond the typical optional essay. We normally tell applicants to use the optional essay only if you need to explain a low undergraduate GPA or other potential blemish in your background. In fact, Wharton's own website calls this essay "truly optional." There's no need to harp on a minor weakness and sound like you're making excuses when you don't need to. However, as schools like Wharton have been cutting down on essays, the role of the optional essay has evolved a bit. No need to monopolize the admissions committee's time, but since Wharton's application now gives you far less space in which you can describe your interests and inject some more personality into your application, this essay provides the perfect place to do that. Have a passion or something else that goes "beyond the resume" and will help Wharton admissions officers get to know you better? This essay gives you room to discuss it and make your application that much more memorable.

Don't ignore glaring weaknesses. Our original advice still holds, too. If you have a blemish that you need address, this is the place to do it. You don't want to leave a glaring weakness unaddressed. However, if you don't have too much explaining to do, don't be afraid to reveal something personal and memorable about yourself here. Re-applicants should focus on those areas that have changed (and hopefully improved!) since their last application.

Recommendations

Instructions for recommendations. Each applicant must submit two recommendations. After filling in some basic information such as the nature of their relationship with you and how long they've had frequent contact with you, your recommenders will provide a quick appraisal of you across three qualities: ability to manage uncertainty, maturity/self awareness, and communication skills. The instructions read, "Please give us your appraisal of the applicant in terms of the qualities listed below. Compare the applicant with others whom you know to have applied to graduate school or with individuals in your organization who are being groomed for positions in senior management." The recommenders will provide one of the following ratings for each attribute: No Basis for Judgment; Below Average; Average (middle 50%); Good (top 25%); Very Good (top 10%); or Outstanding (top 5%). They may also enter additional comments to support these ratings.

Applicant assessment. The only other portion of the Wharton recommendation form is the applicant assessment, where your recommenders will be asked to upload a document that answers the following questions:

1. *How does the candidate's performance compare to those of other well-qualified individuals in similar roles? Please provide specific examples. (300 words)*

2. *Please describe the most important piece of constructive feedback you have given the applicant. Please detail the circumstances and the applicant's response. (250 words)*

3. *(Optional) Is there anything else we should know?*

Selecting your recommenders. Wharton explicitly says the recommendations should come from supervisors, and most schools strongly prefer that one recommender be your current direct supervisor. Wharton also stresses that it is more important to find recommenders who know you well and can answer the essay questions with depth and detail. As stated directly on its website, "Select the two people who really know you and your work, and whom you believe can best address the questions asked, not the two most important people you know." If your recommender is a Wharton graduate, great! He or she knows what the school is looking for. However, the school states, "Please don't seek out alumni who aren't truly qualified to write about you." The message is clear: Pick someone who knows your work, your leadership abilities, and your personal qualities. Don't ask someone because of name, status, or connections to Wharton.

Should I draft it myself? Many applicants to business school are asked by their superiors to draft the recommendation themselves and the recommender will approve it. We strongly recommend that you do not write the recommendation yourself for several reasons. First, your writing style and choice of phrasing are unique, and admissions officers will notice if the recommendations are similar to each other and to your essay(s). If they notice too many similarities, your application could be denied outright. Second, you may tend to be too humble or generic. Your supervisor might use language such as "one of the top analysts I've seen in my entire career" that you wouldn't dare include if writing on his or her behalf. Third, and perhaps most importantly, the admissions officer is looking for a third-party perspective on your candidacy, so writing a recommendation yourself is an unethical breach of trust with the school you are looking to join.

Preparing your recommenders. Instead of writing the recommendation yourself, you should sit down and have candid conversations with your recommenders about the reasons you want to go to business school and why you've selected your target schools, your professional goals, and your experience together. Ask them if they would have the time to write a strong recommendation on your behalf. (This also gives them a nice "out" by telling you that they are too busy rather than saying they don't feel comfortable giving you a positive recommendation.) Bring a copy of your resume and a bulleted list of projects that you've worked on together and accomplishments they have seen you achieve. Let them know that admissions committees prefer to see specific, detailed examples in recommendations. Then, let them know that you'll serve as a "project manager" to follow up and ensure that they are able to submit your recommendation ahead of the deadline.

The Interview

The dreaded team-based discussion. At Wharton, interviews are conducted by invitation only and are a required component of the application. Wharton will again use the innovative, somewhat controversial, and not universally loved team-based discussion model first launched in the 2012–13 application year. Instead of an in-depth, one-on-one interview with an admissions officer, student, or alumni interviewer, groups of five to six candidates will engage in a discussion together. On-campus discussions will typically be conducted by Admissions Fellows, a group of second-year MBA students.

Who is invited? Roughly speaking, approximately 40% of all Wharton applicants will be invited for a team-based discussion and about half of those will be offered admission. The team-based discussion will be required for admission in almost all cases. Dual-degree or specialty applicants (Lauder, Health Care Management, etc.) are required to complete a separate interview.

Where should I interview? The majority of discussions will be held on campus, but admissions officers will travel to select cities globally as well. Wharton goes out of its way to remind applicants that there is no advantage to attending a discussion on campus or off campus, but it encourages applicants to visit campus so they can attend classes, have lunch with current students, take a campus tour, and attend an information session. We at Veritas Prep also encourage candidates to visit the campus if they have the means to do so.

How does it work? The purpose of the team-based discussion is to replicate the experience of working on teams of peers, similar to those you will be working with as a student. The discussion will have a prompt, such as a real-world business scenario, and a purpose. Members of the team will work together toward a tangible outcome. The admissions committee is looking for how you "think, lead, communicate and interact."

Discussion topics tended to center around Wharton's three pillars of Innovation, Social Impact, and Global Education. You'll receive them ahead of time, but they recommend not over-preparing. You want to be ready, but not overly rehearsed. Last year, the prompt remained consistent in each round but evolved somewhat between rounds. After the team-based discussion, applicants have a brief, 10- to 15-minute discussion with a student or admissions officer. This meeting serves both as a de-brief (popular questions run along the lines of "What did you think of the exercise?" and "How would you assess your performance?") and an opportunity to ask questions about the school.

> After the group-based discussion, applicants have a brief, 10- to 15-minute discussion with a student or admissions officer. This meeting serves both as a de-brief and an opportunity to ask questions about the school.

Play nice. Applicants may be tempted to view the team-based discussion as a competition with the other members of the group. If you have a fairly aggressive personality or tend to be long-winded, we caution you not to dominate the discussion. This is an evaluation not only of your critical-thinking skills, but also of your collaboration and teamwork abilities. One way to show leadership but not dominate a discussion is to ask insightful questions that the group may want to consider and to help draw the group to consensus.

That said, Wharton is looking for future leaders, so if you tend to be shy or hesitant to speak up, you may want to make an extra effort to contribute to the discussion when you have a relevant thought or idea, or to draw out others. Don't be afraid to break out of your shell! Remember: This is a bit of an awkward situation for everyone involved, so the other members of your group are going to be just as nervous as you are. Although many applicants dread this interview beforehand, afterward they report that they actually enjoyed it!

COLUMBIA BUSINESS SCHOOL

A finance-driven powerhouse that thrives on the energy of New York City.

◉ NEW YORK, NY

CLASS SIZE
743

PROGRAM FOUNDED
1916

NEWEST ADDITION
STARTUP
LAB

CHARACTERISTICS
HARD-EDGED, FINANCE, BIG-CITY

COLUMBIA

SECTIONS

COLUMBIA BUSINESS SCHOOL SNAPSHOT

What Columbia Is Known For

Finance. Finance. Finance. Columbia sends a high percentage of its graduates into finance, rivaled only by Wharton, Chicago Booth, and NYU Stern. Its location means the school has powerful connections on Wall Street, but the school has made a noted attempt to diversify away from just investment banking over the past several years. These efforts have paid off: Although 16% of the Class of 2014 headed down that path, that figure represented less than half of graduates headed into finance-related roles.

Location. Location. Location. This real estate adage is so relevant to thinking about Columbia, it's traded one geographically centered tagline ("The New York Advantage") for another ("At The Very Center of Business"). NYC has even made a guest appearance in the school's essay questions. But wait! There's another top business school in NYC, you say? You're right, although the "other" New York business school may be closer to downtown's trendy nightlife and financial centers, the reputation and clout of Columbia Business School continue to pull New York's movers and shakers up to Morningside Heights. (The school featured more than 400 guest speakers in one year.)

Culture shift. Back in the day, you might have heard the word "cutthroat" used to describe Columbia's culture. Known as the proverbial shark tank of business schools, Columbia's campus abounded with stories about note-stealing and other sabotage. While the culture is still decidedly "New Yorker" and a bit more hard-edged than the very softest MBA communities such as those at Kellogg, Ross, and Tuck, Columbia now actively seeks out applicants who will be part of a tight-knit community.

Theory *and* practice. Columbia Business School's aim in recent years has been to create "whole" business thinkers who "connect the dots" and understand the importance of bigger-picture frameworks such as globalization. Columbia students also understand the complexity of social (i.e., non-financial) metrics in evaluating the impact of business on the world around them. Research is also important for Columbia's faculty, and bringing theory outside of the classroom and applying it in the real world are key drivers in the curriculum's design.

> Columbia Business School's aim in recent years has been to create "whole" business thinkers who "connect the dots" and understand the importance of bigger-picture frameworks such as globalization.

What Makes Columbia Different

January option. Though its name is clear as to timing, the accelerated January Term—a program unique to Columbia among its peers—warrants a detailed explanation. The curriculum is identical to that used in the "normal" August start. Students enrolling in "J-Term" earn their MBA in 16 months, as opposed to 21 months for students enrolling in August. Classes begin in January and end in May of the following year, continuing throughout the summer (read: no full-time internship). When students who started the previous year return to campus as second-years, the two cohorts merge, taking electives together, going through recruiting together, and eventually walking across the stage together as one graduating class. Although this option eliminates the full-time internship (and the networking opportunities vital to many career switchers), the compacted schedule of the J-Term lowers the opportunity cost of lost salary and is ideal for:

- Entrepreneurs.

- Students who work (or will work) in their family business.

- Students returning to their current employer, whether or not they are financially sponsored. (There are few of these; most sponsored students gravitate toward the EMBA options.)

- Candidates who possess a strong professional network in the industry of their choice.

Value investing. A cornerstone of Columbia's finance program is the Value Investing Program in the Heilbrunn Center for Graham and Dodd Investing. That mouthful of a name is testimony to the historical depth of Columbia's role as an incubator of value investing in terms of mindset and a discipline. Perhaps the most famous value investor in the world is Warren Buffett, a graduate of this program. The basic approach of value investing is evaluating fundamentals against market price to determine intrinsic value for a long-term buy-and-hold strategy.

A variety of value investing classes and resources is available to Columbia's entire MBA and EMBA student bodies, even those not committed to the full program. However, the Value Investing Program is only open to MBA students, with a competitive application process for admission. The advantages? It's taught by more than 25 investors who serve as adjunct faculty. These are practitioners, not just academics. Students also benefit from an impressive roster of guest speakers, and invaluable mentorship and recruiting support. About 40 students are selected based on interest and "aptitude" for investing as expressed in an application essay, mandatory interview, and two-page write-up of a proposed long or short investment. Many classes in the Value Investing Program require students to pitch ideas, usually multiple pitches per class. This type of hands-on training—and the exposure students get to marquee Wall Street firms—puts Columbia's Value Investing Program in a category by itself.

Master classes. These project-based electives are superlative in terms of offering the ability of second-year students to roll up their sleeves and apply what they have learned. This is one element of Columbia's focus on combining theory with practice. Past topics have included "Private Equity & Entrepreneurship in Africa," "Creation of a Retail Enterprise," and "Mergers & Acquisitions in Media."

> **J-Term students earn their MBA in 16 months. The compacted schedule lowers the opportunity cost of lost salary but eliminates the internship.**

COLUMBIA

"CBS Matters." These presentations are very unique and offer faculty and students an opportunity to highlight what matters to them and why. They cover a range of topics: some serious, some lighthearted. Students feel that they provide an opportunity for them to get to know each other on a more personal level and have significantly enriched the business school experience.

An entrepreneurial mindset. Just as at most top programs, entrepreneurship is a popular focus of study at Columbia. However, Columbia Business School takes this even further with an emphasis on entrepreneurial thinking regardless of intended future career or discipline. Columbia proposes to imbue its graduates with an "entrepreneurial mindset for recognizing and capturing opportunity."

Breadth of expertise. While certainly Columbia is known for finance—after all, value investing was invented there—it also has well-regarded faculty from, and deep connections to, media, real estate, retail, marketing, and other fields. The presence on the faculty of media darlings such as Milstein Real Estate Professor and Vice Dean Chris Mayer (who was snatched away from Columbia's competitor to the south, Wharton), Nobel Laureate Joseph Stiglitz, and International Development guru Jagdish Bagwati has served to elevate the school's profile in areas beyond finance.

> The school's global philosophy is also evident in the classroom: 41% of students are from abroad.

Global reach. Columbia's global perspective is the deliberate result of decades' worth of (often-expensive) investments. The school's global philosophy is also evident in the classroom: 41% of students are from abroad, leading every other top program except Stanford (44%) and Berkeley-Haas (43%). Though it is not an admissions requirement, applicants demonstrating either experience abroad or functional ability in a language besides English can hold an advantage, and Uris Hall can at times seem like a modern-day Tower of Babel. In 1991, Jerome Chazen (MBA '50) gave $10 million to found the Institute of International Business at Columbia Business School that now bears his name. (For more on the Chazen Institute, see below.) The popular joint-degree programs with the School for International and Public Affairs offer additional opportunities to Columbia students.

Mini internships. Many students do mini, unpaid internships during the school year at NYC companies. This is very different from just about any other MBA program, and speaks to both the location, and the theory and practice focus of Columbia. Students mention that it can help in breaking into difficult fields like private equity or hedge funds because these companies may not want to take the risk of a full-time, paid, summer internship, but they might be willing to take a risk on you for a part-time role while you're in school.

Early Decision. Columbia is one of the few top programs to offer an Early Decision application option. If Columbia is your number-one choice, you may want to consider applying Early Decision, as that signifies to the admissions committee that you are serious about attending Columbia. This provides a win-win situation for both the school and the applicant, as it enables you to signal your level of interest in the school and allows Columbia to admit applicants who are much more likely to attend, improving their yield. After that, admission is on a rolling basis with no "rounds"—also unusual among top schools.

Startup Lab. A coworking space on campus, the Startup Lab is essentially a team-based incubator available to young alumni of three Columbia schools and for graduating MBA students.

Columbia Business Is a Good Fit for You If...

You are an excellent student and have the transcript to prove it. Columbia places a premium on strong academics. If you did well in college, Columbia may find your profile all the more appealing.

You have a bit more work experience. While Columbia will review any application that comes in, it can be tougher for younger candidates to be successful here. Those with more work experience might see a favorable outcome.

You're not changing careers, and you're in a hurry. As mentioned above, the Columbia J-Term is unique to Columbia (although other schools like Kellogg and Cornell have accelerated programs). It's not the right option for everyone, but if you are committed to your existing career and just need more skills to advance, or if you're an entrepreneur or will be returning to a family business, the J-Term can be an ideal choice.

You want to work on Wall Street. This hardly needs to be mentioned, but in case it's not obvious: Columbia is a major feeder program to the bulge bracket investment banks, hedge funds, and elite financial institutions of the world.

You're not afraid of commitment. With its unique Early Decision application process, the admissions office is looking for students who are committed to Columbia, and being able to demonstrate school fit and a passion for the program itself will serve you well in the application process.

> **If you did well in college, Columbia may find your profile all the more appealing.**

ACADEMICS AT COLUMBIA

What Columbia Is Known For

Areas of study. Columbia does not have formal majors or concentrations. Instead, the flexible curriculum allows students to design their own course of study by choosing from electives under several Areas of Focus, which are not noted on transcripts. Last summer, Columbia made substantial changes to its first-year MBA core curriculum. Four major changes were moving the leadership course to orientation, increasing the opportunity for first-year electives, moving technical components of some courses online, and emphasizing Big Data.

Dual degrees. Columbia University has numerous graduate programs that are among the elite in their respective fields. MBA students can leverage the many strengths of the university as a whole by pursuing one of 11 established of dual-degree tracks. However, you cannot start the two programs simultaneously and Columbia Business School does not offer deferred admission to a future class, so you must apply for the MBA portion of your program for the term in which you plan to enroll. This means that most applicants will have already applied to and started at least the first year of the other graduate program in their intended dual-degree track.

COLUMBIA

COLUMBIA AT A GLANCE

APPLICANTS BY SCHOOL

5,799 hopefuls applied to Columbia last year, the fourth highest of the top-tier schools after Harvard, Stanford, and Wharton. The acceptance rate was 18%.

● Percent admitted

Columbia 5,799	Stanford 7,355	Harvard 9,543	Wharton 6,111	Booth 4,175	Stern 3,890
18.2%	7.1%	11%	20.7%	24%	16%

 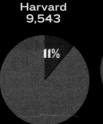 

AVERAGE GPA

3.50 **3.52**
Columbia Stern

GMAT AVERAGE SCORES

716 **721**
Columbia Stern

Columbia's average GMAT score was lower than many of its competitors and lower than its downtown NYC neighbor.

WOMEN

Columbia's percentage of women is right in the middle of pack among the top schools. However, with 36% of the class coming to the program from the finance industry, a traditionally male-dominated field, Columbia has likely had to work particularly hard to recruit female candidates.

Columbia
36%

Stern
36%

Harvard
41%

Sloan
39%

NATIONALITY

59% U.S.

41% International Citizens

AVERAGE AGE

28 Columbia   **27** Harvard

AVERAGE YEARS OF WORK EXPERIENCE

With the bulk of the class having three to seven years of full-time experience, Columbia tends to prefer candidates with more experience.

5 Columbia   **4.3** Stern

UNDERGRAD MAJORS

- ☐ **STEM**
- ☐ **Humanities/Social Science/ Economics**
- ☐ **Business**
- ☐ **OTHER**

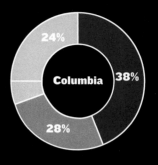

Columbia: 24% / 38% / 28%

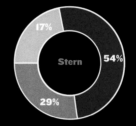

Stern: 17% / 54% / 29%

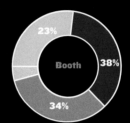

Booth: 23% / 38% / 34%

FROM CONSULTING/FINANCE SECTOR PRE-MBA

Columbia's incoming class has a higher percentage of consultants and bankers than any other top U.S. MBA program. While the admissions committee clearly doesn't shy away from traditional applicants, those from other industries are broadly represented.

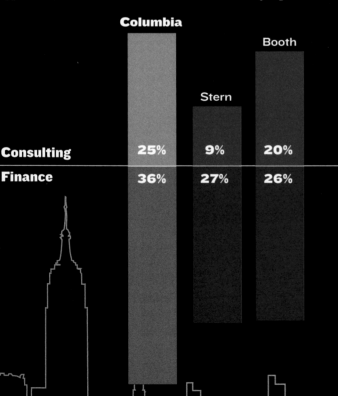

	Columbia	Stern	Booth
Consulting	25%	9%	20%
Finance	36%	27%	26%

CLASS SIZE

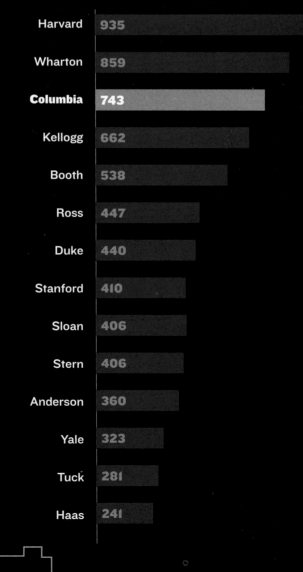

School	Size
Harvard	935
Wharton	859
Columbia	743
Kellogg	662
Booth	538
Ross	447
Duke	440
Stanford	410
Sloan	406
Stern	406
Anderson	360
Yale	323
Tuck	281
Haas	241

COLUMBIA

International programs. Since its founding in 1991, more than 2,500 Columbia MBA candidates have taken advantage of funding provided by the Chazen Institute to study foreign languages (Arabic, Business English, Chinese, French, German, Hindi, Japanese, Portuguese, and Spanish) with a distinct emphasis on applied business contexts. The Chazen Institute also offers Columbia students the chance to spend their third semester at a partner school abroad while earning full credit toward their Columbia MBA. Chazen Institute study trips abroad are also popular. During these seven- to 10-day trips, groups of 20 to 40 students and a sponsoring faculty member meet with business leaders, government officials, and alumni while visiting businesses, factories, and cultural offerings in the foreign destination. Trips often have a specific theme as well. Second-year students can take their interests and develop them further by applying to become Chazen Society Fellows. These fellows receive a stipend to undertake research, interview global business executives, and report on conferences and events in Chazen Global Insights, the Institute's official online publication.

> If your career aspirations tend toward the tangible, Columbia should make your short list.

Real estate. If your career aspirations tend toward the tangible, Columbia should make your short list. The real estate program is built around the three pillars of capital markets, entrepreneurship, and global business. Directed by Professor Lynne Sagalyn, the Paul Milstein Center is Columbia's hub for all things bricks-and-mortar, uniting the theoretical and practical aspects of the field. The Center sponsors events throughout the school year.

You Oughta Know

The cluster system. Even for people as talented as Columbia students, the experience of being dropped into the midst of a class of more than 500 students (or about 200 in the J-Term) could prove intimidating. So, like some of the other larger schools, Columbia uses a cluster system to make it more manageable and to promote opportunities for building relationships among a smaller subsection of the class. The class is divided into 11 clusters of about 65 students each, with eight clusters in the September start and three in the J-Term. Clusters are also assigned second-year student mentors to help navigate processes and protocols. Within each cluster, first-year students are divided into learning teams of about five people from diverse professional and personal backgrounds. Students work in the same learning team for most of their core courses.

Course selection and enrollment. Students use the Business Online Selection System (BOSS) to bid for courses. During bidding rounds a student can bid, change the bid, or drop the bid as many times as desired. Once the round closes, the final bids are processed, and the student's point endowment is modified accordingly. The process is similar to that of many top business schools that use some form of bidding or point allocation to determine spots in the most popular courses.

> Instead of using the A–F scale, Columbia uses the pass system, although there are different shades of passing.

Grading. Columbia students are a talented lot, but graduate school grading can still come as a bit of shock to people with fond memories of being praised throughout college. Instead of using the A–F scale, Columbia uses the pass system, although there are different shades of passing. A forced curve has been adopted by the faculty for core courses only, with 20–25% of the class receiving an H (honors), 50–60% receiving an HP (high pass), and the balance receiving grades of P (pass), LP (low pass), or F (fail). This curve does not apply to elective courses.

Grade disclosure. In 2011, the student body voted to support a nonbinding policy of grade non-disclosure, meaning that students are encouraged not to disclose grades to recruiters until they have already accepted a full-time position. The Career Management Center also encourages recruiters to respect this norm by not asking students about their grades. We suspect that a handful recruiters and students may not abide this policy, but Columbia students have pointed to it as a key factor in changing the cutthroat culture that Columbia was once known for.

Popular Professors

Every top-tier business school has its list of star faculty whom the students adore. The Columbia faculty is populated with many prominent business leaders, researchers, and teachers. Among Columbia students, there is a handful of professors who are considered a "must have" for a class, due to their reputation both as educators and as experts. This list isn't merely a collection of famous names, but rather the instructors that Columbia students deem to be essential for the full experience.

Bruce Greenwald

Robert Heilbrunn Professor of Finance and Asset Management,
Director of the Heilbrunn Center for Graham & Dodd Investing

Among Columbia's luminaries, few professors have reached the rock star or guru level of finance professor Bruce Greenwald. In addition to being the leading authority on value investing—or, as the *New York Times* put it, "the guru to the Wall Street gurus"—Professor Greenwald is an expert on productivity and information economics. The titles of his classes suggest the range of his interests: *Value Investing, Economics of Strategic Behavior,* and *Globalization & Markets & the Changing Economic Landscape.* Not only is he well versed on multiple subjects, but he's also a great teacher in the Socratic Method, so students who are unprepared for class should be on high alert. Year in and year out, Professor Greenwald's classes are significantly oversubscribed, but about 650 students annually find a way into at least one of them. Professor Greenwald is by far the one professor that alumni clubs beg to have sent to them, goosing an event's attendance significantly by his presence. (Quick note: The Columbia finance department has several faculty members whose names are sometimes confused—an error that could cause extreme embarrassment. Bruce Greenwald is the head of the Value Investing Program. Joel Greenblatt and David Greenspan have been on the adjunct faculty of the Value Investing Program in years past. Michelle Greenwald, an adjunct professor in Columbia's marketing department, has no known relation to Mr. Greenwald. However, Ava Seave, also a Columbia marketing professor, is Mr. Greenwald's wife.)

Laura Resnikoff

Senior Lecturer

Professor Resnikoff has a reputation for no-nonsense, focused courses that give students incredible access to leading players in the private equity field. Professor Resnikoff takes these relationships seriously and instills that ethic in her students: If a class member is so much as a few seconds late to the appointed gathering time in the building lobby of a private equity firm, that student is out of luck and might as well head back to campus. Those students who manage to make it on time are starstruck by the people they meet and the ease with which student ideas are evaluated by experienced players in the field. Some of those ideas are nicely validated; others are quite summarily shot down. Though not for the faint of heart, it is a situation many students clearly value. Professor Resnikoff led the inaugural Master Class in private equity and often teaches *Turnaround Management.*

Murray Low
Associate Professor of Management,
Director of the Eugene Lang Entrepreneurship Center
Professor Low stands out as one of the school's most adored teachers. Having started several successful companies himself, Professor Low now devotes himself to studying the context in which entrepreneurship occurs—searching for causal links and debunking supposedly commonsense links. He has helped to increase the school's reputation for turning out entrepreneurs who graduate both with viable business plans and funding, and who in turn circle back to help stoke the cauldron of creativity and process management on campus.

Gita Johar
Meyer Feldberg Professor of Business,
Vice Dean for Research, Cross-Disciplinary Areas
Professor Johar proves that not all beloved Columbia professors teach finance. She teaches courses on consumer psychology and cognition, and how these can be factored into marketing, branding, and advertising activities. Her seminars can entail highly specific "field trips," such as a trek to the Calvin Klein store on Madison Avenue. Recent course titles include *Advertising and Branding, Global Marketing Consulting for Social Enterprise, Research Methods,* and *Consumer Behavior.* Her youthful, low-key teaching style is a large factor in her increasing popularity on campus. Professor Johar was named vice dean of research and is in charge of Columbia's new Cross-Disciplinary Areas.

Laurie Simon Hodrick
A. Barton Hepburn Professor of Economics,
Founding Director, Program for Financial Studies
Professor Simon Hodrick has a distinguished career bridging theory and practice. Selected as "One of Forty under Forty" by Crain's Chicago (while she was a professor at Kellogg), Columbia lured her to New York both for her many prestigious fellowships and for her approachable yet demanding teaching style. She has been awarded the Columbia University President's Medal for outstanding teaching, and students rave that what they learned from her about corporate finance and the market for corporate control has proved valuable over the course of their careers. Professor Simon Hodrick is also launching the new Program for Financial Studies.

Similar Academic Programs

Penn (Wharton). Increasingly flexible in recent years, Wharton now allows first-year students to tailor more of their first-year curriculum. Also very analytical and data-driven, Wharton is another school with a quant reputation trying to diversity its reputation beyond finance. Like Columbia, it has also made investments in academic areas of real estate, global business, and entrepreneurship, to name a few.

Chicago (Booth). Booth's curriculum is even more flexible than Wharton's, with just one required course and multiple options to fulfill all other requirements. Its student body is known for intellectual curiosity, and the school takes great pride in the academic rigor of its program compared to other, "softer" business schools. Also known as a strong finance school, the academics tend to be quite analytical in nature.

NYU (Stern). Stern has just two required courses in its core curriculum, plus the option to choose five additional courses from a "menu" of seven others. This model has become more popular in recent years so that first-year career-changers can tailor their core experience early in their MBA experience to properly prepare for internships in their chosen field. Someone seeking a position in brand management may want to tailor his or her experience differently than a candidate looking to move onto a sales and trading desk.

UCLA (Anderson). You'll find many of the same academic centers at Anderson as you can find at Columbia, including strengths in finance, real estate, media and entertainment, and entrepreneurship. Anderson has made significant investments in building its programs in the technology sector, health care, and global business as well.

EMPLOYMENT & CAREERS AT COLUMBIA

What Columbia Is Known For

Finance. Given the school's New York City location, it's no surprise that Columbia sends a large number of students into finance; 34% of the Class of 2014 went into financial services in some capacity. However, "finance" is a big tent at Columbia, and grads made an array of choices, ranging from research (6%) to internal corporate finance (3%) to investment management (4%) to private equity/venture capital (3%). And, of course, investment banking remains Columbia's largest placement in this industry, with 16% of the class placing into I-banking roles.

Graduates entering the finance industry

Booth	37%
Wharton	36%
Stern	35%
Columbia	**34%**
HBS	33%

Real estate. Although Columbia's 3% placement in the real estate industry may not seem impressive at first glance, this figure is almost triple most business schools, which typically place in the 0.5–1% range into the real estate industry. The only school that exceeds placement in this industry is UCLA Anderson, which placed 4% of its Class of 2014 in this sector. Harvard, Stanford, and Wharton all came close with 2% of their classes placing into real estate. Columbia's strong placement in this industry is not surprising given its solid academic programming in real estate and a center dedicated to the industry.

Graduates entering the real estate industry

UCLA Anderson	4%
Columbia	**3%**
Harvard, Stanford, & Wharton	2%
Stern & Booth	1%

Luxury retail. While Columbia placed 8% of its Class of 2014 into consumer goods and retail, which is somewhat on par with other top-tier schools, Columbia has an edge in the luxury retail goods sector as a school that offers courses dedicated to this niche market and a strong reputation in the field. The school's location also helps. LVMH Moët Hennessey–Louis Vuitton hired multiple Columbia graduates in 2014, as did Estee Lauder, Coach Inc., and Chanel.

Graduates entering the consumer goods/retail industry

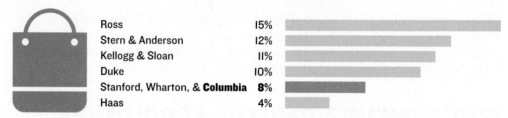

Ross	15%
Stern & Anderson	12%
Kellogg & Sloan	11%
Duke	10%
Stanford, Wharton, & **Columbia**	**8%**
Haas	4%

Media and entertainment. We were surprised to discover that, despite a strong media program at Columbia, the school sends just less than 2% of its MBAs into the field. Nonetheless, students considering a career in this industry should not focus just on this statistic as the school's strong reputation and large class size and its Media and Technology Program mean that it can attract many of the biggest names, including NBCUniversal, Disney, Warner Bros., and Sony.

Graduates entering media and entertainment jobs

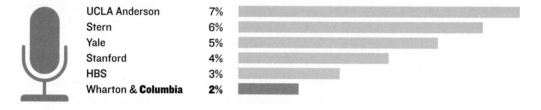

UCLA Anderson	7%
Stern	6%
Yale	5%
Stanford	4%
HBS	3%
Wharton & **Columbia**	**2%**

Consulting. Consulting remains a popular choice for Columbia grads (34% for the Class of 2014). That's actually a higher percentage of the class than at HBS, Wharton, or Stanford.

Graduates entering the consulting industry

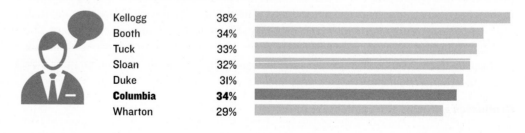

Kellogg	38%
Booth	34%
Tuck	33%
Sloan	32%
Duke	31%
Columbia	**34%**
Wharton	29%

You Oughta Know

Executives in Residence (EIR). Though formally distinct from the Career Management Center, the Executives in Residence program is another key job-related resource available to Columbia students. The EIR was founded almost 30 years ago and is designed to give students access to experienced leaders in key fields such as consulting, investment banking, private equity, real estate, broadcasting, and pharmaceuticals. EIR executives conduct brown-bag lunches with students in groups of 10 to 12, and also assist in setting up interviews with target firms.

Employment statistics. Ninety-seven percent of students in the Class of 2014 seeking full-time employment had offers within three months of graduation; nearly three quarters of students found their opportunity through the school.

Startup Lab. Columbia offers some unique resources on campus for aspiring entrepreneurs. A coworking space on campus, the Startup Lab is essentially a team-based incubator available to young alumni of three Columbia schools and for graduating MBA students.

Salaries. Not that all you care about is money, but surely you want to make sure your MBA investment is worthwhile. So it should make you happy to learn that the overall median salary for the Class of 2014 was $119,400, with consulting leading the way at an average salary of $135,000; private equity was just behind at $132,500. (Just remember to be a bit careful when looking at overall median salary numbers because they can be skewed by high salaries in particular industries. Schools that send fewer students to those industries can be at a disadvantage.) But wait—that's not all! Signing bonuses were also common, with 62% receiving them (median $25,000).

Alumni Career Services. Of late, and partially in response to the challenging economy of the past year, the school has beefed-up its offerings in supporting mid-career alumni. In the process, Columbia has earned some alumni gratitude and strengthened those bonds to the school in the process.

> **97% of Columbia students had employment offers within 3 months of graduation.**

Nuts & Bolts

Career development resources. Similar to all the top business schools, Columbia offers a number of resources to its students to assist them in their job-search process. Students are encouraged to take advantage of these resources from the moment they step onto campus and as alumni. Students give the the team and their services high marks for being "very thoughtful and structured." Columbia's Career Management team offers a number of opportunities for students, including:

> **Professional recruitment.** Like all top-tier business schools, Columbia puts muscle and resources toward ensuring that Columbia students find rewarding jobs after graduation. The Career Management Center (CMC) partners with students to assist them with every phase of their career development, from internship and job searches to lifelong career progress. The Center also makes a concerted effort to teach students lifelong career management skills.

Resume books & club resume books. The career services office publishes and distributes resume books, which are compilations of the resumes of first- and second-year students. Additionally, some student clubs compile their own resume books to circulate the talent to more industry-specific potential purchasers.

CMC individual offerings. From the first week of orientation, CMC has a series of structured offerings that help students tackle and refine the career search. CMC professionals will help students formulate a strategy and tailor a plan that benefits from institutional wisdom. Such offerings include:

- Four-session, non-credit course for first-year students.
- Individual advising sessions, set up on request.
- Workshops and clinics.
- Mock interviews and presentation/public speaking management.

Career Management Library. The CMC maintains a physical library (9 AM–7 PM) of more than 900 volumes of job-search-related books that students can use while on campus. The library also maintains industry job binders with relevant job postings, Wetfeet guides, and 40 periodicals. The virtual career resource center is a portal for online tools that assist both current students and mid-career professionals.

The on-campus recruiting process. On-campus interviews begin in late October, starting with financial firms and bringing all other firms in two days later. Recruiting corporations submit applications to Columbia's COIN (Career Opportunity Information Network) system in September and CMC works with them to ensure that students' schedules are not overbooked. CMC will also go to bat for students to ensure that students do not miss academic commitments for an off-campus interview. They also maintain strict blackout periods that coincide with school holidays and exam periods.

Similar Programs for Professional Opportunities

Penn (Wharton). Columbia and Wharton's placements stats for the Class of 2014 are very similar. Each school sends a large portion of the class into a wide spectrum of finance jobs but is also strong in other areas like consulting and technology, with niche specialties like real estate. Not surprisingly, Wharton sends a large number of students into finance (36%).

Chicago (Booth). Booth sends the highest percentage of its graduates into finance (37% of the Class of 2014) of any top-tier school, and an identical percentage (16%) into investment banking. Booth sends slightly more grads into consulting, but numbers going into technology, consumer goods, and even media/entertainment are right in line with Columbia.

NYU (Stern). Columbia's downtown rival also sends a large number of students into finance (35%). Interestingly, NYU Stern sends a much higher percentage of students into investment banking (27%!) than does Columbia (16%) and Wharton (14%), and a slightly lower percentage of students into consulting than Columbia. Stern is also well-known for its placement in luxury retail and media, and has a similarly strong reputation in both industries, although the overall NYU's range of industry placements is somewhat narrower than either Columbia or Wharton.

London Business School (LBS). A top finance program globally, LBS has perhaps the greatest ties to emerging markets of any leading business school. For candidates seeking finance jobs in Europe, LBS should be at the top of your list.

Dartmouth (Tuck). If you're looking for a slightly different MBA experience outside of the larger cities but with similar career opportunities, you might want to consider Tuck. Interestingly, Tuck sends a large percentage of grads (25%) into finance, and an impressive number of individuals into consulting (35%).

CULTURE & CAMPUS LIFE AT COLUMBIA

What Columbia Is Known For

Life in New York. Although students and alumni benefit from (and generally enjoy) living in New York City, it is worth noting that New York can be a seductive and slightly distracting force—a simultaneous pro and con that more secluded schools like Tuck or Darden rarely contend with. With some Columbia students already residing in NYC upon matriculation, limited on-campus housing, and the sheer enormity of the city, it can be more challenging for Columbia students to form a cohesive group and to schedule team meetings. However, the vast majority of students live on the Upper West Side and in West Harlem, with many choosing to live with their MBA classmates.

Facilities. There is one other drawback of a location in New York: the cost of real estate. At the individual level, this is intuitive. But it also applies to Columbia Business School as a unit of Columbia University. Historically it has proven difficult for Columbia to "think big" about expansion around Morningside Heights; even small projects often arouse intense neighborhood pushback and delays, thereby increasing the cost. The school's primary presence on campus, Uris Hall, is a rather ugly testimony to this fact. Not even the most committed Columbia booster would try to put lipstick on the pig that is Uris Hall. Though the building's exterior was renovated in the mid-1990s, it still looks the uninspired box from the 1950s that it is, even if the large auditoriums for lectures have been updated to include state-of-the art communications technologies. Starting in 1999, some business classes began being held in the new Warren Hall (technically a Columbia Law building), and in 2002, permanent space in Warren Hall was transferred to the business school.

In 2007, Columbia University announced the plans for its Manhattanville Campus, a 17-acre site with trees and tastefully ambitious architecture from big-name star architects. The new site is located in West Harlem between 129th and 133th streets (just five blocks north of the existing campus), with 6.8 million square feet to be fully developed by 2030. The business school will occupy 450,000 of those square feet (up from a mere 280,000 available in existing facilities). This was most definitely helped by a $100 million gift from Columbia Business School alumni Henry Kravis in late 2010, and a second $100 million pledge from Ronald Perelman in May 2013. However, the recession, city red tape, and demolition mishaps have lengthened the overall project time line. As recently as 2013, the school had estimated the new campus to open in 2016, but construction still has not begun, and the school publishes no hints about the new opening date. If you're applying to Columbia this year, don't hold your breath for improved facilities while you're there.

> With some Columbia students already residing in NYC upon matriculation, limited on-campus housing, and the sheer enormity of the city, it can be more challenging for Columbia students to form a cohesive group and to schedule team meetings.

You Oughta Know

More collaborative than it used to be. In recent years, we have heard that Columbia has made attempts to shed its past reputation as a school with a cutthroat culture and is now much friendlier and more collaborative. Recent graduates have told us that this may partially be due to the wider range of backgrounds now represented in the class. The increase in diversity amongst the student body has led to different perspectives and increased inclusiveness. CBS Matters, formed in 2012, allows students to get to know each other and the faculty on a more personal level with less of the "professional façade." Individual students are able to share their passions by conducting presentations on what matters to them most and why with the goal of having your class know who you are as a person. Columbia's recent change to its non-disclosure of grades policy may also have contributed to a less cutthroat environment as students are not aggressively competing against each other. One recent graduate tells us that it is now more common for classmates to study together and share their knowledge from their professional experiences.

Similar Programs Culturally

Chicago (Booth). The most distinguishing factor of Chicago Booth's culture is intellectual curiosity. Professors are not afraid to ask students to pull out calculators and do some calculus in class, and students are encouraged to question everything, even their professors and one another. So you tend to get more intellectual sparring and debating in the Booth classroom than at its rival to the north, Kellogg. Booth is located in Chicago's South Side, which is not the best part of town these days, so students tend to live in clusters in other areas of the city. Although Columbia's students are starting to cluster closer to campus these days, its student body is still more spread out around the city than at many other schools.

Penn (Wharton). Although Wharton is another school that's made a concerted effort to cut back on its competitive reputation, students shouldn't expect a lot of hand-holding through this large MBA program. Wharton's class is even larger than Columbia's, which means similar challenges in forming tight relationships with your classmates. Both schools use the cluster/ cohort system with even smaller learning teams. Wharton students are known for considerable involvement in campus clubs, which is a trend that's starting to catch on at Columbia as well. Years ago, students would quickly abandon campus to hang out with other friends across Manhattan, but now they are far more likely to get involved in student organizations.

NYU (Stern). Even though Stern is historically known for being much friendlier than its uptown rival, the schools share a number cultural similarities simply due to geography. Both schools have strong ties to New York City and emphasize this as a key aspect of their value proposition. The strong culture of New York permeates both schools. In addition, Columbia's culture has been evolving quickly, and so the gap between "friendly" and "cutthroat" has narrowed significantly.

ADMISSIONS AT COLUMBIA

What Columbia Is Looking For

Intellectual, professional achievers. Columbia Business School looks for intellectually driven people from diverse educational, economic, social, cultural, and geographic backgrounds. Its admissions process favors candidates with a history of high academic achievement; those with serious blemishes on their undergraduate record tend to have more difficulty securing an offer from Columbia. Columbia students also share a record of professional achievement, clearly visible on their resumes. Columbia looks for students who are curious and informed about the world, and it tends to favor applicants who are proficient in a language beyond English. Columbia also looks for students who embody leadership, particularly in terms of social intelligence, self-awareness, and behavioral analysis. Effective and polished communications skills are a given—as is the expectation that those baseline levels can (and will) be raised during the Columbia experience.

Admissions criteria. The Columbia admissions process evaluates three dimensions equally:

1. Academic strength, measured by the GMAT and undergraduate/graduate transcripts, as well as any professional certifications like the CFA.
2. Personal characteristics, which need to be demonstrated throughout the essays and recommendations, but most critically coming through via specific examples in your essays.
3. Professional promise, measured more acutely at Columbia than most any other top program. This is Columbia's assessment of whether your career goals are valid, feasible, and achievable.

Professional experience. Columbia also maintains a preference for candidates with at least some work experience. While we have seen Columbia admit superlative candidates straight out of college, this is extremely rare; 99% of the last few entering classes had at least one year of work experience. Veritas Prep recommends two or more years of work experience for Columbia Business School applicants.

Cultural fit. In recent years, Columbia has also emphasized the applicant's cultural understanding of and fit with the school and what differentiates it from other schools. This newfound focus on culture also helps differentiate current Columbia from the Columbia of old, which had a reputation for sometimes being more cutthroat than collaborative. In particular, Columbia now looks for candidates who will actively contribute to the campus community through extracurricular involvement in clubs, cluster activities, and so forth.

Serious about start dates. Finally, Columbia is also quite strict on its "no deferrals" policy. If you're admitted to Columbia and you accept, you better plan on going for the term you applied or you'll end up as a re-applicant like everyone else when you're ready to try again.

> **99% of the last few entering classes had at least one year of work experience.**

 If you are looking for tips on 2016–17 admissions essays, you're in luck! Check out our website at **veritasprep.com/cbs** for our latest advice.

Preparing to Apply

Reading this Essential Guide is a great first step in your preparation. Hopefully, this insider's glimpse has been helpful in understanding the most important aspects of the school. However, nothing can replace gaining firsthand knowledge and experience yourself.

Reach out to current students. Even if you don't have any personal connections to Columbia, you can reach out to current students and get their insight and advice. On the school's Student Organizations page, you'll find a list of all campus clubs. Find a few clubs that fit your personal and professional interests, and reach out to the officers. Remember: These are very busy MBA students, so you don't want to intrude too much on their time, but you could ask for a 10- to 15-minute conversation or elicit some advice via e-mail. Come prepared with specific questions (preferably those that aren't already answered online). If you're planning to visit campus, perhaps you might even arrange a coffee chat or lunch, if they are available. Officers of major clubs like the Finance Club or Management Consulting Club have plenty of responsibilities. You might provide a quick background introduction and ask if there's another member of their club, even one with a similar background, who might be able to offer some insights and advice about his or her Columbia experience.

Visit campus. The school's website can only tell you so much; by far, a personal visit is the best possible research in the application process. If you have the means, we highly recommend you visit the Columbia Business School campus along with the campuses of your other top choices to understand the significant differences in culture, teaching style, student body, recruiting opportunities, facilities, and so forth. You may be surprised at just how different each school can be and how the reality can differ from the perception. We can pretty much guarantee that Uris Hall, the building where most MBA classes are held, will not become a selling point that convinces you to attend Columbia. You'll be hard pressed to find another top-tier program that has worse facilities, although the school has invested in recent years to update some of the classrooms before it moves to the ultramodern Manhattanville campus in coming years.

We encourage you to take advantage of opportunities while you're on campus, including a class visit, information session, and student chats, as available. Because informal and impromptu encounters can be the most informative, don't be afraid to approach students in less-formal settings.

Other events. We know that many applicants will not be able to travel to New York City to visit campus, but you should take advantage of other worldwide admissions events, such as information sessions, virtual sessions, and specific-audience events. In fact, these off-campus events can offer great opportunities for quality time with admissions officers and even other applicants, who can be a great resource and support through the admissions process. Get to know the school and its culture as well as you can, because your familiarity can shine through your application and essays to help you stand out.

You Oughta Know

Early Decision (ED). If you're certain that Columbia is your top choice, Early Decision is the best option for you. But you'd better be 100% sure, because part of the application requires that you agree to the following statement: *I am committed to attending Columbia Business School and will withdraw all applications and decline all offers from other schools upon admission to Columbia Business School.* If you're accepted, you'll have two weeks to submit a non-refundable $6,000 deposit. Though the occasional opportunist does in fact renege on this offer, and the police won't haul you away if you break that promise, the admissions office's attitude is summed up by: "We'll let some other institution handle someone who so casually breaks their word and pledge." Candidates might consider an Early Decision application to Columbia as part of a strategy of Round 1 applications to other schools. However, it doesn't make sense (nor is it ethical) to submit to multiple "early-action" rounds.

The Early Decision option is available only for August Term applicants. There are also no "rules" about how many ED candidates the school will accept. It might vary from a third to almost a half of the August class (so from perhaps to 180 to 270 candidates). Columbia does not break down the statistics of incoming applications based on ED versus Regular Decision versus J-Term.

Rolling admissions (Regular Decision). After the Early Decision deadline (October 7, 2015), Columbia operates on a rolling admissions basis. This process is quite different from most of the other top schools and means three things for applicants:

1. Applications are evaluated in the order received, so there is a significant advantage to applying early, as there is simply more space available in the class.

2. There is no schedule for issuing interview invitations or final decisions; application decisions are released when they are rendered, which can be at any point in the process.

3. Columbia uses the waitlist a little differently than other schools, often as a "holding stage" while they evaluate additional candidates.

How it's different. Because Columbia does not have "rounds" the way its peers do, it's tempting to call the Early Decision cycle "Round 1" and the Regular Decision cycle "Round 2," but this is a misunderstanding of both the process and the implications of applying in one versus the other. Perhaps the most confusing part of the Columbia Regular Decision admissions process is the fact that it appears that there's only one deadline, and it's in April. This is misleading for two reasons:

1. Because of the rolling admissions process described above, applications are evaluated in the order received, which means there are fewer and fewer slots available as time goes by. An application received in March or April simply doesn't have the same odds of success as one that is submitted in October or November.

2. Merit fellowships are only available to those who submit by an early January deadline, so for many candidates, this January date is the "real" deadline they care about, and that's when the bulk of applications is received. Regardless of what the "official" deadline is, international candidates should get their application in as early as possible to make sure they have enough time to secure required visas.

DEADLINES

All deadlines are 11:59PM U.S. Eastern Time on the dates indicated.

Early Decision:
7 Oct 2015

January Term:
7 Oct 2015

Merit Fellowship:
6 Jan 2016

Final Deadline:
13 Apr 2016

COLUMBIA

A GMAT score that's above the school's average will do more for your candidacy than applying in the first week after the Early Decision deadline.

When should I apply? Columbia does admit the bulk of its August-start students through the Regular Decision process, and it's when most people apply. Do not be lulled by that April deadline into thinking that you can delay your application to Columbia. For most of you, it makes sense to submit your Columbia application first, not last. We recommend applying by mid-November or earlier for the best results.

Even though Columbia doesn't have traditional rounds, our standard advice still holds: We recommend that you apply earlier rather than later, especially if you're a traditional applicant from management consulting or finance. With rolling admissions, the flow of applications is harder to predict, and if you wait too long, the school might have hit its limit on CPAs or engineers. If you'd like to be considered for merit-based financial aid, you'll need to meet an early January deadline. Applying as late as March or April means competing for one of the very few seats still open at that point.

Even though it's almost always a good idea to apply as early as possible, this does not mean that you should apply with a rushed application or a mediocre GMAT score. There's no sense in applying early if you're just going to be denied. A GMAT score that's above the school's average will do more for your candidacy than applying in the first week after the Early Decision deadline.

J-Term admissions. The J-Term has some unique elements to note around the admissions process. Specifically:

- There is just one deadline for the J-Term: in early October (which coincides with many schools' Round 1 deadlines).

- There is no Early Decision option for the J-Term.

- The waitlist for the J-Term does not roll over to the August class. If you are placed on the waitlist for the J-Term, the latest date you can expect to get a final answer is usually mid-December (perhaps earlier if you're not a local candidate).

- If you are declined a spot in the J-Term, you can apply in the August Regular Decision cycle during the same admissions season. However, you'll need to significantly improve your profile and fix the weaknesses that caused the original decision or you'll probably see the same results. Veritas Prep recommends waiting to the following application season before you re-apply, and at that point you could apply to either the J-Term or the August start. In both cases you would be considered a re-applicant.

- The J-Term receives far fewer applications than the August class, which means it's easier for an exceptional candidate to stand out, but there are also fewer spots available (usually around 200).

Prioritizing. The Columbia Admissions Office processes applications in the following order. Applications within a category are processed in the order received:

1. J-Term applications are prioritized because the Admissions Office needs to construct that class fast, since they'll be headed to campus just a few months later in order to begin their studies in January. All decisions for J-Term applicants are generally finalized by December.

2. Early Decision applications are processed somewhat in parallel with the J-Term pool.

3. Regular Decision applications are not processed until J-Term and ED applications have all been cleared. The soonest a Regular Decision application will be opened is typically around November or December.

What Does All This Mean?

Here's a mini-decision tree to help you interpret Columbia's policies and evaluate your options:

1. If you are in love with Columbia and see no possibility of falling in love with any other business school, ever, submit in the Early Decision option (early October deadline).

2. If you are in love with Columbia and want to get through business school faster—and are an entrepreneur, will be returning to a family business, or do not otherwise need the summer internship experience—submit to the J-Term (early October deadline).

3. If you really like Columbia but are not comfortable committing to attend Columbia over any other school that might eventually say "yes" to you, submit early to the Regular Decision process (between September and November).

4. If you are an international candidate, submit as early as possible (Early Decision or Regular Decision), and definitely submit no later than March.

5. If you are a re-applicant to Columbia, submit in the Early Decision option to emphasize your commitment to the school.

Identical applications. You will indicate on your application to which program you're applying; it is not dictated by the day you submit your application. The essay questions and application requirements are absolutely the same for all of these options, the only exception being the commitment that binds the Early Decision applicant.

The Essays

Columbia doesn't seem to have received the "streamlined application" memo. While its peer schools are cutting required essays to the bone, it still requires three essays, with one optional essay and one required short answer. (All this work offers a further argument for starting your application early!)

Think of the Short Answer Question as the positioning statement for your short-term career goals.

Short Answer: What is your immediate post-MBA professional goal? (50 characters maximum)

Get to the point! Three years ago, some applicants (and a few MBA admissions consultants) blew a gasket when Columbia introduced this question and gave it a 200-character limit. Two years ago, that limit was cut in half, to 100 characters. Last year, it was 75 characters. Continuing this trend, this year the character limit has been cut down to 50 characters! We think there's surely a bit of "Hey, let's get with what the Twitter kids are doing" in this decision, but the more important takeaway for you is that the Columbia admissions committee truly just wants a super-brief headline about your post-MBA career goals to better understand what to make of you.

Be straightforward. Think of the Short Answer Question as the positioning statement for your short-term career goals. Do you want to be known as the applicant who wants to run a sports team, or perhaps the applicant who wants to launch a renewable energy startup? Columbia provides some examples on its site, and you'll see that there's nothing particularly creative or special about them. Avoid the temptation to get too gimmicky here, but remember that this is the one thing (about your career goals) that you want the admissions committee to remember about you. And stay tuned for next year to see if the limit has shrunk down to a single word: "banking." "Consulting." "Marketing." "Entrepreneur."

Be honest. Some applicants mistakenly think that they need to have off-the-wall goals to be admitted. This couldn't be further from the truth. Columbia wants to see that your goals are realistic and achievable. If you say that you want to start an NGO in the developing world immediately upon graduation, but absolutely nothing in your application would lead the admissions officer to believe that you're setting yourself up to succeed in this goal, you could easily be denied by this one misstep alone.

Essay #1: Through your resume and recommendations, we have a clear sense of your professional path to date. What are your career goals going forward, and how will the Columbia MBA help you achieve them? (Maximum 500 words)

Get beyond the obvious. This essay changed only slightly from last year: It added the words "career goals"; the length is identical. We still would characterize this question as the fairly typical "Why an MBA? Why this school?" question that many top MBA programs ask. Many applicants fail to adequately to explain why Columbia is the best place for them to earn their MBA, given the school's culture, academic strengths, ties to certain industries, etc. Yes, Columbia has a big name and proximity to Wall Street. Those strengths are obvious, and if you write too much about NYC in this response, you might not leave yourself anything for the next question.

Do your homework. What else does Columbia offer that you can't find anywhere else? And why—given your individual background—is Columbia the best place for you to grow as a business leader? This is what the school is looking for when it asks about "fit." Comb through this Essential Guide and the school's website, and, most importantly, seek input from current students and recent alumni to learn about how the Columbia experience differs from its peers. Then, directly tie these advantages to your unique goals.

Don't just rattle off a list of classes. The biggest mistake we see people make with this essay is that they go to the school's website, find some classes that sound interesting, and create a long list here. Your Columbia MBA experience will be much more than just coursework. If there's a particular course, professor, or academic program that Columbia offers that you can't find elsewhere, mention it by all means! However, be sure to get beyond the classroom and explore Columbia's vast offerings in guest speakers, mid-year internships, international opportunities, and beyond.

Essay #2: Columbia Business School's location enables us to bridge theory and practice in multiple ways: through Master Classes, internships, the New York Immersion Seminars, and, most importantly, through a combination of distinguished research faculty and accomplished practitioners. How will you take advantage of being "at the very center of business"? (Maximum 250 words)

New focus on academics. This year, the Columbia admissions committee added information about bridging theory and practice, master classes, and other academic offerings while keeping the portion about being at the very center of business from last year. Clearly, applicants last year had put too much focus on the benefits of a New York City location without tying these things back to specific offerings at Columbia. Instead of focusing solely on the social benefits of going to business school in New York City, we recommend that you show how you'll take advantage of the unique offerings available at Columbia thanks to its location. We believe the admissions committee is using this essay question as a signaling device to show applicants that they believe their location is a key factor in choosing the school over others.

Connections to industry leaders. One of the key advantages that Columbia has is that thousands of successful executives across nearly every industry are just a cab (or town car) ride away. A huge focus of the MBA program is to bring these industry experts to campus in both speaker series and classroom discussions. It's not uncommon for the subject of a business case to quietly listen to the classroom discussion from the back row, only to be brought to the front of the class for a surprise reveal. You'll see this happen at Harvard and Stanford as well, but thanks to proximity, Columbia brings many professionals to class, creating a unique MBA experience.

Get beyond professional. If you want to go into finance, then your answer here will obviously touch upon this fact. Don't limit yourself just to the obvious Wall Street tie-in, however. What other benefits do you expect you will gain from living and learning in one of the biggest cities in the world? (If you're struggling for answers, watch those videos again!) Also, we've noted before that Columbia doesn't want to be viewed as a commuter school in the middle of a huge city; keep this in mind as you spell out how you will fit in at Columbia. Emphasize ways you'd immerse yourself into on-campus life. Especially if you already live in New York (and often, this answer is even more difficult for applicants already living in NYC since they're too far immersed to see the advantages objectively), be sure to emphasize that you're excited about immersing yourself in the Columbia culture.

Essay #3: CBS Matters, a key element of the School's culture, allows the people in your Cluster to learn more about you on a personal level. What will your Clustermates be pleasantly surprised to learn about you? (Maximum 250 words)

Get personal and introspective. This essay is largely unchanged from last year, but the committee added the video and reference to CBS Matters, changing the emphasis of this essay toward the things that matter most to you. This essay offers an opportunity to "sell" yourself, but in a very different way than you might think. It isn't mandatory that this essay be whimsical, but it should present something that's interesting about you as a person, rather than rehashing something that's already in your application or on your resume. Do not focus on professional accomplishments, but instead think about those life moments that have made you the person you are today. Go back to our comments above about fit and about Columbia wanting to build a strong community.

Don't try to impress. This isn't a contest of who has the most impressive arduous experience, nor is it a challenge to present the biggest sob story of your life. Have an unusual hobby or funny story that people enjoy hearing? This may be the place to use it. The purpose of this essay is for the admissions committee to really get to know you on a personal level, not necessarily to convince the admissions committee of how great you are.

Optional Essay: Is there any further information that you wish to provide the Admissions Committee? If so, use this space to provide an explanation of any areas of concern in your academic record or your personal history. (Maximum 500 words)

Our typical advice stands here: Use the optional essay only if you need to explain a potential blemish in your background that isn't fixable (a low undergraduate GPA, time on academic probation, gaps in school or employment history, no recommendation from your current direct supervisor, etc.). There's no need to harp on a minor weakness and sound like you're making excuses when you don't need to. If you do have a red flag in your background, address it here. Otherwise, you can be confident in leaving it blank.

Recommendations

Professional references only. Columbia asks first-time applicants to submit two recommendations, both of which should be professional in nature; re-applicants must submit one. One should come from a direct supervisor, and if that is not possible you should provide an explanation in the optional essay.

Accommodation for youngest applicants. For applicants with less work experience, Columbia advises that you select recommenders who can speak to your managerial abilities and leadership skills. Additionally, one recommendation can be from a college professor, assuming that person can speak to your professional potential.

Start early. The recommendation form is submitted online as part of your application, and must be completed for Columbia to begin reviewing your application. Veritas Prep advises clients to reach out to their recommenders very early in the process, and also to give them some direction and structure around the general themes of and motivations behind your application. Specifically, your recommenders should be aware of why you're applying to business school, and why in particular you feel Columbia would be a good fit, given your goals and career progression to date.

Consolidated questions. Columbia has gotten the "common recommendation" memo and uses the same two questions as several other schools to reduce the burden on your recommenders:

- *How do the candidate's performance, potential, background, or personal qualities compare to those of other well-qualified individuals in similar roles? Please provide specific examples.*

- *Please describe the most important piece of constructive feedback you have given the applicant. Please detail the circumstances and the applicant's response.*

Recommenders are asked to keep their recommendation to 1,000 words or fewer.

Selecting your recommenders. Columbia explicitly says that applicants with more than six months of work experience must submit one reference from their current supervisor and the second from a former supervisor or close associate who can assess your potential. This is a stricter policy than most peer schools, which say that you may explain an alternate recommender if you do not utilize your current supervisor. For both Columbia and peer schools, we highly recommend that you have a conversation with your current supervisor about the possibility of leaving for business school. However, in some rare cases, this may not be possible. If so, we believe that selecting an indirect supervisor, a close mentor at your current company, or the closest possible proxy to your current supervisor would be satisfactory and would not prevent you from being admitted to Columbia. You'll need to explain this choice in the optional essay and provide a compelling reason to the admissions committee why your current supervisor did not offer a recommendation.

Should I draft it myself? (No.) Many applicants to business school are asked by their superiors to draft the recommendation themselves and the recommender will approve it. We strongly recommend that you do not write the recommendation yourself for several reasons. First, your writing style and choice of phrasing are unique, and admissions officers will notice if the recommendations are similar to each other and your essays. If they notice too many similarities, your application could be denied outright. Second, you may tend to be too humble or generic. Your supervisor might use language such as "one of the top analysts I've seen in my entire career" that you wouldn't dare include if writing it on his or her behalf. Third, the admissions officer is looking for a third-party perspective on your candidacy, so writing a recommendation yourself is an unethical breach of trust with the school you are looking to join. Finally, and most importantly, Columbia requires applicants to certify that "I did not write any part of this recommendation, either in whole or part, or have any involvement in its drafting or submission." Need we say more?

Preparing your recommenders. Instead of writing the recommendation yourself, you should sit down and have candid conversations with your recommenders about the reasons you want to go to business school and why you've selected your target schools, your professional goals, and your experience together. Ask them if they would have the time to write a strong recommendation on your behalf. (This also gives them a nice "out" by telling you that they are too busy rather than saying they don't feel comfortable giving you a positive recommendation.) Bring a copy of your resume and a bulleted list of projects that you've worked on together and accomplishments they have seen you achieve. Let them know that admissions committees prefer to see specific, detailed examples in recommendations. Then, let them know that you'll serve as a "project manager" to follow up and ensure that they are able to submit your recommendation ahead of the deadline.

The Interview

Conducted for almost every admit. Interestingly enough, interviews are not 100% required at Columbia. However, Columbia does interview almost every candidate before extending an offer. The exceptions to this mostly come into play for a re-applicant who was interviewed during his or her initial application process. The school only interviews candidates who it thinks have a good chance of being admitted, so receiving an invitation is already a great sign. Because of the rolling admissions policy, Columbia has no cutoffs for extending interview invitations. If you have not yet heard back from the committee, this is likely because they have not yet reviewed your application and not because they are disinterested.

Who will interview me? If you are invited to interview at Columbia, the interview will be conducted by an alumnus in your area, by a current student on campus, or by Skype or phone with a student or admissions officer. You'll typically be given a list of alumni living in your area and can choose the person with whom you would like to interview. It is important to note that although alumni may be very experienced in conducting interviews for the school, it is also likely that they may not be very experienced. This may remove some of the intimidation factors surrounding your interview for a top MBA program.

What should I expect? Interviews are blind, meaning your interviewer will not have seen your entire application, but rather only your resume. Interviews typically last between 45 and 60 minutes, and your interviewer will provide his or her feedback to Columbia within 72 hours. Columbia interviews are quite standard. You'll probably be asked many similar questions to those on the application, such as why you want an MBA, why you've chosen Columbia specifically, and what you would bring to the Columbia community. Be prepared to answer several questions about your professional experience and achievements, so have several stories ready to tell that will showcase your leadership skills, teamwork, abilities to handle complex situations,

When will I hear back? Approximately one to two weeks after the admissions committee renders a final decision, the interviewer will receive an e-mail notification of that decision. If you are offered admission to Columbia, you just might hear from your interviewer via a congratulatory call or e-mail. Please note, however, that if you are placed on the waitlist, your interviewer will not have any involvement or influence in moving you to the admitted or denied list.

> Interviews are blind, meaning your interviewer will not have seen your entire application, but rather only your resume.

COLUMBIA

DON'T TAKE OUR WORD FOR IT

Rich was able to provide insightful feedback and steer me in the right direction. He made sure that everything I did was my own work, which I believe made the applications that much stronger and in line with all of my interviews. **With Rich's help I was able to get into the school we focused on (Booth) in addition to several others (Yale SOM and HBS)** simply because his method and coaching helped me to provide insightful information about myself, something necessary for all the applications.

MATT *Harvard Business School Class of 2017*

Working with Veritas Prep was the absolute best investment I made throughout the whole business school application process. Their team was thorough, timely, professional, and above all—extremely human. Before working with them I did a free consultation with two other MBA consulting firms, which were not half as encouraging, nor did they seem to really care about me as an applicant. Veritas Prep was the absolute opposite. I was admitted to the school of my dreams with a full scholarship for the first year of tuition. Thank you to the team at Veritas Prep!

SHARI *NYU Stern Class of 2017*

I truly believe that **I would not have gotten into my top choice school without the guidance of my Veritas Prep consultants**. They were there with me every step of the way, from my resume preparation and essay development to interview prep, and made me confident in my story. I don't know what I would have done without them!

ASHLEY *NYU Stern Class of 2017*

Michelle was fantastic! From start to finish, she was 100% accessible and extremely timely in communications. Not only did I gain admission to my top choice for business school but **my application process was much less stressful and was better organized with Michelle in my corner**.

BRETT *Columbia Class of 2017*

WHAT ARE YOUR CHANCES?
LET'S TALK.

Call or e-mail us to discuss your candidacy for top MBA programs.

1-800-925-7737 | INFO@VERITASPREP.COM

KELLOGG

With an emphasis on creativity and innovation, it's no wonder Kellogg graduates go on to thrive in marketing and consulting.

EVANSTON, IL

CLASS SIZE
662

PROGRAM FOUNDED
1908

SETTING
SUBURBAN

CHARACTERISTICS
MARKETING, SOCIAL LIFE, DIVERSE

SECTIONS

KELLOGG SNAPSHOT

What Kellogg Is Known For

Marketing. *Kellogg* and *marketing* are nearly synonymous in most MBA circles. However, the school is working hard not to be painted as merely a "marketing school." Indeed, each year nearly twice as many graduates go into consulting as they do marketing, and Kellogg's general management curriculum is perfectly suited for a wide range of career paths. Nonetheless, Kellogg does feature some of the top marketing professors and courses available, and is a natural first choice for anyone looking to specialize in that area.

Collaboration. More than 40 years ago Kellogg pioneered the practice of teamwork in management education and corporate leadership. Today, teamwork is a buzzword at every business school (and corporation) around the world. Despite this widespread adoption, Kellogg continues to remain a leader when it comes to collaborative learning. Many classes have zero individual assignments; every deliverable is submitted as a team. Only one's individual contributions to the classroom discussion would differentiate grades among teammates.

> **More than 40 years ago, Kellogg pioneered the practice of teamwork in management education and corporate leadership. Today, teamwork is a buzzword at every business school (and corporation) around the world.**

A party atmosphere. Whether it's at the weekly on-campus kegger called "TG" (short for TGIF—Thank God it's Friday), on your weeklong, international KWEST trip with fellow students and significant others before school starts, on Ski Trip during winter break, or during the many, many parties and other events, you'll find that Kellogg can have an almost "frat house" feel to it. Some students can be surprised during the three-week pre-term orientation called CIM (Complete Immersion in Management) how quickly some Kellogg students revert back to their undergraduate antics.

What Makes Kellogg Different

A student-driven culture. Prior to Dean Sally Blount's arrival in 2010, nearly every major innovation at Kellogg was the result of a student-led initiative. For example, a student-initiated trip to the Soviet Union in 1990 led to the Global Initiatives in Management (GIM) program. The student-led culture still persists under Dean Blount, but with greater vision and structure. At the suggestion of a Kellogg student, the administration started the Dean's Consulting Alliance, a program in which students earn credit as they learn to manage a team of consultants. The team reports directly to the administration with their results on a specific project to improve the school.

Extremely diverse professional opportunities. At other top-tier MBA programs, 80% of graduates are hired by about 20 to 30 large firms, often in the finance and consulting sectors. For years, Kellogg has emphasized that more than 200 firms hire the same 80% of its graduates. While the Big 3 consulting firms still hire a large number of Kellogg grads, most other firms hire in the single digits. This means that the Career Management Center attracts many more companies to campus than most other schools do, and Kellogg students have a broader range of recruiters to choose from.

An MBA in every flavor. Unlike Harvard Business School, which has carefully protected its MBA brand by offering the degree only in a two-year, full-time program, Kellogg has chosen a portfolio approach to offer the degree in many formats. In addition to its traditional, two-year MBA program, Kellogg is the highest-ranked U.S. business school to offer an accelerated one-year, full-time MBA program. In early 2012, Dean Blount announced that the one-year (1Y) MBA program would grow from 85 students to as many 250 within five years. We think this announcement may have been a bit hasty and that the program is unlikely to break 200 students by 2017, but the 1Y class has been slowly growing. The Class of 2015 included 118 one-years, the largest 1Y cohort in school history. The two-year class is down about 40 students since 2007.

Its top-ranked EMBA program is offered in Evanston, Illinois, and Miami, Florida (targeting Latin American executives). It also has one of the highest-ranked part-time MBA programs, offered in downtown Chicago, which also offers an accelerated track.

Northwestern was one of the early pioneers in offering a three-year JD-MBA joint degree, and it also offers a two-year joint offering with the engineering school called MMM. With its 80-year-old PhD program and the recent addition of a one-year Master of Science in Management Studies for recent college graduates, the Kellogg School has something for everyone.

Kellogg Is a Good Fit for You If...

You're eager to get involved. Kellogg no longer asks a written essay question about why you want to go to Kellogg or what you'll do to contribute, but it does require a video essay about your interest in Kellogg. Admissions officers will also be looking even more closely for evidence of extracurricular involvement during college and throughout your professional life. You're pretty much guaranteed to be asked in your interview about the Kellogg clubs and organizations with which you want to be involved, so be prepared to tell how you plan to actively contribute!

You are not intimidated by a larger program. There's a lot going on at Kellogg, not just with all the various types of students attending in different degree programs, but because it's one of the largest class sizes of any business school in the world. About 650 students are in each full-time two-year class (including 1Y and 2Y MBA, MMM, and JD/MBA students), which is double the size of many more intimate programs like Yale, Tuck, and Haas. It's a great opportunity to make a lot of friends and really expand your network; however, it's also possible to get a little lost in the sea of students and activities.

You have strong work experience. While some top business schools are trending younger, Kellogg continues to prefer applicants with several years of full-time professional experience. The average has been just more than five years. Those coming straight from college or with limited work experience may still apply, although anyone with fewer than two years of post-undergrad, full-time work experience will be interviewed by invitation only. Last year, Kellogg was the only top-tier MBA programs to report zero students with fewer than two years of experience.

You want to go into consulting. Kellogg sends a large number graduates into the field of consulting. In 2014, Kellogg sent an impressive 35% of graduates into consulting roles, which is quite close to the placement statistics of Tuck (35%), MIT Sloan (34%), and Ross (34%). By comparison, Stanford sent 16% of its graduating class into consulting, Harvard Business School 23%, and Wharton 26%.

Kellogg also offers the highest-ranked U.S. one-year full-time MBA program.

NORTHWESTERN (KELLOGG)

You're not looking for a typical "finance school." While Kellogg ranks in the top 10 finance programs every year, it sends far fewer candidates into the field than many peer schools. Last year, Kellogg sent just 14% of graduates into finance, far lower than NYU Stern (35%), Wharton (36%), Columbia (34%), and south-side rival Chicago Booth (37%). In fact, if you're applying to Kellogg with a career goal in finance, the admissions committee is likely to assume that you are also applying to Chicago Booth. Be sure to highlight Kellogg's offerings for your specific career track and experiential learning opportunities such as the Asset Management Practicum, Buy-out Lab, and Venture Lab.

ACADEMICS AT KELLOGG

What Kellogg Is Known For

Teamwork. Perhaps the biggest difference between teamwork at Kellogg and at other schools is that Kellogg students actually like it! Many MBA programs now include team projects as a key part of their curriculum, but we've heard students express dread about teamwork at some other MBA programs, while it's a hallmark of the Kellogg academic experience. Teamwork is so prevalent at Kellogg that study rooms must typically be booked well in advance, as groups must compete not only with other classes, but also teams using the space to organize club activities, conferences, and other events.

Blended teaching. Kellogg offers perhaps the most blended teaching approach of any of the top business schools, dividing its coursework nearly equally: case method (30%), lectures (30%), and team projects (30%), all bolstered by the school's commitment to experiential learning (10%). Classroom participation is one thing that all of Kellogg's class formats have in common. The discussion is extremely collegial, with most students actively avoiding direct contradictions or debates in the classroom like you might see at Harvard or Chicago Booth. The curriculum is constantly evolving with the times and the hot topics of the day.

Experiential learning. Many elite business schools offer their students the chance to study in the field and to get real-world experience, but few incorporate the mantra of "learning by doing" to the extent that Kellogg does. From the number of students who participate in business plan competitions, to the wide range of unique opportunities to create and test new technologies, Kellogg allows every student to find a way to put his or her theoretical learning to the real-world test. The school offers a nearly unparalleled variety of courses and labs that focus almost entirely on experiential learning.

Technically, Kellogg classes are graded on an A-to-F scale (no pluses or minuses), but the curve tends to be extremely generous.

A generous curve. Technically, Kellogg classes are grades on an A-to-F scale (no pluses or minuses), but the curve tends to be extremely generous. There is not a specific curve that is enforced, but in practice about 40% of every class will earn an A, 50% will earn a B, and 10% or less will earn a C or lower. Dean Blount has encouraged a greater focus on academics during her tenure, but this has not affected grades dramatically.

You Oughta Know

Flexibility. Because Kellogg has nine core courses in traditional subjects such as accounting, finance, marketing, statistics, and leadership, the school isn't generally known for its flexible curriculum. However, students may apply for up to seven waivers of core courses, resulting in just two courses that are truly "required." One of those required courses is completed during the three-week pre-term before the first year, so students who majored in Business in college or can demonstrate extensive knowledge in certain fields will have the opportunity to take more advanced electives starting on day one.

Breadth. One advantage of a large MBA program is that the school can offer a wide range of classes. Kellogg offers more than 200 electives across 11 academic departments and professional programs. For example, the Management & Organizations department (typically called Organizational Behavior at other schools) offers courses as varied as *Social Media and Reputation*, *Creativity as a Business Tool*, and *Sports and People Analytics*. With 55 new classes added in the past two and a half years (25% of the current course catalog), the curriculum is constantly evolving.

Social responsibility. The school has a range of opportunities for students to get involved in their local communities while also building strong skills for a future career in social venture or nonprofit. The Kellogg Board Fellows program is an opportunity for students to serve on the board of a local nonprofit. The Social Enterprise program (formerly called SEEK) supports those interested in bringing social benefits to the world through business by offering courses, clubs, conferences, competitions, a speaker series, and a social entrepreneurship lab. In the Aspen Institute's Beyond Grey Pinstripes ranking of MBA programs along metrics of social and environmental stewardship, Kellogg ranks #6 overall and #2 in Business Impact (social and environmental responsibility in for-profit businesses).

Other professional programs. Besides Social Enterprise, Kellogg also has professional programs in Health Enterprise Management, Media Management, and Real Estate. While the school may not be as well known in these areas, the fact that they have dedicated professional programs (similar to academic departments) to these subjects means that the school is serious about its offerings. Applicants interested in any of these industries should consider Kellogg for their shortlist. Each professional program has a corresponding major along with student-led clubs, events, recruiting treks, conferences, and speakers.

Global exchanges. If you'd like to study abroad in an exotic location for a semester, Kellogg has options in every continent on earth (well, not Antarctica). With 30 partner schools, Kellogg's exchange program is the most robust we've seen, and about 125 to 150 students choose to study abroad for a quarter each year. Note, however, that exchanges at the some of the most popular schools, such as London Business School (LBS), INSEAD, IESE, NUS, and HKUST, are quite popular, so you'll need to apply as early as possible in your first year.

The Kellogg Board Fellows program is an opportunity for students to serve on the board of a local nonprofit.

KELLOGG AT A GLANCE

APPLICANTS BY SCHOOL

Kellogg 4,652	Stanford 7,355	Harvard 9,543	Wharton 6,111	Columbia 5,799	Sloan 4,735
23.2%	7.1%	11%	20.7%	18.2%	13.8%

◀ Percent admitted

AVERAGE GMAT SCORES

717	726	728	732
Kellogg	Harvard	Wharton	Stanford

INTERNATIONAL CITIZENS

Kellogg's percentage of international students is a little lower than some schools whose international composition exceeds 40% of the class, but it remains higher than some other schools who bring in a third or lower from abroad.

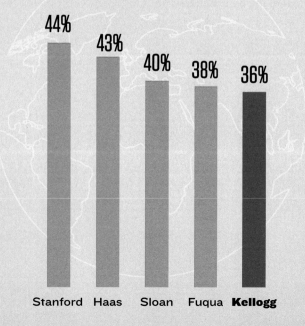

44%	43%	40%	38%	36%
Stanford	Haas	Sloan	Fuqua	**Kellogg**

YIELD

Yield (the percentage of admitted applicants who choose to attend) ticked up at Kellogg last year, from a record low of 54% in 2014.

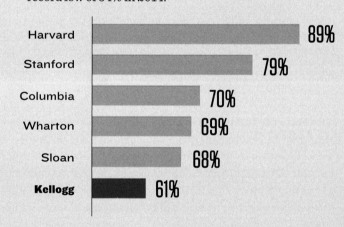

Harvard	89%
Stanford	79%
Columbia	70%
Wharton	69%
Sloan	68%
Kellogg	61%

MARRIED/PARTNERED

Kellogg reports that nearly 40% of their class is married or partnered. At first glance, this is much higher than other B-schools, which typically report ranges between 20 and 30%.

40%	30%	22%
Kellogg	Harvard	Fuqua

AVERAGE AGE

28 Kellogg   27 Harvard   29 INSEAD

YEARS OF WORK EXPERIENCE

Kellogg favors applicants with at least two years of full-time work experience and goes to great lengths to tell applicants that full-time work experience is valued and expected.

 **2-12.5** Kellogg    **0-16** Wharton    **0-15** Stanford

UNITED STATES MINORITIES

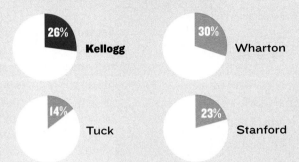

26% Kellogg   30% Wharton
14% Tuck   23% Stanford

WOMEN

Kellogg's percentage of women is slowly creeping up and now stands at 37%. This puts Kellogg in the middle of the road compared to other top-tier business schools.

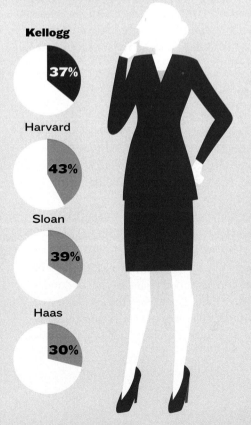

Kellogg 37%
Harvard 43%
Sloan 39%
Haas 30%

AVERAGE GPA

3.54 Kellogg

3.67 Harvard

3.74 Stanford

3.60 Wharton

CLASS SIZE

Kellogg's class size is among the largest. This translates to a large alumni network of nearly 60,000 and an admission rate that tends to be slightly higher than peer schools.

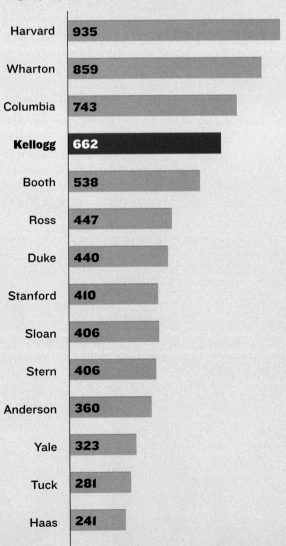

School	Class Size
Harvard	935
Wharton	859
Columbia	743
Kellogg	662
Booth	538
Ross	447
Duke	440
Stanford	410
Sloan	406
Stern	406
Anderson	360
Yale	323
Tuck	281
Haas	241

NORTHWESTERN (KELLOGG)

Majors:

Accounting

Economics

Finance

Managing
Organizations

Marketing

Operations

Strategy

Pathways:

Data Analytics

Entrepreneurship

Growth and Scaling

Health Enterprise
Management

Real Estate

Social Impact

Venture Capital and
Private Equity

Nuts & Bolts

Sections. Each incoming class at Kellogg is divided into eight "sections" of approximately 65 students each. True to Kellogg students' tradition of not taking themselves too seriously, the sections have unusual names, such as the Bucketheads, Moose, Cash Cows, Highlanders, and Big Dogs. These sections are randomly assigned, although Kellogg makes sure that each section has a nice mix of backgrounds. While students at some other business schools remain in their sections for their entire first year, Kellogg's section system really only applies to a few classes in its first quarter, after which students enroll in required courses and electives based on any schedule they choose. (MMM students make up a ninth section for first-quarter classes, but each of these students also belongs to one of the other sections during orientation week activities, etc.)

Majors. A "major" at Kellogg is not like your major in college; majors require just four classes outside the core requirements. At one point, Kellogg students could choose from among 18 different majors, but the school recently streamlined its list of majors and added a new feature called "pathways," discussed below. A major is no longer required, but graduates' majors will be listed on their transcripts and may be mentioned on their resumes for recruiting purposes.

Pathways. Pathways are a new feature at Kellogg to help students navigate the hundreds of available elective courses. Because pathways are simply provided as suggestions for students with particular interests or career aspirations, there are no requirements and they are not listed on transcripts. These pathways are typically organized with foundational courses, in-depth courses, and experiential or field-research courses.

Grade disclosure. Kellogg has no grade non-disclosure policy, which means that recruiters may ask about your grades and students may discuss them. Grades rarely come up in conversation, although finance recruiters are known to ask about them. MBA candidates tend to worry that grade disclosure leads to more competitiveness in the classroom and a more cutthroat culture, but Kellogg certainly shows no signs of these characteristics.

Popular Professors & Courses

Average ratings of all professors are made public to all students, so finding the best professors is not difficult. Kellogg also incorporates student ratings into the tenure process for faculty, so the school takes its teaching very seriously. Below are some of the most popular professors and the courses they teach. Nearly every professor listed here has earned the Professor of the Year award from students over the past few years.

Negotiations
Professor Victoria Medvec
Professor Medvec is not only known as one of the world's leading experts in negotiations, but is extremely dynamic in the classroom. Her sections of *Negotiations* regularly go for hundreds of points in Kellogg's bidding system for elective classes. She also teaches the *Leadership in Organizations* core course to two lucky sections during first-year pre-term. A consultant to many Fortune 500 companies, she brings numerous examples from real-world CEOs into the classroom.

Technology Marketing
Professor Mohan Sawhney

Even students with minimal interest in technology clamor to take Professor Sawhney's course, as it teaches key elements of marketing strategy and incorporates experiential learning using consulting projects with outside tech firms. Professor Sawhney is also a prolific author and consultant for major technology companies.

Marketing Strategy
Clinical Professors Tim Calkins and Julie Hennessy

Marketing Strategy is a classic Kellogg course combining a multi-week simulation competition, case studies, team projects, and lecture. Professors Tim Calkins and Julie Hennessy both teach sections of this course and are wildly popular. Professor Hennessy also teaches the core marketing course, and is among its most popular professors along with Kent Grayson.

Operations Management
Professor Gad Allon

Professor Allon teaches an array of operations courses, and is universally loved by students, faculty, and administrators alike. He teaches the operations core course, which is often postponed until the last possible quarter by Kellogg students, only to discover that Professor Allon is able to make the subject come alive through his oozing passion for the subject and endearing humility. His ability to memorize hundreds of students' names seemingly overnight is renowned.

Customer Analytics
Professor Florian Zettelmeyer

One might think that professors of data analytics would be least likely to hit the list of student popularity. However, Professor Zettelmeyer made his mark on the school quickly. Just two years after teaching his first course at Kellogg, he was named Professor of the Year. He leads Kellogg's Big Data program and continues to delight class after class.

Public Economics for Business Leaders
Professor David Besanko

Professor Besanko once served as a senior associate dean of the Business School, which students regretted because it took him out of the classroom for a period of three to four years. Having returned, Professor Besanko remains one of the most popular professors, seamlessly weaving stories from students' backgrounds into cold calling opportunities!

Similar Academic Programs

There are a number of MBA programs that incorporate a wide range of teaching methods and encourage collaboration and experiential learning into a broad, general management curriculum, although few do it to the extent that Kellogg does. Below are a few programs that take a similar approach.

Penn (Wharton). Kellogg and Wharton are not commonly seen as similar MBA programs, but there are a number of academic similarities. Their core curricula are remarkably similar, and both schools pride themselves on having a broad range of available electives. Wharton has a world-class MBA in Health Care Management, to which applicants must apply to directly. Its Lauder joint-degree program in international studies is also second to none.

MIT (Sloan). Sloan is another program rarely compared directly to Kellogg, but if you are interested in hands-on learning, MIT is a master of it. The school's motto, "Mens et Manus," literally means "Mind and Hand." Sloan pioneered the use of lab classes where students serve as consultants to companies to help solve real-world projects. However, Sloan's core curriculum is known for being extremely analytical and rigorous.

Dartmouth (Tuck). Tuck takes great pride in the variety of teaching methods used in the classroom, and its students tend to be very collegial and friendly in the classroom. The school is known for its general management curriculum and the heavy use of team projects, so the similarities to Kellogg abound.

UCLA (Anderson). With the quarter system and a nine-course core curriculum, the basics at Anderson are nearly identical to those at Kellogg. Elective offerings are also somewhat similar, with specializations that include sustainability, entertainment, health care, and real estate, a rare combination. The classroom environment at Anderson tends to be similar as well. However, experiential learning is more concentrated in the Applied Management Research (AMR) project at Anderson, whereas Kellogg offers more experiential lab and practicum courses.

EMPLOYMENT & CAREERS AT KELLOGG

What Kellogg Is Known For

Marketing and brand management. Given Kellogg's strong reputation in marketing, it may come as a surprise that just 11% of the Class of 2014 took a job with a consumer goods or retail company (the most common industry for brand managers), although 21% described their job function as "marketing/product management." Amazon and Apple both hired a large number of graduates from the Class of 2014, so perhaps some students are pursuing marketing opportunities with these popular tech firms rather than positions with more traditional consumer packaged goods (CPG) companies. In percentage terms, Duke (Fuqua) isn't far behind, with 10% of its class going to consumer goods or retail firms, but Kellogg's class is much larger, so you'll find that these companies are chock full of Kellogg alums. Also surprising is that more Kellogg grads go into finance (14%) than marketing!

Management consulting. Every year, Kellogg sends more grads into the management consulting industry than any other MBA program (with the exception of Tuck, which sent an equal percentage of its graduates into this industry). In 2014, four of the school's five top employers were all consulting firms: McKinsey (29 hires), Bain (24), BCG (21), and Deloitte (26). This year, 35% of the class took a consulting job, which is actually down from the 40% figure for many years.

Graduates entering the consulting industry

Kellogg & Tuck	35%
Sloan, Ross, & Columbia	34%
Duke	30%
Booth & Stern	28%
Wharton, Haas, & Yale	26%

You Oughta Know

There's a lot more to Kellogg than just marketing and consulting. The school has quite a few "hidden gems" when it comes to recruiting opportunities.

Silicon Valley. Shockingly, Kellogg sent more graduates to Silicon Valley firms in 2014 than even Stanford (although Stanford sent a higher percentage of its much-smaller class). From 2013 to 2014, the percentage of students pursuing careers in technology increased from 12% to 18%. The MMM program's recent refocusing on design innovation and technology may be a driver of this trend. Additionally, since many MBAs take product and marketing management roles within tech companies, Kellogg is well-positioned to send its graduates into tech.

In 2014, Kellogg sent more graduates to Silicon Valley than Stanford.

Graduates entering the technology industry

School	%
Haas	43%
Sloan, Anderson, & Texas	28%
Stanford	24%
Kellogg	**18%**
HBS	17%

Manufacturing. Most people don't associate the Kellogg brand with manufacturing, but it sends more graduates into the sector in absolute terms than any other MBA program other than Harvard. The MMM program still has deep connections to the manufacturing industry. General Electric, 3M, and the major auto manufacturers are common recruiters on campus each year.

Graduates entering the manufacturing industry

School	%
Darden	9%
Ross	6%
HBS & **Kellogg**	**5%**
Tuck	3%
Wharton, Booth, & Yale	2%
Sloan & Columbia	1%

Breadth of recruiters. Be careful when you look at hiring numbers and play the percentage game. Just because a school sends a much-higher percentage of its class into an industry doesn't necessarily mean it is "easier" to get a job from those schools. Kellogg takes great pride in the fact that, while 80% of graduates from other schools go to just 20 or 30 companies, the same proportion of its graduates go to 200 firms. This means that the Kellogg alumni network is not nearly as concentrated at individual firms, but you'll have a much higher likelihood of finding an alum who is working for your target company, no matter its size or industry.

Entrepreneurship. In raw figures, an almost identical number of graduates (29) from the Class of 2014 started their own business as did those from MIT Sloan (30). An additional 16 students placed with startups after graduating. Of course, Kellogg's graduating class is quite a bit larger than Sloan's, so the percentage of the class pursuing entrepreneurship is lower (4.4%, vs.

7.4%). However, the school is fairly strong compared to other top-tier business schools, which typically have 1–2% of their class start a business after graduation. In recent years, Kellogg has been taking steps to boost its entrepreneurship offerings and has hired a large number of adjunct faculty with real-world entrepreneurial experience, so it is likely that this trend is set to continue.

Graduates electing to pursue entrepreneurial opportunities

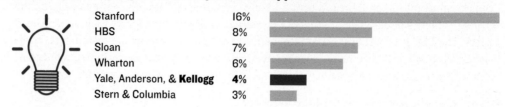

Stanford	16%
HBS	8%
Sloan	7%
Wharton	6%
Yale, Anderson, & **Kellogg**	**4%**
Stern & Columbia	3%

Nuts & Bolts

Open vs. closed list interviews. In an era when big recruiters wield a lot of power in the MBA recruiting process, Kellogg has worked hard to preserve opportunities for career switchers. At least half of a recruiter's interview slots must be reserved for "open list" interviews. This means that students may bid points to secure an interview with an employer, even if their resume may not seem to fit with the role at first glance. Since 80% of the Kellogg class will change industries, job functions, or both, preserving open list interviewing allows these students to make their mark. "Closed list" interviews are conducted at the request of the recruiting company. Interestingly, companies tend to hire equal numbers of open list and closed list interviewees, so this has been an extremely successful policy at Kellogg.

Interview prep. Like at many other schools, interview prep is organized primarily through industry clubs, such as the Finance Club, Consulting Club, and Marketing Club. Each club organizes second-year mentors with a group of first-year students to learn how to tackle case questions, behavioral questions, and so forth. Kellogg students tend to be extremely collegial and collaborative in the recruiting process, even when competing for the same jobs. (However, there are always a few jokes in the end-of-year revue show called Special K! around the fact that students may secretly hope their competition fails!)

Recruiting season. The unprepared may be surprised at how quickly on-campus recruiting starts at Kellogg. In 2015, Fall Quarter classes start on September 21 and recruiters are held at bay for one week. Starting September 28, the school "releases the hounds" and recruiters may start reaching out to first-year students and holding educational events with on-campus clubs. This means that students need to have a strong idea of the kinds of jobs they would be interested in well before school starts.

Similar Programs for Professional Opportunities

Michigan (Ross). Of all top-tier business schools, the recruiting profiles for Kellogg and Ross are perhaps the most similar. Both schools send a large number of graduates into consulting and consumer goods industries, similar numbers of graduates into finance, and a healthy number into both technology and manufacturing. Ross sends more of its class (20%) into tech, with slightly fewer into management consulting, but otherwise the schools are remarkably similar.

Duke (Fuqua). Kellogg and Fuqua often end up together on MBA applicants' short lists for their similar professional opportunities and campus cultures. The most notable difference in recruiting trends is that Duke sends more graduates into health care, although this has narrowed in recent years. Fuqua is known for its strong healthcare program, particularly hospital administration. Fuqua also sends more candidates into the nonprofit and government sectors.

MIT (Sloan). Sloan is another heavy consulting school, with slightly more of its graduating class (37%) taking a consulting-related positionthan Kellogg's class (35%). Fewer MIT graduates go into the management consulting industry, and more go into technology consulting. Significantly more Sloanies go into operations, supply chain, or project management roles than any other MBA program, largely bolstered by its Leaders for Global Operations (LGO) dual-degree program with the engineering school.

Yale School of Management (SOM). Fully 40% of Yale's graduating class identifies their job function after graduation as "consulting," although just more than half of those graduates go into the management consulting sector. This means that more of Yale's graduates serve as consultants in other sectors, such as technology, health care, or nonprofit. Known for its emphasis on the intersection between business and society, Yale sends far more graduates (around one in 10) into nonprofit and government roles than any other MBA program.

Texas (McCombs). For opportunities in technology, consulting, and finance, McCombs's placement statistics are quite similar to Kellogg's. Twenty-eight percent of the Class of 2014 placed in the tech industry upon graduation, which is higher than Kellogg (18%); however, 9% of graduates went into the consumer goods/retail industry, which is not far behind Kellogg's placement of 11%. A solid 25% of the Class of 2014 also placed into consulting.

Indiana (Kelley). For applicants interested in marketing, Kelley is a strong option. The school sends nearly the same percentage of graduates into consumer packaged goods (CPG) firms as Kellogg, and, those graduates earn just $3,000 less on average than their Kellogg counterparts. About 28% of Kelley grads describe their post-MBA position as marketing or sales, higher than every other MBA program in our sample except UCLA Anderson, where many graduates go into technology product management.

CULTURE & CAMPUS LIFE AT KELLOGG

What Kellogg Is Known For

Fun and friendly. Kellogg students have never been known to take themselves too seriously, and the admissions office will look for candidates who fit this fun and casual culture. This isn't to say that they can't buckle down when it's time for interviews, case competitions, and class projects, but even the atmosphere in the classroom tends to be light and casual.

FOMO. Due to the sheer number of competing club events, activities, parties, recruiting events, guest speakers, coffee chats, career fairs, trips, treks, sports—oh, and classes, too—the "fear of missing out" (known as FOMO) runs rampant at Kellogg.

A 24/7 experience. Kellogg offers pretty limited on-campus housing at the McManus Center, where just 250 of the 1,400 full-time students reside. McManus tends to house primarily international students who are unable to come to Evanston to sign a lease in-person before beginning school. However, nearly all Kellogg students live within just a few minutes' walk of the Jacobs Center, concentrated in a handful of apartment complexes southwest of campus. This means that your Kellogg life extends well beyond the classroom; you'll be fully immersed in the Kellogg experience. Married and partnered students only half-joke that they won't see their spouses or partners again for two years!

You Oughta Know

While most schools (and applicants) think of hands-on learning as simply a series of lab courses and consulting projects, Kellogg considers the numerous extracurricular leadership opportunities to be vital elements of its experiential learning experience.

Student leadership. Student-led clubs are the lifeblood of Kellogg. Students lead major portions of the MBA program that are run by the administration of many other schools, including professional conferences (which are usually quite well attended by students and professionals alike), CIM week (new student orientation), Global Initiatives in Management (GIM), Board Fellows (a program for students to sit on local nonprofit boards), leadership expeditions, and many other professional development opportunities. While most schools (and applicants) think of hands-on learning as simply a series of lab courses and consulting projects, Kellogg considers the numerous extracurricular leadership opportunities to be vital elements of their experiential learning experience.

Club participation. Most Kellogg students will actively participate in several clubs and activities throughout the year, often serving in multiple leadership roles. Clubs receive their funding from the school, so students may join as many as they like with no annual dues. Topics range from professional (consulting, investment banking, marketing clubs) to cultural (Black Management Association, Christian Fellowship, Women's Business Association) to social (Kellogg Eatz, The Laughing Stocks, flag football, volleyball, etc.).

Overcommitment. When you combine more than 160 student clubs, conferences, and leadership offices with the fear of missing out, you get classic overcommitment problems. Students are often double- and triple-booked during lunch breaks and popular meeting times with recruiting events, club meetings, event planning meetings, and study groups. Although there are no classes on Wednesdays, this can often be one of the busiest days with extracurricular planning and activities.

Married/partnered students. Nearly 40% of Kellogg students arrive accompanied by a partner. Known as JVs (not Junior Varsities, but rather Joint Ventures), spouses, partners, boyfriends, and girlfriends are invited to attend activities and events, and form a major part of the Kellogg community. Kellogg Kids was an outgrowth of the Joint Ventures Club and provides a support network for families with children.

TG. Each Friday at 5PM., Kellogg hosts a school-wide happy hour called TG (short for TGIF) in its central atrium. The event is completely open, so this is a perfect time for campus visitors to get a glimpse of Kellogg's student culture up-close and personal. Most TGs are sponsored by student clubs. Some are pretty tame, while others are raucous events. Drag TG, sponsored by the Gay & Lesbian Management Association, is typically held early in the year and regularly attracts crowds of more than 1,000 people.

Day at Kellogg (DAK). While there are many, many events that we could describe in this Guide, from KWEST to Ski Trip to Charity Auction Ball, perhaps the most important to prospective students is Day at Kellogg (DAK). The name is deceiving because events now span four days. DAK is the admitted students' weekend where applicants have a chance to experience the program for themselves and decide if this school is the right fit for them. Applicants are broken up into sections, sister sections to those they will join as students. They hear from Dean Blount and other administrators, participate in mini-classes, meet with club leaders, and ask as many questions as possible. Some people hit it off with other prospective students and even sign housing leases together as future roommates. If you've been admitted to Kellogg, DAK is an event not to be missed. It has changed people's perspectives on the school or made them much more confident in their decision to attend.

Popular hangouts. Before it closed in 2013, The Keg was long the most popular hangout for Kellogg students and undergraduates alike, rated the ninth-best college bar in America by *Complex Magazine* in 2012. Now, you'll find most Kelloggians hanging out at World of Beer and JT's Bar & Grill, both located in downtown Evanston. In addition to weekends, Tuesdays tend to be big party nights at Kellogg because no classes are held on Wednesdays.

Similar Programs Culturally

Michigan (Ross). Kellogg and Ross are similar academically, professionally, and culturally. Visitors to Ross often come away with the same perspective as do visitors of Kellogg: that the students are remarkably friendly and the student body incredibly tight-knit despite the size of the programs. Ross's MBA program is quite a bit smaller than Kellogg's, but given its huge undergraduate population and multitude of other masters programs, it feels big.

NYU (Stern). Although NYU may have a few more competitive Wall Street types, its social and party scene resembles Kellogg's. If you're looking to live in New York rather than Chicago, but are still looking for a fun and friendly atmosphere, Stern is the place to be.

Berkeley (Haas). Haas is one of the smallest top-tier MBA programs in the country, so it's no wonder that it has a friendly, tight-knit environment. Given its small size, the admissions committee works hard to weed out applicants who would be a poor fit with their program and culture.

Although NYU may have a few more competitive Wall Street types, its social and party scene resembles Kellogg's.

Stanford GSB. Stanford's MBA program is quite a bit smaller than Kellogg's, but its student body is known for being collegial and down-to-earth. Student clubs don't factor into the culture at Stanford nearly as much as at Kellogg.

Dartmouth (Tuck). If you don't mind living in the middle of nowhere for two years, Tuck's close community is incredibly warm and welcoming. Most students live together in on-campus or nearby housing that's handed down from year to year, and students get actively involved in on-campus clubs (most notably, the ice hockey competitions).

UCLA (Anderson). Taking advantage of the school's Southern California locale, Anderson students are known to have their fair share of fun outside of the classroom. Anderson and Kellogg are often mentioned in the same breath when it comes to enjoyable MBA programs to attend.

ADMISSIONS AT KELLOGG

What Kellogg Is Looking For

Evaluation criteria. Officially, Kellogg states on its website that the admissions committee evaluates candidates on scholastic ability, personal character, motivation, leadership ability, interpersonal skills, career performance, and management potential. These are pretty standard across any MBA program, although the term motivation points to the fact that Kellogg looks for candidates who absolutely *love* the school and have specific, well-thought-out motivations for applying.

> **Kellogg goes to great lengths to tell applicants that full-time work experience is valued and expected.**

Professional experience. All MBA programs will strongly consider your full-time, post-undergraduate work experience in making admissions decisions. At Kellogg, they go to great lengths to tell applicants that full-time work experience is valued and expected. In fact, Kellogg interviews nearly every applicant to the school, no matter their qualifications (which is a herculean task, given the 5,500 applications or so it receives each year). However, any applicants with fewer than two years of full-time work experience since undergrad will be interviewed by invitation only. For a school that prides itself on interviewing every applicant, this serves as a huge signal to applicants that they should wait until they have a least two years of experience before applying. In the Class of 2015, for example, not a single student was admitted with fewer than two years of professional experience at matriculation.

Cultural fit. Early on, Kellogg decided to interview every applicant because it did not have the brand cachet of Harvard, Stanford, or Wharton to entice the top applicants, so it needed to look for "diamonds in the rough"—those candidates who would be overlooked by other MBA programs based on their written applications but who would be very attractive to corporate recruiters. As a result, the school admitted candidates who had much stronger "soft skills" such as teamwork and creative problem-solving abilities.

 If you are looking for tips on 2016–17 admissions essays, you're in luck! Check out our website at **veritasprep.com/kellogg** for our latest advice.

The world was shocked when *Businessweek* released its first ranking of MBA programs in 1988 with Kellogg in the #1 spot. Kellogg's big coup was led in large part because recruiters loved to hire Kellogg grads (a major consideration in the new ranking). The school seeks to maintain this culture of "courageous, driven and supportive" students through the admissions process today. The written elements of the application are used to find students who are successful (driven) and willing to take calculated risks (courageous), while the video essays and personal interviews assess motivations, goals, interpersonal skills, and cultural fit. Never forego an opportunity to show fit with the school in any element of your application.

Preparing to Apply

Reading this Essential Guide is a great first step in your preparation. Hopefully, this insider's glimpse has been helpful in understanding the most important aspects of the school. However, nothing can replace gaining firsthand knowledge and experience yourself.

Reach out to current students. Even if you don't have any personal connections to Kellogg, you can reach out to current students and get their insight and advice. Kellogg has a formalized Ask a Student program where you can reach out to current students for insight. Find a few clubs that fit your interest and reach out to the officers. Remember: These are very busy MBA students so you don't want to intrude too much on their time, but you could ask for a 10- to 15-minute conversation or elicit some advice via e-mail. If you're planning to visit campus, perhaps you might even arrange a coffee chat or lunch, if they are available. Officers of major clubs like the Consulting Club or Investment Banking Club are overloaded with responsibilities. You might provide a quick background introduction and ask if there's another member of their club who might be able to offer some insights and advice about his or her Kellogg experience. There's also a great student-initiated program called You@Kellogg that connects prospective applicants with students who have a similar profile.

Visit campus. If you have the means, we highly recommend you visit the Kellogg campus along with a handful of peer schools' campuses to understand the significant differences in culture, teaching style, student body, recruiting opportunities, facilities, and so forth. A campus visit does not directly impact your admissions chances in any way, but you will be surprised at just how different each school can be. We encourage you to take advantage of the formal on-campus events, including a class visit, building tour, information session, and student lunch, as available. However, we also encourage you to go to the atrium to grab a bite to eat and talk to a few current students informally. The formal program gives a good surface-level experience of Kellogg, but impromptu conversations can be incredibly enlightening about the culture at Kellogg, which is a key differentiator of the school.

Other events. We know that many applicants will not be able to fly to Evanston to visit campus, but you should take advantage of other admissions events, such as information sessions, webinars, and specific-audience events. Get to know the school and its culture as well as you can, because your familiarity can shine through your application and essays to help you stand out.

APPLICATION DEADLINES

**Deadlines: 5PM
U.S. Central Time**

**Round 1:
22 Sept 2015**

Notification:
16 Dec 2015

**Round 2:
6 Jan 2016**

Notification:
23 Mar 2016

**Round 3:
6 Apr 2016**

Notification:
11 May 2016

You Oughta Know

When should I apply? Kellogg uses a standard three-round system for applications. This means that you may submit your application in any of its three rounds for consideration. However, 90% or more of the class will be filled with the first two rounds of applicants, so we do not encourage you to wait until the final round without compelling circumstances. Round 3 candidates will be considered alongside waitlisted candidates from the first rounds. (Waitlisted candidates from Round 1 will be considered with Round 2 applicants, but we've seen a number of R1 waitlistees held on the waitlist again and admitted in Round 3.)

Traditional applicants. If you are a traditional candidate from management consulting or finance, we encourage you to apply in the first round (assuming you have a strong GMAT score), as you'll be competing against many candidates with very similar profiles. In a later round, it's possible that the school may see you as a viable candidate but may have already admitted several other applicants with similar profiles, so it might pass on you to bring greater professional diversity to the class. (Plus, the school knows you've been planning on an MBA since the day you graduated from undergrad, so there's no reason to delay!)

Applying early. Please note that Kellogg encourages you to apply at least two weeks before the deadline to increase your chances of accommodating your interview preference. You may choose an on-campus interview or an alumni interview conducted off campus in your local area (more on that below). Avoiding last-minute procrastination is valuable in any business school application, but with Kellogg there's a concrete benefit.

Don't rush! Even though the top schools encourage you to apply in the earliest round possible, this does not mean that you should apply with a rushed application or a mediocre GMAT score. There's no sense in applying early if you're just going to be denied. A GMAT score that's above the school's average will do more for your candidacy than applying in the first round.

Navigating deadlines. After moving its Round 1 deadline way up last year, Kellogg has only made a minor adjustment this year. If you plan on applying to Kellogg in Round 1, you should get started no later than early August. Why? Because very few applicants are successful when they're writing their essays, managing their recommendation writers, and tracking down transcripts all while also trying to break 700 on the GMAT. And pulling together your applications (and doing it well) will take you at least a few weeks from start to finish.

Note that applying in Round 1 means that you will get your decision by mid-December, which should give you enough time to submit your Round 2 applications for other programs, if you don't get good news from Kellogg. However, we don't recommend that you wait to start other Round 2 applications; rather, prepare all necessary materials beforehand and submit them if you receive bad news in Round 1. The school's Round 2 and Round 3 deadlines are virtually unchanged since last year.

Specialty programs. Applications to the MMM and JD-MBA programs require an additional essay that's pretty straightforward, but don't take it lightly. You have 250 words to explain why the program is right for you, and the joint-degree admissions committees look at these essays closely. For JD-MBAs, if the committee gets the sense that you're only doing it because it adds no more time to a standard three-year law degree, so "why not?" then you have a high likelihood of being denied. The MMM program has far less flexibility when it comes to electives and scheduling than the standard MBA program, not to mention an extra quarter of coursework, so admissions officers want to see a compelling reason for the choice beyond mere curiosity or interest in the subject matter.

1Y vs. 2Y. Candidates applying to Kellogg's two-year program with a business major and significant work experience on their resume who are not changing careers may want to explain why they want to attend the two-year track instead of taking advantage of the growing one-year option. If you're going to business school in order to switch careers, then the opportunity to dip your toe in the water of your new career through a summer internship is reason enough for the two-year program. If you're looking to return to your previous employer or a similar one in your industry, then the one-year program may be the ideal fit.

The Online Application Form

Kellogg's online application form is one of the more intuitive and straightforward that we've seen, but we'll offer a few tips to reduce anxiety in certain sections.

Picking a round. When you create your application, you'll be asked to select a round immediately. If you're unsure, simply select the earliest round you plan to apply. You will have the opportunity to change each time you log in.

Program of interest. Do some research before randomly picking areas of academic interest. Don't worry: You won't be held to these choices when you start school, but if you have some unique interests that fit your background and goals, such as Health Enterprise Management, Media Management, or Real Estate, be sure to mark those majors. The school needs to admit enough applicants to justify the existence of those more niche programs. However, don't just spontaneously dream up an interest in a niche major to try to increase your chances. If it doesn't fit with the rest of your application (such as resume, career goals, etc.), then it will be looked upon extremely dubiously.

Re-applicants are often concerned that they will be viewed skeptically, having failed in their first attempt. To the contrary, we've found that re-applicants are often admitted at higher rates than first-time applicants, although they must show an improvement in one or more areas of their application.

We have not found that having a family member as an alum of the school increases an applicant's chances of admission—unless of course that family member happens to be a multimillion-dollar donor to the school or something.

Personal. There is no advantage nor disadvantage to applying with a spouse or partner. Each applicant is reviewed separately based on his or her own merits. However, if one partner is admitted and the other waitlisted, there may be a slightly higher chance of the waitlisted candidate ultimately receiving an admit because it increases the chances that both partners will attend. Therefore, always include your partner in this section if he or she will be applying this year.

Interview. In our years of experience in MBA admissions, we haven't seen a distinct advantage to selecting an on-campus or off-campus interview in admission rates. Note that Chicago-area residents must select an off-campus interview so that on-campus spots are reserved for applicants who wish to travel to the school and conduct their interview during the same trip.

Employer. Note that when you add an employer, you have a few lines of basic information and a brief section for job duties. Plus, you have just 250 characters to describe your most significant professional accomplishment. Sheesh—a little more than a tweet to say what is most significant to you?! This is a signal that your resume should focus on quantifiable results and achievements so that information about job duties, and so on, is not duplicated in various parts of your application. Ensure that every element of your application is adding additional, valuable information for the admissions officer.

Years of full-time work experience. Most applicants will include only post-undergraduate work experience when calculating this number. However, if applicants took time off from undergrad to work in a professional, full-time job, they may use their best judgment whether to include that time. Remember that this includes work experience at matriculation (when you will start school), not your years of experience at the time of application.

Career goals. Many applicants have heard that they need to differentiate themselves from other applicants, so they feel the need to dream up "unique" career goals to stand out, even if they have no real intention of pursuing those goals. This is a terrible strategy. Kellogg sends about a third of its class into management consulting each year, so stating this "vanilla" goal for your desired position after Kellogg is perfectly acceptable!

> **Many applicants have heard that they need to differentiate themselves from other applicants, so they feel the need to dream up "unique" career goals to stand out, even if they have no real intention of pursuing those goals. This is a terrible strategy.**

The Kellogg application no longer includes an essay about your career goals, so use this section wisely to present a clear plan to connect your previous work experience, realistic post-MBA goals, and your broader, long-term vision for yourself. Kellogg is looking for brave leaders who inspire change, so don't be afraid to dream big in this section. Perhaps the most important question in this section is the last one, which asks about your motivations behind these goals. It's just 250 characters, but utilize them! Tell the admissions committee what would inspire you to give up your income for two years, spend as much as $200,000 on tuition and living expenses, and possibly make a major career change. Depending on your forgone income, this may be a half-million-dollar question or more!

Financing your degree/sponsorship. Financial aid has no bearing on your application, so fill this section out to the best of your knowledge.

Education. The admissions committee looks beyond your GPA alone. They consider the competitiveness of the undergraduate university, your major, difficulty of classes, and overall trends. For example, many students perform poorly in their first year or two as they adjust to life away from home but become outstanding students later in their undergraduate career. Kellogg makes it clear that it also weighs considerations such as whether you were a first-generation college student or needed to work to put yourself through school.

Awards, certifications, and recognition. By allowing applicants to list up to six awards, which is double the number of some other schools, Kellogg shows that it likes applicants with breadth. Feel free to include recognition outside your professional life, including those from undergrad or from current extracurricular pursuits, to show your impact on organizations. Of course, professional certifications and awards are appropriate here as well.

Extracurricular activities. As we've mentioned throughout this Guide, Kellogg looks for applicants who are going to get actively involved. Kellogg allows you to list up to six extracurricular activities, plus six experiences abroad! However, don't feel badly if you have deep involvement in just one or two activities for a period of several years rather than limited involvement in six activities or more. Both depth and breadth of involvement are considered.

Kellogg clubs/interests. Don't be shy in this section; list as many clubs as interest you. It's not uncommon for Kellogg students to be actively involve in seven or eight clubs or more! At some schools, marking this many clubs may be seen as a lack of focus, but not at Kellogg.

Test scores. Kellogg has put greater emphasis on GMAT and GRE scores in the past couple of years. Only 10% of the class had a score of 690 or below. If you scored below 700 and believe you have potential to raise your score, we highly recommend doing so. Note that you must report only your highest test score on the application. This is the score that's used for consideration. Only when the committee has decided to put you on the admit pile will they cross-check your self-reported score with the official GMAC database, which shows all scores from the past five years. Therefore, there's no downside to taking the GMAT multiple times until you get the score you want.

Honor code. Kellogg conducts background checks on admitted applicants each year, so if you have been convicted of a crime or received other disciplinary actions listed in this section, be sure to report it. You may use the optional essay to explain circumstances. At Veritas Prep, we've consulted with many applicants who were convicted of crimes or suspended from school who were admitted to their target schools. This does not need to be a deal-breaker if it is handled appropriately.

The Essays

Essay 1: Leadership and teamwork are integral parts of the Kellogg experience. Describe a recent and meaningful time you were a leader. What challenges did you face, and what did you learn? (450 words)

Emphasize teamwork. This question is new this year, although it's really quite similar to the second essay on last year's Kellogg application, which started with "Leadership requires an ability to collaborate with and motivate others." Note the emphasis on leadership and teamwork here. Both are key traits that the Kellogg admissions team looks for in all applicants. And, even though the second sentence above only mentions leadership, you'd better believe that the admissions committee also wants to see evidence of collaboration and cooperation—in other words, teamwork! Kellogg isn't looking for sharp-elbowed people who lead by ordering others around. Rather, the school wants to find applicants who inspire people to work harder and achieve great things through teamwork and empowerment.

Use the SAR method to tell stories. This essay is a classic candidate for the SAR (Situation–Action–Result) outline that we recommend our clients use. The situation will likely be an opportunity or challenge where you needed to rely on someone in order to get something done.

> Kellogg conducts background checks on admitted applicants each year, so if you have been convicted of a crime or received other disciplinary actions listed in this section, be sure to report it. You may use the optional essay to explain circumstances.

The action will be how you managed to influence them in order to see things your way and to convince them to take up your cause. Perhaps it was an employee or teammate who wasn't motivated, or didn't agree with what you wanted to do. How did you win them over? Finally, the result will be the outcome—not just of that particular situation, but also the positive impact that it had on you as a young leader. Pay particular attention to the last few words of this essay prompt; what you learned may be what admissions committee pays attention to the most.

Essay 2: Pursuing an MBA is a catalyst for personal and professional growth. How have you grown in the past? How do you intend to grow at Kellogg? (450 words)

Show growth. This question is also new this year. However, over the years Kellogg has asked similar questions that have all addressed the ideas of personal growth and change. Assuming you have a good leadership growth story covered in Essay #1, then look for stories that will complement that nicely. How have you matured as a young adult? What was a weakness that you've worked on and have overcome? What strong qualities in others have you been able to emulate? Ask yourself these questions as you consider what makes for an effective topic here.

Show personal introspection. Your story absolutely can come from your personal life—indeed, those often make for the most moving stories in essays like this one—but the more recent, the better. You're still young and you are still evolving, so a story from 15 years ago will likely be less compelling for admissions officers than one that happened in the past few years. (Of course, there are always exceptions to every rule!)

Highlight what you want to do at Kellogg. The second part of the question may require you to drastically shift gears halfway through this essay. Your reasons for wanting to attend Kellogg may have very little to do with the compelling growth story you identified for the first part of this prompt, which is why we don't necessarily love this new question from Kellogg. Sticking these two questions together may leave many applicants tempted to invent a theme in which they dramatically shape the story in the first half to fit what comes in the second half. We actually think a more effective approach is to present a true, impactful story of personal growth in the first part, and then hit the "What do you want to do at Kellogg?" question (which is really a "Why an MBA? Why Kellogg?" question at its core) head-on. Some writers will tie the two together better than others, but remember that this isn't an essay-writing contest.

Don't try too hard to impress. It's far more important for you to help the admissions committee get to know you (and want to admit you!) than to come up with an artful essay theme that doesn't reflect the true you or make a convincing case that Kellogg is right for you.

Additional Information: If needed, use this section to briefly describe any extenuating circumstances (e.g. unexplained gaps in work experience, choice of recommenders, inconsistent or questionable academic performance, etc.) (no word count)

Yes, it's really optional. As we always tell applicants with these optional essays: Only answer this essay prompt if you need to explain a low undergraduate GPA or other potential blemish in your background. No need to harp on a minor weakness and sound like you're making excuses when you don't need any. If you don't have anything else you need to tell the admissions office, it is entirely okay to skip this essay. Don't let yourself get too tempted by that lack of a word limit; less is more!

Choice of recommenders. As we discuss in the next section, Kellogg prefers to have a recommendation from your current supervisor or manager. If you do not include a recommendation from this person, they ask that you briefly explain it here. Many applicants have not yet told their current supervisor there is a chance they will be leaving the company to go to business school. This can be explained with a line as simple as "I have not yet informed my current supervisor that I may leave the company to pursue a business education, as this may affect my project assignments and upcoming bonuses. Therefore, I have selected a professional mentor of three years, John Doe, who serves in a senior-management capacity at our company and can speak to my professional potential from firsthand experience."

The Video Essay

Kellogg introduced a video essay to its application in 2013 and has kept it ever since. There were numerous technical issues last year that required the school to waive the requirement for many applicants, and we hope they've worked out the kinks this year.

How does it work? Once you submit your written application, you'll receive an e-mail with instructions and a link for the video essay. You'll need a computer with a webcam and microphone. You may prepare with the 10 provided practice questions. The format and questions are meant to mimic the actual questions you will be asked. However, once you start the official questions, you'll have just 20 seconds to gather your thoughts for each question and up to one minute to respond.

What are they looking for? Kellogg isn't holding tryouts for the next YouTube sensation, so you don't have to be an expert webcam performer. They are trying to get to know you a little bit better to assess your fit with the culture of the school. They're looking for candidates who are eager and enthusiastic about getting involved, and who are genuinely passionate about Kellogg. For non-native English speakers, they also assess your language abilities to ensure that you'll be able to handle the rigor of a top-tier graduate-level program taught exclusively in English.

What will I be asked? The questions aren't intended to be difficult. One question will ask about why you are interested in Kellogg. With just one minute, you may want to pick one or two aspects of the school and offer some specific examples of what excites you about those things. The second question may be a bit off the wall just to get a sense of your personality, such as "Tell us about your first childhood job" or "If you could have lunch with anyone alive or dead, who would it be and why?" You may not think of a brilliant answer to these questions, and you might even stumble a little bit. That's actually fine. Simply do your best and let them see a glimmer of your personality.

What are some tips for success? We recommend that in addition to the 10 practice questions offered by Kellogg, you practice recording yourself with your webcam in the place where you're going to record the real thing. Are there distracting things in the background? Can they hear you? Do you use lots of filler words (um, er, ya know, etc.)? Again, Kellogg doesn't expect this to be a professional production, but reducing distractions will be helpful. Practice answering questions similar to those we've described. You want to be natural and conversational in the actual recording, so we don't recommend memorizing your answers, or you may come off as stilted. Dress in business attire, as you would in your admissions interview. Lastly, relax! This is meant to be a fun conversation between you and the admissions committee member.

Recommendations

Each applicant must submit two professional recommendations with his or her application. The school generally discourages academic recommendations from college professors unless you've had significant professional experience working with the professor.

First, your recommenders will be asked to fill out basic contact information (pre-populated with information that you provide). Then they will be asked the following questions:

- **Context of Relationship** *[Current Employer, Previous Employer, University/Academic, Extracurricular/Community, Other]*

- **I am the applicant's current supervisor.** *[check box]*

- **Highest Degree Earned** *[Bachelor's, Master's, Doctoral, Other]*

- **Degree Granting Institution**

- **Are you a Kellogg Alumnus?** *[Yes, No]*

- **Year Graduated from Kellogg** *[dropdown of years]*

- **Have known candidate since** *[dropdown of years]*

- **Please comment briefly on the context of your interaction with the applicant and his/her role in your organization.** *[250 characters]*

- **What has been the candidate's most significant contribution to your organization? Provide measurable impact if applicable.** *[250 characters]*

Leadership assessment. *[This is a multiple-choice assessment based on the following skills/qualities: Results Orientation, Strategic Orientation, Team Leadership, Influence and Collaboration, Communicating, Information Seeking, Developing Others, Change Leadership, Respect for Others, and Trustworthiness.]* Each skill/quality has a different description for its 1–5 rating scale. For example, the scale for Results Orientation is as follows: 1) Fulfills assigned tasks, 2) Overcomes obstacles to achieve goals, 3) Exceeds goals and raises effectiveness of organization, 4) Introduces incremental improvements to enhance business performance using robust analysis, 5) Invents and delivers best in class standards and performance.

Note from Veritas Prep: It would be highly unlikely for a genuine recommendation to include a perfect 5 rating on all skills or qualities. In fact, if your recommender simply marks 5s down the page, then the recommendation may be viewed skeptically, as it provides little information about your true strengths and weaknesses.

- **Based on your professional experience, how do you rate this candidate compared to her/his peer group?** *[The best I've encountered in my career, Outstanding (Top 5%), Excellent (Top 10%), Very good (well above average), Average, Below Average]*

- **If needed, please explain any rankings above.** *[250 characters]*

- **Overall, do you recommend this candidate for Kellogg?** *[Do not recommend the candidate, Recommend the candidate with reservations, Recommend the candidate]*

- **Are you willing to speak with an admissions officer about this candidate?** *[Yes, No]*

- Should the candidate accept an offer of admission, I understand I may be contacted by Re Vera Services as part of the application verification process, via phone and/or email, to verify authenticity of this letter of recommendation. *[Box for signature]*

Your recommenders will also be asked to upload a document answering two additional questions:

> ***1. How do the candidate's performance compare to those of other well-qualified individuals in similar roles? Please provide specific examples. (300 words)***
>
> ***2. Please describe the most important piece of constructive feedback you have given the applicant. Please detail the circumstances and the applicant's response. (250 words)***

If your recommenders don't have time to fill out the entire form in one sitting, they may save changes for later and return to their form.

Selecting your recommenders. Kellogg suggests that one of your recommendations come from your current supervisor and the other from "someone who can evaluate your professional performance and your managerial/leadership potential (e.g., former supervisor, previous employer, client)." Even though they will be asked their job title and Kellogg alumni status, don't reach out to distant contacts who happen to have impressive job titles or are alumni of the school. It is far more important to find recommenders who know you well and can answer the essay questions with depth and detail.

Should I draft it myself? Many applicants to business school are asked by their superiors to draft the recommendation themselves and the recommender will tweak and approve it. We strongly recommend that you do not write the recommendation yourself for several reasons. First, your writing style and choice of phrasing are unique, and admissions officers will notice if the recommendations are similar to each other and your essays. Second, you will tend to be too humble or generic. Your supervisor might use language such as "one of the top analysts I've seen in my entire career" that you would never dare include if writing it on his or her behalf. Third, and perhaps most importantly, the admissions officer is looking for a third-party perspective on your candidacy, so writing a recommendation yourself is an unethical breach of trust with the school you are looking to join. We have a three-part series on the Veritas Prep blog about how to get recommenders to write enthusiastic letters.

Preparing your recommenders. Instead of writing the recommendation yourself, you should sit down and have candid conversations with your recommenders about the reasons you want to go to business school and why you've selected your target schools, your professional goals, and your experience to date. Ask them if they would have the time to write a strong recommendation on your behalf. (This also gives them a nice "out" by telling you that they are too busy rather than saying they don't feel comfortable giving you a positive recommendation.) Bring a copy of your resume and a bulleted list of projects that you've worked on together and accomplishments they have seen you achieve. Let them know that the admissions committees prefer to see specific, detailed examples in recommendations. Then, let them know that you'll serve as a "project manager" to follow up and ensure that they are able to submit your recommendation ahead of the deadline.

The Interview

On-campus interviews are typically 30–45 minutes in length, and are conducted from September to April.

Where should I interview? Kellogg takes a unique approach to its interview process in that it requires all applicants request an interview date as part of their application package. Interviews may be requested on or off campus. If you're located outside the Chicago area, it is recommended that you request an on-campus interview, as that is the best way to see the campus and experience firsthand what Kellogg is like. However, choosing an on-campus interview will not impact your admission decision. Chicago residents must request an off-campus interview, as the on-campus spots are limited and reserved for applicants who are not local.

If you request an on-campus interview with your application, you will need to contact the admissions office at (847) 491–3308 to schedule your interview time. On-campus interviews are typically 30–45 minutes in length, and are conducted from September to April. Because on-campus interview slots are limited, the school recommends you submit your application at least two weeks before the deadline to improve your chances of obtaining your choice.

If you plan to interview off campus, you will be contacted within eight weeks of submitting your application. You will be provided with your interviewer's contact information, and you are expected to arrange the interview within 21 days of the assignment. Note that you should e-mail a copy of your current resume to your interviewer in advance of an off-campus interview.

Who conducts the interviews? Admissions officers or current students typically conduct on-campus interviews, while off-campus interviews may be conducted by an alumnus. In either case, the interview is "blind," with your interviewer only having access your resume and not a copy of your application.

It is recommended that you bring a copy of your resume to the interview. While interviews are not technically required for admission and they may sometimes be waived, these instances are very uncommon and candidates whose interviews are waived may at times be given the option to have a phone interview.

Because of the unique process for Kellogg interviews, we recommend reading the admissions website ahead of submitting your application.

What is the interviewer looking for? The interview is simply one more opportunity for the Kellogg admissions committee to get to know you. The interviewer, whether a staffer, student, or alumni member of the admissions organization, will evaluate you based on the same criteria listed on the school's website: scholastic/intellectual ability, personal character, motivations and goals, leadership ability and potential, interpersonal skills, career performance and focus, management potential, and impact on student life.

In all honesty, reports submitted by Kellogg interviewers to the admissions committee tend to be all over the map, especially those from alumni interviews. Some can be extremely valuable while others are not. We at Veritas Prep believe the school introduced the video essays to offer some consistency in evaluating communication skills to supplement interview reports.

What will I be asked? There is no predetermined script for an on-campus or off-campus interview. Since the interviewer will not have access to your application, you will not be asked directly about your answers to essay questions or other information you provided. However, be prepared to walk through your resume in about one to two minutes, offering insights into how you chose your major and decided to work for a particular company, and any career transitions you've made. Talk about the things that you enjoyed most in each role. The interviewer will have read your resume already, so focus less on facts and more on how your personal motivations led you to make decisions that brought you to this point.

You'll want to prepare some additional stories that you can tell from your undergraduate, professional, and extracurricular experiences so that your interview provides additional information beyond that of your application. Practice telling several two- to three-minute stories that can be used as answers to questions about your greatest professional accomplishments, impact on organizations, decision-making processes, use of creativity to solve problems, involvement in organizations outside of work, and successful instances of teamwork, leadership opportunities, and so forth. Some stories may serve to answer any number of these questions. If you have held numerous positions at different companies, try to vary the stories you use to highlight various parts of your resume.

CHICAGO BOOTH

This inventor of the Executive MBA asks all its students to be imaginative.

CHICAGO, IL

CLASS SIZE
538

PROGRAM FOUNDED
1898

NOBEL LAUREATES
6

CHARACTERISTICS
CREATIVE, FLEXIBLE, INTERNATIONAL

CHICAGO (BOOTH)

SECTIONS

CHICAGO BOOTH SNAPSHOT

What Chicago Booth Is Known For

"Why Are You Here And Not Someplace Else?" asks the prominent neon installation on the Chicago Booth campus. Also the title of a series of essays written by Booth professor Harry L. Davis, the question reminds Booth students of the freedom they have to create their own experience.

Nestled close to the shore of Lake Michigan, on the south side of Chicago, Hyde Park is home to the University of Chicago Booth School of Business. Chicago Booth is the second-oldest business school in the United States and was the first to offer an Executive MBA program. Booth has a permanent presence on three continents (including campuses in London and Singapore, as well as access to the University of Chicago's facility just opened in Beijing), creating a global focus and attracting an internationally diverse applicant pool. It was the first business school to have a Nobel Laureate on its faculty, and since 1997 has had six Nobel Prize winners on board.

Booth has a permanent presence on three continents (including campuses in London and Singapore, as well as access to the University of Chicago's facility just opened in Beijing), creating a global focus and attracting an internationally diverse applicant pool.

The Chicago Booth approach to an MBA education consists of rigorous analysis and a focus on demanding facts, questioning assumptions, and assessing problems from all angles. At Chicago Booth, you will learn the tools to examine every idea, evaluate problems and opportunities, and handle uncertainty. Dissent is not frowned upon at Chicago Booth; in fact, it is expected. However, the campus environment is overwhelmingly collegial; you'll often hear the phrase *Ideas compete, not people.*

A focus on research. Research at Chicago Booth grows from the intellectual culture at the University of Chicago. Unlike most universities, Chicago is actually home to more graduate students than undergrads, and those graduate students work with faculty to drive interesting research projects across the university. Chicago Booth encourages its business school faculty to pursue any issue that interests them across a range of disciplines. Such research is regularly featured in the pages of more than 200 economic and business journals.

A focus on ideas. Chicago Booth is known globally for ideas that shape business practice and influence public policy. Focusing on ever-changing theories and principles, Chicago Booth encourages students to question all assumptions. This approach combines the very best in conceptual knowledge and academic theory with practical, real-world application. At Chicago Booth, students are encouraged to continually test ideas and seek proof that leads to new and innovative solutions.

A focus on data. The quant-heavy finance curriculum is certainly well known at Chicago Booth, yet there are actually not enough superlatives to describe the extreme focus at this school on using data in the discipline of marketing. Chicago Booth's relationship with A.C. Nielsen means that researchers have access to a treasure trove of consumer data, and data is the basic tool for decision making deployed across disciplines at the school.

A focus on action. The first school with a formal leadership training program? Chicago Booth. The first school with an experiential component to the classroom? Chicago Booth. A school that led the way 30 years ago with management labs? Chicago Booth. This is a school that works to bring the fruits of its extensive research out into the world and into the hands of its students in a tangible, practical way. At Chicago Booth, you will be busy *doing* your MBA; you won't just be *studying* it.

What Makes Chicago Booth Different

Flexibility. With only one required class, Chicago Booth most definitely takes a different approach to the process of getting an MBA. It does foster training in the "language of business," as Boothies call it—the fundamentals of economics, statistics, and finance—however, the unique setup of the program means that students determine how they will meet the requirements of the degree. Chicago Booth is not a prescriptive environment, and the emphasis on, and appreciation for, ideas make it a place for mavericks and renegades as well as more traditional types.

A quant focus (and not just on finance). Chicago Booth possesses a strong reputation for its rigor, focus on analytics in all fields, and expertise in finance and economics—and marketing. The finance and economics faculty members at Chicago Booth are outstanding, led by professors such as Eugene F. Fama, whom many call "the father of modern finance." Chicago Booth is both deserving and proud of its "quant" reputation, but that tends to overshadow strengths in other areas Booth has been actively improving over the last decade. Not surprisingly, when a Booth admissions representative is asked, "What's the one thing that applicants should know about Chicago Booth?" the answer often mentions Chicago Booth's strengths in academic areas outside of pure finance—particularly entrepreneurship and marketing.

A part-time program that's bigger than the full-time program. Chicago Booth is a big school, with about 3,500 active graduate students enrolled at any one time. The bulk of these students come from the two part-time study options (one evening program and one weekend program), totaling about 1,400 students between them. Another 1,100 students make up the full-time program, with about 550 students per graduating class. The balance of Chicago Booth's students are in the EMBA and PhD programs, and are found around the world at Chicago Booth's other campuses. Full-time and part-time Chicago Booth students often interact and sometimes even take courses together.

A downtown space. In April 2014, Chicago Booth unveiled "Booth 455": a 16,000-square-foot space on the ground level of the famed NBC Tower, across the street from its current Gleacher Center. Although the space is intended primarily for the weekend and evening MBA programs, all MBA students are able to access the study rooms. The new space is especially welcome since most full-time students live in downtown Chicago and not near the Hyde Park campus.

Chicago Booth Is a Good Fit for You If…

You're a quant. The wealth of expertise at Chicago Booth puts it among the top three choices of most candidates interested in finance; the school's data-driven approach extends across the curriculum into areas like marketing and entrepreneurship.

You fall on either side of the work experience distribution. Chicago Booth has been known to be somewhat more open to younger applicants, though not generally those coming straight from university. The Chicago Booth admissions office states that usually one and a half or two years in the workforce is recommended before you'll be ready for the MBA experience. (The only exception to this policy is the Chicago Booth Scholars Program, in which undergraduates from the College at the University of Chicago may apply in their senior year. Much like the 2+2 program at HBS, Booth Scholars are granted a two- to three-year deferment before starting the MBA program.) On the other hand, Chicago Booth also tends to be open to "more experienced" (i.e., older) applicants; it's not unheard of for a class to have a number of students with more than six years of experience.

> Chicago Booth is not a prescriptive environment, and the emphasis on, and appreciation for, ideas make it a place for mavericks and renegades as well as more traditional types.

CHICAGO (BOOTH)

You want to stay in the Midwest. The majority of top American MBA programs are on the coasts. Chicago Booth is one of two top-10 schools in the middle of the country (along with its cross-town rival, Kellogg). If you don't mind the cold—and the wind—Chicago is a dynamic city with plenty of urban attractions and diversions to occupy you when you're not in class. (And in all honesty, the weather really isn't worse than most major cities in the Northeast.) Most recruiters who come to Chicago Booth also go to the other top schools on the coasts, but if you plan to stay in the Midwest after business school, then Chicago Booth is an obvious choice. In fact, more than one third of the Class of 2014 stayed in the Midwest.

> Most recruiters who come to Chicago Booth also go to the other top schools on the coasts, but if you plan to stay in the Midwest after business school, then Chicago Booth is an obvious choice.

You know what you want to do, and you're a self-starter ready to design your own education. The amount of flexibility in the Chicago Booth curriculum is truly unprecedented, which is great for someone who is ready to hit the ground running. However, this can be a bit of a double-edged sword for those students with a less-clear direction on their future goals. It is unfortunately possible to experiment your way all the way through Chicago Booth and end up without the strongest career options when you graduate, due simply to a lack of focus. And if you anticipate needing a lot of hand-holding during business school, Chicago Booth might not be the best choice for you.

You're a career changer. The freedom of curriculum design at Chicago Booth means that career changers can target their first-year experience to gain not just the standard MBA skills of economics, statistics, and finance, but also begin to develop the specialized training they will need for their post-MBA career—before their internship. At Chicago Booth, a well-planned first-year program can potentially result in a more meaningful summer internship experience and dramatically accelerate your progress in your new field, making you more attractive when you compete against candidates from other programs.

You appreciate fewer students in the classroom. Although its graduating class is at the upper end of the range of business school programs, at more than 550 full-time students, the actual class size at Chicago Booth tends to be a little smaller than at other schools, particularly in the core classes. This is because of that flexible curriculum again: Instead of being assigned to a cluster that might be up to 90 students (the extreme end, at HBS) and at least 65 (the average at Kellogg, Columbia, and Wharton), Chicago Booth first-years choose how to satisfy their core requirements from a variety of options. The incoming class naturally scatters out to pursue the core subjects at their appropriate level of difficulty, resulting in fewer than 60 students per class. Electives at Chicago Booth generally have fewer than 50 students. You might still get "lost in the crowd" given how large Chicago Booth is overall, but the classroom experience might be marginally less intimidating with fewer people in the room.

> Electives at Chicago Booth generally have fewer than 50 students.

ACADEMICS AT CHICAGO BOOTH

What Chicago Booth Is Known For

Flexible curriculum. The hallmark of the Chicago Booth experience is its flexible curriculum. Chicago Booth affords students a wide degree of choice. The entire program requires only one class, and that class is *LEAD*, for *Leadership Effectiveness and Development*. Booth still trains graduates in the "language of business"; finance, statistics, and accounting are the tools of the trade. However, students have significant control over the level of difficulty they tackle and even the slant or orientation of approach from which they study these topics based on a menu of courses that are designed to let them choose how to prepare for their future careers.

Finance. A guide about Chicago Booth would never get very far without talking about finance. The emphasis on finance and economics at Chicago Booth is world-renowned. The school claims that modern finance was born there in the 1960s, when Merrill Lynch asked for computing help in a project to analyze 50 years of historical stock prices. This project became what is now the Center for Research in Security Prices, a source of not only data to academic and commercial institutions around the world, but also revenue for Chicago Booth. It has not just one, but two concentrations related to finance: Finance and Analytic Finance—plus two more involving economics: Economics, and Econometrics and Statistics.

> **The emphasis on finance and economics at Chicago Booth is world-renowned.**

The Chicago School. What, Chicago Booth is known for a totally different school? Not exactly. The "Chicago School of Economics" isn't a bricks-and-mortar school; rather, it's a school of thought, subscribing to the free markets theories popularized by Milton Friedman, who was a prime influence on Ronald Reagan's economic policy in the 1980s. Or, as the actual Economics Department explains it, "The unifying thread in all this is not political or ideological but methodological, the methodological conviction that economics is an incomparably powerful tool for understanding society."

You Oughta Know

Class organization. First-year students are broken up into "cohorts" as part of the school's Leadership Effectiveness and Development (LEAD) program that all full-time students are required to complete. Without a more structured program like those found at some other top-tier MBA programs, where students attend most or all of their classes with their cohort, first-years have less opportunity to really bond with their cohort at Booth. Instead, relationships are more commonly formed across the entire student body at Chicago Booth rather than just with a slice of their class.

LEAD. The aim of LEAD is to give students exposure to leadership and team-building concepts, and to help them build relationships, learn to motivate, and affect decisions in the workplace. Incoming students are split up into cohort groups of about 50 students and spend 150 hours over the course of their first year at Chicago Booth engaging in various exercises and retreats. LEAD is the first experience of a new student at Chicago Booth, with many of the initial activities being somewhat similar to what students at other schools go through during their own orientation process. The LEAD program begins in early September of the first year; second-years don't start class until three weeks later.

CHICAGO (BOOTH)

BOOTH AT A GLANCE

APPLICANTS BY SCHOOL

Booth	Stanford	Harvard	Wharton	Columbia	Stern
4,175	7,355	9,543	6,111	5,799	3,890
24%	7.1%	11%	20.7%	18.2%	16%

◄ Percent admitted

AVERAGE GMAT SCORES

724

Booth Stern Columbia Wharton

AVERAGE GPA

3.54

Booth Stern Columbia Wharton

AVERAGE YEARS OF WORK EXPERIENCE

4.6 **Booth** 4.3 Stern 5 Wharton

WOMEN

Booth's percentage of women is right in the middle of pack among the top schools. However, with 26% of the class coming to the program from the finance industry, a traditionally male-dominated field, Booth has likely had to work particularly hard to recruit female candidates.

Booth

36%

Wharton

40%

Columbia

36%

Stern

36%

UNDERGRAD MAJORS

Compared to some other top-tier programs, Booth brings in a large percentage of the class from traditional business and economics backgrounds.

- ■ **Business**
- ☐ **Economics**
- ■ **Humanities/Social Science**
- ☐ **STEM**
- ☐ **Other**

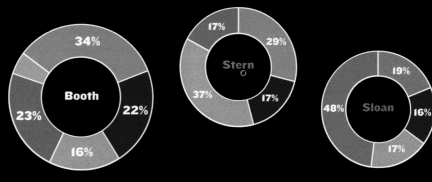

Booth: 34%, 22%, 16%, 23%

Stern: 17%, 29%, 17%, 37%

Sloan: 19%, 16%, 17%, 48%

FROM CONSULTING/FINANCE SECTOR PRE-MBA

More than a quarter of the entering class came from finance and an additional 20% from consulting; the overall class is more diverse than you might think, with consumer products, energy, technology, and government/military all strongly represented.

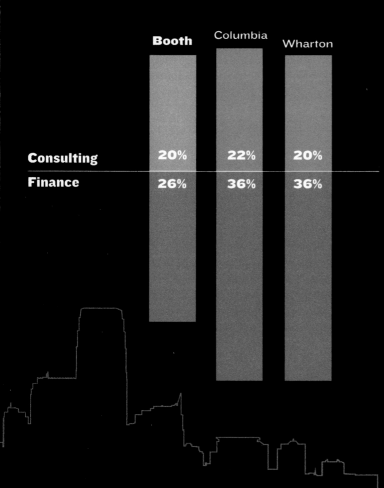

	Booth	Columbia	Wharton
Consulting	20%	22%	20%
Finance	26%	36%	36%

CLASS SIZE

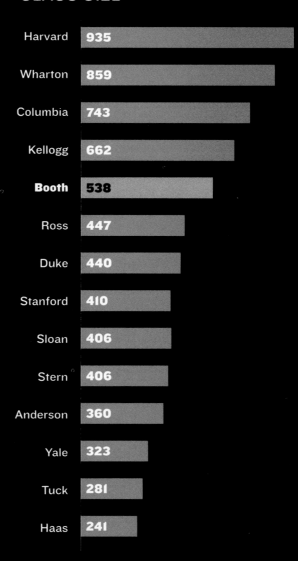

School	Size
Harvard	935
Wharton	859
Columbia	743
Kellogg	662
Booth	**538**
Ross	447
Duke	440
Stanford	410
Sloan	406
Stern	406
Anderson	360
Yale	323
Tuck	281
Haas	241

Concentrations at Booth:

- Accounting
- Analytic Finance
- Analytic Management
- Econometrics and Statistics
- Economics
- Entrepreneurship
- Finance
- General Management
- International Business
- Managerial and Organizational Behavior
- Marketing Management
- Operations Management
- Strategic Management

Lab courses. Chicago Booth offers a series of labs designed to provide students with hands-on business experience, including Management Labs, New Venture/Small Enterprise Labs, and Private Equity/Venture Capital Lab. Lab courses allow students to work as consultants to leaders of sponsor businesses on real-world projects.

Business plan competitions. Like many other prominent business schools, Chicago Booth offers a variety of business plan competitions as a part of the Chicago Booth experience. Some of the most notable competitions are the the Edward L. Kaplan New Venture Challenge (NVC), Glencoe Capital Venture Capital Investment Competition, and Case Writing Competition.

International Business Exchange Program (IBEP). Some Chicago Booth students participate in the IBEP program, which includes 33 schools in 20 countries, such as the London School of Economics and Political Science, and the Stockholm School of Economics.

International MBA. An option available to all Chicago Booth students is the International MBA, or IMBA, which students may declare soon after matriculating. The IMBA is exactly the same credential as the MBA except with a bit of a marketing spin. Essentially, the IMBA is a slightly upgraded version of Chicago Booth's International Business concentration: In addition to a set of classes in international business that the base concentration mandates, the IMBA also requires a semester abroad, plus tested proficiency in another language. IMBA students should begin with a strong foundation in their target language; it is not a language-acquisition program. The IMBA could be seen as a response to Wharton's Lauder dual MA/MBA degree, though the IMBA is not nearly as rigorous, nor is it as competitive.

Concentrations. Chicago Booth offers 13 concentrations. While concentrations are optional, students can claim up to three on their transcripts (although they can accumulate as many as their available credits will allow). Courses can count toward more than one concentration, and most students qualify for at least one concentration even if they were not intentionally working toward one. We consider two of the most popular concentrations in the following paragraphs.

Entrepreneurship. Entrepreneurship is the second-largest concentration at Chicago Booth, with 49% of students qualifying for this concentration upon graduation. The school offers courses taught by renowned faculty such as Steven Kaplan, James Schrager, and Ellen Rudnick, who rank among the top educators in the world. These professors conduct groundbreaking research, collaborate with the entrepreneurial and private equity communities, and bring their own entrepreneurial experiences into the classroom. The Polsky Center for Entrepreneurship at Chicago Booth provides current students, as well as alumni, with industry-specific resources to start companies or support interest in private equity. Booth has also attracted a number of entrepreneurs to teach courses, including Groupon co-founders Brad Keywell and Eric Lefkofsky.

Marketing. Someone interested in a career in marketing may come up against two untrue stereotypes: that marketing is "fluffy" and not quantitative, and that "the other school" in Chicago is the only place to go to study it. Both assumptions would be incorrect. Chicago Booth does not get the recognition it deserves in this field—and boy, does it take marketing seriously. The school's focus on quant-based research is enabled by a longstanding partnership with consumer data provider A.C. Nielsen, and the Chicago Booth marketing department is a storehouse for more marketing datasets than any university in the world. The Kilts Center for Marketing brings researchers from top business schools and universities around the world for its annual Quantitative Marketing and Economics Conference and provides financial incentives to students serious about careers in marketing through subsidies and scholarships.

Nuts & Bolts

Teaching approach. Chicago Booth takes a varied approach to learning. Lectures, case studies, and team projects are determined by the nature of coursework and personal teaching styles of individual faculty members. Full-time students can also engage in labs that deal with real-world business problems. In some courses, experiential learning is utilized to strengthen the connection between theory and practice. Students who are averse to class participation would find the program daunting, given Chicago Booth's strong focus on dialogue and intellectual curiosity in the classroom. Students are encouraged to openly challenge assumptions, even those of fellow classmates or professors. But beware: Expect your classmates and professors to challenge you in return.

Coursework. Chicago Booth places an emphasis on analyzing problems, generating insights, and implementing creative solutions. The highly flexible curriculum means that more than half of a student's courses are chosen from electives. (The rest of the classes are chosen from *Foundations* and *Functions, Management, and Business Environment* courses.) The electives can be taken in other programs at the University or in other countries in conjunction with the International Business Exchange Program (IBEP).

Core classes. Chicago Booth students have mandatory areas of study but do not have specific "required courses." Chicago Booth students in both the full-time and part-time programs must take three foundation courses in the areas of financial accounting, microeconomics, and statistics. Students then select six additional courses from a list of seven categories finance, marketing, operations, management, organizational behavior, strategy, and business environment. The only course full-time students are required to take is *LEAD*, which focuses on leadership and team-building skills, as discussed above.

Though other courses may not be "required," many still serve as prerequisites to higher-level course offerings. Students are permitted to waive course prerequisites at the discretion of the professors, and Chicago Booth also provides a petition process for students to count other courses or previous experience to fulfill requirements. Chicago Booth students can petition to take courses from other schools at the University of Chicago or from a list of affiliate schools located globally.

The school's focus on quant-based research is enabled by a longstanding partnership with consumer data provider A.C. Nielsen.

CHICAGO (BOOTH)

Research and learning centers include:

- Accounting Research Center
- Applied Theory Initiative
- Becker Friedman Institute for Research in Economics
- Center for Decision Research
- Center for Population Economics
- Center for Research in Security Prices
- Fama-Miller Center for Research in Finance
- George J. Stigler Center for the Study of the Economy and the State
- Initiative on Global Markets
- James M. Kilts Center for Marketing
- Polsky Center for Entrepreneurship and Innovation
- Social Enterprise Initiative (SEI)

Research centers. Chicago Booth offers a variety of research centers that engage both students and faculty members in key areas of study. Although many of the centers may not seem to impact the MBA student experience directly, their existence helps prospective students to know where the school is investing resources to understand if there's a good fit with their interests.

Grading policies. In keeping with its reputation as a rigorous program, Chicago Booth does enforce a GPA curve with a mean of 3.33. That means faculty members are limited in the number of high grades they can assign in their classes. Booth's grade non-disclosure policy was adopted by students in 2002, is not an official policy, and therefore is not enforced. Though many students likely don't disclose their grades, it would seem irrational not to expect high-honor students to share their GPAs and their accomplishments with potential employers.

Graduate-Student-at-Large. Unusual at the University of Chicago is the ability for the general public to take courses at the business school without being formally enrolled in a degree program. This is called the Graduate-Student-at-Large program, available through the Graham School of General Studies. Offerings include a variety of finance, accounting, and economics courses. The University of Chicago department of mathematics also offers a one-year master's degree in Financial Mathematics for those wanting to build investing models or start a career in derivatives. Chicago Booth does not have a short-term or accelerated MBA track.

Popular Professors

The Chicago Booth faculty is populated with many prominent business leaders, researchers, and teachers. Among Chicago Booth students, there are a handful of professors who are considered a "must have," due to their reputation both as educators and as experts. Below is a list of highly popular Chicago Booth faculty in various fields.

Steven Kaplan
Neubauer Family Distinguished Service Professor of Entrepreneurship and Finance
Professor Kaplan primarily teaches *Entrepreneurial Finance and Private Equity*. A quarter does not go by without students complaining that they were unable to get into his class prior to graduation. His courses are highly competitive choices during the bidding process, and students are only able to take his courses late in their program, when they have accumulated enough point "wealth." Professor Kaplan consistently attains top scores in Chicago Booth's internal faculty rankings and by students over the last decade.

Eugene Fama
Robert R. McCormick Distinguished Service Professor of Finance
Professor Fama is part of the "Chicago School of Economics," which is not a school per se but is a group of thinkers from the University of Chicago's economics, business, and law schools who promoted free market theories and countered the Keynesian ideals. The percentage of students who take Professor Fama's class is relatively small because his course content is highly specific, is highly rigorous, and has a scope that may go beyond the average Chicago Booth student's interest. Professor Fama has been called "the father of modern finance" and is highly respected both in academic circles and in the outside investment community. Taking a "Fama course" and doing well does wonders for the credibility of a Chicago Booth graduate in the field of finance, but, truth be told, only highly skilled Chicago Booth students with an interest in analytical finance tend to enjoy his classes.

Waverly Deutsch

Clinical Professor of Entrepreneurship

A longtime angel investor and startup consultant, Professor Deutsch teaches *Building the New Venture*, one of the most popular courses at Booth. She developed an award-winning startup simulation game called YourCo, which provides students an experiential learning opportunity while learning how to operate a new venture. The course covers a variety of topics facing entrepreneurs who seek to grow their businesses, including marketing, sales, operations, and team building.

Austan Goolsbee

Robert P. Gwinn Professor of Economics

Professor Goolsbee recently returned from Washington, where he was the chairman of the Council of Economic Advisers and a member of President Barack Obama's cabinet. Goolsbee is highly popular at Chicago Booth and was named a "star professor" in *Businessweek*'s Guide to the Best Business Schools (twice!). An expert in the field of economics, Professor Goolsbee discusses current and relevant issues with a unique sense of humor. A dedicated faculty member, Professor Goolsbee wore a tuxedo to class and then got married that same afternoon. His research has earned him a great deal of professional recognition, and he has collected many awards and accolades.

Sanjay Dhar

James H. Lorie Professor of Marketing

Professor Dhar primarily teaches *Marketing Strategy* and is very active in all of the Chicago Booth MBA programs. Professor Dhar makes this list because his passion in teaching is infectious. He makes the effort to truly know his students, and it is not uncommon for Professor Dhar to have all 65 (or more) students in his class remove their name cards so he may recite their names back on the first day of class. Dhar is the recipient of several awards, such as the McKinsey Award for Teaching Excellence in 2000, and was cited among the outstanding faculty in *Businessweek*'s Guide to the Best Business Schools.

Art Middlebrooks

Clinical Professor of Marketing
Executive Director, Kilts Center for Marketing

Art Middlebrooks is a prime example of a great adjunct faculty member. His teaching method of "learning by doing" is appropriate in his *Services Marketing* and *Product Marketing* classes. As a Chicago Booth alumnus, he really connects well with his students and continually gets top marks in faculty evaluations. Professor Middlebrooks is also the current executive director of the Kilts Center for Marketing and the coauthor of *Innovating the Corporation and Market Leadership Strategies for Service Companies*.

Harry Davis
William H. Abbott Professor of International Business and Economics
Harry Davis, who served as interim dean of Chicago Booth before Sunil Kumar took over, is the type of professor who brings balance and perspective to the MBA experience. His *Business Policy* course is not at all the typical Chicago Booth fare. While most courses at Chicago Booth tend to dominate the left brain, Professor Davis focuses more on right-brain activity: being intuitive, holistic, and metaphorical. Part of the Chicago Booth faculty since the mid-1960s, Professor Davis was once co-dean of the program and was integral to Chicago Booth's push to establish campuses in other countries.

James Schrager
Clinical Professor of Entrepreneurship and Strategic Management
James E. Schrager's *New Venture Strategy* is another highly sought-after course at Chicago Booth. His credibility in the business community equals his reputation as a faculty member at Chicago Booth, and his expertise is on display in multiple mainstream media formats, such as the *Wall Street Journal* and various major television networks. Chicago Booth students across the board absolutely love taking his class.

Similar Academic Programs

MIT (Sloan). Sloan's core curriculum is one of the most rigorous of any MBA program in the world. Leveraging its parent institution's brand in engineering and the sciences, Sloan's academics are very data-driven and analytically focused. Even "softer" subjects such as communications and organizational behavior have a strong analytical bent. However, like at Chicago Booth, the number of required core courses is limited, providing greater flexibility through the first year.

NYU (Stern). Stern has just two required courses in its core curriculum, plus the option to choose five additional courses from a "menu" of seven others. This model has become more popular in recent years so that first-year career-changers can tailor their core experience early in their MBA experience to properly prepare for internships in their chosen field. Someone seeking a position in brand management may want to tailor his or her experience differently than a candidate looking to move onto a sales and trading desk.

Penn (Wharton). Although the Wharton curriculum is somewhat more structured than Chicago Booth's, students there can also expect a rigorous approach where analytics are applied across the board, not just in finance class.

EMPLOYMENT & CAREERS AT CHICAGO BOOTH

What Chicago Booth Is Known For

Finance. Chicago Booth is—and has always been—known as a "finance school," both in terms of the incoming class and the outgoing graduates. Forty-one percent of Booth's Class of 2014 class took finance-related positions at graduation—the highest placement of any top-tier school, with only Columbia and Wharton coming close with 36% of their classes placing into finance roles. Apart from the curriculum and on-campus recruiting efforts, this could also be a result of the incoming class profile: Fifty-six percent of the most recent class came to Booth with some type of business degree (finance, business administration, or economics), and 26% had a professional background in finance.

Graduates taking finance-related positions

Booth	41%
Columbia & Wharton	36%
Stern	33%
Harvard	32%
Yale	30%

Traditional career paths. If you're on track for a "traditional" MBA career in management consulting or finance, you'll be in great company at Booth. Nearly two-thirds of the class (64%) goes into one of these two industries upon graduation, among the highest proportions of top business schools. The school is quick to mention that it sends graduates into a wide variety of industries, which is true. However, beyond the traditional sectors, Booth has no definitive path for which the brand is known like Kellogg (consumer goods marketing), Duke (healthcare administration), Tuck (general management), or Berkeley-Haas (technology). Particularly after the global financial crisis, the school has invested significant energy in developing relationships with consumer goods, technology, and other firms to broaden its base of recruiters and appeal to more nontraditional MBA applicants.

Graduates entering the consulting industry

 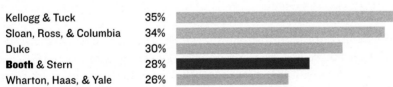

Kellogg & Tuck	35%
Sloan, Ross, & Columbia	34%
Duke	30%
Booth & Stern	28%
Wharton, Haas, & Yale	26%

You Oughta Know

Diversified industry placement. At first glance, Booth's employment report doesn't look much different than those at peer schools. There are schools that send more people into consulting, health care, media, energy, technology, manufacturing, or other specialized industries. However, not many other top-tier schools have as much representation in *all* of those industries. An Booth degree will serve you well in pretty much any industry.

Diversity of industries entered by graduates

Technology	14%
Consumer goods/retail	8%
Energy	3%
Manufacturing	2%
Health care	2%

Employment statistics. Nearly 90% of the Class of 2014 who were seeking employment had accepted a job by graduation; three months later, that number was up to just under 98%. This is an improvement over the previous year's statistics, with 91% of the Class of 2013 securing employment three months after graduation. Just more than 76% of full-time job offers were school-facilitated, either through an on-campus interview, a job posting, or a student or alumni relationship.

Salaries. Not that all you care about is money, but surely you want to make sure your MBA investment is worthwhile. So it should make you happy to learn that the median base salary for Chicago Booth's Class of 2014 was $120,000, with consulting hires landing the highest base of approximately $135,000. Just remember to be a bit careful when looking at overall average salary numbers because they can be skewed by high salaries in particular industries. Schools that send fewer students to those industries can be at a disadvantage.

Grade disclosure. The Class of 2002 adopted an ad hoc grade non-disclosure policy, which was never rescinded. It is not an official policy and therefore not enforced. Though many students likely don't disclose their grades, we wouldn't be surprised if recruiters from banking and consulting firms ask for them.

Midwestern roots. More than one third (35%) of Booth graduates stayed right in the Midwest. That's a higher percentage than at any other top-tier school, with only its Chicago neighbor, Kellogg, coming close, with 33% of the Class of 2014 electing to stay in the Midwest. About one fifth of the class went to the Northeast, and just 18% headed West (one of the lowest percentages among the top-tier schools).

Even top-rated business schools tend to place the majority of their graduates close to home. While this is often a result of stronger relationships with employers in a school's region, graduates often choose to attend a business school where they ultimately wish to live post-MBA. Most schools have mobility and strong alumni networks across the country and globally, but applicants would be wise to consider placement statistics by location when considering which schools to target.

Similar Programs for Professional Opportunities

Penn (Wharton). The similarities in the financial sector make comparisons between the two schools inevitable (and necessary), but the two schools are remarkably similar across the board, also sending similar percentages of grads into consulting, consumer goods, nonprofit, and technology.

Columbia. And, surprise, another strong finance school. But as with Wharton, the similarities between Columbia and Chicago Booth don't end there. The two schools also send very similar numbers of grads into consulting, technology, and consumer goods/retail.

NYU (Stern). Columbia's downtown rival also sends a high percentage of students into finance (35%). In addition, it sent an identical percentage of its Class of 2014 into the consulting industry (28%). NYU's overall range of industry placements, however, is somewhat narrower than Booth, Columbia, or Wharton.

Dartmouth (Tuck). Located in rural New Hampshire, Tuck couldn't be more different than Booth when it comes to environment and surroundings, so the two schools are rarely compared. However, when it comes to professional opportunities, candidates who are attracted to Booth should give Tuck a close look. Sixty percent of Tuckies enter the consulting or finance industry after graduation, with the rest pretty evenly spread across technology, consumer goods, manufacturing, health care, and so on. It is perhaps best known for placing candidates into general management and leadership rotation positions, with almost one in five landing such jobs.

Cornell (Johnson). Nearly every aspect of the Johnson MBA program is geared toward professional recruiting, and it shows. Ninety percent or more of its graduates each year accept jobs within three months of graduating, and its career services are always highly rated by students. About a third of its class goes into finance roles every year, although more Johnson grads go into corporate finance positions than those from Booth.

CULTURE & CAMPUS LIFE AT CHICAGO BOOTH

What Chicago Booth Is Known For

A storied history. Chicago Booth traces its history back to the late 19th century, when the University of Chicago opened the College of Commerce and Politics. The school went through several name changes until 2008, when a $300M gift from alumnus David Booth gave the school its current identity. Chicago Booth has certainly had many firsts in its long life, including being the first school to award a PhD in business to a woman, in 1929.

Community of graduate schools. Booth is one of many prestigious graduate schools at the university, which has more graduate students than undergraduates. The university is also home to a renowned law school, medical school, and even a divinity school. The university's many centers and institutes show the school's breadth and diversity.

Friendly, Midwest vibe. Although the vast majority of students come from outside the Midwest, the school tends to maintain its region's characteristically friendly and welcoming energy. The Booth environment tends to be much less formal than peer schools on the East Coast, such as Harvard, Wharton, and Columbia. Although Booth students are intellectual and accomplished, they're incredibly down-to-earth and don't give you the sense that they're constantly trying to impress.

A commuter school. Although some students live in Hyde Park, the majority of students live downtown ("the Loop" to insiders), often even in the same buildings. Other popular spots include the South Loop and northern neighborhoods of River North, Old Town, and Lincoln Park. The campus itself tends to clear out by early evening. Nighttime study sessions take place at the school's downtown facilities or in individual apartments.

You Oughta Know

Student environment. As one student put it, "We work hard and we play hard." Chicago Booth offers plenty of opportunities to have fun, but given the rigorous curriculum, the students also hit the books. Sleep is usually the casualty between these forces, with even former investment bankers reporting they have more to do than they have time to do it! Booth's collaborative environment features students who enjoy hanging out and professors who aren't above auctioning themselves off for charity.

Lack of cohort structure. Because of the flexible curriculum, after the *LEAD* course, Chicago Booth doesn't have the strong cohort/learning team structure that you might find in other schools. Instead, teams tend form on an ad hoc basis and vary by class. The benefit is that you end up with broader relationships than you might have at another school, but they might not be quite as deep as if you'd spent your first semester or year with the same tight-knit group.

> **The Booth environment tends to be much less formal than peer schools on the East Coast, such as Harvard, Wharton, and Columbia.**

Relationships across classes. At other schools, you may get to know very few students outside your graduating class other than a few mentors and leaders of various clubs. At Booth, because you can take advanced courses starting in your very first quarter, first-years and second-years interact more than you might typically see. Student-to-student mentorship is key, although this is common among MBA programs. Second-years mentor first-years on everything from course selection, to career advice, to interview preparation. For example, during "Winterview," a Saturday in the winter, second-years prepare first-years for upcoming interviews.

Leadership opportunities. Chicago Booth offers more than 70 student-led clubs and activities. Students enjoy collaborating outside the classroom, seeing it as an extension of the collaboration that goes on inside the classroom. Students created all existing student organizations and run them with limited involvement from faculty or staff. However, North Shore rival Kellogg offers twice as many student-led clubs and activities, highlighting the increased level of expected involvement. Most Booth students are involved in two to four clubs across professional and personal interests.

Most students are involved in two to four clubs across professional and personal interests.

Social events. A popular activity on Thursday evenings is "TNDC," or—you guessed it—Thursday Night Drinking Club, when students explore a different neighborhood bar each week. For casual hangouts, River North tends to be the default spot because it's close to the Loop and has a young-professional vibe to it. Students also explore bars and restaurants in Wicker Park, Old Town, Lincoln Park, West Loop, and Wrigleyville. Additionally, the Rock 'n Roll McDonald's (the huge, two-story McDonald's in downtown Chicago) is a prime late-night "after party" spot since it's open 24 hours.

Facilities. The Charles M. Harper Center is, literally, the center of campus life for Chicago Booth. The glass-enclosed structure was built in 2004 and includes classrooms, study rooms, a student lounge, a business center, outdoor terraces, and faculty offices. The Harper Center is often seen as the first big leap forward in business school facilities, followed by an "arms race" in new construction at Stanford, Wharton, NYU Stern, Yale, Kellogg, and soon at Columbia. Booth's facilities continue to wow visitors and draw applicants even a decade later.

CHICAGO (BOOTH)

Similar Programs Culturally

MIT (Sloan). Chicago Booth and Sloan aren't only similar academically: Not only do both schools take pride in the intellectual nature of their students, but they're also located in urban areas where students tend to scatter throughout the city rather than live exclusively on campus or within walking distance. MIT Sloan tends to be seen as one of the friendliest MBA environments, which may come as a surprise to those who know its parent institution only for its strength in engineering and sciences.

Yale. Yale School of Management (SOM) students and alumni consider one another family, similar to Booth's Midwestern, friendly vibe. However, Yale SOM's class is about half the size of Booth's, so students tend to know pretty much everyone in their class incredibly well. Both schools put a premium on attracting extremely intelligent and curious applicants, so its admitted students tend to share these characteristics.

Duke (Fuqua). Like the Midwest, the South is known for its friendly people and warm hospitality. Fuqua is no exception here; the program is known for its active, social, and friendly student body. However, we've heard from some applicants and students that there can be a little bit of an atmosphere of exclusivity. Located in Durham, North Carolina, Duke has a much more isolated, "college town" feel than the urban University of Chicago campus.

Virginia (Darden). Darden students are also known for their "work hard, play hard" determination. Like Booth, Darden sees itself first and foremost as a strong academic institution, and this permeates the school's culture. Both universities have long and storied histories, although this sense of prestige may be felt even more strongly at Darden.

ADMISSIONS AT CHICAGO BOOTH

What Chicago Booth Is Looking For

As Chicago Booth has climbed to the top of business school rankings, it has attracted a larger number of applicants, some of whom may not be a great fit with the school. The obvious benefit is that the admissions office can choose from an even stronger, more diverse pool. But the school's challenge is to figure out who really belongs at Chicago Booth, as well as who really wants to attend. Be honest with the admissions committee (and with yourself) about why you are considering Chicago Booth. Then, be sure to demonstrate your fit with the program and how you will contribute to the school's community.

Showing that you fit. Despite the fact that the school's 24% acceptance rate (for the Class of 2016) is higher than that of any other top program, candidates should not assume that the Chicago Booth admissions committee is easy to impress. Much care is given to figuring out whether applicants have the chops to survive in what is one of the most rigorous and analytical MBA programs. Furthermore, the school wants to make sure that incoming students are on board with the various elements of the Chicago Booth approach, and that they have the kind of robust work experience and professional development that will suggest strong performance in group projects. They also value innovation, creativity, and problem-solving skills. These are just a few of the reasons that Chicago Booth includes the "photo" essay question option.

Admission criteria. Other important factors Chicago Booth considers when admitting candidates are those that should already be familiar to applicants interested in elite business schools. Chicago Booth is looking for academic ability, proper motivation, preparedness, intellectual curiosity, communication skills, and professional success. It finds these traits among the usual application components: GPA, GMAT, essay, recommendation letters, resume, and, later in the process, interview. Successful candidates use each part of the written application to present a unique aspect or element of their candidacy, so that the entire package fits together as a complete picture. Wherever possible, avoid regurgitating facts from one place to the next. Instead, let each piece build on and reinforce the others so the admissions team can see more of who you are and why you're right for Chicago Booth.

Re-applicants. Chicago Booth has a slightly different policy for those who are trying again: You are considered a re-applicant if you submitted in either of the previous two years. (Other schools define a re-applicant as someone who applied in the just-prior year only.) This can be an advantage, because someone in this position would not have to write the essay and get all new recommendations. However, a re-applicant definitely needs to demonstrate how her profile has changed and her candidacy improved if she's going to be successful in her second attempt. Chicago Booth has a specific re-applicant essay question that invites candidates to explain how their "thinking has changed" about their goals and their desire for an MBA. This is an interesting angle and indicates the type of insights or self-reflection that the school expects re-applicants to demonstrate.

APPLICATION DEADLINES

All deadlines are 5PM U.S. Central Time on the date indicated. (not in bold, please)

Round 1:
17 Sept 2015
Notification:
10 Dec 2015

Round 2:
5 Jan 2016
Notification:
24 Mar 2016

Round 3:
5 Apr 2016
Notification:
19 May 2016

CHICAGO (BOOTH)

V If you are looking for tips on 2016–17 admissions essays, you're in luck! Check out our website at **veritasprep.com/booth** for our latest advice.

Preparing to Apply

Reading this Essential Guide is a great first step in your preparation. Hopefully, this insider's glimpse has been helpful in understanding the most important aspects of the school. However, nothing can replace gaining firsthand knowledge and experience yourself.

Reach out to current students. Even if you don't have any personal connections to Chicago Booth, you can reach out to current students and get their insight and advice. On the school's Student-led Groups page, you'll find a list of all campus clubs. Find a few clubs that fit your personal and professional interests, and reach out to the officers. Remember: These are very busy MBA students so you don't want to intrude too much on their time, but you could ask for a 10- to 15-minute conversation or elicit some advice via e-mail. Come prepared with specific questions (preferably those that aren't already answered online). If you're planning to visit campus, perhaps you might even arrange a coffee chat or lunch, if they are available. Remember that officers of major clubs like the Finance Club or Management Consulting Club have plenty of responsibilities. You might provide a quick background introduction and ask if there's another member of their club, even one with a similar background, who might be able to offer some insights and advice about his or her Chicago Booth experience.

Visit campus. The school's website can only tell you so much; by far, a personal visit is the best possible research in the application process. If you have the means, we highly recommend you visit Chicago Booth in person along with the campuses of your other top choices to understand the significant differences in culture, teaching style, student body, recruiting opportunities, facilities, and so forth. You may be surprised at just how different each school can be and and how the reality can differ from the perception. We encourage you to take advantage of opportunities to visit campus; because informal and impromptu encounters can be the most informative, don't be afraid to approach students in less-formal settings.

Other events. We know that many applicants will not be able to travel to Chicago to visit campus, but you should take advantage of other worldwide admissions events, such as information sessions, virtual sessions, and specific-audience events. In fact, these off-campus events can offer great opportunities for quality time with admissions officers and even other applicants, who can be a great resource and support through the admissions process. Get to know the school and its culture as well as you can, because your familiarity can shine through your application and essay to help you stand out.

Get to know the school and its culture as well as you can, because your familiarity can shine through your application and essay to help you stand out.

You Oughta Know

When should I apply? Chicago Booth uses a standard three-round system, meaning that you may submit your application in any of its three rounds for consideration. However, 90% or more of the class will be filled with the first two rounds of applicants, so we do not encourage you to wait until the final round without compelling circumstances.

Traditional candidates. We mentioned earlier that Booth tends to attract a lot of traditional candidates, and the school is seeking to broaden its appeal. It still admits many students from the management consulting and finance industries, but we encourage you to apply in the first round (assuming you have a strong GMAT score). In a later round, it's possible that the school may see you as a viable candidate but may have already admitted several other applicants with similar profiles, so it might pass on you to bring greater professional diversity to the class. (Plus, the admissions committee knows you've been planning on an MBA since the day you graduated from undergrad, so there's no reason to delay!)

Applying early vs. applying right. Please note that even though the top schools encourage you to apply in the earliest round possible, this does not mean that you should apply with a rushed application or a mediocre GMAT score. There's no sense in applying early if you're just going to be denied. A GMAT score that's above the school's average will do more for your candidacy than applying in the first round.

Deadlines. Once again Booth has moved its Round 1 deadline forward by a week, making Booth the latest top business school to have its first deadline come in mid-September. The good news is that applying to Booth in Round 1 means that you will get your decision back by December 10, which gives you almost a month before most business schools' Round 2 deadlines come in early January. Booth's Round 2 and Round 3 deadlines each moved only slightly compared to last season. This season's deadlines are September 17, 2015; January 5, 2016; and, for procrastinators, April 5, 2016. Note that applications are due at 5PM U.S. Central Time. Applications for each round are considered after each deadline, so there is no advantage to applying earlier in the round. That said, we recommend that you submit at least a couple of days before your target deadline to avoid the last-minute crush. Recommendations need to be submitted by the deadline as well.

The Essay

After years of whittling down its essay count to just one single essay last year, Booth returns with one essay this year, although it's a new one. Booth has always been one of the pioneers in using unusual essay prompts, and it's good to see that continue. The way Booth goes about it this year is a little different (and perhaps not ideal), but we dig into that in much more detail below.

Chicago Booth values individuality because of what we can learn from the diverse experiences and perspectives of others. This mutual respect creates an open-minded community that supports curiosity, inspires us to think more broadly, take risks, and challenge assumptions. At Booth, community is about collaborative thinking and tapping into each other's different viewpoints to cultivate new ideas and realize breakthrough moments every day.

Using one of the photos provided, tell us how it resonates with your own viewpoint on why the Booth community is the right fit for you.

> Booth still admits many students from the management consulting and finance industries, but we encourage you to apply in the first round (assuming you have a strong GMAT score).

CHICAGO (BOOTH)

This essay prompt is new this year, although at its core, it's not that different from last year's essay. The Booth admissions team wants to get to know you better, and this is their way of doing it. Why did they change the essay prompt? Our bet is that they actually liked what they saw from applicants last year, but they seemed determined to make their essays a moving target because of all of the coaching resources that applicants have access to (such as this Essential Guide!). This is their way of trying to keep it fresh while not messing with the formula too much.

Let your personality shine through. We always tell applicants that they have to do two things to be successful: Stand out from other applicants, but also show fit with their target MBA program. With this essay prompt Booth is going after the latter; it explicitly asks you to show why the Booth community "is the right fit for you." But, how you show fit is one way you can stand out versus other applicants. Don't simply use this response to just show off professional achievements that you already cover elsewhere in your application. Don't be afraid to get creative here! Remember: The reason Booth asks this question is because it really is the admissions committee's best chance to get a sense of your personality, so let that personality shine through here!

Don't get too hung up on the photo. The addition of the "react to one of these photos" idea is...interesting. We have a feeling that a lot of applicants will end up forcing the explanation of why a photo of Eugene Fama resonates with them. At a high level, our advice is not to get too hung up on your choice of photo. Don't just randomly pick one and then use editorial duct tape to attach that your own story, but remember that the admissions committee really wants to learn about you here, not about what you think of one of these photos. Any one of Booth's thousands of applicants can write about those photos, but only you can tell Booth about you.

Reapplicant Question: Upon reflection, how has your perspective regarding your future, Chicago Booth, and/or getting an MBA changed since the time of your last application? (300 words maximum)

Focus on improvement. This question gets at the heart of what MBA admissions officers at any school care about when they see a re-applicant: What has changed since last time? While we don't believe the Chicago Booth admissions committee did it deliberately, we do think that the phrasing here can be a bit misleading. An important thing to think about: The way this question is written, it may lead some applicants to believe that they didn't get in before because of something wrong in the way they answered the "Why an MBA? Why Booth?" question and that this is their chance to make another run at answering that question. But, that may not at all be why they were rejected last time. Maybe you had a weakness in your application that had nothing to do with your research on Chicago Booth or your reasons for wanting to earn an MBA, such as a low GMAT score or lack of leadership experience at work. While you do need to answer the question, you will also need to make it obvious that your application weaknesses have been strengthened since your previous application.

Do I have a chance if I re-apply? Chicago Booth actually tends to have a positive view of re-applicants, especially if the application has significantly strengthened since the prior attempt. Perseverance is seen as a sign of passion and commitment to the school, and re-applicants are often admitted at higher rates than first-time applicants.

Recommendations

Whom should I ask? Similar to many other top programs, Chicago Booth requires that all applicants submit two letters of recommendation. One of these must be professional in nature and should come from your current supervisor. If you're unable to acquire such a recommendation, the admissions committee asks that you explain why. The second letter of recommendation does not need to be professional and could come instead from a club, organization, team, or volunteer project, if appropriate.

Does title or status matter? As many top business programs claim, Booth is more concerned with the content and quality of your recommendations than the reputation or title of your recommenders. Choose individuals who know you well, can speak to your qualifications as an MBA candidate, and can add "valuable insights to your application." We see candidates try to call in favors to try to get their company's CEO to write a letter on their behalf. In general, the admissions committee will be far more impressed by a genuine and passionate letter from a middle manager with whom you work every day than a polite letter from a well-known CEO that lacks depth and detailed anecdotes about you. The latter will likely be discounted or completely ignored. In fact, Chicago Booth says outright, "Avoid choosing people simply based on their title or status."

What will they be asked? The actual "letter" of recommendation is submitted through an online form. Once you begin your online application you will provide the names and email addresses of your recommenders and they will receive a link to complete the online form.

First, your recommenders will be asked to fill out basic contact information (pre-populated with information that you provide). Then they will be asked the following questions:

- *For how long have you known the applicant? [text box]*
- *Do you have an MBA degree? [Yes/No]*
- *If yes, did you receive your MBA from Chicago Booth? [Yes/No]*
- *If yes, graduation year [text box]*
- *Are you affiliated with Chicago Booth or the University of Chicago in any way? [Yes/No]*

Skills assessment. [This is a multiple-choice assessment based on the following skills/qualities: *Ability to adapt to change, Awareness of self and others, Maturity, Openness to feedback and constructive criticism, Interpersonal skills (with colleagues/subordinates), Interpersonal skills (with superiors/executives), Confidence, Initiative/Self-Motivation, Collaboration/Teamwork, Critical Thinking Skills, Intellectual Curiosity, Problem Solving Skills.*] Each recommender will be asked to rate you on each skill with the following scale: *Unable to Assess, Area of Concern, Opportunity for Development, Solid/Meets Expectations, Strength/Exceeds Expectations.* The recommender is advised that "most candidates will have a range of marks; it is extremely rare for a candidate to exceed expectations in all areas."

> As many top business programs claim, Booth is more concerned with the content and quality of your recommendations than the reputation or title of your recommenders.

CHICAGO (BOOTH)

Your recommender will then be asked:

- ***Based on your professional experience, how does the candidate rate within his/her peer group?*** *[Recommender to select one of the following: Unable to Assess, Below Average, Average (top 50%), Very Good (top 25%), Outstanding (top 10%), Truly Exceptional (top 5%), The best I've encountered in my career].*

Recommendation letter. Finally, your recommender will be asked to answer the two "common app" questions adopted by several other schools this year:

> ***How does the applicant's performance, potential, background, or personal qualities compare to those of other well-qualified individuals in similar roles? Please provide specific examples.***

> ***Please describe the most important piece of constructive feedback you have given the applicant. Please detail the circumstances and the applicant's response.***

What should they say? Booth admissions officers are looking for specific examples of your performance, teamwork, and leadership qualities to shine through in your letters of recommendation. Your recommenders should be up to speed on the overall theme of your application and should be aware of your reasons for getting an MBA and applying to Booth to ensure consistency throughout your application. The use of specific examples combined with genuine enthusiasm about your candidacy is the key to a successful letter.

Should I draft it myself? Many applicants to business school are asked by their superiors to draft the recommendation themselves and the recommender will approve it. We strongly recommend that you do not write the recommendation yourself for several reasons. First, your writing style and choice of phrasing are unique, and admissions officers will notice if the recommendations are similar to each other and to your essay. If they notice too many similarities, your application could be denied outright. Second, you may tend to be too humble or generic. Your supervisor might use language such as "one of the top analysts I've seen in my entire career" that you wouldn't dare include if writing it on his or her behalf. Third, and perhaps most importantly, the admissions officer is looking for a third-party perspective on your candidacy, so writing a recommendation yourself is an unethical breach of trust with the school you are looking to join. Some schools even require applicants to certify that they have not been involved in drafting their recommendations.

Preparing your recommenders. Instead of writing the recommendation yourself, you should sit down and have candid conversations with your recommenders about the reasons you want to go to business school and why you've selected your target schools, your professional goals, and your experience together. Ask them if they would have the time to write a strong recommendation on your behalf. (This also gives them a nice "out" by telling you that they are too busy rather than saying they don't feel comfortable giving you a positive recommendation.) Bring a copy of your resume and a bulleted list of projects that you've worked on together and accomplishments they have seen you achieve. Let them know that admissions committees prefer to see specific, detailed examples in recommendations. Then, let them know that you'll serve as a "project manager" to follow up and ensure that they are able to submit your recommendation ahead of the deadline.

The Interview

Who is invited to interview? Chicago Booth interviews are by invitation only. Being invited to interview is a good sign, as Booth usually interviews slightly less than half of its applicants. It has a lot of seats to fill and often will interview a wider assortment of candidates than some other schools might. Interviews can be conducted on campus (usually by a second-year student) or by an alumnus in the applicant's hometown (when available).

What should I expect? Of course, being asked to interview is only the first step: Of those interviewed, fewer than half are admitted. If you are one of the lucky ones to be offered an interview spot there are a few things to keep in mind as you prepare. First, interviews at Booth can vary significantly. For the most part, interview content is up to the interviewer. Usually the questions will be fairly typical ("Walk me through your resume."; "Why an MBA?"; "Why Booth?"), but you can also expect a few more challenging questions ("Discuss your leadership style."; "What is your greatest weakness?"; "What role do you take in a team?"). And, from time to time, you may get something outside the box ("What stocks would you invest in and why?"; "What is your thought on our current monetary policy?"; "How would you spend a million dollars if you couldn't spend it on yourself?"). This means your Booth interview may be one of the most challenging of your MBA interviews.

Who will conduct my interview? The variance in questions is in part due to the fact that many interviews are conducted by second-year students or local alumni rather than exclusively by admissions staff members. (Staff members tend to be more consistent, but all interviews hold the same weight.) Student interviewers may think it is fun to see how you react when thrown a curveball. There is no right answer to this type of interview question; interviewers usually just like to see if you can maintain your composure and back up your answer with data or some concrete examples.

What will my interviewer know about my background? It is also important to note that interviews at Booth are blind. This means that your interviewer will not be familiar with your GMAT scores or other elements of your application. The interviewer will have your resume. Even though the interviewer has not read your essay, try not to use the same stories over and over again. You want the admissions committee (Adcom) to have as many data points as possible so rehashing what you wrote in your essay is not additive. Some points will be reiterated (why you want an MBA; why you like Chicago Booth), but to the extent possible avoid repetition.

What questions should I ask? Most interviewers will ask if there is anything you'd like the Adcom to know that you were not able to put in your application. This is a perfect time to stress your sincere desire to attend Booth. Remember to prepare a few other questions for your interviewer. Insightful questions not only give you a better idea of the school but also enable you to finish the interview on a strong note. You could ask about popular professors by saying something like, "I've heard that no one should go through their Booth experience without taking courses from Professors Kaplan and Fama (or others that you're interested in). Would you agree? What others would you recommend?" Even if you feel your questions about the school have been answered, you can always ask the interviewer what she wishes she had known before coming to Booth, or what she has enjoyed most about the Booth experience.

DUKE
FUQUA

A rising program that emphasizes collaboration and global awareness.

 DURHAM, NC

CLASS SIZE
440

PROGRAM FOUNDED
1969

PRONOUNCED
FEW-kwa

CHARACTERISTICS
HEALTH CARE, COLLABORATION, GLOBAL CAMPUSES

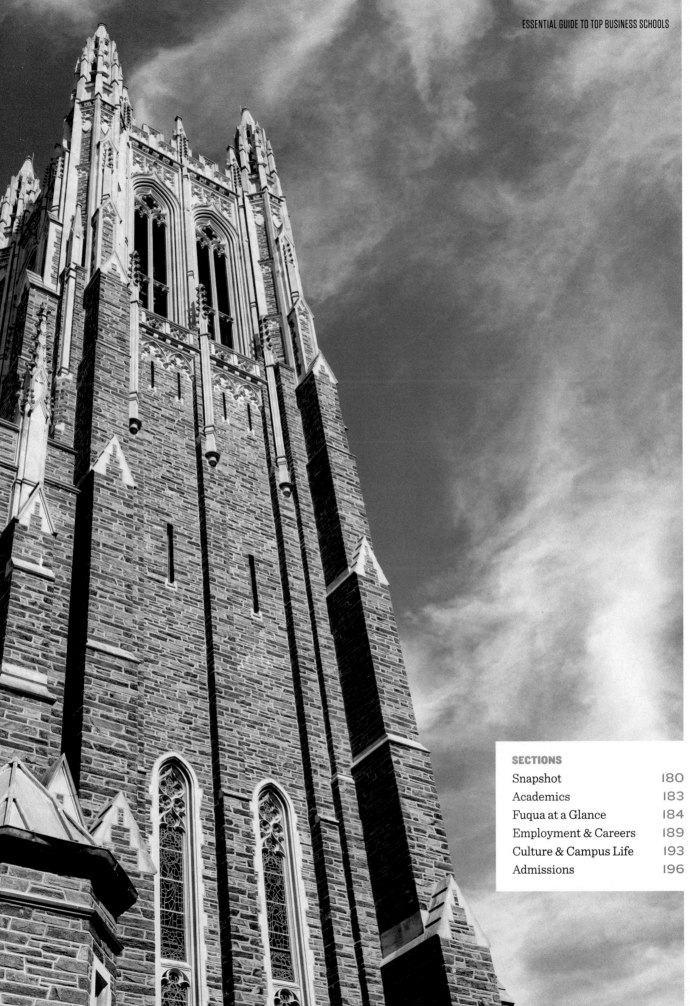

SECTIONS

FUQUA SNAPSHOT

What Fuqua Is Known For

Healthcare administration. If you're coming from the healthcare industry, or hoping to enter it upon graduation, Fuqua should definitely be on your list. The school maintains one of the top reputations for health care in the nation and even offers multiple ways to integrate healthcare study into your curriculum. You can add a Health Sector Management (HSM) concentration or certificate to each of the four separate MBA programs. Duke HSM makes tremendous use of the Research Triangle area of North Carolina, home to many leading biotechnology, pharmaceutical, and other healthcare organizations. HSM courses are taught by Fuqua School of Business and Duke Hospital faculty, including those from the renowned graduate schools of nursing and medicine. Nine percent of graduates go into health care, the highest of top business schools.

"Team Fuqua" is an expression you'll hear often.

....

Team-oriented culture. The collaborative, team-oriented approach infuses all aspects of the learning and social environments at Fuqua; "Team Fuqua" is an expression you'll hear often. In the classroom, team-based projects are common; the environment is competitive (this is a business school, after all) but not in a cutthroat way. This concept extends beyond the student body. During popular "Fuqua Fridays" students, staff, and faculty members enjoy food and beverages. The school has taken some criticism for being too collaborative and supportive, and therefore not preparing the students for the "real world." However, the school points directly to this strength as the reason for its #1 spot in the 2014 Bloomberg *Businessweek* ranking of top full-time MBA programs.

Options, options, and more options. In addition to the popular daytime, full-time MBA, Fuqua also offers the Cross-Continent MBA, Global Executive MBA, Weekend Executive MBA, two Master of Management Studies (MMS) programs, a PhD program, and a handful of joint-degree offerings. This represents the most diverse and globally-oriented set of degree offerings of any U.S. business school.

What Makes Fuqua Different

Collaborative leadership. One of Fuqua's key differentiating factors is its emphasis on collaborative leadership. Other than Kellogg and perhaps UCLA Anderson, few business schools can cite that as the program's most distinguishing feature to the degree that Fuqua can. At Duke, collaboration is evident in the "Team Fuqua" philosophy and in the emphasis on student involvement across the educational experience. Many business schools emphasize leadership, but Fuqua's simultaneous emphasis on collaboration sets it apart from many of the school's peers.

Expanding reach. Fuqua claims to be "rethinking the boundaries of business school," and has systematically broadened its reach geographically, being the only school that has a firm presence in major centers around the world. It has also expanded its demographic reach by offering compelling options to students in various phases of their careers and from different populations. The latest example is its new Master of Management Studies (MMS) offered at the Duke Kunshan University in Kunshan, China. The MMS is a 10-month program designed for students coming directly from undergraduate with little or no work experience.

Leaders of consequence. Duke has a stated goal to create so-called "leaders of consequence," a phrase that we believe was coined by Dean Blair Sheppard around 2008 when he assumed leadership. The phrase has since been refined to "global leaders of consequence." This concept is so important, in fact, that it comes into play within the Fuqua admission criteria. While a concrete definition is lacking, suffice it to say that Duke feels a leader of consequence is adaptable, down to earth, and ethical. In terms of an application, Duke's admissions team is looking for applicants who have made a difference in their jobs and in their communities, and who seek an MBA from Fuqua in their quest to make a real impact on the world in the future.

Open Interviews. Another unique feature of the Duke MBA is its Open Interview process: The school strongly encourages candidates to travel to Durham and visit campus to interview with a student. This Open Interview option is available only in the earliest part of the admissions cycle each year, and is scheduled for September 8 to October 12, 2015. Scheduling opens in August for these limited slots. You need not have your application completed in advance of the Open Interview; it is characterized more as an "evaluation" than an interview. Participating in the Open Interview process is a great opportunity not only to explore campus and meet students, but also to demonstrate your interest in the program.

Among top business schools, only the Tuck School at Dartmouth College has a similar open interview offering. Both programs have very distinct, tight-knit cultures located off the beaten path, and the schools want candidates to come experience it for themselves before deciding to apply. This also helps improve the quality of the applications, since candidates can really get to know the program and speak with some authority about how they will best leverage Fuqua opportunities and resources. Additional details on interviewing at Duke are provided below in the Interview section.

> **Participating in the Open Interview process is a great opportunity not only to explore campus and meet students, but also to demonstrate your interest in the program.**

Fuqua Is a Good Fit for You If...

You've got some work experience under your belt. Fuqua traditionally prefers that students in the Daytime MBA have about five years of work experience, though there is some flexibility on this requirement for stellar candidates. Just three admits (not 3%—three people!) from the Class of 2014 had no work experience at all.

You're a younger candidate who wants core management training. The MMS degree is a great option for those coming straight from college. These degrees have been popular in Europe, and Duke is one of the early adopters in the U.S. The Cross-Continent MBA also sometimes accepts students with a little less work experience (though some professional experience—and a current job—are definitely required).

You're interested in a truly unique international MBA education. If your career has already put you in the international arena, Duke's Cross-Continent MBA and Global Executive MBA programs are definitely worth investigating. Duke's focus on global business is evident across the entire school, making the North Carolina campus more diverse than might be expected.

> **If your career has already put you in the international arena, Duke's Cross-Continent MBA and Global Executive MBA programs are definitely worth investigating.**

You want to go into health care. There are few other programs that offer the depth and breadth of healthcare management that is available at Duke. For those looking to accelerate their progression in an existing career, or for someone interested in transitioning over to hospital management, clinical outcomes, or the payer side, Duke's Health Sector Management MBA and the other educational options are hard to beat.

You want to go into energy, including alternative and renewable energy. If you want to go into investment banking and become a sell-side commodities analyst, you want to push innovations in alternative energy, or you care about sustainability in business, Duke may be the right place for you. Fuqua is increasing its attentions in these critical areas, and it could therefore be a great choice to launch or reposition your career.

You are a woman or a U.S. minority. Fuqua has been actively catering to these different populations, perhaps even more so than other top American business programs.

You're willing to visit the campus. Duke knows that it is often a "safety school" for top candidates and has struggled with yield in its admissions. If you're willing to go to lengths to show that if accepted you'll actually attend, you'll become a very attractive candidate. Things like visiting the campus, participating in the Open Interview process and mentioning that Duke is your top-choice school can go a long way here. If you don't have the means or opportunity to visit campus, you can develop a rapport with admissions officers at one of the school's many global informational sessions.

ACADEMICS AT FUQUA

What Fuqua Is Known For

General management. Fuqua first introduced concentrations in 2008, but unlike majors at some other business schools, Fuqua students are not required to declare a concentration. Students frequently earn multiple concentrations, as there are many overlapping required classes among them. While Fuqua is known as a general management program, the school's marketing classes and professors rival those of other top schools, and therefore the marketing concentration is very popular. Finance classes and concentrations are also popular.

Diversity of instruction. As has become increasingly common among innovative business schools, Duke's courses feature a blended teaching approach that includes an almost equal distribution of case studies, lectures, and team projects. Each class is typically more than two hours long, allowing ample time for a highly interactive case discussion, followed by a course lecture. Duke professors conduct leading research and are adept at integrating relevant and topical business issues into every class. Team projects are absolutely integral to each course, and select groups are called upon to present insights and strategic recommendations as a way to launch a class discussion. Class participation is expected and is a prominent grading criterion.

Experiential learning. While Duke's experiential learning options may not feature as prominently as those of Ross or Tuck, it does offer numerous courses to help students apply the theory they learn in the classroom. These classes impart knowledge and experience by assisting real-world businesses in such areas as consulting, strategic planning, marketing strategy, and business plan development. Recently Fuqua introduced a global consulting practicum pairing teams of interested first year students with international clients to complete impactful semester-long projects. Faculty members guide and participate in strategy sessions with the students to reinforce the translation of academic concepts to practical solutions.

Global perspective. *Global* is a major MBA buzzword in this day and age, but few schools come close to the international emphasis and flavor that Fuqua promotes. Each incoming MBA class begins with the Global Institute, a one-of-a-kind program that is held in the summer before the first year and that introduces students to the global business environment and the world economy structure. Students tackle current global business issues and are exposed to diverse backgrounds and perspectives while also gaining exposure to more traditional "orientation" concepts such as leadership and team building. Fuqua also offers study abroad programs and the increasingly popular *Global Academic Travel Experience*, or GATE, a course in which students study international business trends from select regions and then travel to designated locations for hands-on experience.

FUQUA AT A GLANCE

APPLICANTS BY SCHOOL

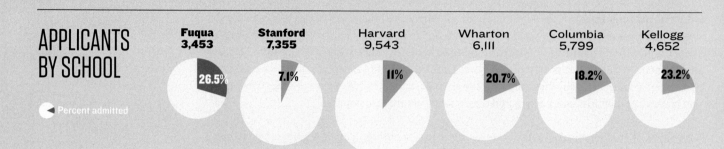

◀ Percent admitted

Fuqua 3,453	Stanford 7,355	Harvard 9,543	Wharton 6,111	Columbia 5,799	Kellogg 4,652
26.5%	7.1%	11%	20.7%	18.2%	23.2%

UNDERREPRESENTED MINORITIES

Fuqua has been actively catering to different populations, perhaps even more so than other top American business programs. Despite these efforts, Fuqua's U.S. minority statistics are a little lower than some other programs.

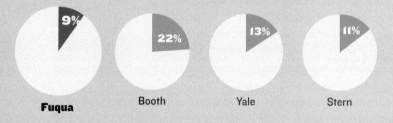

Fuqua	Booth	Yale	Stern
9%	22%	13%	11%

INTERNATIONAL CITIZENS

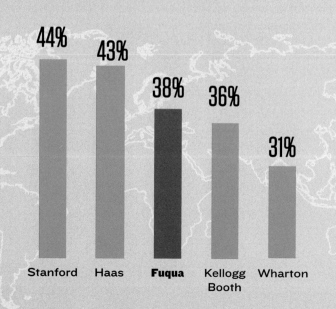

Stanford	Haas	Fuqua	Kellogg Booth	Wharton
44%	43%	38%	36%	31%

WOMEN

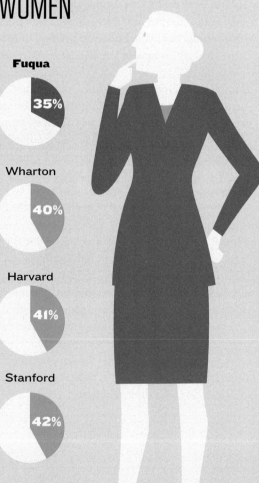

Fuqua	35%
Wharton	40%
Harvard	41%
Stanford	42%

UNDERGRAD MAJORS

32% of class have a STEM degree, which is high (and unexpected for Fuqua, which is often seen as a "softer" MBA program).

- ■ **STEM**
- ■ **Humanities/Social Science**
- ■ **Business**
- ■ **Economics**
- □ **Other**

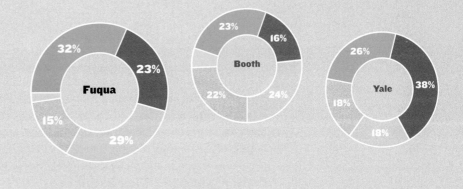

GMAT SCORE RANGE

Fuqua places less emphasis on standardized test scores than peer schools, resulting in a lower average GMAT and wider range of scores among admitted students.

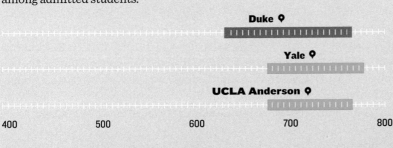

GPA RANGE (MIDDLE 80%)

Fuqua's GPA range between the 10th and 90th percentile of its admitted class is a bit wider than the range at other top schools, and the school tends to be more open to candidates with lower GPAs. The bottom 10th percentile of Fuqua's class entered with a 3.0 GPA or lower, compared to 3.2 at UCLA Anderson and Chicago Booth, and 3.36 at Berkeley-Haas.

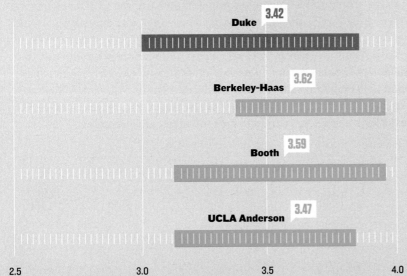

CLASS SIZE

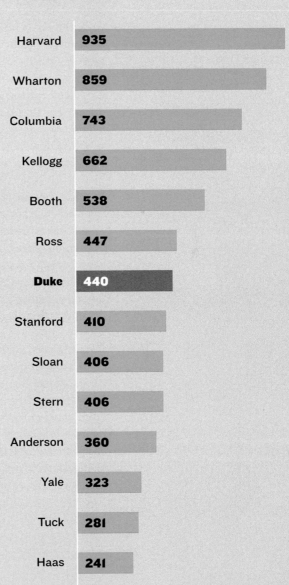

School	Size
Harvard	935
Wharton	859
Columbia	743
Kellogg	662
Booth	538
Ross	447
Duke	**440**
Stanford	410
Sloan	406
Stern	406
Anderson	360
Yale	323
Tuck	281
Haas	241

DUKE (FUQUA)

Nuts & Bolts

Class organization. Incoming classes are divided into six sections of approximately 70 students each. Students remain in sections for core classes during the first two terms. Each section has a unique history and distinctive features that are passed down from class to class. For instance, one section substitutes the standard hand clap with a thunderous stomp of desks and tables, while another section shouts the word *deuce* in unison any time the number two appears on a screen or slide. These eccentricities provide an example of the distinct and tight-knit Fuqua environment. Classmates are very proud of their sections, and friendly competition exists across sections. Students are randomly assigned to sections, although Fuqua ensures that each section is made up of diverse backgrounds.

ILE Teams. Within each section, students are divided into Integrative Learning Experience Teams (ILE Teams) that consist of five-to-six-person groups. During core classes, most team projects are completed in the pre-assigned ILE Teams. Just as each section includes diverse backgrounds, ILE Teams reflect Fuqua's diversity of nationalities, career backgrounds, ethnicities, and gender. Beyond the core classes, teams are either assigned by the professor or are self-formed.

Six-week terms. Fuqua courses span four six-week terms: Fall Term 1, Fall Term 2, Spring Term 1, and Spring Term 2. This structure allows students to take more courses during the academic year than many other top business schools, providing a broader knowledge base upon which to draw during interviews and internships. However, classes move very quickly, with midterms just three weeks into each course. This pace may not be ideal for every student.

Weekly schedule. Classes meet every Monday, Tuesday, Thursday, and Friday. Although there are no classes on Wednesday, students are busy working with teams, orchestrating club events, and attending career service activities. All classes include two hours of instruction with a 15-minute break between the first and second hour. Typically, the first hour of class is dedicated to case discussions and group presentations, whereas the second hour is devoted to lectures. Students complete the majority of core classes during the first two terms, which allows for many elective courses during Spring Term 1 and Spring Term 2. These electives provide additional training and tools prior to summer internships.

Core classes. Each student begins the core with the three-week Global Institute, where students are introduced to the collaborative Fuqua environment and exposed to global business issues. Global Institute counts as two core classes: *Leadership, Ethics and Organizations* and *Global Institutions and Environment*. Students can waive a core class by performing well on an exemption exam prior to the term or, more rarely, by receiving an administrative exemption that requires incoming students to furnish documentation of relevant coursework or work experience. Students are required to maintain a 3.0 GPA and complete 79 units to graduate. Most students complete well more than half of this requirement by the end of the first year and elect to take fewer classes during the second year in order to focus on their career search.

Course enrollment. Incoming students are automatically enrolled in core classes. Second-year students have priority over all electives and are provided an enrollment date and time. Elective courses are then added on a first-come, first-serve basis, compared to the bidding systems that many other top MBA programs employ. Although popular electives fill quickly, they are offered on multiple days and at multiple times so students who enroll on the first day of enrollment rarely have a problem securing a class. Wait lists are offered for full classes, and multiple spots usually open during the beginning of the term as students are adjusting their schedules by adding and dropping courses. This policy makes it easier for students to take their desired courses than at some other top business schools.

Popular Professors

The Fuqua faculty is populated with many prominent business leaders, researchers, and teachers. Among Duke MBA students, a handful of professors are considered a "must have" due to their reputation both as educators and as experts. This list isn't merely a collection of famous names, but rather the instructors that Fuqua students deem to be essential for the full experience. These notable professors include:

Dan Ariely

James B. Duke Professor of Behavioral Economics
Professor Ariely is a fairly recent addition to the Fuqua School of Business, hailing from MIT's Sloan School of Management. Although he first began teaching in 2007, his classes immediately reached capacity with extensive waiting lists. Unregistered students are sometimes spotted in his classroom just to hear his lectures. Students rave about Professor Ariely's behavioral economics class and his highly acclaimed book, *Predictably Irrational*, which has been hailed as the next *Freakonomics* and is used extensively in his course. Professor Ariely focuses on how people actually act in the marketplace as opposed to how rational people are expected to behave. He has also provided commentary for the *New York Times* and CNN, with his research being cited in *New York Magazine*, the *Washington Post*, and *Financial Times*.

Doug Breeden

William W. Priest, Jr. Professor of Finance
Professor Breeden is the former dean of the Fuqua School of Business and a highly respected Fuqua faculty member. He is also the founder and chairman of the successful Smith Breeden Associates, a global asset management firm with more than $10 billion under management. Smith Breeden frequently hires Fuqua interns and graduates. Professor Breeden donated generously during Fuqua's recent building expansion, and Breeden Hall was named in his honor. In 2010, Professor Breeden was elected into the Society of Fellows of the American Finance Association, a select group of distinguished finance scholars. With Professor Breeden's acclaimed academic and professional background, his finance classes are in high demand and fill up immediately.

DUKE (FUQUA)

David Robinson

William and Sue Gross Distinguished Research Fellow, Professor of Finance

Professor Robinson is a very popular instructor due to his keen finance and entrepreneurial insight as well as his engaging discussions and unique sense of humor. His *Entrepreneurial Finance* class is always in high demand. The class features guest speakers including successful entrepreneurs and venture capitalists as well as a consulting firm, which presents a live case. Professor Robinson is very approachable and often provides guidance to students interested in entrepreneurial pursuits.

Shane Dikolli

Assistant Professor of Accounting

Professor Dikolli hails from Australia and has established himself as a highly demanded professor. His passion and ability to make abstract concepts easy to understand make him very popular. Students rave about his interesting lectures, in which he provides unique and relevant examples to explore academic theories. He has won the DaimlerChrysler teaching award multiple times and was named the fourth-most-popular professor in a 2011 *BusinessWeek* survey. He frequently attends Fuqua Fridays and other events to enjoy social and academic conversations with current students.

Similar Academic Programs

Michigan (Ross). Similar to Fuqua, Ross places a great deal of emphasis on developing practical leaders through a heavy emphasis on teamwork and an unparalleled practicum through its Multi-disciplined Action Project (MAP).

Berkeley (Haas). Fuqua has a strong emphasis on global business leadership, and Haas offers global consulting projects through its International Business Development program as well as significant exchange opportunities. Its student body is also known for being very collegial and friendly.

Penn (Wharton). You don't see many comparisons between Fuqua and Wharton, which tend to attract very different MBA candidates, but their core curricula are remarkably similar. Each school offers students significant flexibility while focusing on very traditional MBA subjects of statistics, accounting, finance, economics, marketing, and so forth. With Wharton's increased emphasis on management communications, the two schools' core requirements have become even more similar in recent years. Both schools also have strong programs in health care.

Vanderbilt (Owen) and Yale. Vanderbilt and Yale are also strong healthcare schools with an emphasis in the business of health care with collaborative and collegial learning environments.

EMPLOYMENT & CAREERS AT FUQUA

What Fuqua Is Known For

Breadth, not depth. Fuqua doesn't like career stereotypes. When it comes to career placement, it's not a "finance" school or a "marketing" school or an "anything else" school; rather, the school sends new grads to a wide range of industries in a variety of locations.

Health care. Fuqua sends a greater percentage of graduates (9%) into health care than nearly any of other top-tier program with the exception of UNC Kenan-Flager, which place 13% of its graduates into this industry. Fuqua offers a certificate in Health Sector Management and attracts all the major healthcare companies to recruiting, including Medtronic, GlaxoSmithKline, Amgen, Becton Dickinson, Genentech, and many more.

Graduates entering the healthcare industry

UNC Kenan-Flagler	13%
Fuqua	**9%**
Wharton, Tuck, Sloan, & Kellogg	6%
Harvard	5%
Stanford, Haas, & Yale	4%

Marketing. Fuqua sends 21% of its class into marketing and product management roles after graduation, which is the same proportion as Kellogg, widely seen as the top consumer marketing program. UCLA Anderson sent a higher percentage of graduates (32%) into this field than any other top-tier school, although many of those graduates tend to go into technology product management roles rather than consumer packaged goods (CPG) marketing. Because MBA programs report marketing and product management as the same job function in their employment reports, Anderson, Berkeley-Haas, Stanford, and other tech-heavy programs tend to skew these statistics.

Graduates taking marketing/product management positions

UCLA Anderson	32%
Haas	27%
Stanford	24%
Ross & Texas	22%
Fuqua & Kellogg	**21%**

Energy. Although the sheer numbers of Fuqua graduates entering the energy industry isn't large (3% of graduates), the school is regarded as having one of the top energy programs in the country. The school offers MBA concentrations in Energy & Environment and Energy Finance, while most MBA programs don't even offer a single course specific to the energy sector.

You Oughta Know

Technology. Most applicants don't associate Fuqua with the technology sector like they might Stanford, MIT Sloan, or UCLA Anderson, which have historically sent large percentages of graduates into this industry after graduation. However, Duke sent 20% of its Class of 2014 grads into tech, which isn't far behind Stanford's 24%, and more than double the percentage that other top-tier schools such as NYU Stern (6%) and Yale (10%) send into this industry.

Graduates entering the technology industry

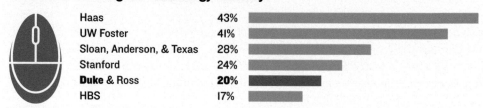

Haas	43%
UW Foster	41%
Sloan, Anderson, & Texas	28%
Stanford	24%
Duke & Ross	**20%**
HBS	17%

Liked by recruiters. Because Duke MBA students bring strong teamwork skills and a lack of entitlement found at some other MBA programs, they are well liked among recruiters. This reputation was a strong driver behind the school's surprise leap in the Bloomberg *Businessweek* ranking to the #1 full-time MBA program in 2014. While we at Veritas Prep don't endorse the overall ranking, we think it shows the value of Duke's collaborative culture in the eyes of recruiters.

Salaries. Not that all you care about is money, but surely you want to make sure your MBA investment is worthwhile. So it should make you happy to learn that the overall median salary for the Class of 2014 was $111,000, with consulting leading the way at an average salary of $135,000. Fuqua's average salary lagged Harvard's and Stanford's by about $15,000, which we see as a better indicator of how recruiters value graduates of each program. Just remember to be a bit careful when looking at overall average salary numbers because they can be skewed by high salaries in particular industries. Schools that send fewer students to those industries can be at a disadvantage. But wait—that's not all! Signing bonuses were also common, with 81% receiving them (median $25,000).

87% of students in the Class of 2014 had full-time job offers at graduation. By August, more than 94% had offers.

Employment statistics. Eighty-seven percent of students in the Class of 2014 seeking full-time employment had offers at graduation; by August that number reached 94%. Seventy-two percent of full-time offers were Fuqua-facilitated.

Grade disclosure. Although schools like Wharton and Columbia have grade non-disclosure policies that prevent recruiters from asking about your grades, Fuqua has a full disclosure policy. So be prepared to talk grades during your recruiting interviews, particularly with finance companies.

Nuts & Bolts

Career Development Resources

The Career Management Center (CMC) provides tools, services, and other resources to all students. In fact, the CMC contacts incoming students prior to arrival to prepare students for job search–related activities. The CMC has numerous counselors specializing in different industries. Each CMC counselor has strong relationships with many top corporations. Students are encouraged to take advantage of these resources from the moment they step onto campus and as alumni.

Fuqua's Career Management team offers a number of opportunities for students, including:

On-campus recruitment. The majority of Fuqua students secure jobs and internships via on-campus interviews. Students submit cover letters and resumes to target companies, and some are selected by the company for interviews. Students who aren't selected have the option to bid for an interview slot using a finite number of points they are granted at the beginning of the school year. If a student unsuccessfully bids for an interview slot, those points are returned to the student.

Alumni network. Fuqua's alumni network of more than 19,000 is extremely loyal and very approachable. Fuqua students have access to the alumni network database as well as access to the University-wide network of more than 130,000 alumni. The Fuqua alumni network also provides ongoing workshops and networking events for all Fuqua alumni. Additionally, there are numerous alumni clubs in various cities around the world.

Week-in-Cities. Organized by the different student functional clubs, these trips offer students the opportunity to make less-formal visits to companies prior to the interview season so that they can research the companies and connect with current employees. The trips usually take place over the break between second and third term. For example, past marketing club Week-in-Cities events have included trips to companies such as Unilever, PepsiCo, Diageo, and J&J, to name a few. These occur in different cities such as New York and Chicago, the Bay Area, etc.

Similar Programs for Professional Opportunities

Northwestern (Kellogg). Kellogg's and Fuqua's placement statistics are remarkably similar across the board, emphasizing breadth rather than depth. Neither is known as a finance school (14% of the Class of 2014 for Kellogg; 18% for Fuqua), but both schools have nearly identical numbers in consulting, consumer products, technology, and even energy.

Michigan (Ross). Ross and Fuqua are also near-twins when it comes to industry placement, posting essentially matching numbers in consulting, consumer goods, finance, and manufacturing.

Berkeley (Haas). Haas also shares a number of similarities, since both it and Fuqua send relatively few candidates into the finance industry, at 18% and 12% respectively. Four percent of the Berkeley-Haas Class of 2014 went into health care, driven by strong recruiting in the the Bay Area's booming biotech industry. Haas also sends more than one in 10 graduates into the energy sector, so it should certainly be on the shortlist of any applicant with aspirations in that industry. The key difference is in technology, where a whopping 43% of Haas grads head after school, compared to 20% of the Fuqua class. However, Fuqua's placements in technology doubled for the Class of 2014, and are higher than many other top-tier schools.

Penn (Wharton). Again, this comparison isn't made frequently, but the two schools' strong connections to the healthcare sector make Duke and Wharton comparable, at least in that field.

UNC (Kenan-Flagler). For opportunities in finance, consumer goods/retail, and health care, UNC's placement statistics are quite similar to Duke's. Twenty-four percent of the Class of 2014 placed in the finance industry upon graduation, which is a little higher than Duke's placement of 18% in this industry. In addition, 10% of each school's class pursued opportunities in the consumer goods/retail industry. What makes the schools remarkably similar is their niche placement in health care. UNC placed 13% of its Class of 2014 in the healthcare industry, compared to 9% from Duke—both high placements compared to other top-tier business schools. In comparison, Stern and Booth placed 2% into the healthcare industry.

CULTURE & CAMPUS LIFE AT FUQUA

What Fuqua Is Known For

Duke University and Durham. Duke's home of Durham, North Carolina, is in the heart of the famous Research Triangle that includes Raleigh, Durham, and Chapel Hill. This is a beautiful area that is very cosmopolitan and intellectually rich with a growing restaurant and indie music scene. Duke's rigorous undergraduate program is one of the best in the nation and is consistently near the top of every ranking system: In 2015, *U.S. News & World Report* ranked Duke's undergrad program eighth overall. Duke University also has noteworthy graduate school programs in business, law, and medicine; the basketball program is also, well, kinda famous. Duke also features an enormous campus (known as the "Gothic Wonderland") relative to the school's student population—nearly 9,000 acres for less than 14,000 total students.

Team Fuqua. You'll hear the term *Team Fuqua* used on a near-daily basis around campus. Not only is teamwork strongly emphasized in academics, but the student body is known for its friendly and tight-knit nature. The admissions committee specifically seeks out applicants who they think will fit well with this friendly group, so a natural outcrop of this selection process are numerous social events, clubs, and activities. Although many schools boast of their collaborative environments, if you're looking for a strong dose of activities and parties, Fuqua ranks among the top. We'll go into greater detail about several of them in the You Oughta Know section below.

Blue Devils basketball. What do you get when you combine the collaborative culture of Fuqua with a university that's passionate about basketball? The Campout experience. It's unique to Duke but makes sense given the strong basketball history at the school. Graduate students camp out in RVs for 36 hours over one weekend to enter a lottery for season basketball tickets, and, in true Team Fuqua spirit, typically form large teams to increase their chances of winning and then split up the tickets to the games among everyone. People rent trucks and RVs, and bring lots of food, drinks, music, and other entertainment (if this is starting to sound like a weekend-long tailgate...). The legendary "Coach K" has been known to make an appearance to thank the students for their support.

You Oughta Know

Must-attend events. As we mentioned, Fuqua is a fun environment and the students host many, many social events throughout the year. Below are some of the activities that students have said you "must attend" to have a complete Fuqua experience. This will give you just a small taste of life at Fuqua, and how it differs from many other business schools.

- **Fuqua Fridays.** The aforementioned Fuqua Fridays offer a weekly opportunity for students, faculty, and staff to mingle; many are often themed, so it's not only food and drink. Different student clubs often choose to host one, and themes have included celebrations of different cultures (Indian, Asian, Latin, African-American), a marketing brand challenge that pits branded products against private label brands in creative ways, and Casino Night, where students get to play games such as blackjack, poker, and roulette.

DUKE (FUQUA)

- **FuquaVision.** Many business schools produce an end-of-year follies show to highlight all the awkward moments, inside jokes, and common experience of the year. At Fuqua, they produce a show after every quarter! Each FuquaVision production includes skits and videos lampooning all aspects of Fuqua life.

- **Winter ski trip.** First-year and second-year students descend upon a different ski resort each year for the annual ski trip. Everyone goes all-out for their costumes during the themed parties each year, particularly the perennial '80s party.

- **MBA Blue Cup.** Each year, Fuqua competes against cross-town rival, UNC Kenan-Flagler, in a series of intense competitions for the MBA Blue Cup title. Events include golf, ping pong, bowling, volleyball, and other sports, with bragging rights extending a full year!

- **MBA Games.** Fuqua invites business schools from around the country to compete against one another in various light-hearted competitions to raise money for Special Olympics. MBA Games events include dance-offs, tug-of-war, the izzy dizzy bat race, the business suit relay, and briefcase toss, among others. The weekend also includes a couple of parties and good times had by all.

- **LDOC.** LDOC (Last Day of Class) is a campus-wide event hosted by Duke undergraduates featuring A-list musicians performing on the campus quad.

- **Beach Week.** Hundreds of second-year students invade the beach homes of North or South Carolina in the gap between their final classes and graduation. This is the last big party for Fuqua students before they have to face "the real world" again.

> **The cost of living in Durham is substantially lower than in cities like New York, Boston, and San Francisco, meaning students can maintain a relatively comfortable standard of living without breaking the bank or maxing out student loans.**

Where to live. Almost all Fuqua students live off campus, and the majority live in just a handful of complexes. American students without families tend to live in Station 9, Trinity Commons, and the Lofts at Lakeview, which are closer to Fuqua and near nightlife. International students and Americans with families more often live at Alexan Place, Pinnacle Ridge, and Alexan Farm, which are about 15 minutes away from Fuqua but are much less expensive.

Getting around. The cost of living in Durham is substantially lower than in cities like New York, Boston, and San Francisco, meaning students can maintain a relatively comfortable standard of living without breaking the bank (or maxing out their student loans). However, public transit is minimal, and many of the apartments are far enough from campus that you'll need a car, so make sure to budget for that—and if you're a city kid without a license, that's one more test you'll have to take (after the GMAT, of course). The driving averse will want to consider the one of the several apartment complexes within biking distance to campus.

Facilities. The Fuqua School of Business has grown significantly in the past 30 years and, at roughly 500,000 square feet, it is quite an impressive sight. What began as one large building is now several state-of-the-art buildings all linked together. These buildings house innovative technology to enhance productivity, teamwork, and strategic decision making. Ample team rooms fill the Fuqua School along with the newly expanded Ford Library, computer center, auditoriums, and classrooms. All of the Fuqua MBA programs, from the full-time program to the numerous executive programs, are housed in the Fuqua complex, although some of the executive degrees are distance-learning programs. At the heart of Fuqua is the Fox Student Center. Opened in 2002, the Fox Center, with its indoor winter garden and outdoor terraces, has been compared to a grand hotel lobby.

The Fuqua complex also includes the R. David Thomas Executive Conference Center, a 112,000-square-foot facility named after the founder of Wendy's. The center includes guest rooms, executive suites, a 230-seat luxury dining room, and a full bar where many Fuqua students congregate prior to Fuqua Friday events. The Thomas Center is primarily used by the school's executive education and executive MBA students. One of the newest additions to the Fuqua Campus is Breeden Hall, added in 2008. The new building spans 91,400 square feet with state-of-the-art classrooms, team rooms, auditoriums, and a rooftop terrace. With this new addition and the expansion of the Ford Library, the Fuqua School of Business occupies an impressive 500,000 square feet adjacent to the Duke School of Law on the Duke University West Campus.

Cross-campus interaction. Although the Fuqua School of Business resides in close proximity to other distinguished Duke University graduate schools, there is little interaction between Fuqua students and other Duke graduate students. This is partly due to the business school's self-contained facility, which hosts an abundance of Fuqua-related activities and services. Because the center boasts a state-of-the-art facility and robust activity calendar, graduate students from other Duke University programs are often spotted enjoying Fuqua amenities. Undergraduate Duke students and Fuqua students also rarely interact, partly because there is no formal undergraduate business school. Nevertheless, the business school's convenient location relative to the football stadium, lacrosse field, and ever-popular Cameron Indoor Basketball Stadium provides ample opportunities to enjoy the full collegiate experience with the entire student body.

Similar Programs Culturally

Dartmouth (Tuck). If you're looking for a very tight-knit student body whose strong culture builds lifelong bonds among its students, Tuck's concentrated social and academic environment creates a deep sense of connection with the school and the highest alumni giving rates of any top-tier school. Like Duke, its campus is not located in a major urban center.

Berkeley (Haas). Although it has a smaller enrollment, Haas's student body is also known for being very collegial and friendly with an emphasis on teamwork.

Northwestern (Kellogg). If you're interested in a student-run and teamwork-focused general curriculum with a particular strength in marketing and consulting placement, you can't miss with Kellogg.

DUKE (FUQUA)

Michigan (Ross). Ross, Kellogg, and Fuqua are often mentioned in the same breath. Fuqua students are found at every Blue Devils basketball game, and many Ross students are equally obsessed with Michigan football.

UCLA (Anderson). Student involvement is at the core of Anderson's culture, where the ideas of shared success and "paying it forward" are key. Students certainly make the most of Anderson's Southern California location, with frequent beach activities and other events throughout Westwood, Santa Monica, and West Los Angeles. Andersonians are a lively crew, holding professional and interest-based social events throughout the week, ranging from tailgate parties at Bruins football games to "Dinner for 8" networking events with prominent alums.

ADMISSIONS AT FUQUA

What Fuqua Is Looking For

Fuqua uses four criteria for admission to its programs:

- Applicants who they believe will be successful in the program. (This typically means that you've proved you can do the academic work and that they can help you with your career goals.)

- Applicants who will add significant value to the program and the school throughout their professional, personal, and academic experiences. (This is another way of asking how you'll contribute and how the learning environment will benefit from your presence. Remember: Community is an integral part of the school's culture.)

- Applicants who believe diversity in thought and background are important within their community.

- Applicants who demonstrate competence, character, and purpose, and have the strongest potential to be a *leader of consequence*.

(If you're paying attention, you've noticed that "leader of consequence" phrase cropping up pretty regularly. If you're not paying attention, now might be a good time to start reflecting on how you meet that criterion.)

 If you are looking for tips on 2016–17 admissions essays, you're in luck! Check out our website at **veritasprep.com/fuqua** for our latest advice.

Preparing to Apply

Reading this Essential Guide is a great first step in your preparation. Hopefully, this insider's glimpse has been helpful in understanding the most important aspects of the school. However, nothing can replace gaining firsthand knowledge and experience yourself.

Reach out to current students. Even if you don't have any personal connections to Fuqua, you can reach out to current students and get their insight and advice. On the school's campus groups page, you'll find a list of all campus clubs. Find a few clubs that fit your personal and professional interests, and reach out to the officers. Remember: These are very busy MBA students so you don't want to intrude too much on their time, but you could ask for a 10- to 15-minute conversation or elicit some advice via e-mail. Come prepared with specific questions (preferably those that aren't already answered online). If you're planning to visit campus, perhaps you might even arrange a coffee chat or lunch, if they are available.

Visit campus. The school's website can only tell you so much; by far, a personal visit is the best possible research in the application process. If you have the means, we highly recommend you visit Fuqua in person along with the campuses of your other top choices to understand the significant differences in culture, teaching style, student body, recruiting opportunities, facilities, and so forth. You may be surprised at just how different each school can be and and how the reality can differ from the perception. We encourage you to take advantage of opportunities to visit campus, including a tour, lunch with students, class visit, and special panel discussions, as available. Because informal and impromptu encounters can be the most informative, don't be afraid to approach students in less-formal settings.

Open Interview period. Early in the fall, Fuqua will allow you to request an admissions interview even before your application has been submitted. We recommend that you take advantage of the Open Interview period, if possible, as this shows your genuine interest in the school. We discuss the interviews in greater detail later in this section.

Other events. We know that many applicants will not be able to travel to North Carolina to visit campus, but you should take advantage of other worldwide admissions events, such as information sessions, virtual sessions, and specific-audience events. In fact, these off-campus events can offer great opportunities for quality time with admissions officers and your fellow applicants, who can be a great resource and support through the admissions process. Get to know the school and its culture as well as you can, because your familiarity can shine through your application and essays to help you stand out.

> **We recommend that you take advantage of the Open Interview period, if possible, as this shows your genuine interest in the school.**

DUKE (FUQUA)

You Oughta Know

When should I apply? Duke uses a standard three-round system for applications, plus an added Early Action round. This means that you may submit your application in any of its four rounds for consideration. However, 90% or more of the class will be filled by Round 2, so we do not encourage you to wait until the final round without compelling circumstances.

Traditional candidates. If you are a traditional candidate from management consulting or finance, we encourage you to apply in Early Action or Round 1 (assuming you have a strong GMAT score), as you'll be competing against many candidates with very similar profiles. In a later round, it's possible that the school may see you as a viable candidate to the school but may have already admitted several other applicants with similar profiles, so it might pass on you to bring greater professional diversity to the class. (Plus, the school knows you've been planning on an MBA since the day you graduated from undergrad, so there's no reason to delay!)

Don't rush! Please note that even though the top schools encourage you to apply in the earliest round possible, this does not mean that you should apply with a rushed application or a mediocre GMAT score. There's no sense in applying early if you're just going to be denied. A GMAT score that's above the school's average will do more for your candidacy than applying in the first round. Fuqua itself advises, "Given the competitive applicant pool, you are encouraged to apply in the round in which you can submit your 'best' application."

Deadlines. Fuqua's admissions deadlines are virtually unchanged versus last year: There's an Early Action round ending September 15, 2015, and three "regular" rounds with deadlines on October 14, 2015; January 5, 2016; and March 22, 2016. One important note about the school's Early Action deadline: Even though it's called "Early Action," which most schools interpret as "non-binding," Fuqua considers it to be a binding agreement that you will attend the school if admitted. So, we only recommend applying in this round if Fuqua is clearly your first choice. If it's not, save your application for Round 1; you'll still receive your final decision from the admissions committee before the holidays. Interview invitations are issued approximately four weeks after the deadline, and admissions decisions are sent four weeks after that. You'll want to apply in the earliest round possible for full consideration for financial aid.

The Essays

We've focused on the short answer and essay questions asked in Duke's Daytime MBA program, but the concepts can be applied to its myriad other programs, too. Duke hasn't added or cut the number of required essays this year for the Daytime program, although it did add a new option for the second required essay. The "25 Random Things" prompt remains, which makes us happy! (And probably makes you happy, too, since it's fun to write.)

Short Answers. These three prompts are unchanged from last year.

1. What are your short-term goals, post-MBA? (500 characters maximum)

This short answer question is very straightforward and should be seen in some sense as a "Why an MBA?" question. However, your response should be specifically targeted to your post-MBA role. The admissions committee is evaluating several things with this essay:

Unambiguous. First, do you understand and can you articulate directly what you want to do? They are looking for you to state with clarity and conviction your ideal choice of function and industry. If you seem vague or wavering, it may be a red flag that you don't know why you want an MBA.

Realistic. Second, they are evaluating whether your goal is realistic based on your prior experience and background. Career switching is very common among MBAs, but if you are interested in a highly quantitative role, for example, it would be expected that you have demonstrated ability through test scores, coursework, or prior experience. Conversely, if you write that you want to move into social impact investing, you should show a track record of community engagement.

Balanced. Finally, they will be using this essay to shape their class and ensure a diverse set of interests that generally align with their recruiter pipeline. There is no "right answer," but Fuqua heavily encourages diverse and non-traditional post-MBA goals. They want to see that your interests align with a foreseeable recruiting opportunity, and expect that not every student wants to be a consultant or brand manager. That said, it's more important to be honest and realistic than to be unique here. There's plenty of space available for aspiring management consultants and investment bankers.

2. What are your long-term goals? (500 characters maximum)

Tie things together. It is understood that MBA graduates will change jobs during their career—whether they're pursuing the C-suite, an entrepreneurial opportunity, or other plans. This is where the admissions committee is looking to see if you have thought things through, even though they know you may change your mind down the road. Again, you should be as specific as possible with the roles and industries in your future plans. However, you don't need to spell out that you're going to spend four years in marketing at P&G before launching your own startup. What the admissions committee will be looking for is whether you can "tie it all together" into a coherent and plausible story.

Be ambitious. While you want to provide a vision that makes sense, don't be conservative here. If you have big dreams, be sure to spell them out and convince the admissions committee that you're capable of achieving them. Help them catch a glimpse of the world through your eyes. Your short-term goals should be extremely realistic and achievable; your long-term goals should be more visionary and ambitious.

3. Life is full of uncertainties, and plans and circumstances can change. As a result, navigating a career requires you to be adaptable. Should the short-term goals that you provided above not materialize what alternative directions have you considered? (500 characters maximum)

Connect to your experience. Many applicants consider this question to be a curve ball, but this sort of adaptability is important to show. No one knows how exactly their career will unfold, and with this question Fuqua wants to see if you "get it" and have at least thought through some alternatives. Your answer should be a viable alternative to your top short-term goal, but one that is still aligned with your general professional interests. For example, students interested in investment banking in the healthcare industry might also consider corporate finance in the healthcare industry. Note, however, that certain career tracks, including consulting, investment banking, and private equity, have distinct and demanding recruiting guidelines and are not recommended as alternative directions to one another.

Headlines to your application. This trio of short questions (and really short answers!) should add up to only about 300 words, if it's easier for you to think about them that way. With the three short questions, the admissions team really is just looking for the facts. That doesn't mean that you shouldn't put any thought into these responses, but rather that they're looking for less hand-waving and "big picture"–speak and for more headlines to help them quickly get a read on why you're even applying to Fuqua in the first place. Think of this as your chance to make the admissions team's job a little easier. Rather than having to sort through your application essays to figure out why you're applying, you're spelling it out in three bold, "can't miss" headlines.

Essay 1:
Answer the following question—present your response in list form, numbered 1 to 25. Some points may be only a few words, while others may be longer. Your complete list should not exceed 2 pages.

The "Team Fuqua" spirit and community is one of the things that sets The Duke MBA experience apart, and it is a concept that extends beyond the student body to include faculty, staff, and administration. When a new person joins the Admissions team, we ask that person to share with everyone in the office a list of "25 Random Things About Yourself." As an Admissions team, we already know the new hire's professional and academic background, so learning these "25 Random Things" helps us get to know someone's personality, background, special talents, and more.

In this spirit, the Admissions Committee also wants to get to know you—beyond the professional and academic achievements listed in your resume and transcript. You can share with us important life experiences, your likes/dislikes, hobbies, achievements, fun facts, or anything that helps us understand what makes you who you are. Share with us your list of "25 Random Things" about you. (2 pages maximum, no less than 10-point font)

Be yourself. This question also carries over unchanged from last year. This exercise makes many applicants uncomfortable since it's so far removed from the "typical" MBA admissions essay, but we like it. While you shouldn't generate a completely frivolous list, you also shouldn't simply rehash what else is in your application. Seemingly random facts such as "I once narrowly lost a pizza-eating contest to the eventual state champion" are relevant and reveal something important about you (that you're fun!), whether you realize it or not.

Not every element must stand out. We have seen some advice out there that tells applicants that all 25 items must be "unique" and "ownable," but it would be a mistake to apply that rule to all 25 items. If the favorite part of your week is spending a couple of hours on Sunday morning reading the paper, then it would be crazy for that not to make it into this list, whether or not other applicants might possibly say the same thing. For us, a good rule of thumb is that approximately half of this list should reinforce your application themes (which you should have nailed down long before drafting this list) and the other half can be more "fun." Don't run the risk of putting the admissions committee to sleep with your list. Finally, take a look at the examples that Fuqua admissions officers and students have posted about themselves; you'll see that they're far from 100% serious!

Show how you'll contribute to the culture. In composing your answer to this question, you would also be well served to carefully read and consider the preamble to the essays that clearly lays out characteristics that the admissions committee considers core to the "leaders of consequence" they hope to cultivate at Fuqua. While your list should certainly contain examples of your leadership, impact, and teamwork, you would also be well served to highlight your individuality, passions, and personality. A big part of Fuqua is its colorful and inclusive student-led culture, something that former dean Blair Shepherd believes is essential to making a Fuqua MBA a "transformative" rather than "transactional" experience. The admissions team is looking for people who will bring unique experiences to class discussions, become founders and leaders of clubs, and be active members of the Fuqua community. Applicants are encouraged to show that they understand Fuqua's unique culture and consequently express how they might contribute.

Essay 2:
Please answer only one of the following two questions. (2 pages maximum; 1.5 line spacing; do not include the question in the document.)

Option 1. When asked by your family, friends, and colleagues why you want to go to Duke, what do you tell them? Share the reasons that are most meaningful to you.

Do your homework. This question also carries over unchanged from last year, and that's a strong hint that the Fuqua admissions team likes what it's been getting from applicants. The purpose of this question is really to assess your fit with the school. The school used to simply ask, "Why Duke?" in an essay, but this question is still about fit: This is your opportunity to demonstrate that you have really researched the program, understand its culture, and really want to spend the rest of your life as a member of the Fuqua community. The first eight words of this question are the Fuqua admissions committee's way of saying, "Please don't just tell us what you think we want to hear."

Get personal. Some pragmatic components to your response are totally fine; it has strong ties to the healthcare industry, or has a specific research center that interests you, for instance. That's a completely real, honest response. But the school wants you to go beyond rattling off lists of professor and course names from its website, and convince admissions that you will be eager to attend Fuqua if you're admitted. Conversations with current students or recent alums would help you make this essay much more personal.

Option 2. The Team Fuqua community is as unique as the individuals who comprise it. Underlying our individuality are a number of shared ideas and principles that we live out in our own ways. Our students have identified and defined six "Team Fuqua Principles" that we feel are the guiding philosophies that make our community special:

- *Authentic Engagement: We care and we take action. We each make a difference to Team Fuqua by being ourselves and engaging in and supporting activities about which we are passionate.*
- *Supportive Ambition: We support each other to achieve great things, because your success is my success. The success of each individual member of Team Fuqua makes the whole of Team Fuqua better.*
- *Collective Diversity: We embrace all of our classmates because our individuality is better and stronger together.*
- *Impactful Stewardship: We are leaders who focus on solutions to improve our communities both now and in the future. We aren't satisfied with just maintaining the status quo.*

- ***Loyal Community:*** *We are a family who looks out for each other. Team Fuqua supports you when you need it the most.*
- ***Uncompromising Integrity:*** *We internalize and live the honor code in the classroom and beyond. We conduct ourselves with integrity within Fuqua, within Duke, and within all communities of which we are a part.*

At the end of your two years at Fuqua, if you were to receive an award for exemplifying one of the Principles above, which one would it be and why? Your answer should reflect the research you have done, your knowledge of the Fuqua program and experience, and the types of activities and leadership you would engage in as a Fuqua student.

Show your involvement. This question is new this year, and it's another example of how much emphasis Fuqua places on fit and a desire to find applicants who truly want to attend the school. Fuqua is the classic example of a top business school that's not quite in the uppermost echelon of MBA programs, despite its top spot on the *Businessweek* 2014 rankings. It attracts a lot of applicants, but Fuqua often loses out to other schools when an applicant has multiple offers to choose from. That's not a knock on the school at all; rather, it underscores how tough it is for the Fuqua admissions team to try to determine just how enthusiastic an applicant is for the school. The more you can tailor your responses specifically to Fuqua's offerings, the more the admissions committee will be convinced that their application is not at the bottom of your priority list.

Use examples. Don't just regurgitate what you read in Fuqua's brochures and on its website. This question is your chance to show that you really, truly are enthusiastic about Fuqua, so much so that you see yourself embodying one or more of the traits that Fuqua's own students have identified as the community's core principles. Bring out specific examples of your own past experiences that demonstrate how you embody one of these important traits. There are few more effective ways to show how much you want to be a part of the Fuqua community than by using examples to show you're already a great fit.

Optional Essay:
If you feel there are extenuating circumstances of which the admissions committee should be aware, please explain them here (e.g. unexplained gaps in work, choice of recommenders, inconsistent or questionable academic performance, significant weakness in your application). Note that you should NOT upload additional essays nor additional recommendations in this area. The Optional Essay is intended to provide the admissions committee with insight into your extenuating circumstances only. (1 page maximum; no less than 10-point font; 1.5 line spacing; do not include question in document)

It's really optional. We tell applicants to only use the optional essay if you need to explain potential blemish in your background that isn't fixable (a low undergraduate GPA, time on academic probation, gaps in school or employment history, no recommendation from your current direct supervisor, etc.). There's no need to harp on a minor weakness and sound like you're making excuses when you don't need to. If you do have a red flag in your background, address it here. Otherwise, leave this essay blank.

Recommendations

Fuqua asks first-time applicants to submit two recommendations, both of which should be professional in nature; re-applicants must submit one. One should "reflect your performance in your most recent professional setting"; the school mentions that your volunteer work or community involvement can be "excellent sources" of recommendations.

What they'll be asked. Your recommenders will be asked to answer the following questions:

- *Relationship to applicant [Please select: Advisor, Board Member, Business Associate, Business Partner, Client, Colleague, Current Immediate Supervisor, Department Head, Employee, Former Colleague, Former Manager, Friend, Manager, Mentor, Professor]*
- *How long have you known the applicant?*
- *Are you an alumnus/alumna of Duke University? [Yes, No] If so, please state the year you graduate and the degree received Include name of program, if relevant.*
- *Do you have an MBA from a school other than The Fuqua School of Business? [Yes, No] If so, from what school?*

Leadership behavior grid. Instructions: The grid will facilitate your evaluation of the applicant's competencies and character traits that contribute to successful leadership and program success. *[Multiple-choice assessment based on the following skills/qualities: Results Orientation, Strategic Orientation, Team Leadership, Influence and Collaboration, Communicating, Information Seeking, Developing Others, Change Leadership, Respect for Others, Trustworthiness, Stress Management and Resilience, Global Competence, and English Language Skills (for non-native English speakers).]* Each skill/quality has a different description for its 1–5 rating scale. For example, the scale for Results Orientation is as follows: *5) (Low) Fulfills assigned tasks; 4) Overcomes obstacles to achieve goals; 3) Exceeds goals and raises effectiveness of organization; 2) Introduces incremental improvements to enhance business performance using robust analysis; 1) (High) Invents and delivers best in class standards and performance; or, No Basis.*

Letter of reference. *Instructions: In your letter of reference, please provide insight about the applicant in the areas described below. Help us understand the applicant's leadership potential and highlight the traits and skills the applicant possesses that will contribute to success. Please be specific and provide concrete examples where possible. We ask that you refrain from using material provided by the applicant so as to present only your unique view of his/her potential. We recognize the time and effort this request constitutes and we are most appreciative of your investment in this process.*

1. *Comment briefly on the context of your interaction with the applicant.*
2. *How do the applicant's performance, potential, or personal qualities compare to those of other well-qualified individuals in similar roles?*
3. *What do you perceive as the applicant's areas for growth? Describe the applicant's awareness of these areas and his/her response to constructive feedback.*
4. *Please include additional comments you feel will be helpful to the Admissions Committee.*

Please limit your letter of reference to two pages, double spaced. Outdated or general letters that do not address the points above do not strengthen the candidate's application.

DUKE (FUQUA)

Selecting your recommenders. Fuqua explicitly says that "the most valuable recommendations come from people who know your professional skills and abilities." In other words, don't ask your company's CEO, whom you might or might not have met once in the cafeteria. And hopefully you don't need to be told this, but Fuqua discourages recommendations from friends and relatives. Fuqua allows applicants to submit additional recommendations from current students or alumni; if these are submitted soon enough, you could even get your application fee reduced!

Should I draft it myself? Many applicants to business school are asked by their superiors to draft the recommendation themselves and the recommender will approve it. We strongly recommend that you do not write the recommendation yourself for several reasons. First, your writing style and choice of phrasing are unique, and admissions officers will notice if the recommendations are similar to each other and your essays. If they notice too many similarities, your application could be denied outright. Second, you may tend to be too humble or generic. Your supervisor might use language such as "one of the top analysts I've seen in my entire career" that you wouldn't dare include if writing on his or her behalf. Third, and perhaps most importantly, the admissions officer is looking for a third-party perspective on your candidacy, so writing a recommendation yourself is an unethical breach of trust with the school you are looking to join.

Preparing your recommenders. Instead of writing the recommendation yourself, you should sit down and have candid conversations with your recommenders about the reasons you want to go to business school and why you've selected your target schools, your professional goals, and your experience together. Ask them if they would have the time to write a strong recommendation on your behalf. (This also gives them a nice "out" by telling you they are too busy rather than saying they don't feel comfortable giving you a positive recommendation.) Bring a copy of your resume and a bulleted list of projects that you've worked on together and accomplishments they have seen you achieve. Let them know that admissions committees prefer to see specific, detailed examples in recommendations. Then, let them know that you'll serve as a "project manager" to follow up and ensure that they are able to submit your recommendation ahead of the deadline.

The Interview

Visiting campus. The interview is a big deal at Duke—mostly because they really, really want you to come to campus to do it. Other schools conduct interviews almost at the convenience of the applicant, with even phone or Skype interviews being offered in some cases. Not at Duke. They feel that Team Fuqua is a part of the evaluating process, and Team Fuqua is on campus. They want you to come to campus and experience it for yourself, so they can sell you on Duke at the same time as you're trying to sell yourself to them. Duke offers two types of interviews: Open and Invitation.

Open Interviews. Open Interviews are applicant-initiated, meaning you sign up for it yourself, even before you've submitted your application. Although the window for them this season is September 8, 2015–October 14, 2015, applicants from any round are eligible for an Open Interview. These interviews are more evaluative in nature and are conducted by a current student on campus. Duke offers these Open Interviews as a way to have a more "open" admissions process and also to encourage candidates to get involved in their campus community before applying.

Interview invitations. If you don't schedule an Open Interview, you may be invited to interview after submitting your application. Interviews are not technically required for admission at Duke (in fact, until just a few years ago they were optional), though 99.9% of admitted students go through the interview process. The exceptions (still in rare cases) may be active military or other significant extenuating circumstances. Interviews can be conducted on campus at Duke (the admissions committee explicitly prefers that candidates come to Durham to interview) or in select cities around the world on a specific schedule published by the admissions committee ("hubs" and "non-hubs"). International interviews may be conducted by almost anyone involved in the Fuqua community: a member of the admissions committee, an alum, or a current student.

Book it fast. Interviews need to be scheduled very quickly once an invitation is issued, so it pays to check the schedule carefully before you even submit your application to ensure that you will be available if and when that invite comes. The Duke admissions committee is quite clear that they expect invited candidates to be available on those pre-announced dates and asks you not to submit an application in a particular round if you know you will be unavailable.

What can I expect? Like many top schools, interviews at Duke are "blind," meaning the interviewer has not read any part of the application except for the resume. Interviewers are trained to structure interviews as a conversation among colleagues, and not to try to intimidate or trip up candidates. The questions are designed to get to know the candidate and include the standard questions: Tell me about yourself (aka walk me through your resume); Why an MBA?; Why Duke?; Discuss your team and leadership experiences. Each interviewer may have a different style or approach and could potentially ask other, more unique questions.

Ask questions. Additionally, since this is a conversation, it's also encouraged that you get to know your interviewer a little bit and be prepared to ask him or her questions relevant to your interests. Be mindful that despite interviewers' approachable and collegial demeanor, this is still an interview and candidates must remain professional at all times.

MIT SLOAN

Hands-on learning that's always pushing the boundaries of innovation.

📍 CAMBRIDGE, MA

CLASS SIZE	PROGRAM FOUNDED	SETTING
406	1914	URBAN

CHARACTERISTICS

FRIENDLY, ENGINEERS, LAB COURSES

MIT (SLOAN)

SECTIONS

MIT SLOAN SNAPSHOT

What MIT Sloan Is Known For

Learning by doing. The MIT Sloan approach to management education can be summarized with the Institute's motto: "mens et manus," or "mind and hand." More than just a token motto, this is a way of thinking that permeates the culture across all programs at MIT. Both in and out of the classroom, "learning by doing" is very much a part of the MIT Sloan culture. Called "Action Learning," this philosophy is best evidenced in the wide offering of lab courses in which students conduct consulting projects for real companies and organizations.

A challenging curriculum. The first semester at MIT Sloan is notoriously challenging—more so even than at other top schools. All students take the same set of five required core courses in that first term, and it's known to be grueling. Most schools have a fixed core that extends over two semesters and, while challenging, it typically isn't quite as brutal as the one-semester core at MIT Sloan.

Collaboration. A lesser-known fact among many potential applicants is that MIT Sloan enjoys a deeply collaborative culture. From the first moments of the intense "One-Semester Core" experience, to the launch of fledgling startups upon graduation, the desire to work with and help fellow students is shared by most Sloan students throughout their MBA experience. MIT Sloan views the art of developing high-performing teams as crucial to addressing today's business challenges, and strives to cultivate effective teams and leaders through action-based learning in the field.

What Makes MIT Sloan Different

Following the rigorous first-semester core, students are given the remaining 75% of their time at Sloan to craft their own curriculum.

Entrepreneurship and self-direction. The MIT Sloan MBA program is customizable, allowing for each student to focus on developing specific leadership and analytical skill sets while pursuing a unique set of interests. Following the rigorous and intense experience of the first-semester core, students are given the remaining 75% of their time at Sloan to focus on a certificate program of their choice or create an informal specialization of their own. The Sloan admissions committee targets students who are proactive, creative, and comfortable with ambiguity. These entrepreneurial traits are all helpful in this environment, in which each individual student has a higher degree of responsibility of making the most of their time at Sloan.

Technology. Given the strength of MIT and engineering, it's no surprise that MIT Sloan has a superior offering in the area of tech ventures and IT. Innovation is a buzzword at many top business schools, but Sloan embodies it, particularly in the area of high tech. Support for an entrepreneur in launching a new venture at business school is stronger at MIT than almost anywhere else.

Sustainability. Sloan has a concerted focus on "green" business, and the relatively new Certificate in Sustainability is one of the few formal programs of its kind at any top school. MIT Sloan also has a track record for putting its money where its mouth is: Not only is the new E62 building at Sloan LEED Gold certified for environmental friendliness, but MIT's admissions team also recently converted Apple iPads in order to make their entire admissions process paper-free.

Open access to information. Not just Sloan, but all of MIT believes in sharing information, and the school is a pioneer in the way it's made its educational content—nearly all of it—available for free on the web through the MIT OpenCourseWare initiative. This includes a vast array of Sloan courses, from undergraduate to graduate to PhD. These course materials are open to everyone, though the school does not grant degrees or certificates, or provide any proof of completion. (It is no substitute for the actual MBA experience.)

Sloan Fellows. Most schools keep their executive MBA students totally separate from their full-time students—even sequestered in a separate building or a totally separate campus. But not Sloan. The Sloan Fellows are a select group of highly experienced, mid-career students who take classes right along with the full-time students, adding valuable real-world insights to the classroom.

MIT Sloan Is a Good Fit for You If...

You're an engineer or a techie. Nearly half of MIT Sloan's Class of 2016 had undergraduate degrees in STEM fields. On the flip side, if you're an engineer, you'll have to work that much harder to stand out in a crowded field. Of course, since half the class came from other fields, contrary to popular opinion, you don't have to be an engineer to get in. The Sloan admissions team does not specifically seek out engineers, but the brand name of MIT tends to attract more of them in the application pool.

You're an entrepreneur (or want to be one). While it's probably obvious that MIT Sloan would be a good school for someone interested in tech ventures, what may be surprising to some is that Sloan is strong on all things entrepreneurial. No matter what type of entrepreneurial business you want to launch, you'll find good support for it at MIT, including its $100K Business Plan Competition.

You're interested in finance. Many people may not realize how extensive the finance resources are at MIT, nor how deep its roots are in the field. Regardless of where you earn your MBA, you will likely learn about the Black-Scholes formula to model the market for a particular equity. Fischer Black and Myron Scholes originated this model, and Robert Merton published a paper on it—all of them professors at MIT. MIT offered courses in finance before most other schools, and it remains a strength of the program, even though relatively few graduates (less than 15%) move into finance careers each year.

> Sloan Fellows, a select group of highly experienced mid-career students, take classes right along with the full-time students.

MIT (SLOAN)

You're not afraid of quant. While MIT Sloan is not just looking for "quant jocks," its curriculum incorporates analytical and quantitative practices into every field, including those that may seem "softer." You certainly can't be afraid of the more analytical and quantitative aspects of business! MIT Sloan was the birthplace of Marketing Science, and its undergraduate degree is a bachelor of science in Management Science. Its intense first-semester core curriculum includes *Economic Analysis; Data, Models, and Decisions; Organizational Processes* (focusing on analytical tools needed for organizations); and *Financial Accounting.*

You're interested in operations or supply chain management. With the LGO (Leaders for Global Operations) program and the opportunity to take classes campus-wide at MIT, Sloan students interested in a career in manufacturing or logistics have a wealth of resources and the best academic researchers in the world at their disposal.

You're interested in "green" business. With the Certificate in Sustainability at MIT Sloan and its institute-wide sustainability initiative, MIT is leading the way in a focus on "green" business. While plenty of other schools have strong social venture programs, with more popping up all the time, the emphasis at Sloan is cutting-edge and integrated.

You're a woman. While strong female candidates are well received at most schools, MIT Sloan often gets fewer applications from women because of the misperception that it's strictly a techie school. Female applicants still need to present a strong profile, including a good GMAT score and academic history. The Class of 2016 had 39% women (higher than Columbia, Yale, Duke, Berkeley-Haas, Ross, and Tuck), a strong number indicating that female applicants who do meet Sloan's admissions criteria have an exceptionally good chance of getting an offer from MIT.

40% of MIT Sloan's most recent incoming class were non–U.S. citizens.

Your passport says something other than "USA." A whopping 40% of MIT Sloan's most recent incoming class were non–U.S. citizens. That's one of the highest of any of the top-tier MBA programs, with only Stanford and Columbia bringing in a larger percentage of international citizens. The MIT brand is recognized worldwide, so the business school sees large numbers of qualified international applicants.

ACADEMICS AT MIT SLOAN

What MIT Sloan Is Known For

Analytical rigor. MIT Sloan's MBA curriculum grew out of "the conviction that, in education as in business, leadership belongs to those who reject the comfort of the status quo." The curriculum offers a high degree of flexibility, and encourages freedom and experimentation. After the intense, shared experience of the first-semester core, students are free to build a highly personalized course of study. Courses are designed to be rigorous analytically, but also to push students to think in new ways and experiment with their own development as leaders, managers, and team members. Throughout the wide variety of courses, there is an effort to balance innovative ideas and theories with real-world application.

Action Learning. While case studies and lectures have their place in the Sloan curriculum, its emphasis on Action Learning is unparalleled. Don't get us wrong, "experiential learning" has caught on across top business schools, but Sloan has an amazing array of offerings. It provides project-based lab classes focused on global entrepreneurship, innovation, and sustainability that pair student teams with companies and organizations around the world. Popularity continues to grow, and MIT Sloan most recently added Operations Lab (Ops-Lab) to its Action Learning program, giving students the chance to partner with local small and medium-sized business.

Responsive faculty. The faculty also embraces the idea of learning by doing, whether piloting experimental classes to share their groundbreaking research, or making significant adjustments to flagship courses based on student and partner feedback. Going beyond theoretical discussion to take action is a deeply ingrained aspect of the MIT Sloan culture.

Intellectual curiosity. During the month of January, the typical academic schedule is suspended for MIT's Independent Activities Period (IAP). This unique session gives students an opportunity to set their own educational agenda or participate in independent projects. This is often the time when MIT Sloan students travel for lab projects, and there are also ample opportunities to take a variety of courses for credit across the greater MIT campus. The Sloan Innovation Period (SIP) is another unique offering that replaces one week in the middle of each semester with an intense week packed full of shorter courses. Students have an opportunity to explore leadership courses, take workshops on negotiation, or learn more about faculty research. SIP provides another element of flexibility and customization of learning opportunities at Sloan. See more details about how these periods work in the Nuts & Bolts section below.

Global focus. MIT tends to have a more recognized brand internationally than many other top-tier schools such as Booth, Kellogg, Haas, Tuck, and others that struggle to gain global recognition. Recently, the school has sought to further leverage the MIT brand around the world by encouraging students and alumni to refer to the program as "MIT Sloan" in every instance, rather than the more casual moniker, "Sloan." Global courses continue to be added such as *China Lab, India Lab,* and *Global Entrepreneurship Lab* that allow Sloan students to gain hands-on experience overseas as part of their MBA education.

> **While case studies and lectures have their place in the Sloan curriculum, its emphasis on Action Learning is unparalleled.**

MIT (SLOAN)

MIT SLOAN AT A GLANCE

APPLICANTS BY SCHOOL

Sloan 4,735	Stanford 7,355	Harvard 9,543	Wharton 6,111	Columbia 5,799	Kellogg 4,652
13.8%	7.1%	11%	20.7%	18.2%	23.2%

 Percent admitted

AVERAGE GMAT SCORES

Sloan's incoming GMAT average is lower than most other top-tier schools and is more on-par with tech-heavy schools such as UCLA Anderson and Haas.

713	724	717
Sloan	Booth	Haas

WOMEN

MIT Sloan has one of the highest percentages of women in its class compared to other top-tier schools, with women making up 39% of the Class of 2016.

AVERAGE GPA

3.6	3.67	3.62	3.74
Sloan	Harvard	Haas	Stanford

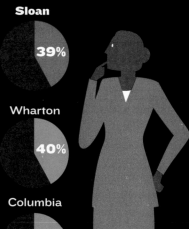

Sloan 39%

Wharton 40%

Columbia 36%

Haas 43%

Yale 37%

NATIONALITY

With 40% of the class comprised of non–U.S. citizens, MIT has one of the most international classes of any of the top-tier schools.

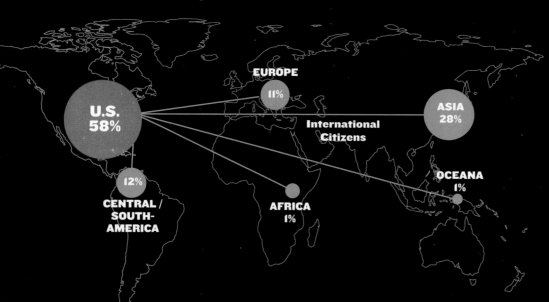

EUROPE 11%

ASIA 28%

U.S. 58%

International Citizens

OCEANA 1%

CENTRAL / SOUTH-AMERICA 12%

AFRICA 1%

UNDERGRAD MAJORS

Unsurprisingly, MIT attracts the highest percentage (48%) of students with STEM backgrounds of any top-tier program. Interestingly, schools not traditionally known for engineering and technology including Haas (36%) and Harvard (40%) are catching up!

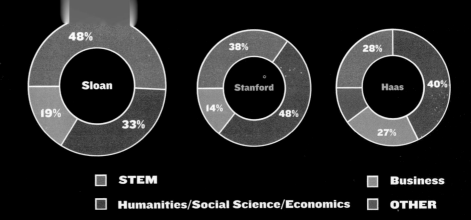

Sloan — 48%, 19%, 33%

Stanford — 38%, 14%, 48%

Haas — 28%, 40%, 27%, 27%

- ◻ **STEM**
- ◻ **Humanities/Social Science/Economics**
- ◻ **Business**
- ◻ **OTHER**

YEARS OF WORK EXPERIENCE

0–13 Sloan

0–16 Wharton

2–12.5 Kellogg

INTERNATIONAL CITIZENS

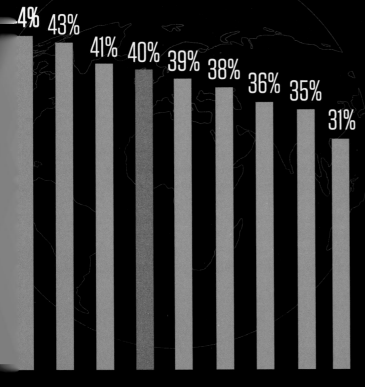

44% • 43% • 41% • 40% • 39% • 38% • 36% • 35% • 31%

Stanford Haas Columbia **Sloan** Yale Stern Kellogg Harvard Wharton

CLASS SIZE

Sloan's incoming class is small compared to similarly ranked schools, and its alumni network is still maturing at 23,500 strong.

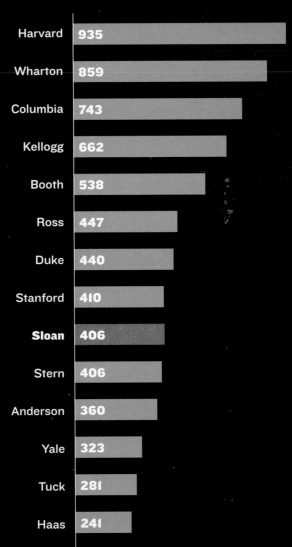

School	Class Size
Harvard	935
Wharton	859
Columbia	743
Kellogg	662
Booth	538
Ross	447
Duke	440
Stanford	410
Sloan	406
Stern	406
Anderson	360
Yale	323
Tuck	281
Haas	241

MIT (SLOAN)

You Oughta Know

Cross-registration. One huge advantage of MIT Sloan is that students can cross-register at Harvard Business School (HBS), at Harvard Kennedy School (HKS), and across other MIT departments, giving them the flexibility to pursue a wide range of subjects outside of Sloan's curriculum. If HBS is your top choice, you may want to put MIT Sloan on your list as well.

Track Certificates. As part of the standard MBA degree, MIT Sloan students may optionally pursue a Track Certificate in one of three areas:

Entrepreneurship & Innovation (E&I). This is one of the most popular programs at MIT and it's the main reason many students apply there in the first place. All Sloan students are free to bid on and take courses in entrepreneurship, but participants of the E&I program benefit from direct exposure to a rich network of influential players in the entrepreneurial community.

Enterprise Management (EM). The Enterprise Management certificate is a relatively new offering for MIT Sloan, with a focus on training students for management careers in large organizations (consulting, functional roles, product development, and rotational management programs, for example). The recommended set of courses in this certificate track aims to provide students with a cohesive skill-set including marketing, operations, and strategy. The track includes a project-based seminar during the first semester in which students work on a consulting project for a large organization, and provides exposure to practitioners in the field through speaking events, seminars, networking events, and on-site visits. This track offers a solid foundation for students who are looking to transition into a consulting or industry job.

Finance. The Finance track consists of a set of required courses, electives, and extracurricular activities designed to explicitly prepare MBA students for careers in the finance industry. MIT was the first business school to offer a specialized finance education, and many pioneers of finance and today's leading theories got their start at Sloan.

Certificate in sustainability. In addition to the three separate tracks, MIT Sloan also offers a certificate in sustainability. Sloan's Sustainability Certificate was launched in early 2010 to offer an integrated curriculum across Sloan and leverage MIT's strengths in the physical sciences, social sciences, and technology for those interested in tackling the challenges of adapting business to the changes in the world around us. This certificate, and related classes and initiatives, are strong examples of MIT's efforts to have robust offerings and a focus on sustainability in recent years.

Business plan (and other) competitions. Most MBA students have a competitive streak, but MIT Sloan takes the idea of friendly competition to an entirely new level. The MIT $100K Entrepreneurship Competition is one of the world's premier business plan competitions. Since the inception of the competition 20 years ago, the amount awarded to winners has grown from $10K to $100K and has spawned more than 120 companies with a collective market cap of more than $10 billion. Some notable companies with roots in this competition are Akamai, Zipcar, and Harmonix, developer of the popular Guitar Hero and Rock Band video games. The Competition spans most of the academic year, and is designed to encourage students and researchers across the MIT community to act on their talent, ideas, and energy to produce tomorrow's leading firms.

Nuts & Bolts

Class organization. First-year MBA students enjoy the camaraderie, classroom contributions, and support of their cohort (called "Oceans," because each one is named after an ocean or sea), a group of roughly 67 students who take all core courses together. Each "Ocean" is further broken down into 10 teams of six or seven students (each named after a sea-going bird). The school spends substantial time and energy to make sure the groups are highly diverse, and they're carefully matched to include a mix of international students and women.

There is one notable exception in the core, which is the 30-person *Communication for Leaders* class. In this course, students typically have small discussion sections or recitations in which they have the opportunity to discuss conceptual issues and work on problem sets. Elective subjects typically have 25 to 60 students (although a few number as high as 90), and seminars may have even fewer students.

One-semester core. MBA students build the foundation of their MIT Sloan education during the first-semester core. Students develop foundational skills through required courses including economics, accounting, managerial communication, business statistics, and organizational processes (as well as an elective in marketing, finance, operations, or strategy).

A unique aspect of the MIT Sloan MBA program is that the required core is only one semester long. This allows students great freedom and flexibility to pursue their unique goals and interests throughout the rest of their time at MIT Sloan. The core courses overlap and build off of one another at a number of points. For example, students will give presentations in *Communications* based on assignments from *Economics* or *Organizational Processes*. Much of this work is done within core teams, which are intentionally assembled to represent a wide range of skills, personalities, and experience. Learning how to manage this broad and rigorous workload effectively as a team is a very important part of the core experience.

The **MIT $100K** Entrepreneurship Competition is one of the world's premier business plan competitions. Companies with roots in this competition include Zipcar, Akamai, and Harmonix.

MIT (SLOAN)

Course enrollment. When enrolling in elective classes, students rely on a computerized bidding system that aims to fill classes as fairly as possible based on student preferences and priority. (Sloan students get placement priority over non-Sloan students, as do second-year students over first-year students.) Starting with 1,000 points each, students place bids on courses based on their level of interest and the perceived level of demand of the rest of the student body. In typical Sloan fashion, students tend to experiment with ways to gather and share information at nearly every bidding cycle so that the community can make informed decisions and maximize the power of their bid points.

Grading policies. The MIT Sloan grading system is based on a 5.0–point scale, with a 5.0 being equivalent to an A. (A 4.0 is a B, and so on, although an F is a zero.) An average of a 4.0 or higher is required of every student in order to graduate. The school has not adopted the grade non-disclosure policy common at many schools, so recruiters and employers do indeed have access to students' academic records (although students report that prospective employers rarely ask about grades). Faculty members are given the freedom to grade in whatever method they feel is most appropriate, and which they discuss with the class at the start of each course. Despite the assumption of widespread grade inflation in business schools, some 3.0s (Cs) are given out every year. While MIT Sloan is known for its academic rigor, students are rarely competitive about grades. It is much more common to find students focused on learning and personal goals, and the general culture tends to be one of cooperation and collaboration, especially when course-loads get demanding.

Sloan Innovation Period. At MIT Sloan, the traditional 13-week semester breaks for a unique and intense week of workshops and seminars during the Sloan Innovation Period (SIP). During this week, students break from their regular course schedule in order to learn about groundbreaking faculty research, explore new subjects areas, and take part in experiential learning exercises. This week provides students with a chance to enrich their studies with a variety of new and different ideas, and gain some healthy perspective about the world outside of their intense course-load. The sections of each semester before and after SIP week are referred to as H1 and H2, respectively. A certain number of SIP credits are required for graduation, and students bid on SIP workshops using a similar process as they do for classes. In the spring, SIP week aligns with spring break, which means two weeks to travel for many of the popular lab classes.

Independent Activities Period. Across all of MIT, the month of January is dedicated as the Independent Activities Period (IAP), a time where students can broaden their educational horizons and explore personal interests. Course offerings over IAP include both credited and non-credited classes, seminars, how-to sessions, forums, lectures, films, recitals, and tours on a wide variety of topics. IAP courses cover everything from the philosophical to the scientific to the less serious; the Annual Mystery Hunt and Charm School are always two of the most popular IAP offerings among MIT students. IAP provides a nice break from the academic grind of the fall and spring semesters, and is another unique opportunity for creativity and flexibility in learning. Students can create their own educational agendas, pursue independent projects, meet with faculty, or pursue many other options not possible during the semester. Faculty members are free to introduce innovative educational experiments as IAP activities or to work with students on independent study projects. Many students travel internationally during IAP either on independent trips or as part of class work through programs such as the Global Entrepreneurship Lab ("G-Lab").

Popular Professors

The MIT Sloan faculty is populated with many prominent business leaders, researchers, and teachers. Among Sloan students, there are a handful of professors who are considered a "must," due to the level of instruction and teaching style of the faculty members.

John Sterman

Jay W. Forrester Professor of Management

Professor Sterman's *System Dynamics II* is a popular and engaging course that expands the way students approach complex problems. Using stocks, flows, and feedback loops, students taking *System Dynamics* learn how to model the interconnectedness of complex systems and begin to map the non-linearity found in so many modern-day problems. The class has a notoriously challenging workload to match the elaborate vocabulary, but Professor Sterman teaches with an enthusiasm and clarity that students enjoy and appreciate. He has won multiple awards for teaching excellence from MIT Sloan students. Professor Sterman's other claim to fame: He invented the beer game. (If you don't know what this is just yet, wait. You'll know soon.)

Andrew Lo

Charles E. and Susan T. Harris Professor of Finance
Director, Laboratory for Financial Engineering

Professor Lo teaches multiple classes in the finance department, including *Finance Theory, Financial Market Dynamics and Human Behavior,* and *Financial Management.* He has significant publications, and his list of awards would require its own separate guide!

Paul Asquith

Gordon Y. Billard Professor of Finance

Professor Asquith's *Finance II* course is considered by many to be among the most engaging and popular courses at Sloan due to both his teaching excellence (he has been awarded the MIT Sloan student award an incredible 13 times) as well as his expertise in areas such as corporate finance and control, mergers, dividend policy, financial distress, and market efficiency.

Kristin Forbes

Jerome and Dorothy Lemelson Professor of Management

Professor Forbes has recently rotated between academia and policy positions in the United States government. She has served as a member of the Council of Economic Advisers to the White House and as a deputy assistant secretary in the U.S. Treasury Department in addition to her academic duties. As such, she possesses an incredible amount of real-world experience in her area of expertise. As one of Sloan's "rock-star" professors, her new course *Global Economic Challenges and Opportunities* is certain to be in high demand.

Robert Pindyck

Bank of Tokyo-Mitsubishi Ltd. Professor in Finance and Economics

Professor Pindyck works a great deal on irreversible investment decisions, the role of network effects in market structure, and the behavior of commodity prices. His course is known to be demanding, but is also consistently one of the classes with the highest points bid when the time comes to select courses. Professor Pindyck is also the coauthor of one of the most widely used microeconomics textbooks across universities around the world.

Roberto Rigobon

Society of Sloan Fellows Professor of Management

A Venezuelan economist, Professor Ribogon's research focuses on international, monetary, and development economics; he teaches applied macro and international economics. Highly popular with students, he has won both the "Teacher of the Year" award and the "Excellence in Teaching" award at MIT three times since joining the school in 1997.

Similar Academic Programs

Penn (Wharton). Also an extremely rigorous environment that infuses quant and analytical elements across disciplines with a moderately flexible core curriculum and a hybrid case/lecture model, Wharton has also placed a renewed emphasis on experiential learning with its new motto, "Knowledge for Action."

Chicago (Booth). Booth's curriculum is even more flexible than MIT's, with just one required course and multiple options to fulfill all other requirements. Its student body is known for intellectual curiosity, and the school takes great pride in the academic rigor of its program compared to other, "softer" business schools. Also known as a strong finance school, the academics tend to be quite analytical in nature.

Northwestern (Kellogg). Perhaps the only other school as dedicated as MIT Sloan to experiential learning opportunities is Kellogg, with new labs and experiential courses added every year. In addition, Kellogg offers a joint degree with Northwestern's McCormick School of Engineering and Applied Science called the MMM, which is similar to MIT's LGO program.

Harvard. Harvard Business School (HBS) focuses strongly on the case method while MIT Sloan emphasizes action learning, but these programs are just two T (subway) stops away from each other, and students may cross-enroll in courses. Sloanies take a variety of courses at HBS, and Harvard students tend to head to MIT for labs.

EMPLOYMENT & CAREERS AT MIT SLOAN

What MIT Sloan Is Known For

Entrepreneurs. MIT's location in Kendall Square makes Sloan an attractive destination for aspiring entrepreneurs. Home to biotech companies, tech startups, and research labs, Kendall Square is a vibrant, energetic community. Nearly 8% of the Class of 2014 reported they were starting their own business right out of school, which is high compared to Columbia (3%), Yale (4%), or Stern (3%). Many other programs encourage their graduates to "make their mistakes on someone else's dime" by taking a job for another company before striking out on their own, but many Sloan graduates discover business opportunities among MIT's other innovative graduate programs and start building a business upon cutting-edge technologies right away. Among top-ranked business schools, only Stanford and Harvard graduates more entrepreneurs.

Graduates electing to pursue entrepreneurial opportunities

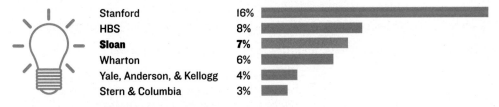

Stanford	16%
HBS	8%
Sloan	**7%**
Wharton	6%
Yale, Anderson, & Kellogg	4%
Stern & Columbia	3%

High tech. Twenty-eight percent of the Class of 2014 headed to technology, which is a significantly higher percentage than schools like Columbia, Wharton, and Kellogg. It beat out competitor Stanford (24%) this year, but it's below Berkeley-Haas and on par with UCLA. In 2014, four of MIT Sloan's top-10 hiring companies were tech-related: Amazon, Microsoft, Apple, and Google.

Graduates entering the technology industry

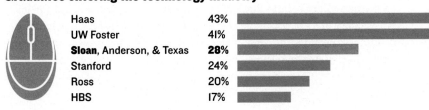

Haas	43%
UW Foster	41%
Sloan, Anderson, & Texas	**28%**
Stanford	24%
Ross	20%
HBS	17%

You Oughta Know

Consulting. Sloan doesn't always come immediately to mind when many candidates think of "consulting schools," but it's a veritable powerhouse in the space. More than a third of the Class of 2014 chose this career path; the two top hirers at MIT that year were McKinsey and Bain, with BCG and Deloitte also in the top 10.

Graduates entering the consulting industry

Kellogg & Tuck	35%	
Sloan, Ross, & Columbia	**34%**	
Duke	30%	
Booth & Stern	28%	
Wharton, Haas, & Yale	26%	

Operations, logistics, and supply chain. Despite the fact that most business schools have academic departments in operations, very few graduates tend to go into operations-related roles. However, at MIT Sloan, more than one in 10 graduates will take such a job, thanks largely to Leaders for Global Operations (LGO), a dual-degree program with the engineering school.

Graduates entering operations, logistics, and supply chain positions

Sloan	11%	
Texas	10%	
Stanford	8%	
Yale & Ross	6%	
Darden	4%	

> **86% of students in the Sloan Class of 2014 had full-time employment offers at graduation.**

Employment statistics. Eighty-six percent of students in the MIT Sloan Class of 2014 seeking full-time employment had offers at graduation; by August that number reached nearly 95%. Seventy-five percent of full-time offers were school-facilitated.

Salaries. The overall median salary for the Class of 2014 was $121,000, with consulting leading the way at an average salary of $135,000. (Just remember to be a bit careful when looking at overall median salary numbers because they can be skewed by high salaries in particular industries. Schools that send fewer students to those industries can be at a disadvantage.) Signing bonuses were also common, with 77% receiving them. The median bonus varied by industry from $20,000 to $45,000.

Grade disclosure. Although schools like Wharton and Columbia have grade non-disclosure policies that prevent recruiters from asking about your grades, MIT Sloan believes that "students own their grades" and can disclose (or not) as they please.

Nuts & Bolts

The MIT Sloan Career Development Office (CDO) is the primary student resource for navigating the search for internships and employment. The CDO provides opportunities to learn about career options, teaches the skills students need to market themselves successfully in the professional marketplace, and maximizes employment opportunities for the community. The CDO runs the Career Resource Center (CRC), which features a variety of databases and materials all filtered through industry-specific resources. Additionally, the CDO provides a series of career management offerings to MIT Sloan students.

Career core. Part of the first-semester core, this fusion of theory and practice is intended to help students develop career management skills. By working with both faculty members and the CDO, Sloan students gain experience in things like career mapping, networking, interviewing, and negotiation.

MIT Sloan Alumni Network. As with most elite business schools, the MIT Sloan alumni network of more than 20,000 people provides an outstanding career-management resource for students. Specifically, the MIT Sloan Alumni Office offers the Alumni Student Mentor Program, which pairs first-year students with an alumni mentor.

Similar Programs for Professional Opportunities

Northwestern (Kellogg). Like MIT Sloan, Kellogg sends a large percentage of the class into consulting, and percentages pursuing careers in finance, consumer goods, manufacturing, and even health care are nearly perfectly aligned.

Michigan (Ross). MIT Sloan and Ross are both known as strong operations schools, but the similarities don't end there. In terms of class percentages, the two schools are nearly identical in the number of graduates going into consulting, consumer goods, finance, manufacturing, and technology.

Stanford. If you want to work in technology or start your own business, but the idea of a New England winter makes you want to curl up and hibernate until spring, Stanford offers an excellent (and warmer) alternative, although other career placement stats (consulting, finance, etc.) don't match up nearly as well.

Berkeley (Haas). Given its Bay Area location, Haas sends a large number of candidates into the technology sector. Like MIT Sloan, it has strengths in biotech and entrepreneurship, so applicants to MIT Sloan often find themselves applying to Berkeley-Haas as well.

UCLA (Anderson). Another West Coast school with strong ties to technology, Anderson sends an identical percentage of graduates into this sector as does MIT Sloan. Like MIT Sloan, Anderson's largest employers include the likes of Amazon and Google, with additional strong ties to consulting firms such as Deloitte.

CULTURE & CAMPUS LIFE AT MIT SLOAN

What MIT Sloan Is Known For

A social community. The student body at MIT Sloan is known to be highly social, collaborative, and down to earth. Sloan students love to go out together, travel, help each other in team projects, etc. The collaboration is tangible, even during recruiting: Sloan students are competitive within themselves, but not with each other. Because of MIT's reputation in engineering, Sloan tends to receive a large number of applicants with a STEM (science, technology, engineering, math) background. Particularly if you're coming from these fields, be sure to highlight your ability to connect well with others to ensure you showcase a good cultural fit with the school.

The "friendlier" school in Cambridge. We've met numerous Sloanies who have attended parties and other social gatherings with Harvard Business School (HBS) students, only to find that the HBS students didn't know each other! Given MIT Sloan's smaller, generally friendlier atmosphere, this often comes as a big surprise. These experiences highlight the difference between MIT's class of about 400 students and Harvard's of more than 900.

Heritage. Sloan's history began in 1914 with a single course: *Engineering Administration*. In 1950, a $5M gift from the Alfred P. Sloan Foundation established the "School of Industrial Management"; the name changed to "Sloan" in 1964. Through the years, some of the top names in business have taught at Sloan, including Myron Scholes and Fischer Black.

You Oughta Know

Leveraging the broader MIT community. With their main building in a far corner of the Institute campus, many MIT Sloan students tend to stay focused on their business school experience and are generally autonomous from the rest of the MIT student body. However, the school has made great strides to integrate deeply with its parent institution and better leverage the MIT brand. It asks students to refer to the program as "MIT Sloan" rather than just "Sloan," and has encouraged greater participation in multidisciplinary courses, labs, clubs, and events. It has now has two web pages focusing on how cross-campus integration enhances the student experience. MIT Sloan is one of the few elite business schools to allow undergraduate students to take classes side-by-side with MBA students. While this adds a layer of diversity to the classroom experience, it is worth noting, since not every MBA candidate is eager to include undergrads in the educational process.

Facilities. The early 2000s saw a boom in business school construction worldwide, and MIT was no exception. Opened in fall 2010, the 215,000-square-foot building known as "E62" is the flagship of the MIT Sloan campus. Considered the greenest building at MIT, E62 includes 35 breakout rooms, numerous gathering spaces, classrooms, and the Siteman Dining Room, overlooking the Charles River and the Boston skyline.

Housing. Some MBA programs offer significant on-campus housing or the vast majority of students live in a few buildings nearby. Sloanies are a bit more spread out. About one-third of students utilize MIT graduate student housing, which offers a location near campus, better affordability, and interaction with many classmates. The other students live off campus, often preferring the Beacon Hill area in Boston or the Central Square and Kendall Square neighborhoods in Cambridge. The campus is located in Cambridge, so these areas are quite close. The key to getting around Boston is to live near a T (subway) line to make commuting easier.

Popular hangouts. Beacon Hill Pub (known as BHP) is Sloan's favorite dive bar. It's located on the Boston side of Beacon Hill, and Sloanies are known to take over every Wednesday night. The Muddy Charles Pub has been located on MIT campus since 1968. Many students go to hang out, grab a beer, and sometimes do homework. For those students who want to show off their best moves, Middlesex Lounge, Havana Club, and Phoenix Landing are popular dance clubs.

Clubs and activities. The Action Learning philosophy extends beyond the classroom to extracurricular opportunities run by Sloan students. Among the roughly 60 student clubs and numerous other activities are some of the largest U.S. conferences run by students, such as the Venture Capital Private Equity Conference and the Sports Analytics Conference.

C-Functions. When you speak with Sloanies about the events that are critical to their MIT Sloan experience, inevitably you'll hear about C-Functions. These are weekly, informal after-hours parties held every Thursday where all students are invited to embrace the school's diversity and learn about other cultures. Each C-Function features a new theme, such as "Japanese C-Function" or "LGBT C-Function." The evening begins with a performance and continues with free food and beer throughout.

Other events. Besides C-Functions, popular Sloan events include Fall Ball and Spring Fling, formal galas organized by the student activities committee, student treks over the Independent Activity Period (IAP) and spring break, study tours that incorporate a strong educational component, and spontaneous weekend trips, including those to far-off places like Iceland!

Similar Programs Culturally

Dartmouth (Tuck). If you're looking for a very tight-knit student body whose strong culture builds lifelong bonds among its students, Tuck's concentrated social and academic environment creates a deep sense of connection with the school and the highest alumni giving rates of any top-tier school. Unlike MIT Sloan, however, the campus is not urban in nature.

Chicago (Booth). Booth attracts intellectuals who enjoy a more casual environment than you might find in the harder-charging schools like Wharton, Columbia, and Harvard. Both Sloan and Booth environments emphasize rigorous academics balanced with a welcoming, friendly student body.

Ross (Michigan). Perhaps it's the cold weather, but there's something about these Midwest and Northeastern schools that instills a culture of unity, humility, and fun. Ross is no exception. Located in idyllic Ann Arbor, Michigan, the Ross School has a greater connection to its undergraduate traditions than many business schools, largely thanks to its large bachelor's of Business Administration program and the University of Michigan's dominant sports programs.

Berkeley (Haas). Although it has a smaller enrollment than MIT Sloan, Haas's student body is also known for being very collegial and friendly with an emphasis on collaboration and teamwork. Its parent university, University of California, Berkeley, is also a highly regarded research institution. Both business schools are located on the outskirts of their respective campuses, and both leverage the technology and biotech strengths of their parent institutions to form cross-campus initiatives and organizations.

MIT (SLOAN)

ADMISSIONS AT MIT SLOAN

What MIT Sloan Is Looking For

Not just quants. Some applicants mistakenly assume that the MIT admissions committee screens the applicant pool with an eye for "quant jocks" and math whizzes. The ability to manage the academic rigors of Sloan is one important factor, but the admissions committee is interested in learning much more about potential students than simply test scores and undergraduate grades. Senior Director of Admissions Rod Garcia and the other members of the admissions committee are looking for principled and motivated individuals who will contribute to a dynamic, engaged, and vibrant community.

Admissions criteria. To identify these people, the committee looks for demonstrated success in past performance (work experience, GMAT or GRE score, and undergraduate grades) and then digs deeper. Specifically, they seek candidates who demonstrate:

- A natural sense of leadership, ambition, and an ability to inspire others,
- A collaborative spirit, focus on community, and enhancement of others,
- Intellectual curiosity, analytical strength, and academic achievement,
- Creativity to generate new solutions to existing challenges,
- Interpersonal and communication skills,
- Growth in both professional and personal endeavors, and
- Pursuit of meaningful goals.

Evaluation process. More than any other MBA program, MIT Sloan believes that past performance is the best indicator of future success. You'll find that MIT Sloan asks almost nothing about your future goals throughout the application process. Other schools may ask questions about your short- and long-term goals, why you want an MBA, or other questions to determine whether you have a clear plan for how to get the most out of your MBA experience. Instead, MIT Sloan wants to see examples—ideally, recent examples—of how you've succeeded in the past.

Work experience. While Sloan does accept applications from those fresh out of school, and work experience is not technically required for an application, professional experience is seen as vitally important to the MIT Sloan MBA experience. Its average for each new incoming class is usually around five years of full-time, post-undergraduate experience. We estimate that about 80% of admitted students have between three and seven years of experience, although the student body includes admits with zero to 13 years. Those without work experience need to show incredible initiative during college such as starting their own business, running major campus operations, or otherwise providing evidence that they bring personal and professional maturity beyond their years.

 If you are looking for tips on 2016–17 admissions essays, you're in luck! Check out our website at **veritasprep.com/sloan** for our latest advice.

College seniors. MIT Sloan does not have an official application program for college seniors such as Harvard's 2+2 program, but it does encourage college seniors to apply for deferrals. This means that if you're a college senior, you could apply by the standard Round 1 or Round 2 deadline, note in your optional essay that you would seek a deferral to gain work experience, and then attend Sloan in a future class. Most MBA candidates believe Harvard and Stanford are the only options to receive deferred admission, but MIT Sloan is an excellent option.

Student involvement. Unlike many of its peer schools, Sloan handles its admissions process entirely within the Sloan admissions committee. Students and alumni are very actively involved with admissions initiatives and activities with prospective students but do not participate in the evaluation of applicants for admissions purposes. Some off-campus interviews are conducted by outside professionals. These interviews tend to be extremely formal, with little rapport building or insight into the school. If you have the misfortune of experiencing one of these interviews, don't get a bad impression! These "hired hands" do not exemplify the warm and friendly culture on campus.

Preparing to Apply

Reading this Essential Guide is a great first step in your preparation. Hopefully, this insider's glimpse has been helpful in understanding the most important aspects of the school. However, nothing can replace gaining firsthand knowledge and experience yourself.

Reach out to current students. Even if you don't have any personal connections to MIT Sloan, you can reach out to current students and get their insight and advice. On the school's Clubs page, you'll find a list of all campus clubs. Find a few clubs that fit your personal and professional interests, and reach out to the officers. Remember: These are very busy MBA students so you don't want to intrude too much on their time, but you could ask for a 10- to 15-minute conversation or elicit some advice via e-mail. Come prepared with specific questions (preferably those that aren't already answered online). If you're planning to visit campus, perhaps you might even arrange a coffee chat or lunch, if they are available. For larger clubs, you might provide quick background information and ask if there's another member of their club, even one with a similar background, who might be able to offer some insights and advice about his or her MIT Sloan experience.

Visit campus. The school's website can only tell you so much; by far, a personal visit is the best possible research in the application process. If you have the means, we highly recommend you visit MIT Sloan in person, along with the campuses of your other top choices, to understand the significant differences in culture, teaching style, student body, recruiting opportunities, facilities, and so forth. You may be surprised at just how different each school can be and and how the reality can differ from the perception. We encourage you to take advantage of opportunities to visit campus and to engage through the Ambassadors Program. Because informal and impromptu encounters can be the most informative, don't be afraid to approach students in less-formal settings.

Other events. We know that many applicants will not be able to travel to Massachusetts to visit campus, but you should take advantage of other worldwide admissions events, such as information sessions, virtual sessions, and specific-audience events. In fact, these off-campus events can offer great opportunities for quality time with admissions officers and even other applicants, who can be a great resource and support through the admissions process. Get to know the school and its culture as well as you can, because your familiarity can shine through your application and essays to help you stand out.

You Oughta Know

When should I apply? Sloan's Round 1 deadline has moved up by almost a week, pushing into mid-September for the first time ever. And, the school's Round 2 deadline comes almost a week later than it did last year. If you apply to Sloan in Round 1, you will receive your decision by December 16, which will give you plenty of time to get Round 2 applications ready for other MBA programs, if needed.

The other interesting thing here is that Sloan has added a Round 3! For a while, Sloan had been unique among top U.S. business schools in that it only had two admissions rounds. For instance, last year, if you hadn't applied by January 8, then you weren't going to apply to Sloan at all. Now stragglers actually have a chance of getting in to MIT Sloan, although our advice about Round 3 is always the same: There are simply fewer seats available by Round 3, so only truly standout applicants have a real chance of getting in. Plan on applying in Round 1 or 2 to maximize your chances of success.

Overrepresented applicants. Candidates from traditional MBA feeder industries such as management consulting or finance, or applicants with technical and engineering backgrounds tend to be strongly represented in the MIT Sloan applicant pool. This doesn't mean that you can't get in if you're coming from these industries; a quick glance at the class profile will tell you there's plenty of room in the class for consultants, bankers, and engineers. However, we encourage you to apply in the first round (assuming you have a strong GMAT score), as you'll be competing against many candidates with very similar profiles. In a later round, it's possible that the school may see you as a viable candidate to the school but may have already admitted several other applicants with similar profiles, so it might pass on you to bring greater professional diversity to the class.

Don't rush! Please note that even though the top schools encourage you to apply in the earliest round possible, this does not mean that you should apply with a rushed application or a mediocre GMAT score. There's no sense in applying early if you're just going to be denied. A GMAT score that's above the school's average will do more for your candidacy than applying in the first round, even if you're coming from an overrepresented industry or demographic.

The Essays

Only one required essay. While hardly any top business schools have cut essays this year (after several years of doing so), Sloan actually did cut an essay, going down to just one required essay this year. But, here's a twist: The Sloan admissions team has added a second essay just for those who are invited to interview. So, you're still going to need to write two strong essays to get into Sloan, and we break down the essay prompts below.

Essay 1: We are interested in learning more about how you work, think, and act. In your response, please describe in detail what you thought, felt, said, and did.

Question: Tell us about a recent success you had: How did you accomplish this? Who else was involved? What hurdles did you encounter? What type of impact did this have? (500 words)

Focus on past performance. This question is new to MIT Sloan's application this year. What we like about it is how it very explicitly spells out what Sloan's admissions team wants to see. For these types of questions, we always advise applicants to use the "SAR" method: Spell out the Situation, the Action that you took, and the Results of those actions. There is no hard and fast rule for how many words you should devote to each section, but the situation is where you want to use up the fewest words; you need to set the stage, but with only 500 words to work with, you want to make sure that you give the bare minimum of background and then move on to what actions you took. And, make sure you leave enough room to discuss the result ("What type of impact did this have?"). Your individual actions and the impact that you had are what the admissions committee really wants to see.

Show successful collaboration. Because MBA applicants feel pressure to impress the admissions committee, we see a lot of essays that focus on "me." You certainly need to play the primary role in your own essay, but you don't need to present yourself as the "knight in shining armor," riding to save the day from your incompetent coworkers. Instead, the best essays tend to show what you learned from others through this experience and how a collaborative effort led to success. You can list all of your greatest successes on your resume; the purpose of this essay isn't to show how great you are, but to give the admissions committee a glimpse into what you consider to be a success (either professional or personal) and the process you took to achieve it.

Make it personal. Don't only think about the impact that you had on your organization, but also spend some time thinking about the impact that the experience had on you. What did you learn? How did you grow as a result? And, how did you put this lesson to work in a later experience? That may be a challenge to fit into a 500-word essay, but this is the type of introspection and growth that any business school admissions committee loves to see.

Essay question for those who are invited to interview: The mission of the MIT Sloan School of Management is to develop principled, innovative leaders who improve the world and to generate ideas that advance management practice. Please share with us something about your past that aligns with this mission. (250 words)

Why Sloan? The wording of this prompt has changed slightly since last year, but the biggest change (other than the fact that it's become the essay only for those invited to interview) is that the word count has dropped from 500 to 250 words. At its core, this is a "Why MIT Sloan?" question. The admissions committee wants to see that you have done your homework on Sloan, that you understand what the school stands for, and that you really want to be there.

How you will contribute. When Sloan asks you to share something that "aligns with" its mission, it's not just asking about what you will do while you're in school for two years, but also about how you plan on taking what you've learned (and the connections you've built) and going

> The best essays tend to show what you learned from others through this experience and how a collaborative effort led to success.

farther than you could ever have without an MIT Sloan MBA. Note the very last part of the question: The key to a believable essay here will be to cite a specific example from your past when you got involved and made things better around you. Don't be intimidated by the high-minded ideals in the first part of the essay prompt; making an impact (rather than just standing idly by and being a follower) is what they want to see here, even if it's on a relatively small scale.

Optional Question: The Admissions Committee invites you to share anything else you would like us to know about you, in any format. If you choose to use a multimedia format, please host the information on a website and provide us the URL.

Not your standard optional essay. For most optional essays, we tell applicants to answer them only if they have extenuating circumstances such as gaps in work experience, poor academic performance or test scores, disciplinary actions, and so forth. However, this essay is wide open. This is a great opportunity for the admissions committee to get a glimpse of your personality. Feel free to think outside the box here! If you have a creative side, and you'd like to show it off, perhaps you point to a fun blog post or YouTube video. However, don't feel pressured to use multimedia simply because the option is available.

> **Be focused on a particular goal: Think about your personal brand and showcase something specific that you want the admissions committee to learn about you.**

Have a clear goal in mind. Don't submit just anything here, simply because you can. Be focused on a particular goal: Think about your personal brand and showcase something specific that you want the admissions committee to learn about you. Ask your friends or impartial observers who don't already know you to review it before you submit. What is the the impression they get about you? What did they learn? Is this what you want the admissions committee to take away?

Be yourself. If you choose to write an essay, we would expect it to have a lighter, more personal tone. Some applicants may be tempted to focus on adversity they have experienced prior to business school, such as surviving cancer or overcoming a death in your family during a particularly trying time. We recommend highlighting something positive about yourself such as a fun passion, unique perspective, personal value system, or something else that would contribute to the vibrancy and diversity of the MIT Sloan class. If you feel that a story about adversity would really show the admissions committee how you became the person you are today, briefly mention the incident itself and then focus exclusively on the lessons, passions, change in personal motivations, or impact that it had on your life.

Be brief. This should not be a long essay or multimedia presentation. While no word limit or time limit is mentioned, we would recommend no longer than a 250- to 300-word essay or 90-second video. Be mindful of the admissions officer's time and attention, and don't abuse this opportunity to tell the committee a little more about yourself.

Recommendations

MBA applicants must submit two letters of recommendation. Professional recommendations are preferred and should come from individuals who are able to speak with certainty about your professional achievements and potential. Recommenders must submit recommendations online. Sloan does not accept mailed recommendations. Recommendations may be in either letter or short-answer format and should not exceed two pages each.

Your recommenders should be prepared to answer the following questions:

MIT affiliation. Recommenders may select if they have graduated from MIT or MIT Sloan, or whether they serve on faculty or staff. However, applicants are not recommended to try to find a recommender who happens to be affiliated with the school.

Preferred contact. *[Email/phone]* MIT Sloan may occasionally reach out to a recommender for clarification or verification. These are rare instances where the school suspects that the applicant wrote his or her own recommendation or something else in the recommendation causes concern.

Applicant rating. Your recommender will then be asked to rate you "in relation to other high potential people [they] know" on the following criteria: leadership potential, creativity and resourcefulness, intellectual curiosity, energy and initiative, ability to work in a team, oral and written communication skills, presence, and analytical thinking and reasoning. They will rate you on a 1 to 6 scale: *1) Outstanding – Top 2%, 2) Very Good – Top 10%, 3) Above Average – Top 25%, 4) Average – Top 50%, 5) Below Average – Bottom 50%, or 6) Unobserved.* Pay close attention to these attributes on which your recommenders will rate you. These align perfectly with the type of candidates MIT Sloan is looking for, so you'll want to find ways to showcase them in your resume, online application, and essays, if possible.

Recommendation letter. Your recommenders will then upload a document that responds to several questions. We include the instructions and questions below so that you may select recommenders who can most thoroughly answer the admissions committee's questions:

> *We are interested in specific examples of intellectual and professional achievement and how they might relate to graduate study in management and in a career as a manager or business leader. In addition, we are very interested in the character of the applicant and will be helped by any information in that regard.*
>
> *We have posted a series of questions and scenarios for you to answer. The letters that are most helpful to the applicant are those that utilize the template below and point to actual observations of the candidate's actions. If you do not feel sufficiently informed to answer a particular question, please indicate 'not observed' or 'not applicable'.*

Please compose your answers to the following questions in one document and then upload below. Recommendations should be no longer than two pages.

- *How long and in what capacity have you known the applicant?*
- *How does the applicant stand out from others in a similar capacity?*
- *Please give an example of the applicant's impact on a person, group, or organization.*
- *Please give a representative example of how the applicant interacts with other people.*
- *Which of the applicant's personal or professional characteristics would you change?*
- *If you are an academic/technical recommender, please tell us how well the applicant mastered the subject you taught or supervised and in what ways did the applicant demonstrate this mastery.*
- *Please tell us anything else you think we should know about this applicant.*

Selecting your recommenders. The admissions committee strongly prefers professional recommenders to academic ones, such as a former professor. The best recommenders are people who can provide very detailed examples of your actions and behavior. In general, the admissions committee will be far more impressed by a genuine and passionate letter from a middle manager who is your supervisor than a polite letter from a well-known CEO, that lacks depth and detailed anecdotes about you. Look for people who can speak very clearly about your performance in relation to peers. In other words, don't ask your company's CEO, whom you might or might not have met once in the cafeteria. And hopefully you don't need to be told this, but MIT Sloan does not accept recommendations from family members.

Should I draft it myself? Many applicants to business school are asked by their superiors to draft the recommendation themselves and the recommender will approve it. We strongly recommend that you do not write the recommendation yourself for several reasons. First, your writing style and choice of phrasing are unique, and admissions officers will notice if the recommendations are similar to each other and your essays. If they notice too many similarities, your application could be denied outright. Second, you may tend to be too humble or generic. Your supervisor might use language such as "one of the top analysts I've seen in my entire career" that you wouldn't dare include if writing on his or her behalf. Third, and perhaps most importantly, the admissions officer is looking for a third-party perspective on your candidacy, so writing a recommendation yourself is an unethical breach of trust with the school you are looking to join.

> **Instead of writing the recommendation yourself, you should sit down and have candid conversations with your recommenders about your experience together.**

Preparing your recommenders. Instead of writing the recommendation yourself, you should sit down and have candid conversations with your recommenders about the reasons you want to go to business school and why you've selected your target schools, your professional goals, and your experience together. Ask them if they would have the time to write a strong recommendation on your behalf. (This also gives them a nice "out" by telling you that they are too busy rather than saying they don't feel comfortable giving you a positive recommendation.) Bring a copy of your resume and a bulleted list of projects you've worked on together and accomplishments they have seen you achieve. Let them know that the admissions committees prefer to see specific, detailed examples in recommendations. Then, let them know that you'll serve as a "project manager" to follow up and ensure that they are able to submit your recommendation ahead of the deadline.

The Interview

How will it work? Interviews are by invitation only and are held on campus, in key cities internationally, and, occasionally, by Skype. The MIT Sloan admissions committee conducts nearly every the interview themselves, although they employ professionals to conduct some of the interviews in key cities. They do not have students or alumni handle any interviewing tasks. The focus of this experience is the Behavioral Event Interviews, based on the idea that past behavior is a reliable indicator of future responses in similar situations. As with the application essay questions, the interview will focus on specific experiences in recent years and on what applicants said, felt, and did in each instance.

Non-blind interviewers. Unlike at most elite business schools, the interview process is not "blind"; interviewers review applications prior to the interview, and it is not unusual for them to ask additional questions about application materials and essays. The admissions committee is interested in learning about what makes candidates tick—what motivates them, what guides their decisions and actions, and what their passions are. Sometimes the result of this is a greater emphasis on feelings, thought processes, and some of the softer competencies than one might find in other business school interviews. Sloan offers the same advice as we do for answering interview questions: Use the Situation––Action––Results (SAR) method. Present the situation (S), discuss what actions (A) you took to achieve the result, and then summarize the results (R), or the impact, of those actions.

What will they ask? Every candidate is different, so interview questions will vary as well, with no one standard set of questions for applicants. The admissions committee will use the interview to learn more about candidates and fill in any gaps that they might have based on what they have already learned from the application. It is not uncommon for the interview to start with some general background questions, such as asking that you walk through your resume and note what you did in each role. If you have written about a particularly unique interest or experience in your application, they might probe more deeply to learn more.

What are they looking for? Behavioral questions in the interview usually come in the form of "Tell me about a time when you _____." Here, they are asking you to identify a very specific experience or event (for example, a time when you had to convince a group or another person, a time when you were under a lot of pressure, or a time when you had to make a decision with limited information). Again, it will help to have practiced describing your experiences broken down into the situation, action, and results. You should be prepared to discuss the situation in detail since the interviewers usually drill down to learn more specific information. Even if the interviewer doesn't specifically ask for such details, proactively prepare for and offer answers to the following questions: What were you thinking and feeling at the time? What information did you consider that impacted your decisions? What action did you take, and what was the impact?

It's not an interrogation. Interviews can be nerve-wracking, but it helps to remember that the admissions committee is never going to try to trick you or pummel you with tough questions. They are genuinely trying to learn more about you and how you might fit into the program and community. Most people come out of MIT Sloan interviews feeling like they had a pleasant and interesting conversation with the admissions officer.

MEET SOME OF THE TEAM

Veritas Prep has the world's most accomplished MBA admissions team. Every Head Consultant™ has insider experience in MBA admissions at a top-tier business school.

AARON *Harvard*

Aaron earned his MBA from Harvard Business School, and has advised prospective MBA students for more than 8 years. As a minority student liaison to the HBS Admissions Committee, Aaron has worked with minority prospective students to help develop their applications and was involved in recruiting both on and off campus. In 2008, Aaron began working with Veritas Prep and has successfully helped dozens of clients gain admittance to the nation's most selective MBA programs. Aaron works with all types of candidates, but specializes in working with women and minority clients and those with non-traditional backgrounds.

KARA *Wharton*

Kara started her career as a venture capitalist. She has a talent for identifying and investing in promising teams and helping them grow into successful businesses. This skill extends to her clients, as well. Kara works closely with applicants to understand their unique strengths, and to highlight and position these assets within their applications. Kara got her MBA from Wharton, where she was an Admission Fellow. As a student member of the admission committee reviewing hundreds of applicants, Kara gained valuable insights into how Admissions Committees evaluate candidates. She used her MBA to transition to the operations side, and has been working in marketing and partnerships for small and large startups since then. Most recently, this Boston transplant was lured back to San Francisco for its dynamic entrepreneurial industry.

MATT *Stanford*

The admission process is stressful no matter your accomplishments or test scores. Matt recognizes and remembers this first-hand, having gone through this process first at Princeton, and then at the Stanford GSB. Matt worked both in investment banking at Goldman Sachs in New York and at several startups in Silicon Valley, so he is familiar with the resume and pedigree of a traditional business school applicant. Also having taught in the UK and worked for a major U.S. politician, Matt knows what it means to be a non-traditional applicant. What is more, he sat on the board of trustees of an Ivy League university, where he became intimately aware of how admissions decisions are made and how applicants are viewed. A passionate reader and writer, Matt is excited about helping applicants find their natural voice and craft essays and applications that are authentic. He strives to make the process less stressful and uses lots of humor to do so!

PURVI *Yale SOM*

Purvi has one overarching philosophy: She wants to showcase each client's individual talents and virtues. She'll get to know your thoughts and will help to craft your application in a way that will allow it to stand out from the thousands of others. Her clients have gained admission to top business schools, including Harvard Business School, and her specialty is taking your unique story with your own voice and bringing out the successful applicant. Purvi also has vast industry experience in the finance, healthcare, entrepreneurship, and non-profit/social enterprise sectors, and has a passion for career counseling. She wants your path to be an informed one, and will make it so you also come out of your sessions together with an understanding of how to get the most out of business school. At Yale SOM, she was a student member of the admissions committee and continues to interview potential applicants for the school. She looks forward to getting you in to your dream school as well!

*Meet the rest of our team at **veritasprep.com** and find the consultant who's right for you.*

NYU STERN

Diverse, hands-on, and fast-paced—this program could only exist in New York City.

 NEW YORK, NY

CLASS SIZE
406

PROGRAM FOUNDED
1900

SETTING
URBAN

CHARATERISTICS
DIVERSE, REAL WORLD, WALL STREET

NYU (STERN)

SECTIONS

NYU STERN SNAPSHOT

What NYU Stern Is Known For

Real-world perspective in New York City. Leveraging its physical location at the heart of New York City, NYU Stern strives to encompass all of the dynamic energy of the "world's business capital" in its MBA programs. Stern prides itself on a real-world approach to business education, and on the balance the school's programs provide between theoretical learning and practical, "roll-up-your-sleeves" engagement in the broadly defined business community. For example, a case study developed by now–Distinguished Service Professor of Management Emeritus Richard Freedman on New York's Metropolitan Opera has given numerous students open access to and in-depth understanding of the venerable institution (and a great chance to soak up some culture as well!).

Highly diverse, highly collaborative community. Stern is proud of the exceptional diversity of its student body, and students thrive in the rich, multicultural environment it affords. The school publicizes the fact that it has a student body representing nearly 60 different nationalities and has long enjoyed significant ethnic and racial diversity, as well as a relatively high percentage of women. Despite the fact that more than a third of its students in any given year are aiming for post-MBA employment in a finance-related sector, Stern is by no means one-dimensional in terms of its academics, nor is it looking for competitive "lone stars" to feed into the banking industry. Participation in student organizations is prolific, with most students involved in two or more clubs on campus. Academic collaboration is also a cornerstone of the Stern programs, and students actively engage with each other and with the faculty, administration, and staff in all aspects of the MBA experience. In fact, many prospective students who visit the campus are surprised at the high degree of collaboration and mutual support among Stern classmates and within the broader community, even relative to other comparable programs.

Broad-based and balanced MBA curriculum. Although it is best known for its finance department, Stern takes a balanced and general approach to management education. In their first year, MBA students are required to study a rigorous core curriculum covering all fundamental areas of business. In the second year, students can customize the Stern curriculum to meet specific academic and professional goals by choosing up to three specializations (or none at all), taking electives during the day or in the evening with students from the part-time MBA program, leveraging one of the many study abroad offerings, or registering for elective courses at other NYU graduate schools.

> **Academic collaboration is also a cornerstone of the Stern programs, and students actively engage with each other and with the faculty, administration, and staff in all aspects of the MBA experience.**

Relevant course content and evolving teaching methodology. Stern's teaching methodology particularly emphasizes team projects, case studies, experiential learning, and lectures. The school's strong research emphasis is evident in class content, which is regularly updated to reflect relevant developments in the business world as well as Stern's belief in the integration of MBA subject matter. The highly engaged (and engaging) professors encourage students to challenge their assertions and create a healthy back-and-forth dialogue in the lecture halls and classrooms on a daily basis. In addition, the world outside of the classroom serves as a very real and regular venue for testing skills and theories. Some examples of this real-world learning include: studying a local company as the basis for a group project, advising New York City nonprofits through the Stern Consulting Corp (SCC), making investment decisions through the Michael Price Student Investment Fund, and obtaining funding for a new venture through the annual Entrepreneur Business Plan Competition.

Values. Like many other business schools, Stern has been working to communicate and market its points of differentiation, and increasingly this comes down to culture. The Stern community is known as collaborative and friendly, and the school is focused on producing leaders who will influence the world in a positive way. It does this through four articulated values:

1. **Academic Excellence:** Stemming from the skilled faculty, the academic environment is rich and demanding.

2. **Collaborative Community:** Teamwork is more than just a buzzword at Stern.

3. **IQ + EQ:** An emphasis on interpersonal skills as much as intellectual power.

4. **The Energy of a Global Hub:** Using the resources of New York City to its advantage, for both business and fun.

Successful applicants to Stern generally are able to express their appreciation for and support of these values in their application (or the interview!), either implicitly or explicitly.

What Makes NYU Stern Different

An agile and responsive faculty, with a focus on research. Stern was quick to move during the global financial crisis. Not only were its professors speaking to the media on a daily basis as the events unfolded, but by the first quarter of 2009, a major collaborative effort by 33 faculty members resulted in 18 policy white papers, a book on the financial crisis (*Restoring Financial Stability*), and a new course offered by the white paper authors. In late 2010, Stern published the next book in this series, *Regulating Wall Street*, which discusses the impact of the Dodd-Frank Act and identifies flaws in this sweeping regulation on the financial industry. Most recently, *Guaranteed to Fail* was released, blasting Fannie Mae and Freddie Mac as the underlying culprits of the mortgage crisis and our economic woes. Stern's faculty is heavily engaged in research of critical issues of the day, and few schools have been so quick to publicize analysis of and policy recommendations for these very significant events.

> **The Stern community is known as collaborative and friendly, and the school is focused on producing leaders who will influence the world in a positive way.**

NYU (STERN)

An oasis for career changers. Stern is considered one of the best possible destinations for those looking to move from one field to another by way of their MBA education. The Industry Mentoring Initiative (IMI) allows Stern students to apply for a very unique mentoring program that puts career changers into roles that will educate them about a new industry or function, and that will in turn provide a great opportunity for networking. It is a competitive application process and one that requires a clear move from one career to another, but for those students who participate, it can be a lifesaver. The IMI program features tracks in six different industries: consulting, luxury and retail, marketing, media and entertainment, investment banking, and sales and trading. Although any business school can serve as the launch pad into a new career, the significant resources available for students at Stern make this a natural choice for many.

The best part-time MBA in the Northeast. Although this Guide focuses on the full-time program, Stern was one of the first graduate business schools to offer a part-time program, and it remains the only top program in the region to have one. If you're looking to attend part-time at a top-10 business school, the next closest option is at the Fuqua School of Business at Duke University, all the way down in North Carolina.

> **Stern was one of the first graduate business schools to offer a part-time program, and it remains the only top program in the region to have one.**

A focus on emotional intelligence. While many schools are grappling with the issues that created the economic problems a few years ago and seeking to redefine their place in business and society, NYU Stern has focused on identifying the traits of individuals they want to invite into their collaborative community. Stern looks to evaluate candidates' "EQ"—or emotional intelligence—just as much as their IQ to determine whether or not the candidate will be a good fit with the school.

NYU Stern Is a Good Fit for You If...

You want to go into sales and trading (S&T). Stern is, after all, a finance school, and those interested in pursuing even specialized finance careers can find support here. At any school, there are generally fewer jobs available in S&T through on-campus recruiting compared to investment banking. So if you're interested in trading, you'll want to go to a school that has the relationships in place to facilitate your career switch. Stern is one of the few schools (along with others like Wharton, Columbia, Booth, and LBS) that reports placements into sales and trading every year, and Stern has the right electives for those interested in this career.

> **Stern is one of the few schools (along with others like Wharton, Columbia, Booth, and LBS) that reports placements into sales and trading every year, and Stern has the right electives for those interested in this career.**

You want to work in luxury goods. Very few top business schools have specialized offerings in luxury retail and brand management, and Stern is one of them. (Others include HEC Paris and ESSEC in France, along with some lesser-known programs in Europe such as SDA Bocconi.)

You're interested in media and entertainment. If you want to pursue a career in media, you probably need to be in New York or Los Angeles. Columbia, UCLA, USC, and NYU are the best choices for anyone looking to do something in the entertainment industry, the music business, sports, publishing, or broadcasting, and Stern has a specific program designed to support students and graduates.

You're interested in nonprofit. Stern has an active and growing presence into the nonprofit world—in New York City and beyond—as well as a strong social enterprise curriculum. New programs include the Stern Board Fellows, which appoints second-year students to serve as non-voting members on the boards of local charities, and classes such as *Examining the Non-profit Capital Market*, a course that teaches students how to apply best practices in business to the challenges of a nonprofit model.

You're in the New York City area and you want to keep your job. Trying to work full-time and complete your MBA part-time makes for a very hectic and sometimes-stressful life, but if you can't or would rather not give up your income, Stern has one of the best part-time programs in the country, with classes in both Manhattan and nearby Westchester County, New York. If you're looking to change careers, you'll want to stick with the full-time program since the part-time program won't include an internship.

You're applying right out of college. Since most MBA programs recommend at least two years of work experience before pursuing your MBA, opportunities for college seniors to go directly into business school are limited. The chairman of NYU Stern's Board of Overseers, William Berkley, donated $10 million in 2013 to fund a scholarship for college seniors who wish to move directly into business school to receive their MBA degrees. Called Berkley Scholars, about four to six college seniors will be selected each year and offered full-tuition scholarships, a housing stipend of $18,000 per year, and an additional $10,000 per year for books and other expenses. Although four to six seniors out of a class of 400 doesn't appear to be much, Stern's average number of years of post-college work experience (4.3) is lower than most top-tier programs, which suggests it is open to admitting fresh graduates and early career applicants.

STERN AT A GLANCE

APPLICANTS BY SCHOOL

◄ Percent admitted

Stern 3,890	Stanford 7,355	Harvard 9,543	Wharton 6,111	Columbia 5,799	Kellogg 4,652
18%	7.1%	11%	20.7%	18.2%	23.2%

AVERAGE GPA

3.52 3.50

Stern Columbia

AVERAGE GMAT SCORES

721 716

Stern Columbia

WOMEN

Stern's percentage of women is right in the middle of the pack among the top schools. However, with 37% of the class coming to the program from finance or technology, traditionally male-dominated fields, Stern has likely had to work particularly hard to recruit female candidates.

Stern

36%

Columbia

36%

Harvard

41%

Wharton

40%

AVERAGE YEARS OF WORK EXPERIENCE

Stern has one of the youngest incoming classes of any top-tier school with the exception of Stanford, which brought in a class having an average of 4 years of work experience before starting the program. Most schools have an average closer to 5 years of work experience.

4.3 Stern

4.6 Booth

5 Wharton

5 Columbia

UNDERGRAD MAJORS

Perhaps surprisingly, Stern admits more humanities and social science majors (37%) than any other top MBA program except Yale (38%). A few other programs report higher social science admits, but they combine social science with economics, a common field of study for management consultants.

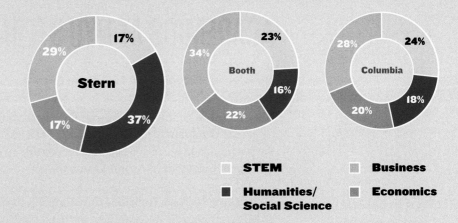

Stern 17% 29% 17% 37%

Booth 23% 34% 22% 16%

Columbia 24% 28% 20% 18%

- ☐ **STEM**
- ■ **Humanities/ Social Science**
- ▨ **Business**
- ▨ **Economics**

FROM TRADITIONAL SECTORS PRE-MBA

Although Stern is seen by many applicants as a veritable rotating door to and from Wall Street banks, its incoming class is significantly more diverse than other "finance" schools.

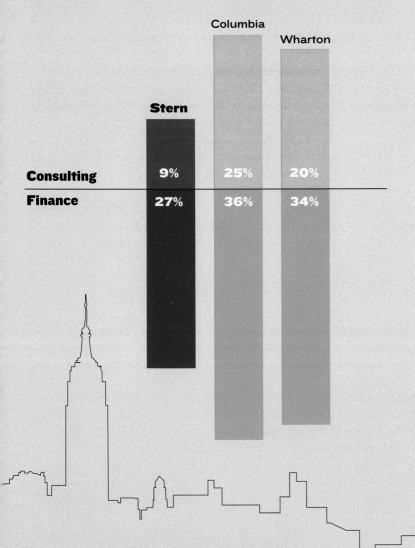

	Stern	Columbia	Wharton
Consulting	9%	25%	20%
Finance	27%	36%	34%

CLASS SIZE

The class size for Stern's full-time MBA program is relatively small compared to peers, but thanks to its robust part-time and EMBA programs, it boasts an alumni network of more than 100,000 strong in 125+ countries.

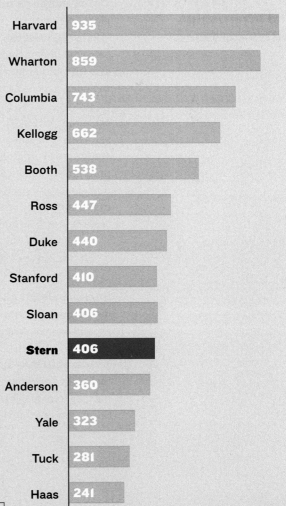

Harvard	935
Wharton	859
Columbia	743
Kellogg	662
Booth	538
Ross	447
Duke	440
Stanford	410
Sloan	406
Stern	406
Anderson	360
Yale	323
Tuck	281
Haas	241

NYU (STERN)

ACADEMICS AT NYU STERN

What NYU Stern Is Known For

Finance-plus. Stern has a long-standing reputation in finance and increasingly has been recognized for its strength in all other areas of MBA education. One of the most notable aspects of the program is how Stern integrates its powerhouse research faculty, its internationalism, its entrepreneurship, and its diversity into the day-to-day classroom experience.

Leveraging its New York location. Probably the factor that most impacts how Stern delivers its MBA education is its location in the center of New York City, including the strong ties it has to the city's immense and dynamic business community. Stern's location and community allow for a real-world component to just about any business subject being studied, and students are able to test their skills in short-term projects and internships with local firms. Despite the ties to New York City (Stern's "home, campus, classroom, and laboratory"), the school's administration prides itself on the broadly applicable nature of the education it delivers, stating that "Stern students develop the skills they need to succeed in any business environment, anywhere in the world."

> **Stern's location and community allow for a real-world component to just about any business subject being studied, and students are able to test their skills in short-term projects and internships with local firms.**

Doing Business in.... Stern is one of several business schools to turn its focus outward to a global perspective. In doing so the school has carved out a unique and popular offering called "Doing Business in..." (DBi). Held during extended breaks, such as January before the second semester and during spring break, DBi is either a 1.5- or a 3-unit course that features an intensive immersion into a foreign location for either one or two weeks. Recent DBi locations have included Argentina, Australia, Beijing, Hong Kong, India, Ireland, and Italy. One truly unique program is Stern's *Craft and Commerce of Cinema* course, held each year in Cannes during the acclaimed international film festival of the same name, during which students study film development, financing, distribution, and marketing. Additionally, Stern offers more traditional study abroad programs, whereby students can spend a semester studying with one of 44 partner programs in almost 30 countries. Most Stern students are a bit reluctant to spend one of their four semesters studying in a city other than New York (often a strong reason for choosing Stern in the first place), which is why the school moved to the DBi program as an alternative for those seeking international experience.

You Oughta Know

Summer Start. All full-time applicants are considered for NYU Stern's Summer Start academic program, designed to give non-traditional students (those from non-business backgrounds or who might have been out of school for a while) a head start on the first term.

Leadership Development Initiative. Incoming students begin work on the 360 assessment tool of the Leadership Development Initiative even before school starts. After individual coaching, participants create an Individual Development Plan to serve as a guide for their time at Stern. The program also includes workshops, speakers, and leadership simulations.

Core classes. From the first semester, Stern takes a balanced and general approach to management education. In their first year, MBA students are required to study a fairly rigorous core curriculum covering all fundamental areas of business. Out of 60 credits required for graduation, more than half are electives.

Electives. Stern offers one of the most extensive lists of elective courses of any business school. The adjunct professors, visiting scholars, and executives-in-residence who complement the tenured faculty add to the experienced and insightful practitioners in the community.

Specializations. Stern students graduate with an MBA in General Management, but have the flexibility to select up to three areas of specialization (or majors), or none at all. A specialization requires three courses (nine credits). The wide variety of course combinations (more than 200 electives) within the specializations enables students to pursue very specific educational objectives tailored to meet individual short- and long-term career goals. For example, Stern has five different finance-related specializations, four product/marketing specializations, plus resources in media, real estate, and business law, among other niche interests.

Nuts & Bolts

Class organization. At the Stern School, each incoming MBA class is divided into six "blocks" of 60–70 students who work closely together during the entirety of their first year. Blocks are further divided into diverse study groups of five or six students. Students identify themselves as members of their respective blocks, and, although great effort is made to have each block be as diverse as the overall class itself, each takes on a character of its own based on the personalities and interests of its members. Block members share an intense and transformative period of personal and professional growth and, whether or not they become enduring friends and key members of each other's networks, they maintain a strong connection post-MBA. Each block elects three "block leaders" (one international) to organize block activities, represent the block to the Stern Student Government (SGov), and administer the block budget. Blocks also stick together outside of class, for opportunities like Monday Block Lunches (guest speakers), the MBA Challenge (community involvement), and Block Olympics (self-explanatory).

Teaching methods. Stern's teaching methodology is a combination of the team projects (30%), case studies (25%), experiential learning (20%), lectures (20%), and other methods (5%). The school has a strong emphasis on research through such world-renowned centers as the Salomon Center for the Study of Financial Institutions, the Berkley Center for Entrepreneurial Studies, and the Glucksman Institute for Research in Securities Markets. This is evident in class content, which is regularly updated to reflect relevant developments in the business world. Professors encourage students to challenge assertions, and they create a healthy back-and-forth in the lecture halls and classrooms. At Stern, the world outside the classroom serves as a venue for testing real-world skills and theories.

NYU Stern Specializations:

Accounting

Banking

Business Analytics

Corporate Finance

Digital Marketing

Economics

Entertainment, Media and Technology

Entrepreneurship and Innovation

Finance

Financial Instruments and Markets

Financial Systems and Analytics

Global Business

Law and Business

Leadership and Change Management

Luxury Marketing

Management

Management of Technology and Operations

Marketing

Product Management

Quantitative Finance

Real Estate

Social Innovation and Impact

Strategy

Supply Chain Management and Global Sourcing

NYU (STERN)

Course enrollment. Course selection and enrollment can be tricky when you're trying to ful-fill requirements and satisfy multiple specializations in four semesters. Stern has academic ad-visers who help enrolled students understand their program requirements and options to make the process a bit easier. Stern uses a lottery system for course registration because for some popular classes there is more demand than seats available. The course enrollment process is done online, and MBA students have an approximately one-month lottery submission period, followed by an add/drop period about a month later, after the lottery results are made public. This system is actually referred to as a "weighted lottery," because it takes into consideration the program and expected date of graduation of each student, and in some cases the student's specialization(s). The weighted lottery system gives all students with the same graduation date an equal chance of getting into the classes they choose, allowing them to place emphasis on the courses that are most important to them.

> *Note:* The daytime sections of the core courses are reserved for full-time students, and the evening and weekend sections of these courses are reserved for Langone (part-time) students. Non-core courses are open to all Stern graduate students, regardless of meeting time, when space is available and prerequisites are met.

Grading policies. Stern uses a pretty typical scale of letter grades, and core courses are graded on a relatively rigid curve, with a maximum of 35% of the class receiving a letter grade in the "A" range. Although there has been much discussion of this policy, the school has determined that it keeps students focused on intellectual and academic rigor in acquiring basic skills and that it allows recruiters to identify the "best of the best" when trying to differentiate among candidates for post-MBA jobs. Some departments—in particular the Finance Department—encourage fac-ulty members to utilize curves for elective courses as well in order to truly differentiate among students. Corporate recruiters drive this to some extent; there has been a real desire on the part of firms recruiting at Stern to be able to identify those students who have truly excelled in fi-nance classes (in an overall strong pool of talent). The downside is that some students feel that this level of competition detracts from the collaborative spirit at the school (and some would say it is an indication that there is still a range of skill levels in the MBA class, as opposed to at some other elite schools where no numerical grades are used). Grades are turned around by teaching staff pretty quickly, and professors do a good job of communicating in advance the specific cri-teria that grades will be based on in their classes.

Popular Professors

Stern prides itself on the intellect, teaching skills, research accomplishments, and approachability of its faculty. The Stern faculty is populated with many prominent business leaders, researchers, and teachers. Among Stern students, there are quite a few professors who are considered a "must" to have for a class, due to their reputation both as educators and as experts. This list isn't merely a collection of famous names, but rather the instructors that NYU students deem to be essential for the full experience. Some of these notable professors include:

A. Michael Spence

William R. Berkley Professor in Economics & Business, Nobel Laureate

Dean Henry recruited Professor Spence from Stanford in 2010. Professor Spence won the Nobel Prize in 2001 and is a former dean of the Stanford Graduate School of Business. He joined NYU Stern to teach economics and to continue his research in economic policy in emerging markets. Dr. Spence is the author of *The Next Convergence*, a publication about emerging markets in the "post-crisis period."

Aswath Damodaran

Kerschner Family Chair in Finance Education

Professor Damodaran, an immensely popular faculty member whose status has risen to that of "guru," teaches corporate finance and equity valuation courses in Stern's MBA programs, with research interests focused on valuation, portfolio management, and applied corporate finance. At least one of his books on these topics (*Damodaran on Valuation, Investment Philosophies, The Dark Side of Valuation, Strategic Risk Taking,* and *Applied Corporate Finance: A User's Manual,* to name just a few) is almost certain to be found on any Stern MBA's bookshelf. Despite his prolific research and writing, Professor Damodaran's great love is teaching, and it shows. On the Stern faculty since 1986, he received the Stern School of Business Excellence in Teaching Award (awarded by the graduating class) in 1988, 1991, 1992, 1999, 2001, 2007, and 2008. Perhaps most importantly, Professor Damodaran is seemingly always available. He can be seen roaming the halls of the business school at all hours and is known for his quick e-mail replies—even in the middle of the night.

Edward Altman

Max L. Heine Professor of Finance

Staying current on Professor Altman's views and quotations in the media is almost a sport at Stern, especially in the present environment. In addition to being a hugely popular teacher, being the founder of the ZScore for predicting bankruptcy, and chairing the Stern MBA program for 12+ years, Professor Altman has directed the research effort in fixed income and credit markets at the NYU Salomon Center for Research in Financial Institutions and Markets since 1990, and is currently the vice director of the Center. Professor Altman has published or edited more than 20 books and well in excess of 100 articles in scholarly finance, accounting, and economic journals. He has consulted with numerous institutions and governments, and was a founding member of the board of trustees of the Museum of American Financial History.

Robert Engle

Michael Armellino Professor of Finance
Director of the Center for Financial Econometrics
Affiliated Faculty, Statistics Group

Professor Engle, an expert in time series analysis with a focus on financial markets, joined the Stern faculty in 2000 and is a 2003 Nobel Prize winner in economics for his research on the innovative statistical method ARCH. Professor Engle, the author of multiple books and journal articles, applies his methods to the analysis of equities, options, currencies, and interest rates. He is founding co-president of the Society for Financial Econometrics (SoFiE), housed at the Salomon Center for Research in Financial Institutions and Markets.

Eitan Zemel

W. Edwards Deming Professor of Quality and Productivity
Vice Dean of Strategic Initiatives

Professor Zemel, the founding chairman of the Information, Operations and Management Sciences Department at Stern, teaches *Operations Management* and *Operations Strategy*, and has published numerous articles and books on these topics. Professor Zemel's research involves complex computations and algorithms relating to areas such as supply chain management, operations strategy, service operations, and incentive issues in operations management. Internally, however, he is equally known for his involvement in the strategy and operational issues impacting the Stern School through his position as vice dean of strategic initiatives, a role that allows him significant exposure to and involvement with the broad Stern community.

Scott Galloway

Clinical Professor of Marketing

Scott Galloway is a clinical professor of marketing at NYU Stern School of Business, where he teaches *Brand Strategy* to second-year MBA students. He often hits lists of the world's best business school professors and is universally loved at Stern. He is also the author of the Digital IQ Index®, a global ranking of prestige brands' digital competence. Professor Galloway is the founder and CEO of L2, a think tank for prestige brands. Professor Galloway is also the founder of several firms, including Firebrand Partners, Red Envelope, and Prophet Brand Strategy.

Paul Romer

Professor of Economics

Paul Romer is professor of economics at Stern and director of its Urbanization Project. The Urbanization Project addresses a truly historic challenge and opportunity: welcoming an additional three to five billion people to urban life in less than a century. The Project's first initiative helps existing cities plan for expansion. Its second initiative fosters the creation of entirely new cities, because history shows that a new city offers a uniquely important opportunity to implement systemic social reform and speed up progress. Prior to joining Stern, Romer taught at Stanford's Graduate School of Business, where he took an entrepreneurial detour to start Aplia, an education technology company dedicated to increasing student effort and engagement. Romer is a research associate at the National Bureau of Economic Research and a fellow of the American Academy of Arts and Sciences. In 2002 he received the Recktenwald Prize for his work on the role of ideas in sustaining economic growth.

Similar Academic Programs

One of the most unique aspects of the Stern education is its integration with the surrounding community. Some courses will meet at local businesses to study how their operations differ based on industry, market pressures, competencies, and so forth. While this is quite unique among business schools, each of the following schools shares at least one similarity to Stern in the way it presents academics.

MIT (Sloan). Sloan has one of the most rigorous core curricula of any MBA program in the world. Leveraging its parent institution's brand in engineering and the sciences, Sloan's academics are very data-driven and analytically focused. Even "softer" subjects such as communications and organizational behavior have a strong analytical bent. However, like at NYU, the number of required core courses is quite limited, providing greater flexibility through the first year, and a learn-by-doing philosophy (called "action learning" at Sloan) permeates the curriculum.

Chicago (Booth). Booth's curriculum is even more flexible than NYU's, with just one required course and multiple options to fulfill all other requirements. Its student body is known for intellectual curiosity, and the school takes great pride in the academic rigor of its program compared to other, "softer" business schools. Also known as a strong finance school, the academics tend to be quite analytical in nature.

Cornell (Johnson). Johnson is also has a strong finance curriculum yet is rooted in general management. Stern and Johnson also share an emphasis on experiential learning and a blended teaching method. Johnson uses an "immersion learning" method to target first-year courses to student's professional goals.

Columbia. One can hardly mention Stern without its neighbor to the north coming up in conversation. The two programs are quite different, but both schools are extremely integrated in New York City. Columbia also allows students the opportunity to work in local (often unpaid) internships during the school year. This is quite uncommon at schools outside of New York City.

EMPLOYMENT & CAREERS AT NYU STERN

What NYU Stern Is Known For

Finance. As mentioned, Stern is a financial powerhouse, sending a large percentage of students to traditional roles in investment banking, sales and trading, and corporate finance. As well, many students move on to less-traditional careers in venture capital, private wealth management, private equity, and real estate. In fact, 35% of the Class of 2014 went into a finance-related field; that's more than fellow quant powerhouse Columbia, and on par with other top-tier finance schools including Wharton and Booth. Interestingly, Stern sends a much higher percentage (27%) into investment banking than Columbia (16%), Wharton (14%), and Booth (16%).

Graduates entering the finance industry

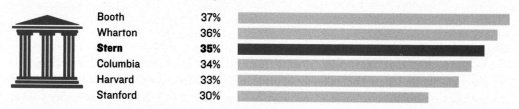

Booth	37%
Wharton	36%
Stern	**35%**
Columbia	34%
Harvard	33%
Stanford	30%

Media, entertainment, and technology. Access to major media, entertainment, and technology companies in New York City and beyond makes NYU Stern an ideal destination for career success in those industries. Over the last decade the school has brought companies such as Apple, Google, and Microsoft to campus. This, along with the leagues of alumni working in traditional media, is one of Stern's undeniable strengths. Twelve percent of the Class of 2014 accepted jobs in these industries.

Graduates entering media and entertainment jobs

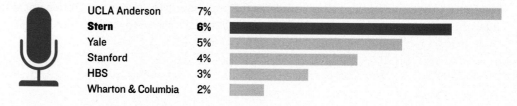

UCLA Anderson	7%
Stern	**6%**
Yale	5%
Stanford	4%
HBS	3%
Wharton & Columbia	2%

Luxury and retail. Although it might not be obvious from raw placement statistics, Stern has a strong Luxury and Retail program that garners a lot of attention. It is one of just a handful of MBA programs with dedicated resources for a luxury and retail career path. Given the strong network of luxury retailers in New York City, the school is well positioned for candidates who are looking to advance in this field or switch into it.

You Oughta Know

Entrepreneurship and innovation. NYU Stern's Berkley Center for Entrepreneurship and Innovation offers a comprehensive program of courses and practical experience for future entrepreneurs. Stern's culture encourages an entrepreneurial approach from academics to on-campus clubs. More and more students are pursuing this path during their time at Stern; 3% of the Class of 2014 reported starting their own businesses after graduation.

Graduates electing to pursue entrepreneurial opportunities

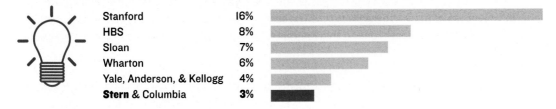

Stanford	16%
HBS	8%
Sloan	7%
Wharton	6%
Yale, Anderson, & Kellogg	4%
Stern & Columbia	**3%**

Industry Captains in Residence. This mentoring program brings NYU alumni back to campus for one-on-one conversations with MBA students. Past Industry Captains have come from a diverse list of companies including Apple, HBO, and West Elm Brand.

Ignite. The Office of Career Development (OCD) holds an innovative Ignite program that prepares students to meet potential employers. Ignite meets on Fridays (when no classes are in session) and includes industry panels, resume critiques, networking workshops, and mock interviews.

Salaries. Not that all you care about is money, but surely you want to make sure your MBA investment is worthwhile. So it should make you happy to learn that the average base salary for Stern's Class of 2014 was $112,096, with real estate hires landing the highest base of approximately $136,000, followed by consulting at $126,000. (Just remember to be a bit careful when looking at overall median salary numbers, because they can be skewed by high salaries in particular industries. Schools that send fewer students to those industries can be at a disadvantage.) But wait—that's not all! The average signing bonus was just more than $31,000.

Grade disclosure. Stern does not have a grade non-disclosure policy during recruiting, so recruiters may ask about grades. Future investment bankers in particular report being asked to report their GPAs. Combined with a fairly strict grading curve, this policy results in more a more competitive academic environment than at most business schools.

Similar Programs for Professional Opportunities

Penn (Wharton). The finance similarities make comparisons between the two schools inevitable (and necessary), but the two schools also send a similar percentage of grads into consulting and consumer goods/retail.

Columbia. Although NYU Stern's uptown neighbor actually sends a slightly smaller percentage of grads into finance than NYU, the two schools share many specialties: finance, media and entertainment, technology, even retail. A decision between the two schools may come down to culture (see the next section).

Chicago (Booth). Along with Wharton, Columbia, and Stern, Booth is known for finance. More than a third of the class goes directly into the finance industry upon graduation, with another 4% taking finance roles in other industries. Booth sends more than a quarter of its class (28%) into the management consulting industry, which is identical to Stern's placement in this industry.

Dartmouth (Tuck). Many applicants wouldn't think of Tuck as being very similar to NYU Stern, since Tuck is located in rural New Hampshire, far from the hustle and bustle of New York City. However, when it comes to professional opportunities, Tuck holds its own in the finance sector. One quarter of the Tuck class goes into the finance industry, and the school has done an excellent job of maintaining its ties to the sector. The differences lie in general management, where Tuck sends nearly one in five graduates, whereas Stern sends just 3% of its grads into such roles.

UCLA (Anderson). The West Coast media and entertainment powerhouse, UCLA sent 7% of the Class of 2014 into "the industry"—almost identical to the proportion of Stern's class. UCLA, however, sent more than a quarter of graduates into technology—far more than Stern's 6% placement in this industry. If you're looking for finance jobs on the West Coast in particular, Anderson should be at or near the top of your list as a school that sent 28% of its graduates into finance roles.

CULTURE & CAMPUS LIFE AT NYU STERN

What NYU Stern Is Known For

A vibrant community. As one of the world's premier management education institutions, NYU's Stern School of Business is a collaborative community of energized and entrepreneurial individuals. Located in the heart of New York City, the school benefits from its multitude of intellectual, commercial, cultural, and human resources, and it frequently cites its NYC location as a key differentiator. Stern students, alumni, faculty, and staff are passionate about their school, and there is a never-ending discussion of how to continuously improve, and how to clearly demonstrate the school's myriad strengths and differentiating factors to the outside world. In some ways, the school's story is analogous to that of its benefactor and namesake, Leonard N. Stern, billionaire son of the German immigrant who founded the Hartz Mountain Pet Company.

Ties to Wall Street. New York University's "Wall Street Division" was in close proximity to the many financial institutions whose employees made up a large component of the student body—a connection that significantly influenced the school's focus and culture. Following a $30 million landmark gift from Mr. Stern and another $10 million gift from alum Dr. Henry Kaufman, Stern's undergraduate and graduate programs were consolidated at NYU's Washington Square campus in a state-of-the-art facility, the Henry Kaufman Management Center, in the 1990s.

Heritage of diversity. The Stern School's roots trace back to 1900 and downtown Manhattan, when the school opened as the School of Commerce. Attention, female applicants: The first women matriculated that very year (1900). That's two decades before women in the United States were allowed to vote! The school hired its first female faculty member in 1913. Today, the school is one of the most active partners in diversity-related organizations, including the Consortium for Graduate Study in Management, Management Leadership for Tomorrow (MLT), Robert Toigo Foundation, Graduate Horizons, and Forte Foundation.

Warm and welcoming culture. The composition and personality of the student body reflect the school's eclectic downtown neighborhood; it's diverse and welcoming. Despite the urban setting and lack of centralized housing, students form tight-knit groups thanks to the school's collaborative, friendly culture. Most students tend to live off campus, although limited on-campus housing is available.

You Oughta Know

Connection to parent university. Stern's Graduate School of Business is one of many prestigious NYU graduate programs. The brightest stars in the constellation of NYU programs include the consistently top-five-ranked law school, the Wagner School of Public Service, the Tisch School of the Arts, and the Courant Institute of Mathematical Sciences. These and other programs at NYU boast world-class faculties, facilities, and resources, making Stern's eight dual-degree programs all the more attractive.

Lively life on campus. The new student guide offers a helpful "How Do I Find the Bar?" guide. Need we say more? This is a school that likes to have fun, and especially in downtown New York City, that's not hard to do. Beer Blasts bring full-time, part-time, and EMBA students together from 6PM to 10PM each Thursday night in an unusual show of inter-MBA unity. The "Beer Blast Room," located in the Kaufman Management Center, always seems to have a never-ending supply of kegs at the ready.

Newly renovated facilities. With the completion of the Concourse Project in 2010, Stern students benefit from a beautifully renovated space full of light and compelling urban design elements. The Concourse Project unites and synthesizes Stern's three buildings (Kaufman Management Center, Tisch Hall, and Shimkin Hall) through renovated lobbies and the lower and upper concourses that span the three buildings. The visual and practical effects of the project, which included new pathways to link the school's three buildings, plaza skylights, floor-to-ceiling windows, and state-of-the-art classrooms to yield flexible learning environments, are dramatic. However, despite the facelift, Stern's facilities still feel a bit claustrophobic compared to the sweeping new buildings at Chicago Booth, Wharton, and Yale.

Similar Programs Culturally

Northwestern (Kellogg). Yes, you can get a great education at Kellogg, but you also won't lack for social events (read: parties). Its energy and vibrancy go toe-to-toe with NYU Stern's despite its location in the sleepier Chicago suburb of Evanston, Illinois. Even though its full-time MBA class is two-thirds larger than NYU's, Kellogg is known for its friendly and collegial atmosphere and fun-loving students.

Duke (Fuqua). Although the campus atmosphere at Fuqua is decidedly suburban, not urban, it's also a fun-loving, tight-knit culture with a plethora of on-campus events in which students,

> Despite the urban setting and lack of centralized housing, students form tight-knit groups thanks to the school's collaborative, friendly culture.

> This is a school that likes to have fun, and, especially in downtown New York City, that's not hard to do.

NYU (STERN)

faculty, and staff mix and mingle. An added dimension at Fuqua is the Blue Devils basketball team, which creates strong ties between Fuqua students and Duke University.

Berkeley (Haas). Haas has one of the smallest classes among world-class MBA programs, and this leads to a very friendly and welcoming vibe among students. Like Stern, Haas focuses strongly on building a diverse class of students with wide-ranging backgrounds and perspectives. It is an active participant in many diversity-related recruiting organizations.

UCLA (Anderson). Student involvement is at the core of Anderson's culture, in which the ideas of shared success and "paying it forward" are key. Students certainly make the most of Anderson's Southern California location, with frequent beach activities and other events throughout Westwood, Santa Monica, and West Los Angeles. Andersonians are a lively crew, holding professional and interest-based social events throughout the week, ranging from tailgate parties at Bruins football games to "Dinner for 8" networking events with prominent alums.

ADMISSIONS AT NYU STERN

What NYU Stern Is Looking For

Two decades ago, upon receiving Leonard N. Stern's transformative naming gift of $30 million, the Stern School implemented an initiative to attract the elite caliber of student that would support its ambitious goals. Since that time, the profile of the average Stern MBA student has strengthened significantly, and admissions criteria have become increasingly stringent. The Stern School's admissions committee claims to evaluate each candidate "holistically," paying careful attention to three clearly defined factors:

Academic profile. Students should be "confident in their ability to master the required material and excel in the classroom," and are assessed based on past academic performance (as well as the institutions they attended) and general aptitude as measured by the GMAT and GPA. Successful candidates come from a wide range of academic backgrounds, and Stern has no minimum criteria for accepting an application. In reality, though, most applicants whose profiles are outside the middle-80% range of GMAT scores (currently, the bottom 10th percentile is a 680), or who have a low undergraduate GPA (10th percentile is a 3.2), will have a tough time gaining an offer at Stern. Specifically, Stern is looking for the following in terms of your GMAT and GPA:

> **Successful candidates come from a wide range of academic backgrounds, and Stern has no minimum criteria for accepting an application.**

- **GMAT or GRE.** Stern accepts scores from either test for applicants to the full-time or part-time MBA program. Like other schools, Stern encourages MBA candidates to re-test if they feel their score does not reflect their full potential. There is no minimum GMAT/GRE score for admission, though the average GMAT is an impressive 721. Note that no test score at all is required to apply to the Stern EMBA program.

- **GPA.** While Stern has no minimum GPA, it does seek students who have proven their ability to perform in an academic environment. For older applicants, the GPA is usually not weighted quite as much as it is for younger ones. However, anything less than a 3.0 (on the U.S. 4.0 scale) means that the candidate should provide additional evidence of academic ability.

Professional achievements and aspirations. Students who will "share their experiences with classmates and perform as future business leaders" are valued at Stern. Therefore, students who have interesting and significant work experiences and who have progressed in their jobs are attractive candidates. The Stern admissions committee also feels strongly that time spent at Stern should be used to pursue specific, defined short- and long-term goals, not to first identify them. Accordingly, it seeks candidates whose past experiences (and personal passions) have led them to future goals and who have a clear understanding of how an MBA will assist them in achieving those goals. Stern assesses candidates' essay content, resumes, work histories, and professional recommendations. In the interview, the admissions team evaluates candidates' ability to express themselves in a professional setting. Although work experience is not required to apply to Stern, most applicants have "material" work experience (between one and 10 years). No one type of professional experience is prized over others, and a diversity of backgrounds is sought for each incoming class.

Personal characteristics. Stern has long had a reputation with outsiders as a meritocratic institution, rich with "scrappy," self-made individuals. Stern claims that it values "participants and leaders" who will "contribute to the supportive and diverse Stern community." The admissions committee looks for candidates who demonstrate leadership ability, maturity, character, and strong communication skills, and who will develop into truly engaged and passionate "Sternies," with enduring pride in and commitment to the school. They look to assess candidates against these criteria by reviewing essay content, professional recommendations, and past activities and achievements, and through the interview process.

Fit with Stern. In addition to the above three factors, the Stern admissions committee wants to be convinced that applicants have "done their homework" on Stern, NYU, and New York City. Candidates should demonstrate that the overall environment is one in which they will thrive and to which they can make significant contributions. To assess candidates in this area, the admissions committee focuses on how aware candidates seem to be of Stern's culture, program offerings, facilities, faculty, placement record, and alumni network, and of how these aspects of the school appeal to them and meet their specific needs. Stern students tend to be energetic, driven, outgoing, sociable, entrepreneurial, and open-minded, and candidates possessing such characteristics are desirable for the admissions committee.

Commitment to Stern. Of course, this focus on "fit" is of critical importance to the admissions committee in filling out the MBA class; they want to feel relatively certain that a great number of admitted students consider Stern their "first choice" and will accept their offer of admission. Therefore, if there is any sign in your application that you'd actually prefer to go to that other school uptown—such as reusing an essay and forgetting to change the school name to Stern—this will likely result in an instant pass by the Stern admissions committee. Similarly, two of the most important points of emphasis in an interview with Stern are a genuine interest in the school and an ability to express how you would contribute to the culture and the community. These are best developed through significant firsthand research into the school via networking and attendance at the school's outreach events.

> The admissions committee looks for candidates who demonstrate leadership ability, maturity, character, and strong communication skills, and who will develop into truly engaged and passionate "Sternies," with enduring pride in and commitment to the school.

NYU (STERN)

Preparing to Apply

Reading this Essential Guide is a great first step in your preparation. Hopefully, this insider's glimpse has been helpful in understanding the most important aspects of the school. However, nothing can replace gaining firsthand knowledge and experience yourself. Stern places more emphasis on this kind of research than perhaps any other business school, so you'll need to explain to the school the steps you've taken to prepare in Essay 1.

Reach out to current students. Even if you don't have any personal connections to NYU Stern, you can reach out to current students and get their insight and advice. On the school's Student Clubs page, you'll find a list of all campus clubs. Find a few clubs that fit your personal and professional interests, and reach out to the officers. Remember: These are very busy MBA students, so you don't want to intrude too much on their time, but you could ask for a 10- to 15-minute conversation or elicit some advice via e-mail. Come prepared with specific questions (preferably those that aren't already answered online). If you're planning to visit campus, perhaps you might even arrange a coffee chat or lunch, if they are available.

Visit campus. The school's website can only tell you so much; by far, a personal visit is the best possible research in the application process. If you have the means, we highly recommend you visit NYU Stern in person along with the campuses of your other top choices to understand the significant differences in culture, teaching style, student body, recruiting opportunities, facilities, and so forth. You may be surprised at just how different each school can be and and how the reality can differ from the perception. We encourage you to take advantage of opportunities to visit campus; but, because informal and impromptu encounters can be the most informative, don't be afraid to approach students in less-formal settings.

Other events. We know that many applicants will not be able to travel to New York to visit campus, but you should take advantage of other worldwide admissions events, such as information sessions, virtual sessions, and specific-audience events. In fact, these off-campus events can offer great opportunities for quality time with admissions officers and even other applicants, who can be a great resource and support through the admissions process. Get to know the school and its culture as well as you can, because your familiarity can shine through your application and essays to help you stand out.

You Oughta Know

When should I apply? Stern has a unique, four-round application process. As we always tell applicants, you should only apply when you're absolutely ready, so don't rush to hit that Round 1 deadline if it means putting in anything less than an airtight application. However, note that applying in Round 1 means that you will be notified whether or not you will receive an interview by December 15, giving you several weeks to prepare Round 2 applications to other schools if you get bad news from Stern. Many applicants find the Round 1 deadline appealing for this reason.

Notifications. Note that Stern uses the term *Notification Deadline* differently than many other MBA programs. You'll only be notified of an invitation to interview, waitlist offer, or denial of admission at this point. You'll have to wait another three weeks or so to conduct your interview and receive your final decision.

Don't wait until Round 4. Stern actually advertises a benefit to applying in an earlier round. Successful Round 1 and Round 2 candidates receive priority consideration for merit scholarships and off-site interviews, and those admitted in Rounds 1, 2, and 3 receive notification in time to attend the school's "Pre-View" admitted student event held in April. Applying during the last round at any business school requires careful examination of the pros and cons, but the fact that Stern highlights missed opportunities of later rounds is a soft indicator that Round 4 may be more challenging at NYU than it is at other top schools, especially now that it's offering four total rounds. Stern also encourages international candidates to apply by its November 15 deadline to facilitate visa arrangements and to have priority consideration for off-site interviews.

Deadlines. If you're applying to NYU, just remember "15." Its four deadlines are October 15, 2015; November 15, 2015; January 15, 2016; and March 15, 2016. This approach is so logical. (Other schools: Take note please!) Unlike most other schools, Stern is known to take a peek at applications as they come in, so submitting even a few days before the deadline can have some slight advantages.

The Essays

The content of NYU's application essays hasn't changed at all since last year, so our advice mostly remains the same. However, the admissions committee no longer gives you a choice between two prompts for their famous "Personal Expression" essay. Thankfully, Stern is still sticking to reducing the total amount of "stuff" that you will submit to the school. Note that the part-time and EMBA programs have different questions and applications.

Stern provides applicants with admissions tips on its website, including podcasts, to help you clarify your story. These are great resources for any Stern applicant.

Essay 1: Professional Aspirations (750 word maximum, double-spaced, 12-point font)

- *Why pursue an MBA (or dual degree) at this point in your life?*

- *What actions have you taken to determine that Stern is the best fit for your MBA experience?*

- *What do you see yourself doing professionally upon graduation?*

Connect the dots. An MBA may seem like an obvious choice to you, but don't just assume that the admissions committee will understand why it's the right choice. They want to hear your decision-making process in your own words. Clearly connect the dots among what you've done to this point, what you want to do in the future, and why you need an MBA from Stern to get there. Don't feel like you need to address each bullet point in the order that they are presented. Perhaps the reason why you decided to pursue an MBA is closely tied to your professional goals, so make that connection explicitly between "Why pursue an MBA?" and "What do you see yourself doing professional upon graduation?" Then you can address why Stern is the best fit in the last portion of your essay.

Do your homework. Be sure to answer clearly the actions you have taken to determine that Stern is the best fit for your MBA experience; Stern clearly wants to see that you have done your homework and are applying to the school for reasons that go beyond the obvious. Besides look-

NYU (STERN)

ing at the rankings or seeing that Stern places a lot of graduates in investment banks every year, what have you done to be sure that Stern is a good fit for you, and vice versa? (Hint: Check out the other sections of this Guide!) Like most top-ranked business schools, Stern places a good deal of emphasis on fit, and you need to demonstrate that you have done the same.

Be specific. Also note the emphasis on specifics. Don't describe your knowledge of Stern in generalities, and don't just copy language from the school's website. What do you know about NYU Stern that convinces you that it's the right school for you, and how do you know that you're the ideal Stern student? This essay is your chance to convince the admissions committee that you will be a good fit with their program. Moreover, looking at this kind of essay question early in the process will hopefully provide the impetus you need to really do your homework. And, note the title of the essay: Professional Aspirations. You must be very clear about your career goals, and you must specifically identify how a Stern MBA will help you achieve those goals.

Outline realistic goals. There are several pitfalls to avoid when it comes to post-MBA goals. First, don't be so open-ended that it's clear you have no idea what you want to do. We see a lot of goals that say, "I'm looking for a management position at a Fortune 500 company." This says almost nothing about what you want to do; it just says you want a job—pretty much anywhere. Stern wants to see that you've put extensive thought into what motivates you, what you're passionate about, and how your previous experience will translate into future endeavors.

Second, don't feel like you need to differentiate yourself through your career goals by inventing something outlandish. A quick glance at Stern's employment numbers will tell you that plenty of candidates go into very traditional roles such as investment banking, consulting, and retail goods. Honest, realistic, and achievable goals are better than false ones ones every time.

Third, don't feel like you're trapped into one course by writing it down. The school is most interested in seeing if you have a clear vision for how you'll achieve your ambitions. However, by highlighting one path, this doesn't mean that there aren't other opportunities you may explore while at Stern as well. If your "Plan A" is a fairly high-risk career path, then you might mention a backup plan here as well.

Essay 2: *Personal Expression*

Please describe yourself to your MBA classmates. You may use almost any method to convey your message (e.g. words, illustrations). Feel free to be creative.

See the NYU Stern website for additional guidelines and restrictions in submitting your Personal Expression.

Express your true self. Stern has used this question for years, meaning that the admissions committee must feel that it's effective in helping them get to know candidates. Stern truly wants to learn about what makes you unique. The school's admissions officers are almost begging you to stand out here, which is a reminder about how you can make their job easier by helping them remember the real you. There is no pressure to link this essay or submission directly to business school in any way.

Submit anything. As you'll see in Stern's instructions, you may physically mail them an item that you feel best represents you. Be careful in what you select, however, because the item will not be returned. (In fact, they now have a whole room full of objects that have been submitted over the years!) Finally, while this essay prompt truly is wide open in terms of what you can submit, note that there are a few parameters (e.g., nothing perishable!) that you need to observe.

An essay is perfectly fine. Just because this question allows you to use any medium doesn't mean that you need to submit something other than the written word. If that's your best medium, use it. "Being memorable" means more than just sending them something outrageous; the most effective submissions really are the ones that leave admissions officers feeling like they know you better.

Essay 3: Additional Information (optional)

Please provide any additional information that you would like to bring to the attention of the Admissions Committee. This may include current or past gaps in employment, further explanation of your undergraduate record or self-reported academic transcript(s), plans to retake the GMAT, GRE and/or TOEFL or any other relevant information.

As we always advise our clients when it comes to optional essays, only use this essay if you need to explain a low undergraduate GPA or other potential blemish in your background. No need to harp on a minor weakness and sound like you are simply making excuses when you don't need any. If you don't have anything else you need to tell the admissions office, it is entirely okay to skip this essay. If you have gaps in your employment, poor academic performance, undergraduate disciplinary actions, or other things to explain in your profile, do so in a straightforward way. Simply explain the circumstances and take responsibility for your actions, focusing on how this experience helped you learn, grow, and mature.

Recommendations

Two recommendations are required with your application to Stern. Specifically, professional recommendations are strongly preferred over academic recommendations. One recommendation must come from your current supervisor. If a recommendation from your current supervisor cannot be included, you must provide an explanation in the optional essay. Stern does allow additional recommendations as long as they add a new perspective.

Recommender information. Your recommenders should be prepared to answer the following questions:

- *Is the applicant currently employed by your organization? [Yes, No]*
- *Are you an alumna/alumnus of the NYU Stern School of Business? [Yes, No]*
- *If yes, what year did you graduate? [Year (YYYY)]*
- *If yes, what was your degree? [Degree]*

> **"Being memorable" means more than just sending them something outrageous; the most effective submissions really are the ones that leave admissions officers feeling like they know you better.**

Scaled assessment. Your recommender will be asked to rate you on the following traits in relation to your peers: analytical/quantitative ability, oral communication skills, written communication skills, initiative, integrity, leadership, maturity, teamwork, professionalism. Each trait is rated on the following scale: *Outstanding (Top 5%), Excellent (Top 15%), Good (Top 1/3), Average (Middle 1/3), Below Average (Bottom 1/3), Unable to Judge.* The admissions committee would be surprised to see an Outstanding rating listed for every attribute. Recommenders should genuinely rate your strengths and weaknesses to make the most impact on your admission.

Finally, your recommender will be asked to make an overall recommendation regarding your admission to Stern:

- ***Please make your overall recommendation regarding this applicant's admission to NYU Stern:*** *[I strongly recommend this applicant for admission, I recommend this applicant for admission, I recommend this applicant for admission with some reservation, I do not recommend this applicant be admitted.]*

Written assessment. Your recommender is given the following questions with these instructions: *Please respond to the following questions, using specific examples when possible. You may answer each question separately in the boxes provided OR upload a Word document or PDF document which includes all of your responses.*

- *How long have you known the applicant and in what capacity? [1000 characters]*
- *How do the candidate's performance, potential, background, or personal qualities compare to those of other well-qualified individuals in similar roles? Please provide specific examples. [3000 characters]*
- *Please describe the most important piece of constructive feedback you have given the applicant. Please detail the circumstances and the applicant's response. [3000 characters]*
- *How would you describe the applicant's interpersonal skills? [1000 characters]*

Selecting your recommenders. The best recommenders are people who can provide very detailed examples of your actions and behavior. In general, the admissions committee will be far more impressed by a genuine and passionate letter by a middle manager who is your supervisor than a polite letter from a well-known CEO that lacks depth and detailed anecdotes about you. In other words, don't ask your company's CEO, whom you might or might not have met once in the cafeteria. And hopefully you don't need to be told this, but NYU Stern discourages recommendations from family members, family friends, and close friends. Look for people who can speak very clearly about your performance in relation to peers.

Should I draft it myself? Many applicants to business school are asked by their superiors to draft the recommendation themselves and the recommender will approve it. We strongly recommend that you do not write the recommendation yourself for several reasons. First, your writing style and choice of phrasing are unique, and admissions officers will notice if the recommendations are similar to each other and to your essays. If they notice too many similarities, your application could be denied outright. Second, you may tend to be too humble or generic. Your supervisor might use language such as "one of the top analysts I've seen in my entire career" that you wouldn't dare include if you're writing it on his or her behalf. Third, and perhaps most importantly, the admissions officer is looking for a third-party perspective on your candidacy, so writing a recommendation yourself is an unethical breach of trust with the school you are looking to join. NYU Stern requires applicants to certify that they have not been involved in drafting their recommendations either in whole or in part.

Preparing your recommenders. Instead of writing the recommendation yourself, you should sit down and have candid conversations with your recommenders about the reasons you want to go to business school and why you've selected your target schools, your professional goals, and your experience together. Ask them if they would have the time to write a strong recommendation on your behalf. (This also gives them a nice "out" by telling you that they are too busy rather than saying they don't feel comfortable giving you a positive recommendation.) Bring a copy of your resume and a bulleted list of projects that you've worked on together and accomplishments they have seen you achieve. Let them know that the admissions committees prefer to see specific, detailed examples in recommendations. Then, let them know that you'll serve as a "project manager" to follow up and ensure that they are able to submit your recommendation ahead of the deadline.

The Interview

Who is selected to interview? Interviews at Stern are by invitation only, and only about 30% of all applicants receive an invitation, which is quite low compared to other schools. The Stern interview is typically conducted on campus, although some off-site interviews are possible—in particular in India, England, and China, depending on the specific candidate pool each year. (The school will also help candidates schedule lunch with a current student while visiting campus, which provides another opportunity to gain insight into the program.) Only trained admissions professionals conduct Stern interviews; alumni and students are not part of the process. This allows the school to standardize the experience and make sure that the assessment is consistent across all candidates.

How does it work? Stern interviews are not "blind," so the interviewer will be highly familiar with your application package, including your essays. During the interview, you'll be expected to articulate key aspects of your academic and professional profiles, your short- and long-term goals, and why Stern is a good fit for you. The interview will be highly candidate-specific and will make good use of the relatively short time frame. Otherwise, there is no particular interview style used by admissions officers or any specific line of questions that can be expected.

How many people are admitted? Being invited to interview should be viewed as a very positive development, as nearly 70% of those interviewed are ultimately admitted. The most common reason for a candidate to make it to the interview stage and not receive an offer of admission is lack of knowledge about the school and how one will contribute to its vibrant culture. If you haven't done your homework, admissions officers will assume that NYU is merely a backup school and not your top choice. Interviewers also look for a level of polish that will impress corporate recruiters once you're admitted.

> **Being invited to interview should be viewed as a very positive development, as nearly 70% of those interviewed are ultimately admitted.**

NYU (STERN)

DARTMOUTH TUCK

The first school to offer a master's degree in business, Tuck emphasizes fundamentals.

📍 HANOVER, NH

CLASS SIZE
281

PROGRAM FOUNDED
1900

SETTING
RURAL

CHARACTERISTICS
QUAINT, TRADITIONAL, FAMILY ATMOSPHERE

DARTMOUTH (TUCK)

TUCK SNAPSHOT

What Tuck Is Known For

Quaint New England setting. Located in picturesque Hanover, New Hampshire (population 11,000), on the campus of Dartmouth College, the Tuck School of Business offers an Ivy League experience in a uniquely close-knit and supportive community. The intimacy of the community is also enhanced by the fact that most first-year students live in dormitories on campus, typically referred to as a "residential MBA." This arrangement is not common at other full-time programs, where students tend to be more spread out, especially those in urban environments.

Strong general management program. One of three professional schools at Dartmouth, Tuck is consistently recognized as a strong general management program whose students are known for teamwork and leadership. The program ranks as a world-class business school, coming in at #9 on *U.S. News & World Report's* most recent rankings and #15 on *Businessweek's* latest rankings. Tuck also occupies the #2 spot on *The Economist's* "Which MBA?" list, which heavily weighs student evaluations of their MBA experience.

Consistency. Tuck is the oldest graduate school of management in the country (Wharton was the first business school, but for undergraduates), and its original teaching philosophy and instructional model continue to influence other top graduate management schools. Tuck has stayed true to a fairly rigid first-year core at a time when many schools are scrambling to roll out a flexible curriculum; it also has maintained a heavy case method approach in the face of increasingly diverse program choices. While this approach may seem limiting at first glance, Tuck students often find that it actually alleviates stress about juggling options, since the Tuck curriculum guides them through a tried-and-true path.

> With fewer than 300 students per graduating class, Tuck is one of the smallest elite business schools in the world.

Individual attention. Because of the small class size, Tuck offers an intimate, personal culture, with faculty and administrators personally available to advise and customize a student's learning experience and career development. Tuck professors are readily available to meet with students, and they enjoy doing so. With fewer than 300 students per graduating class, Tuck is one of the smallest elite business schools in the world. It's also one of most remote locations of any top school, and probably the only one without the likes of even a Marriott hotel in driving distance. (Although in keeping with the quaint New England culture, you'll find plenty of B&Bs and inns nearby.)

What Makes Tuck Different

One big Tuck family. Though most business schools spend lots of time talking about their cultures, few of them can demonstrate a truly tangible "culture" the way that Tuck does. Visitors get a sense of the family-like community the minute they set foot on campus. Small class sizes foster close bonds among students, encouraging teamwork and a collaborative, intellectual environment. Tuck's remote location also lends to a concentrated social environment that creates early bonds that last most Tuck grads a career and a lifetime.

Access to faculty. Tuck's small size also translates to an impressively low 10:1 student-to-professor ratio and allows unprecedented student access to the faculty, whether it's in a seminar setting or at a Tuck social event. Eighty-six percent of Tuck's classes are taught by full-time faculty members, as opposed to visiting professors, lecturers, and adjuncts, more than at most MBA programs. This helps foster the student-professor relationship, although we don't see the statistic alone as an inherent strength. Many students at other MBA programs find lecturers and adjunct faculty members to be their favorites, largely thanks to their recent and ongoing connections to industry.

Helpful alumni. The other key difference at Tuck is the commitment to the school found among alumni. Tuck graduates give back to the school at a rate higher than any other, with a 20-year track record of more than 60% of alumni donating. This level of alumni involvement also translates into a significant resource for current students, who often end up in internships and first jobs that result from an alumni referral or connection. For alumni effectiveness, Tuck ranks #1 in *The Economist*'s "Which MBA?" poll of current and recent students.

Dedication to diversity. Tuck's Minority Business Executive Education program was the first diversity-focused program of its kind. Tuck launched this initiative more than 30 years ago, and the school remains dedicated to its mission of attracting students across all ethnographic and demographic groups. Tuck sponsors a by-application Diversity Conference, affectionately dubbed "Div Co," each fall. The school also participates in conferences hosted by National Black MBA, National Hispanic MBA, and Reaching Out MBA (for the LGBT community). And, Tuck is the second-highest-ranked member of The Consortium for Graduate Study in Management, behind only Berkeley-Haas according to *U.S. News* rankings. All that said, Tuck still seems to have trouble consistently attracting minorities compared to some of its peers, with just 14% of the Class of 2016 being U.S. minorities, the lowest of any school included in this Guide.

Unique admissions policies. Tuck doesn't seem to be trying to do things differently just to be different (as we sometimes suspect at other schools), but the school is quite thoughtful in how it approaches admissions. We'll discuss in further detail in the Admissions section, but highlights include the applicant's ability to report multiple test scores, initiate an on-campus admissions interview, receive feedback on denied applications, and obtain a deferral for extenuating circumstances.

Tuck Is a Good Fit for You If...

You come from an underrepresented group—or another country. We've already covered Tuck's support of and interest in minority applicants. If you're an international candidate, you may also want to consider Tuck more closely. Despite its ranking, international applicants sometimes tend to overlook the school, possibly due to lack of familiarity with the location. And the foreign nationals who do apply often do not understand how Tuck is different, and thus they do not show an appreciation for Tuck when writing their application. This makes it very difficult for the admissions committee to accept them. Because of this, well-qualified international candidates who have done the legwork and know how Tuck can help them achieve their goals can find themselves strongly positioned in the admissions process.

You bring strong professional experience. Although some other business schools in its backyard have been welcoming younger and younger students, Tuck has held steadfast on its requirement for significant work experience prior to matriculation. The average age of a first-year is 28, and not a single person entered Tuck straight from college this year; 100% have some work experience. The age range for the Class of 2016 was 23 to 35 years old at matriculation.

You want to work in New York, Boston, Chicago, or San Francisco. Graduates who stay in the U.S. are most frequently found in these cities, with 22% of the Class of 2014 heading to the New York City area.

You want to work in Japan or the UK. Because of the smaller size of the overall network, Tuckies are not as easily found all around the world. However, due to the school's outreach and attention in past decades to both Japan and the UK, more Tuck alums are found in these countries than others. Five percent of the Class of 2014 placed in Europe, which is high compared to other top-tier schools, which typically place between 1 and 3% in this region.

You have a military background. Tuck appreciates the men and women who have unparalleled leadership and team experience (and often international experience) via the military, U.S. and otherwise. (China and Israel seem to be the top supplier of military applicants outside of the U.S.) Tuck is extremely pro-military and accepts the Yellow Ribbon education funding from the U.S. government for qualified applicants. The Armed Forces Alumni Association is the student club for military students and alumni.

You are bringing a partner and/or a family with you to business school. Nearly a third of Tuckies (32%) come to campus with a spouse or partner, which is among the highest of top-tier business schools. Like many business schools, Tuck has a club, outreach, and resources available for partners of students to minimize the sense of alienation that can be felt when your significant other disappears from your life for a good two years. Tuck is an inclusive community, and spouses, partners, and children usually report feeling very welcome and engaged. However, Hanover is a small town, so employment options for a partner may be limited.

Not a single person entered Tuck this year straight out of college; 100% of the class have some work experience.

Tuck is extremely pro-military and accepts the Yellow Ribbon education funding from the U.S. government.

You love the outdoors (and the snow!). Your years of business school will be a lot of work, but why not also go to a school where you know you'll be able to play? If you're into winter sports and love the beauty of the mountains, Tuck might be more enticing than any other school. Dartmouth is one of just two colleges in the country to own its own ski resort, called the Dartmouth Skiway. In addition, the Tuck Hockey Club is one of the most popular clubs on campus. Approximately 150 Tuck students and partners of all skill levels form eight ice hockey teams each fall term and six teams each winter. Whether you play hockey now or not, you may find yourself learning the sport while at Tuck!

You're switching careers. Tuck doesn't shy away from or discourage those who want to use business school as a catalyst to change direction—or even jump the tracks. With the increased attention on career development that begins for new Tuckies literally the day school starts, the school is ready and able to provide the in-depth support and concentrated attention to help traditional and nontraditional students alike realize their dreams. About two-thirds of Tuckies change careers as they go through the program, which is higher than many other schools report. The dean has said that business school is the proper platform for all types of career-changers, including the more "challenging" types like those coming from an arts background and looking to transition into business. You still need to express your goals well in your application, whatever direction that might lead; don't feel like only certain paths are "acceptable" at Tuck.

You want to go into finance. One doesn't typically think that going to the secluded hills of New Hampshire would be an ideal path to Wall Street. However, 25% of the Class of 2014 went into the finance industry, bested only by finance heavy hitters like Wharton, Columbia, and NYU Stern. Plus, Tuck's strength in private equity seems to be a well-kept secret—unless you're in private equity. In this exclusive industry, "who you know" can really matter, and the Tuck alumni network is vital. The school even has a research institute specifically for private equity; no other business school has anything quite like it.

You're interested in energy. When you think of "energy" schools, Tuck might not be the first one that comes to mind. But if that's your chosen field, you should carefully consider heading to Hanover, thanks to the Dartmouth Energy Collaborative, an association formed among Tuck and several other schools (both at and outside of Dartmouth), and the Revers Energy Initiative, formed in 2012.

You appreciate the small size and strong relationships. Tuck definitely has all of the advantages of a small school in terms of community and network, and it works hard to mitigate the challenges of the remote location (in terms of attracting teaching talent and recruiters) and the smaller alumni network. There's a lot to be said for being able to disconnect from the world for two years to "immerse" in the business school education, and, for the right type of person, Tuck can be an excellent choice. If you already went to Dartmouth for undergrad, even better: Tuck tends to look favorably on applications from Hanover alumni.

You're not afraid to work hard. Tuck is known to be a place where students roll up their sleeves and dive in. The workload at Tuck is tough, even compared to other very challenging programs. If you enjoy the company of hardworking people, Tuck may be just the place for you.

TUCK AT A GLANCE

APPLICANTS BY SCHOOL

Tuck receives fewer applications than any of its peer schools, likely due to its remote location. As a result, the admissions committee admits more than 22% of applicants.

 Percent admitted

Tuck 2,437	Harvard 9,543	Stanford 7,355	Wharton 6,111	Fuqua 3,453	Ross 2,443
22.1%	11%	7.1%	20.7%	25.1%	33.7%

AVERAGE GPA

Tuck **3.5**   Harvard **3.67**   Haas **3.62**   Stanford **3.74**

GMAT SCORES

Tuck **716**   Stern **721**   Yale **720**   Duke **690**

NATIONALITY

65% U.S.

35% International Citizens

 23 Countries Represented

WOMEN

At 32%, Tuck had the smallest percentage of women of any business school's Class of 2016 in our research except UCLA Anderson (30%). However, that number jumped to 42% for the Class of 2017.

Tuck
 32%

Harvard
41%

Stanford
42%

Haas
43%

UNDERGRAD MAJORS

Nearly half of Tuck's incoming class has an undergraduate background in business or economics, demonstrating that the Tuck applicant pool tends to comprise fewer non-traditional applicants than at many of its peers.

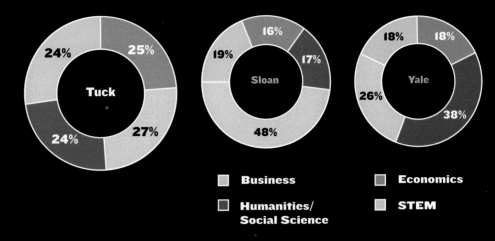

Tuck
- 25%
- 27%
- 24%
- 24%

Sloan
- 16%
- 17%
- 48%
- 19%

Yale
- 18%
- 18%
- 38%
- 26%

- ■ **Business**
- ■ **Economics**
- ■ **Humanities/ Social Science**
- ■ **STEM**

FROM CONSULTING/FINANCE SECTOR PRE-MBA

Tuck's admitted class includes a higher percentage of applicants from the finance industry (35%) than any school other than Columbia (36%). However, many of these people choose to switch industries post-MBA, frequently to management consulting.

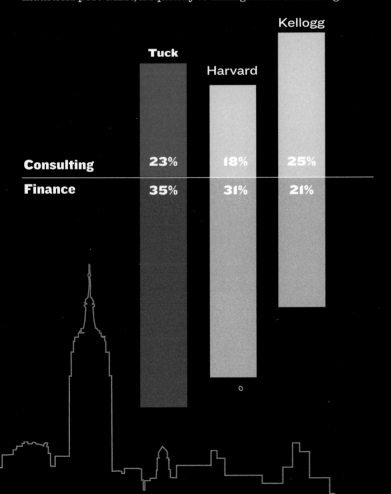

	Tuck	Harvard	Kellogg
Consulting	23%	18%	25%
Finance	35%	31%	21%

CLASS SIZE

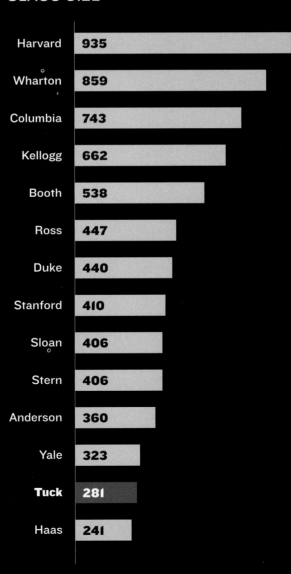

School	Size
Harvard	935
Wharton	859
Columbia	743
Kellogg	662
Booth	538
Ross	447
Duke	440
Stanford	410
Sloan	406
Stern	406
Anderson	360
Yale	323
Tuck	281
Haas	241

DARTMOUTH (TUCK)

ACADEMICS AT TUCK

What Tuck Is Known For

One school, one degree. Whereas other schools take pride in diversifying their academic offerings, expanding to Executive MBA, part-time MBA, evening MBA, weekend MBA, online MBA, and even other degrees like MSx or MSc Finance, you won't find those at Tuck. A la Henry Ford, any customer at Tuck can have any degree he or she wants, as long as it's a full-time MBA. This focus means that your experience will be highly cohesive; your classes won't be infiltrated with students from other degree programs. The school does, however, offer a number of joint-degree and dual-degree options, some in conjunction with other institutions.

Rigid core curriculum. Tuck has an integrated and rigorous first-year core curriculum with a general management focus that prepares students for virtually any role in business. This 31-week, full-year core is slightly longer than those at other business schools. Students with extensive experience may waive just one core course and take an elective instead, placing Tuck's policies among the least flexible in business schools today.

60% of the core is taught using the case method teaching style.

Case method. Tuck is one of the few business schools (along with HBS and Darden) that continues to use the case method teaching style as the predominant method, especially for core courses during the first year. Sixty percent of the core is taught via the case method, with the balance of the classes featuring the usual business school alchemy of lectures, experiential learning, and group projects. Class participation is another important component of the Tuck academic experience, often representing 30 to 50% of a student's grade.

You Oughta Know

A new dean. After one of the longest tenures at the helm of any top business school, Dean Paul Danos announced his retirement in 2014. In 2015, the college appointed Matthew Slaughter to take his place, a longtime Dartmouth professor. The founding faculty director of the school's Center for Global Business and Government, Dean Slaughter has already announced a new program called "Tuck GO," which promises to ensure every Tuck student graduates with a global mindset. However, since Dean Slaughter has taught at the school for some time, we don't anticipate any dramatic departures from the course Dean Danos has forged.

Rigorous workload. The school combines theoretical and experiential learning with a focus on leadership, teamwork, and globalization. These elements inform each and every aspect of the Tuck academic experience as well as the type of recruitment that occurs on campus. Many come to visit the school or even begin the program expecting to find a laid-back, "summer camp" atmosphere, but while the culture is uniquely close-knit, the academic workload is actually very intense and focused.

Experiential learning projects. One of the most interesting elements of the Tuck curriculum is that while it is a fairly case method–heavy school, it is also at the forefront of experiential learning. An entire term of the first year is devoted to the First Year Project, in which outside companies engage student teams to help solve a real-world business problem. This extensive offering is augmented by a second-year project that is shorter in duration but equally impactful in the way that students get exposure to actual, real-time issues.

Leadership and teamwork. While it may not be as widely known for combining leadership and teamwork as schools like Kellogg and UCLA Anderson, Tuck is a business school that puts a premium on developing leaders who are also valuable team players. The school recognizes the business adage that a leader is "only as good as the people around him." Students expect a great deal out of one another, and an honor code emerges that drives students to greater levels of achievement.

Leadership Fellows. In addition to putting its students into team scenarios that foster leadership, Tuck has stepped up its commitment to leadership in its Center for Leadership. The Tuck philosophy is that all of its students have leadership potential, and it therefore provides courses, individual coaching, and practical exercises (including self-assessments, peer assessments, goal-setting, and individual leadership development plans) to develop and draw out these qualities. Second-year students may serve as Leadership Fellows who learn how to develop others through coaching and mentoring first-year students.

Electives. In the second year, Tuck offers more than 75 electives, allowing students to focus on and master specific functional disciplines. With just 50 full-time faculty members, the selection of electives is much narrower at Tuck than at larger schools, which may offer 200 courses or more. The teaching style also shifts from case method to include lecture, small groups, group projects, and experiential/simulation approaches.

Entrepreneurial opportunities. The entrepreneurial clubs of both Dartmouth and Tuck sponsor an annual business plan competition at the end of the Spring Term. The winning team gets $50,000 and the support of the Barris Incubator program. More importantly, winning candidates gain the opportunity to present their business idea to an impressive and influential audience of judges including successful entrepreneurs and venture capitalists.

Global Insight Requirement. Tuck students are required to complete a global immersion (officially termed the Tuck Global Insight Requirement). Most other schools adopted similar requirements years ago, but since Tuck has numerous other requirements in the core curriculum and first-year project, we don't fault them for waiting to add even more.

Nuts & Bolts

Class organization. Each incoming class at Tuck is divided into four sections of approximately 60–70 students each. These sections are randomly assigned, although Tuck makes sure that each section has a balanced mix of backgrounds. The sections are reassigned every term, so by the end of the first year, students have worked closely with everyone in their class.

Study groups. The MBA Program Office also assigns study groups in the first year to ensure a balance of professional expertise and background diversity. One twist on the typical section model is that during first year, study groups change each term. In the second year, students can pick their elective courses and their study groups.

DARTMOUTH (TUCK)

Course enrollment. At the end of the first year, Tuck distributes a list of upcoming electives for the second year. Students can rank courses in which they are interested. Based on interest levels, Tuck will sometimes provide a second section of a popular course. While Tuck can guarantee that students will get to take the courses that interest them the most, they cannot guarantee a specific professor. This is one of the huge benefits to Tuck's small size and personalized approach, as students are not forced to run through the bidding gauntlet or lottery systems present at so many other top schools.

Grading policies. There are four passing grades at Tuck: Honors (H), Satisfactory Plus (S+), Satisfactory (S), and Low Pass (LP). The distribution considers both absolute and relative standards. Faculty members outline expectations at the beginning of each course, and students rarely receive failing grades. Nearly all students apply themselves to their studies, so most students are likely to be disappointed if they "loop" a class (i.e., receive a grade of LP, or low pass). However, many students who arrive at Tuck are interested in the overall experience and are willing to accept a grade of S if it means that they can have more time for other activities that contribute to their Tuck experience. In keeping with Tuck's supportive atmosphere, students do not typically discuss or advertise their grades.

Grade disclosure. Companies recruiting at Tuck are permitted to ask students about grades and request transcripts from job candidates. However, candidates do not have to respond to grade inquiries, nor are they required to comply with transcript requests during the interview process. However, if candidates divulge information about their grades, they are bound by Tuck's Honor Code to provide data that accurately reflect their school record.

On the one hand, the school's partial-disclosure policy supports the atmosphere of teamwork and cooperation that characterizes the Tuck community. On the other hand, the academic and recruiting environment at Tuck remains competitive, because students are aware that recruiters may inquire about their grades.

Popular Professors

Tuck has attracted a world-class faculty to Hanover, in part because the faculty-student relationship is so central to the learning environment at Tuck. This element of the culture is often just as appealing to elite academics as it is to prospective students. Among the students, certain Tuck professors are considered a "must have" for a class, due to their reputation both as educators and as experts. Their dynamic personalities and unique teaching styles make even rigorous academics a fun and memorable learning experience. Some of these notable professors include:

Kusum Ailawadi
Charles Jordan 1911 TU'12 Professor of Marketing
Known for her remarkable ability to make marketing science methods relevant to business practice, Professor Ailawadi sets high expectations of her students in the classroom, encouraging them to learn from each other in a way that echoes Tuck's core values. Within the field of marketing, her expertise also includes econometrics and statistics. Professor Ailawadi's marketing electives offer students a unique opportunity to bridge the creative thought process with practical research and rigorous analysis.

Paul Argenti
Professor of Corporate Communication

Nothing is more indicative of Professor Argenti's passion for communication than the manner in which he practices what he preaches. His annual first-year lecture on *Time Management for MBAs* is just the introduction to what he offers Tuck students in the realms of general management, corporate communication, and corporate social responsibility. Tuck has consistently received high marks in communication instruction due to the scholarship and teachings of Professor Argenti and his colleagues, including his wife, Professor Mary Munter. (The two of them are sometimes dubbed "The Armuntis" by students.)

Ella Bell
Professor of Business Administration

A dynamic speaker, Professor Bell has a way of motivating students to take action. Her friendly, no-nonsense demeanor encourages students to honestly examine their own views as they develop capacities for embracing diverse perspectives in her popular second-year elective, *Leadership Out of the Box.* Her approach to organizational behavior is molded by her research on issues such as work-life balance and challenges faced by women (and especially women of color) in the corporate world. Outside of the Tuck community, she is also known for her column, "Working It," in *Essence* magazine and her book, *Our Separate Ways: Black and White Women and the Struggle for Professional Identity.*

Kenneth French
Carl E. and Catherine M. Heidt Professor of Finance

Among his many accolades, Professor French is best known for his work in developing the Fama-French Three Factor Model, completed in conjunction with Eugene Fama of the University of Chicago. Given Professor French's expertise in the areas of portfolio theory, asset pricing, dividend policy, and capital structure, it is no surprise that students flock to his classroom for a taste of the perspective he brings to investing in the capital markets. Students especially benefit from his balance of professor and practitioner, serving as the director of investment strategy at Dimensional Fund Advisors. In turn, he is impressed by the manner in which Tuck students negotiate a balance between studies and activities, since he himself enjoys cycling, snowshoeing, and hiking, offering further proof of how Tuck really does facilitate exchanges "outside" of the classroom.

Vijay Govindarajan
Coxe Distinguished Professor of International Business
Director of Tuck's Center for Global Leadership

Fondly referred to as "VG" by his students and throughout the business community, Professor Govindarajan has been recognized as a thought leader and top-ranked professor of strategy by numerous publications, such as *Businessweek, Forbes,* and *The London Times.* He was voted the #3 greatest business thinker in the world by Thinkers50 in 2011 and #5 in 2013. In the most recent ranking, he was ranked the #1 Indian management thinker. His electives for second-year students are among the most popular courses at Tuck. After taking a year-long leave of absence to serve as GE's first "professor in residence" and chief innovation consultant, VG returned to Tuck in 2009. True to Tuck form, and in spite of his stature outside of Tuck, VG remains accessible to students. He is also the co-author with Chris Trimble of the highly acclaimed book, *Reverse Innovation.*

DARTMOUTH (TUCK)

Similar Academic Programs

Harvard. If the general management emphasis and case study approach sound appealing, you'll of course want to look into the ultimate case study school. Other than teaching method, though, the two schools are quite different, particularly in class size. (HBS is the largest of the top-tier schools and Tuck is one of the smallest.)

Yale. Yale School of Management offers a small class size and an integrated core curriculum that focuses on the various stakeholders in business, including the customer, investor, manager, employee, and so forth. If Tuck's broad, general management curriculum interests you, then be sure to check out Yale as well.

Virginia (Darden). Darden shares a strong emphasis on teaching and academics, particularly in its usage of the case method and emphasis on participation. Students and faculty also interact frequently, in part due to Darden's smaller class size (~325), another similarity to Tuck.

Michigan (Ross). While Ann Arbor is a larger college town than Hanover, Ross shares a similar climate and culture with Tuck. Its Multidisciplinary Action Project (MAP) is the closest parallel to Tuck's first-year project, and it shares a strong general management focus.

Western Ontario (Ivey). Ivey also remains committed to the case study method, feeling that it best prepares students to tackle real-world problems. The only case-based business school in Canada, Ivey also offers a winter climate similar to Tuck's.

EMPLOYMENT & CAREERS AT TUCK

What Tuck Is Known For

> Tuck's culture of being a transformative and a life-changing experience means that it is more tolerant of driven applicants who may not have totally locked down their post-MBA goals.

A transformative experience. Tuck prides itself on being transformative and life-changing, and assumes that its graduates will leave as very different people than when they arrived. For that reason, Tuck has a much higher tolerance than other elite programs when it comes to talented and driven students who may not be as clear on their career goals. It is the ultimate "come as you are" business school. However, applicants who are uncertain about their post-MBA goals need to show some overall direction in their careers; the school is not interested in attracting aimless dilettantes. Therefore, while Tuck may be more flexible than most MBA programs in its philosophy, you still have to present a natural and clear career path to gain admission.

General management. Nearly one in five Tuck graduates (18%) takes a general management position coming out of school. This may not seem like a high number, given the fact that graduates of every MBA program get an education in "management." However, Tuck sends the largest proportion of its class into general management and rotational programs of any top business school. On the flip side, it sends almost no one into operations, supply chain, or strategic planning roles.

Graduates entering general management positions

Tuck	18%
HBS & Cornell	13%
Yale	11%
Sloan & Anderson	10%
Kellogg, Haas, & Duke	9%
Stanford	7%

Consulting. Although Tuck encourages students to find their own way, nearly half (40%) of them pursued a career in consulting/strategic planning, with 35% pursuing positions in the management consulting industry. Tuck and Kellogg placed the highest number of graduates into consulting roles compared to other top-tier programs, although the industry remains a popular destination for graduates across nearly every elite business school.

Graduates entering the consulting industry

Kellogg & **Tuck**	**35%**
Sloan, Ross, & Columbia	34%
Duke	30%
Booth & Stern	28%
Wharton, Haas, & Yale	26%

You Oughta Know

The herd mentality. Students support each other throughout the recruiting process. Students are discouraged from developing the "herd mentality" that sometimes pervades the recruiting process and leads a large number of students to interview with only a handful of recruiters. However, Tuck still sends 60% of its graduates into the traditional MBA industries of consulting and finance, one of the highest proportions of any business school. Ironically, it is the "herd mentality" that contributes to the need for some recruiters to have to employ an especially rigorous screening process that involves inquiring about a student's grades.

Connections. Coupled with its small-town charm and the inherent insular bubble of Dartmouth is the fact that Tuck offers legitimate access to top recruiters and networks, both in the Northeast as well as throughout the U.S. and abroad. The school has strong ties to Manhattan in both the finance and consulting sectors, and these connections produce results. More than 700 companies, both domestic and international, actively recruit at Tuck (even though each class has fewer than 300 students). Ninety-one percent of the Class of 2014 who were seeking employment had accepted a job by graduation; three months later, that number was up to 98%. These are the highest employment rates of any top-tier school we've seen, including the likes of Harvard and Stanford.

Private equity. As we mentioned in the Tuck Snapshot section, Tuck is not usually mentioned in lists of "finance schools," but it is quite well regarded within finance circles. Twenty-five percent of Tuck students go directly into the finance industry upon graduation, which isn't too far behind more traditional finance schools like NYU Stern (35%), Wharton (36%), Columbia (38%), and Chicago Booth (37%). It's known particularly in private equity circles as a "hidden gem" among business schools. The school's strong connections and deep roots in the industry contribute to its reputation in this notoriously insular industry.

Graduates entering the private equity industry

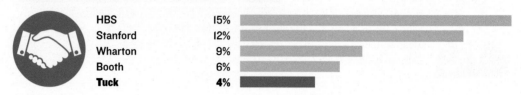

HBS	15%
Stanford	12%
Wharton	9%
Booth	6%
Tuck	**4%**

A little bit of everything. Unlike business schools that have established a clear brand in finance, or technology, or marketing, Tuck grads' career paths are distinguished by their breadth across disciplines. Of the remaining class who did not pursue finance or consulting jobs, popular choices were technology (18%) and consumer goods (7%). However, given its small class size, it's surprising to see decent representation going into health care (6%), manufacturing (3%), and energy (2%). Most schools its size send no graduates at all into many of these industries.

Northeast dominance. Nearly half (45%) of the Class of 2014 remained in the Northeast; that's higher than any other top-tier school except Yale (59%) and NYU Stern (70%). Even top-rated business schools tend to place the majority of their graduates close to home. While this is often a result of stronger relationships with employers in a school's region, graduates often choose to attend a business school where they ultimately wish to live post-MBA. Most schools have mobility and strong alumni networks across the country and globally, but applicants would be wise to consider placement statistics by location when considering which schools to target.

Salaries. Not that all you care about is money, but surely you want to make sure your MBA investment is worthwhile. So it should make you happy to learn that the median base salary for Tuck's Class of 2014 was $116,000, with consulting hires landing the highest base of approximately $135,000. (Just remember to be a bit careful when looking at overall median salary numbers, because they can be skewed by high salaries in particular industries. Schools that send fewer students to those industries can be at a disadvantage.) But wait—that's not all: The average signing bonus was $25,000, with 87% of the class reporting a signing bonus.

Similar Programs for Professional Opportunities

Yale. It's not a complete surprise that another general management school in the Northeast with a relatively small class would have a career statistics similar to Tuck; what may be surprising is just how closely the numbers align. If you're looking for a smaller school that sends its graduates into a variety of industries and roles, Yale is worth a look. Many applicants don't realize the ties that Yale has to New York City, including a strong pipeline into finance companies. Several second-year students even choose to live in the City and commute to New Haven for class.

Cornell (Johnson). Johnson's class size is nearly identical to that of Tuck, and yet it is also extremely successful in securing jobs for its graduates every year. The school puts more resources into career management per student than perhaps any other U.S. business school. As a result, its placement numbers rival Tuck's, and its distribution of industries is remarkably similar. One-third of Johnson graduates go into finance roles upon graduation.

Chicago (Booth). Located in urban Chicago, Booth couldn't be more different from Tuck when it comes to environment and surroundings, so the two schools are rarely compared. However, when it comes to professional opportunities, candidates who are attracted to Tuck should give Booth a close look. More than 70% of Booth graduates land in a consulting or finance-related role after business school, compared to 65% at Tuck. The remaining Booth grads spread fairly evenly among marketing/product management, general management, strategic planning, business development, and other roles.

Harvard. Harvard has a strong general management curriculum and sends graduates into a wide variety of industries. Given its reputation and prestige, it's often the top-choice school for many applicants. However, given the many similarities in academics and professional opportunities, Tuck is often a close second. However, the two programs couldn't be more different culturally, so make sure you understand what it means to become a "Tuckie" before applying.

UNC (Kenan-Flagler). Known for a student body that's exceptionally friendly and down-to-earth, the culture also closely mimics that of Tuck. Kenan-Flagler sends about 12% of its class into general management roles, highlighting a similarly strong academic emphasis on general management.

CULTURE & CAMPUS LIFE AT TUCK

What Tuck Is Known For

Ivy League roots. Founded in 1900 as the first graduate business school in the U.S., Tuck has a decidedly "Ivy League" image. Dartmouth College was founded in 1769 and maintains a strong focus on undergraduate education and liberal arts. In addition to Tuck, the other professional schools at Dartmouth are the Thayer School of Engineering and the Geisel School of Medicine.

An isolated location. The setting in Hanover is dramatic and very different from the urban landscapes you'll find at many other elite MBA programs. Each New England season drapes the campus in memorable colors: the brilliant reds and oranges of autumn, the whitewash of winter, and the vivid greens and chocolate browns of what Hanover residents call "mud season," when the frozen New England ground gives way to spring. In spite of the cold, Tuck students are active year round, taking advantage of everything that New Hampshire's Upper Valley has to offer.

However, Hanover is two hours from Boston, three hours from Montreal, and nearly four-and-a-half hours from New York City. As with many aspects of Tuck, the location glass can be either half full or half empty. If your glass is half full, you'll focus on the beautiful surroundings, an ample opportunity for outdoor activities, the cohesive community that the location fosters, and the lack of distractions that encourage you to focus on studying. The half-empty glass can't get past being two hours from Boston and four-and-a-half hours from New York City, which complicates travel for breaks and recruiting and limits social opportunities.

> A small school located far beyond the bright lights of the big city, Dartmouth encourages a sense of community that can be either incredible or intimidating, depending on one's personality and expectations.

A cohesive community. Tuck is known for building a close-knit community full of friendly, innovative people who love being "Tuckies." A small school located far beyond the bright lights of the big city, Dartmouth encourages a sense of community that can be either incredible or intimidating, depending on one's personality and expectations. With a class of fewer than 300 students, just one or two people who don't thrive in the Tuck lifestyle can affect the whole group. As a result, the admissions committee is very vigilant in selecting candidates who understand what they're getting themselves into! (Read more in the Admissions section.)

Difficulty attracting a diverse population. While the school boasts a decent international population and a fair number of female students, it is not as diverse as most of the top schools. Only 14% of the students come from minority groups in the U.S. However, this isn't due to a lack of effort. Tuck is well-known for its diversity initiatives.

You Oughta Know

A truly residential campus. More urban schools tend to struggle with getting students to engage in campus life, but that's not an issue at Tuck, where many students live right on campus. You won't find everyone rushing out after class to catch the next train or bus home. Many first-year students live on campus in modern residence halls such as the Living and Learning Complex, which features 145 furnished rooms with a private bath and shared spaces such as lounges, study rooms, conference rooms, laundry rooms, and kitchen and dining areas. The fabulous Living and Learning building even features a resource center complete with a copier, fax machine, and supplies that come in handy when students are working late at night on a case with their study groups. An exercise facility, lockers, showers, and changing rooms are available in Whittemore Hall for use by the Tuck community.

Opened in 2009, the Achtmeyer and Pineau-Valencienne Halls are the latest addition to Tuck's evolving residential village. With demand for on-campus housing growing, Tuck uses the lottery system to assign students to the residence halls, which are only available to single students. Numerous off-campus housing options, including Sachem Village, are available nearby for second-year students and Tuck students with partners or families. Many students live nearby in grand private homes, such as the affectionately named "Burrito Barn" and the "Sky Box," which are owned by Tuck alumni, with leases passed down from class to class.

Facilities. Although some business schools are moving to one large building, Tuck's campus of several smaller, yet interconnected, buildings maintains the New England charm of the campus. Living and learning spaces are integrated. Tuck's academic buildings are equipped with the latest in desktop and mobile computing, including facilities for video conferencing and multimedia production.

Leadership opportunities. Tuck's smaller size translates into greater opportunities to get involved in the school. It boasts a large number of professional, cultural, service, and athletic clubs offering opportunities for involvement and leadership, and the administration sees this involvement as a natural part of the leadership development journey at Tuck. Much of your development will come outside of the classroom, so be sure to mention the extracurricular opportunities you plan to get involved with while writing your admissions essays.

Tuck 'Tails. Since there aren't any classes on Fridays, Tuckies get together pretty much every Thursday evening for a sponsored happy hour called Tuck 'Tails. Each week is sponsored by a different club or organization on campus.

Winter Carnival. If you can't beat (or escape) the weather, go play in it. The annual Tuck Winter Carnival is typically held in February and has become a business school tradition, attracting 14 schools from across the country to compete in various events, parties, and competitions. Although ski races are the premier event, the less athletic will find plenty of activities to enjoy, some even indoors.

Small Group Dinners. A mainstay of the Tuck culture are Small Group Dinners, where students can get to know one another in a friendly and intimate way. This universally beloved tradition is a chance for students, faculty, or staff to host six guests for a casual meal, and it exemplifies the family-like atmosphere that permeates the Tuck culture. In fact, one class felt that this tradition was so core to their Tuck experience that they created a gift to fund one Small Group Dinner every year.

Other must-attend events. In addition to Tuck 'Tails, Winter Carnival and Small Group Dinners, Tuckies say the other must-attend events include Fall Formal, Tucktober Fest, Diwali (a celebration of Indian dance), the Frosty Jester comedy show, and Tuck Follies musical revue.

Similar Programs Culturally

Yale. Yale School of Management (SOM) students and alumni consider one another family, similar to Tuck's intimate learning environment. The class sizes at the two schools are nearly identical, so students tend to know pretty much everyone in their class incredibly well. Both schools put a premium on attracting extremely intelligent and curious applicants, so their admitted students tend to share these characteristics.

Cornell (Johnson). Nestled in Ithaca, New York, Cornell boasts a culture and surroundings remarkably similar to those you'll find at Tuck. Students tend to be the types who don't mind the quiet isolation but look for more individualized attention and deep ties to fellow classmates and faculty members.

Duke (Fuqua). IIf you're attracted to the close-knit community and fostering of teamwork that Tuck provides, you should also consider the Fuqua School of Business at Duke University. Both programs are similar in terms of their emphasis on teamwork and collaborative leadership. However, the Fuqua experience has a less "Ivy League" feel to it; for example, students camp out for days to get their Blue Devil basketball season tickets.

UCLA (Anderson). Another school known for its focus on teamwork and its strong general management curriculum is the Anderson School of Management at UCLA. If you're attracted to a smaller class size and community but want to be in a big city, you should explore the MBA programs at Anderson.

Virginia (Darden). Given its location in beautiful Charlottesville, Virginia, Darden is also seen as an escape from the big-city urban life, although it couldn't be more different from Tuck when it comes to climate! The student culture at Darden is more "blue blazer country club" as opposed to Tuck's "turtleneck mountain cabin" kind of feel.

ADMISSIONS AT TUCK

What Tuck Is Looking For

Fanatical about fit. Perhaps more than any other MBA program, Tuck is fanatical about "fit" with the program. Whether it's visiting campus for an interview, applying in the Early Action round, or simply speaking to a number of current students or recent alumni and including many school-specific elements in your essays, you want to do everything in your power to signal to the admissions committee that you understand the school and its culture, and want to contribute to it. Reading this Guide is a good first step in understanding the pros and cons of the Tuck experience. However, nothing can replace gaining firsthand knowledge and experience yourself.

Admission criteria. Besides demonstrating a strong fit with the school, successful candidates to Tuck showcase many of the same skills and attributes as those to other top schools:

- **Academic excellence.** Outstanding academic ability, intellectual curiosity, and a mastery of quantitative concepts.

- **Demonstrated leadership.** Leadership in extracurricular activities, the workplace, and/or community, as well as future leadership potential.

- **Notable accomplishments.** Significant academic, professional, and community achievements that have had an impact.

- **Interpersonal skills.** Personality, maturity, and communications skills conveyed via interview, essays, and recommendations.

- **Diverse background/experience.** Demographic and geographic diversity, as well as range and mix of professional experiences.

- **Global mindset.** Fluency in a second language, as well as work, study, or extensive travel outside of one's home country, can help a candidate stand out.

Work experience. On average, those admitted to Tuck have five years of full-time work experience. The admissions office almost never grants admissions to students straight out of college. Tuck strives for a diverse student body and seeks qualified applicants from all backgrounds. However, Tuck recommends that applicants coming from non-business backgrounds prepare by taking classes in microeconomics, financial accounting, statistics, finance, and even Microsoft Excel.

> The admissions office almost never grants admissions to students straight out of college.

 If you are looking for tips on 2016–17 admissions essays, you're in luck! Check out our website at **veritasprep.com/tuck** for our latest advice.

Preparing to Apply

Reach out to current students. Even if you don't have any personal connections to Tuck, you can reach out to current students and get their insight and advice. You can find a list of all campus clubs and activities on the school's website. Find a few clubs that fit your personal and professional interests, and reach out to the officers. Remember: These are very busy MBA students so you don't want to intrude too much on their time, but you could ask for a 10- to 15-minute conversation or elicit some advice via e-mail. Come prepared with specific questions (preferably those that aren't already answered online). If you're planning to visit campus, perhaps you might even arrange a coffee chat or lunch, if they are available. Or you might provide a quick background introduction and ask if there's another member of their club, even one with a similar background, who might be able to offer some insights into and advice about his or her Tuck experience.

Visit campus. Admissions officers at Tuck strongly encourage everyone to visit campus before attending. If you don't have the opportunity to visit before applying, they will invite you to come for an on-campus interview. A school's website can only tell you so much, and they want you to fully understand what you're getting yourself into! If you have the means, we highly recommend you visit Tuck in person before applying along with the campuses of your other top choices to understand the significant differences in culture, teaching style, student body, recruiting opportunities, facilities, and so forth. You may be surprised at just how different each school can be and and how the reality can differ from the perception. We encourage you to take advantage of formal opportunities to visit campus, including an applicant-initiated interview where you can speak with admissions officers before submitting your application. Because informal and impromptu encounters can be the most informative, also don't be afraid to approach students in less-formal settings.

Other events. We know that many applicants will not be able to travel to New Hampshire to visit campus, but you should take advantage of other worldwide admissions events, such as information sessions, virtual sessions, and specific-audience events. In fact, these off-campus events can offer great opportunities for quality time with admissions officers and even other applicants, who can be a great resource and support through the admissions process. Get to know the school and its culture as well as you can, because your familiarity can shine through your application and essays to help you stand out.

You Oughta Know

When should I apply? Tuck has an Early Action round followed by three standard rounds. You may submit your application in any of these four rounds for consideration. However, we do not encourage you to wait until the final round without compelling circumstances.

Early Action. Unlike schools like Columbia, Tuck's Early Action round is non-binding, although if you are admitted you will need to send in a $4,500 deposit by January 15 if you plan to enroll. Anyone accepted in that round is welcome to continue applying elsewhere until the January response deadline. The Early Action deadline is October 7, 2015. The key advantage of the Early Action deadline is the ability to signal to the school that it is one of your top choices by working on its application so early in the season.

Applying early vs. applying right. Please note that even though the top schools encourage you to apply in the earliest round possible, this does not mean that you should apply with a rushed application or a mediocre GMAT score. There's no sense in applying early if you're just going to be denied. A GMAT score that's above the school's average will do more for your candidacy than applying in the first round.

Deadlines. This season's regular deadlines are November 4, 2015, January 6, 2016, and April 4, 2016. Note that applications are due at 5PM ET. Applications for each round are considered after each deadline, so there is no advantage to applying earlier in the round. That said, we recommend that you submit at least a couple of days before your target deadline to avoid the last-minute crush. Recommendations need to be submitted by the deadline as well.

Unusual admissions policies. As we mentioned earlier in this Guide, Tuck tends to do things a bit differently. Below are several policies that differ at Tuck from most other MBA programs.

- **Test scores.** If you have taken the GMAT or the GRE multiple times, Tuck will allow you to "cherry-pick" the best overall score, and will consider the best quant or verbal score from different sittings of the test. (You cannot combine different components of the GRE with those of the GMAT, however.) This approach is definitely different from other schools'.

- **Former MBA recipients.** Tuck does not accept applications from anyone already holding an MBA, which disqualifies a large number of Indian candidates who went straight to business school after college, and now, after working for a while, realize that they would benefit from another run-through at a formal business education. Some other schools are open to this applicant profile; Tuck is not.

- **Applicant-initiated interviews.** Tuck is one of the few remaining schools that still allows applicant-initiated interviews, a strategy that works for both the school and the applicant. Applicants who might be attracted to the traditional New England setting but are a bit apprehensive about the location may find that the campus sells itself with bucolic charm and a friendly and approachable community. Applicants also gain a distinct advantage by demonstrating their interest and adding another (hopefully positive) element to their application before it is reviewed by the admissions committee. And the admissions committee gets to meet a variety of interesting applicants for whom the confines of the application might not tell the entire story.

- **Ding analysis.** Tuck, in keeping with its friendly and accessible culture, encourages re-applications. This fact is not unusual in itself; in fact, re-applicants are admitted at higher rates than first-time applicants at most business schools. However, if an applicant is denied ("dinged," in the MBA admissions world), the admissions team offers feedback calls if requested (usually provided May through July) to offer suggestions for improvement.

- **Scholarship essay.** Probably the biggest difference that can be overlooked—and the one that can potentially matter most to applicants—is the fact that the Tuck scholarship application requires another essay in addition to the standard application essays. Other schools often do not require anything further to be considered for fellowships and scholarship funding. However, the essay is short (less than 500 words) and isn't harshly judged or scrutinized if you overlap content with your formal admissions essays.

APPLICATION DEADLINES

Deadlines: 5PM Eastern Time

Early Action round:
7 Oct 2015
Notification:
17 Dec 2015

Round 1:
4 Nov 2015
Notification:
12 Feb 2015

Round 2:
6 Jan 2016
Notification:
11 Mar 2016

Round 3:
4 Apr 2016
Notification:
13 May 2016

DARTMOUTH (TUCK)

- **Deferrals.** Another nuance is that Tuck does occasionally permit deferrals from time to time, so if you gain an offer of admission and some life event arises that prevents you from attending business school on the originally planned schedule, you may see some flexibility from the admissions department. (Other schools are much more strict about refusing deferrals in any situation.)

The Essays

Tuck stuck with two required essays this year, and the questions are substantially the same, although both of them have been reworded a bit for this year's application. These small changes suggest that the Tuck admissions team was mostly happy with the responses they saw from last year's applicant pool.

Essay 1: *What are your short- and long-term goals? Why do you need an MBA to achieve those goals? Why are you interested in Tuck specifically? (500 words)*

Clear, concise career goals. This question has been substantially reworded since last year, although at its core, it's still the same fairly standard "Why an MBA? Why this school?" question that many business schools ask. One notable change is actually the addition of the second question in there ("Why do you need an MBA?"), and the fact that the Tuck admissions team added this part suggests that perhaps not enough applicants were addressing this fairly obvious question last year. For example, an applicant might write, "I seek an MBA to improve my financial and business skills to make a career transition into an organization that will enable me to utilize my talents and improve my skills." Generic statements like this provide almost no clarity, and in essence tell the admissions committee that you haven't really thought through your future goals at all beyond going back to grad school. The application process is intended to cause (almost force) applicants to explore potential career paths before they start their MBA program.

Short-term goals. A "short-term goal" in this context refers to the job you hope to gain directly out of business school. This trick is to not make this goal so narrow that there's only one job in the entire world that will satisfy you, while not making it so broad that you seem directionless. An example of a goal that's too narrow would be: "Upon graduation, I will seek to be the Corporate Product Manager for Kiva Microfunds, focused on business development in the Latin American region." The admissions committee might be concerned that if you are not successful in obtaining this position, you'll be unhappy with your MBA experience. Instead, you might say something like:

> *I seek to leverage my experience in finance with my demonstrated passion for developing nations. Ideally, I would apply for a business development role for a philanthropic organization such as Kiva, Grameen Bank, or even traditional lenders such as Bank of America, which has started a microlending practice. Understanding that these positions are in high demand, my Plan B is to transition into Management Consulting in the developing world.*

Long-term goals. Don't be afraid to be ambitious with your long-term goals. How do you want to make an impact in your industry, in a new industry, or on the world? Over the course of their careers, more than 70% of Tuck alumni achieve top management positions such as CEO, CFO, partner, managing director, or owner. So don't be afraid to dream big while offering a couple of thoughts on how you plan to utilize your MBA to achieve your goals.

Demonstrating fit. The other subtle change is how the last part of the prompt changed from "Why are you the best fit for Tuck?" to "Why are you interested in Tuck specifically?" No matter how the question is asked, Tuck really is still trying to get at the concept of fit here. What about Tuck interests you enough that you would consider devoting two years of your life to the program? Tuck takes the concept of fit very seriously when evaluating candidates—which makes sense, given its small class size and remote location—so you need to take it seriously, too.

Think of why Tuck is the best MBA fit for you academically, professionally, and culturally. You may decide to comment on the structure of academics, particularly strong professors and courses that fit with your goals, recruiting opportunities for which Tuck has great connections, and elements of campus life that are particularly appealing. Keep in mind that anyone can browse the school's website and drop some professors' and clubs' names into this essay; a response that will really stand out is one that is believable, shows that you've done your research, and reveals something unique about you. In this way, the wording in last year's essay prompt can be a great guide to writing a great response to this year's question. In this portion of the essay you might weave together experiences from your campus visit, information sessions, or conversations with current students with your own needs:

> *As I spoke with members of the real estate club, I was impressed with how helpful the Tuck alumni are in securing internships and full-time positions. This is particularly valuable to me as I seek to make a career transition into the insular world of real estate finance.*

Essay 2: *Tell us about your most meaningful leadership experience and what role you played. How will that experience contribute to the learning environment at Tuck? (500 words)*

This question has also been tweaked for this year's application. The meaningful difference is in the second part: While last year's question asked you what you learned about yourself, this year's version squeezes in the part that was dropped from Essay #1. Why does this matter? Because the part that was dropped ("What did you learn about your own individual strengths and weaknesses through this experience?") is still actually pretty important, and it's hard to imagine writing a great essay that doesn't at least briefly cover that material this year.

Show introspection and growth. You only have 500 words in which you need to describe what the situation was, what action you took, and what the results were (Situation–Action–Result, or SAR). However, don't forget to devote at least a few sentences to how you grew or changed. What exactly happened is very important, but evidence of how you grew and how you got to know yourself better is even more critical. A great essay tells about how you learned something valuable about yourself, such as a shortcoming or lack of experience, and how you were able to act and improve upon it. That's the type of response that has the potential to stick with the application reader.

Let your leadership qualities shine. Are you grasping for a story to use for this essay? Don't lose sight of that important word in the first part of the question: *leadership*. Keep in mind that leadership shows itself in many forms, not just from being the official manager of a team. Perhaps you took on a tough problem that no one else wanted to deal with. Maybe you faced a tough ethical decision that kept you up at night. Or maybe you spotted an opportunity for how something could be done in a better way, and you convinced your peers to come around to this new way of doing things. All of these could make for rich stories to use in this essay! Finally, remember to tie it back to Tuck. Our advice here is not to force it (e.g., *...and that is why I will be a natural to lead the Tuck Finance Club*). The key is to tell a story that demonstrates your growth as a young, developing leader, and then to demonstrate that you understand what Tuck's respectful, collaborative culture is all about.

Essay 3 (Optional): *Please provide any additional insight or information that you have not addressed elsewhere that may be helpful in reviewing your application (e.g., unusual choice of evaluators, weaknesses in academic performance, unexplained job gaps or changes, etc.). Complete this question only if you feel your candidacy is not fully represented by this application.*

It's *really* optional. As we always tell applicants when it comes to the optional essay for any business school, only answer this essay prompt if you need to explain a low undergraduate GPA or other potential blemish in your background. No need to harp on a minor weakness and sound like you're making excuses when you don't need any. If you don't have anything else you need to tell the admissions office, it is entirely okay to skip this essay!

Recommendations

Whom should I ask? Similar to many other top programs, Tuck requires that all applicants submit two letters of recommendation. Although Tuck does not require that one recommender be your current direct supervisor, asking your boss for a recommendation is standard practice for business school applicants. So, if you are able, we recommend reaching out to your current supervisor. As do most schools, Tuck discourages academic recommendations from undergraduate professors.

Does title or status matter? As many top business programs claim, Tuck is more concerned with the content and quality of your recommendations than the reputation or title of your recommenders. Choose individuals who know you well, can speak to your qualifications as an MBA candidate, and can add "valuable insights to your application." We see candidates try to call in favors to try to get their company's CEO to write a letter on their behalf. In general, the admissions committee will be far more impressed by a genuine and passionate letter from a middle manager with whom you work every day than a polite letter from a well-known CEO that lacks depth and detailed anecdotes about you. The latter will likely be discounted or completely ignored.

What will they be asked? The actual "letter" of recommendation is submitted through an online form. Once you begin your online application, you will provide the names and e-mail addresses of your recommenders, and they will receive a link to complete the online form. The next few sections describe the questions your recommender will be asked to answer.

Traits assessment. *Please compare the applicant on the scale below with others in his/her peer group whom you have known during your professional career. [Effectiveness of leadership; effectiveness of teamwork; effectiveness of communication skills; positive attitude; ethics and integrity; ability to handle conflict; ability to cope with pressure; ability to inspire and motivate others; ability to see opportunity and take initiative; organization and time-management skills; quantitative ability; analytical ability; intellectual curiosity; ability to think creatively; self-confidence; resilience and ability to cope with setbacks; overall drive, motivation, and energy level; professional impression, poise, and presence; cultural sensitivity; comfort with risk-taking; maturity/self-awareness.]* For each trait, your recommender is asked to rate you compared to others in your peer group using the following scale: *Top 5%, Top 10%, Top 20%, Top 50%, Bottom 50%, Bottom 20%, or N/A.*

Characterization of support. *How would you categorize your support for this candidate? [Champion, Strongly support, Support, Moderately support, Oppose.]*

Questions. *In one document, please answer the following questions. To be sure to address all of the questions, you may wish to number your responses (i.e. 1,2,3, and so on).*

1. *How long have you known the applicant and in what context? Have you served as the applicant's supervisor? If so, please provide approximate dates. Please comment upon the frequency and nature of your interactions with the applicant.*

2. *What are the applicant's three principal strengths? Please provide an example of each.*

3. *In which three areas can the applicant improve? Please provide an example of each. How has the applicant worked to address these areas?*

4. *How does the applicant respond to constructive criticism?*

5. *Describe the impressions this candidate makes in meetings, presentations, interviews other important interactions.*

What should they say? Tuck admissions officers are looking for specific examples of your performance, teamwork, and leadership qualities to shine through in your letters of recommendation. Your recommenders should be up to speed on the overall theme of your application, and should be aware of your reasons for getting an MBA and applying to Tuck to ensure consistency throughout your application. The use of specific examples combined with genuine enthusiasm about your candidacy are keys to a successful letter.

Should I draft it myself? Many applicants to business school are asked by their superiors to draft the recommendation themselves and the recommender will approve it. We strongly recommend that you do not write the recommendation yourself for several reasons. Your writing style and choice of phrasing are unique, and admissions officers will notice if the recommendations are similar to each other and to your essays. If they notice too many similarities, your application could be denied outright. The admissions officer is looking for a third-party perspective on your candidacy, so writing a recommendation yourself is an unethical breach of trust with the school you are looking to join.

When it comes to Tuck, the answer to this question is an emphatic *no*. The school specifically states the following:

> *Letters of recommendation are to be completed by the recommender and no one else. Drafting, writing or translating your own recommendation, even if asked to do so by your recommender, is inappropriate and a violation of the terms of our application process and Tuck's Academic Honor Principle. Applicants are expected to inform recommenders of this policy.*

Preparing your recommenders. You should sit down and have candid conversations with your recommenders about the reasons you want to go to business school and why you've selected your target schools, your professional goals, and your experience together. Ask them if they would have the time to write a strong recommendation on your behalf. (This also gives them a nice "out" by telling you that they are too busy rather than saying they don't feel comfortable giving you a positive recommendation.) Bring a copy of your resume and a bulleted list of projects that you've worked on together and accomplishments they have seen you achieve. Let them know that admissions committees prefer to see specific, detailed examples in recommendations. Then, let them know that you'll serve as a "project manager" to follow up and ensure that they are able to submit your recommendation ahead of the deadline.

The Interview

How does it work? Unlike most top business schools, Tuck says interviews are not required, although on-campus interviews are strongly encouraged. And, we suspect that all accepted students were in fact interviewed at some point in their application process. As we mentioned before, applicants to Tuck have the unique opportunity to initiate on-campus interviews by scheduling them online. Tuck (and Veritas Prep, too!) most definitely recommends that you do so. Applicant-initiated interviews are scheduled on a first-come, first-served basis and are only conducted on campus. You should certainly make the effort to go to Hanover if you're really serious about Tuck. It will help you understand the unique program and help the school get a better feel for how you might fit in there.

Understanding the school. There is no obligation to submit an application before the interview, and going through the entire campus visit and interview will likely either radically inspire you that Tuck is the place you want to be (thus allowing you to infuse this enthusiasm into your essays), or will educate you that perhaps it's not the best environment for you. In either case, you come out ahead. In its official *Tuck 360* blog, the admissions office strongly recommends interviewing prior to submission.

Interview invitations. For those who apply without interviewing first, the Tuck Admissions Office will issue invitations when they are interested to know someone better. These Tuck-initiated interviews can be conducted on campus, off campus, or occasionally by Skype. Off-campus interviews are conducted by admissions committee members, admissions associates, or alumni. Tuck states that all interviews, no matter how conducted or when, are evaluated equally and that they understand that in certain cases applicants will not be able to travel to New Hampshire.

What should I expect? Of course, being asked to interview is only the first step: Of those interviewed, fewer than half are admitted. If you are one of the lucky ones to be offered an interview spot, there are a few things to keep in mind as you prepare. First, Tuck will be heavily assessing your "fit" with the school, so do your homework beforehand. The format is very casual, with no "gotcha" questions, but the interviewer will be evaluating intangible skills such as communication, leadership, teamwork, introspection and self-awareness, and clarity of goals—aspects that are more difficult to assess in the written application alone.

Who will conduct my interview? On-campus interviews are conducted mostly by select second-year students (called Tuck Admissions Associates), though sometimes admissions committee members do them, too. Candidate-initiated interview appointments are on a first-come, first-served basis. The interview can be combined with a class visit, student lunch, or campus tour, and we recommend taking advantage of all these opportunities while you're there. In addition, be sure to chat more informally with as many students as you can. Ask them about their experience at Tuck, where they live, what their academic and extracurricular schedule is like, how they like Hanover, how recruiting has gone, and so forth. Do everything you can to get a sense of the school from different perspectives.

What will my interviewer know about my background? If you interview prior to submitting your application, the interviewer will have only your resume. If your interview is invitational, a member of the admissions committee will have already read your application and deemed you worthy of the next round of evaluation. However, it's unusual for the same officer to read your application and conduct your interview, so it's rare to be asked about specific elements of your written application. Invitational interviews cover the same topics and skills as in applicant-initiated ones, mentioned above.

What questions should I ask? Most interviewers will ask if there is anything you'd like the admissions committee to know that you were not able to put in your application. This is a perfect time to stress your sincere desire to attend Tuck. Remember to prepare a few other questions for your interviewer. Insightful questions not only give you a better idea of the school but also enable you to finish the interview on a strong note. Always make sure to ask questions that are genuine and sincere, and those that you couldn't have found the answer to on your own (especially on the school's website!). Even if you feel your questions about the school have been answered, if the interviewer is a student, you can always ask her what she wishes she had known before coming to Tuck or what she has enjoyed most about the Tuck experience.

DARTMOUTH (TUCK)

YALE SCHOOL OF MANAGEMENT

This relatively young MBA program focuses on the nonprofit sector and small class sizes.

📍 NEW HAVEN, CT

CLASS SIZE
291

PROGRAM FOUNDED
1976

NEWEST ADDITION
NEW BUSINESS FACILITY

CHARACTERISTICS
NONPROFITS, INTEGRATED LEARNING, TIGHT-KNIT

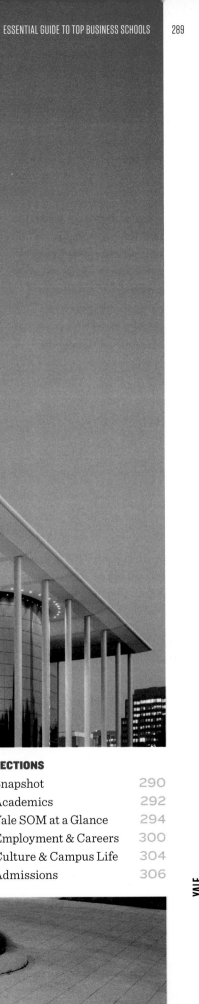

YALE

YALE SCHOOL OF MANAGEMENT SNAPSHOT

What Yale SOM Is Known For

The school is known for its strength in the nonprofit sector and has taken a very different approach to management education than most business schools.

Intersection of business and society. If you asked people knowledgeable about MBA programs one thing they knew about Yale School of Management, they'd probably say "nonprofit." The school is known for its strength in the nonprofit sector and has taken a very different approach to management education than most business schools. Although the vast majority (92%) of its graduates go into for-profit companies upon graduation, the school's mission is "to educate leaders for business and society," emphasizing that it stands for more than merely maximizing corporate profits. This theme of both "business and society" permeates much of the SOM experience.

Small class size. Even though its MBA classes have grown since moving into a new facility, Yale's MBA program remains one of the smallest among the top tier. The total class size grew by 41% in just three years, from 229 students in the Class of 2013 to 323 in the Class of 2016. The Class of 2016 is SOM's largest class ever. However, there's plenty of room in the 350-seat Zhang Auditorium for the new-student orientation activities, and admissions statistics have remained essentially unchanged. Class size is expected to remain just more than 300 students for the foreseeable future, so we expect the program to continue to maintain its intimate, tight-knit feel. Among top-15 U.S. MBA programs, only Berkeley (Haas), Dartmouth (Tuck), and Texas (McCombs) have smaller classes.

The Class of 2016 is the largest SOM class ever, topping 300 students.

Global brand. Opening its doors in 1976, SOM is the youngest of top-tier U.S. business schools. However, it burst onto the business school scene bolstered by the cachet of its parent institution, Yale University, and has shot up through the rankings. Now, one of Dean Ted Snyder's key initiatives is to leverage the school's brand advantage by further integrating SOM with Yale University.

What Makes Yale Different

Integrated curriculum. Several top MBA programs have "revamped" their curricula over the past few years, releasing new core courses and requirements that have been terribly underwhelming. They proudly announce that the marketing requirement can be fulfilled by *Intro to Marketing* or *Advanced Marketing!* (Yawn.) Enter Yale School of Management. Back in 2006, the school upended management education and introduced an integrated curriculum that remains truly innovative to this day. Gone are the traditional silos of marketing, accounting, finance, statistics, etc., replaced by management perspectives called *Customer, Competitor, Investor,* and *Employee,* among others. We'll discuss the core curriculum in detail in the Academics section.

Global network. Many top business schools boast of their global focus, but as with many things in management education, Yale has a different take. In 2012, Dean Ted Snyder formed the Global Network for Advanced Management, now a network of 27 international business schools. The Global Network offers online courses taught by faculty at any of its member schools and attended by students worldwide. Students must learn to work in global teams, handling issues such as time zones, language barriers, cultural differences, and technology struggles, just as they will in today's multinational corporations.

Leadership development. At Veritas Prep, we've visited dozens of MBA programs and spoken with hundreds of faculty members and administrators, but we were most impressed by the direction the Leadership Development Program is moving at Yale SOM. Each first-year student must create a plan for their individual leadership practicum, to be executed throughout their second year. Although the program was designed by the former head of behavioral sciences and leadership at West Point, students caution that it is still new and developing at this point.

Yale SOM Is a Good Fit for You If...

You value a small, tight-knit network. Yale students can expect to receive a lot of help, both while completing their studies and when looking for that key internship or first job. This is partly because of the small class and the close bonds that form during the business school experience, and also because of the tilt toward "doing good" that attracts many to Yale in the first place. The faculty and administration remain directly involved in their students' careers and are well connected with industry, making for win-win relationships that benefit the entire SOM ecosystem.

You're a strong academic. Undergraduate grades and test scores matter more at Yale than at many of its peers. While we don't want to discourage an otherwise-strong candidate from considering Yale, the truth is that only 20% of the Class of 2017 had a GMAT score of 690 or lower! Of course, there are always exceptions, but be aware that schools with larger classes can more easily absorb candidates with a wider spectrum of profile statistics. Like the rest of Yale University, SOM genuinely looks for passionate intellectuals, so its admissions officers will look for evidence of intellectual curiosity beyond statistics throughout your application, video questions, and interview.

You want to get your MBA straight out of college. Unlike similar programs for college seniors such as HBS 2+2 and Stanford's deferred enrollment, Yale Silver Scholars does not require a deferral period before starting your MBA directly out of college. Just a small handful of incredibly intelligent and mature college seniors are admitted to the program each year. Successful applicants must use concrete experiences to demonstrate their leadership potential, intellectual curiosity, passion, and compassion.

You are interested in the public or nonprofit sectors. If you're interested in a job in government or nonprofit, Yale should be at the top of your list. Before 1999, SOM did not even confer an MBA degree, instead offering a master's degree in Public and Private Management (MPPM). Consistently ranked #1 in nonprofit by *U.S. News & World Report*, SOM is also right up there with Ross and Stanford in scoring on the social responsibility and corporate ethics scales. Nearly one in 10 SOM graduates will take a position at a nonprofit or government organization, leading every other top-tier school.

> The faculty and administration remain directly involved in their students' careers and are well connected with industry, making for win-win relationships that benefit the entire SOM ecosystem.

YALE

You'd like to pursue a joint degree. As Dean Snyder seeks to integrate SOM more deeply with the broader Yale community, he proudly trumpets the fact that approximately 15% of the student body consists of joint-degree candidates. Among top business schools, only Stanford has more joint-degree students, at 20%. Currently, SOM offers joint degrees in law, environmental management, forestry, global affairs, medicine, public health, architecture, drama, divinity, and religion, or a custom joint degree in sciences or humanities.

In the Class of 2016, 54% of students are from outside the U.S. or hold dual citizenship, a dramatic increase from previous years.

You're from outside North America. Dean Snyder regularly emphasizes SOM's goal to become "the most global U.S. business school." In the Class of 2016, 54% of students are from outside the U.S. or hold dual citizenship, a dramatic increase from previous years. The Master of Advanced Management, a one-year program for graduates of Global Network schools, has also grown from just 20 students two years ago to 62 students today. This gives SOM a significantly more international feel than in previous years.

In addition, SOM is the first top-tier MBA program to no longer require international applicants to take the TOEFL, IELTS, PTE, or any other language-proficiency test. The program has also adopted a sliding scale for admissions fees for applicants with incomes less than $20,000 USD. Given Yale University's strong brand reputation across the globe, now is the perfect time for applicants outside of North America to apply.

ACADEMICS AT YALE SOM

What Yale SOM Is Known For

Because Yale's curriculum is integrated, students are unable to waive any classes. Everyone must go through the entire curriculum from start to finish.

Integrated curriculum. As we mentioned earlier, the School of Management's integrated curriculum really sets it apart from any other business school. If Yale is on your target list, you should carefully understand how the curriculum works to see whether it would be a good fit for your learning style. At Veritas Prep, we really like it. (And we can still claim to be unbiased: The new curriculum was introduced after our co-founders graduated from the program in 2002.) However, don't just take our word for it. Here's what one member of the Class of 2015 had to say about her first-year experience:

> In brief, my year at Yale SOM was transformative. I came in with five years of mid-management experience in the legal industry and was rather skeptical about the value the integrated curriculum could add to my preconceived notions of sound leadership. That skepticism was shattered as each integrated class (Customer, Investor, Competitor, etc.) provided me with insights into various stakeholder perspectives in a business that I wasn't aware of. The process of opening up those new angles on the same problem was rigorous. It was the first time I feared I wouldn't be able to meet—forget about exceed—educational requirements.

One thing to remember about Yale's curriculum is that because it's integrated, students who have a strong background in finance, accounting, or marketing are unable to waive any classes. All students must go through the entire curriculum from start to finish.

Raw cases. A key part of the integrated curriculum is SOM's use of "raw cases," a teaching method it pioneered in 2007 and continues to refine. Traditional cases, such as those written at Harvard Business School, consist of a multi-page narrative of a business situation, usually followed by a series of exhibits that may include relevant data. Students analyze the issue and data and then present a clear recommendation or "answer."

In contrast, Yale's raw cases contain various web-based sources of information about a situation as a manager would receive it, including extensive data that has not necessarily been carefully curated. Rather than proposing a solution to a single decision point, students must synthesize the various internal and external sources of information to create their proposal. This may require skills across accounting, finance, marketing, organizational behavior, and other disciplines.

You Oughta Know

Cohorts. For decades, the SOM class has been divided into four cohorts: Blue, Silver, Green, and Gold. With the growth of the class to more than 320 students in 2015, the school decided to add a fifth cohort, Red. The size of each cohort had grown to 80 students, but with the addition of the Red cohort, each is a much more manageable 65. You'll go through a weeklong orientation with your cohort and attend all core classes together, so your cohort is a big part of your SOM experience. You'll get to know one another really well! Recently, the school introduced the Cohort Cup, a series of fun, sports-related competitions throughout the year among the cohorts.

Learning teams. Within your cohort, you'll be assigned to a seven- or eight-person learning team with whom you'll work on core course assignments and cases. Learning teams tend to participate in small social gatherings together outside of class as well.

Varied learning methods. Even though the school loves to talk about its raw case method to drive differentiation from other schools, its professors use a wide range of teaching methods. Except for a select group of MBA programs that teach almost 100% case method, most MBA programs incorporate a variety of learning methods, so this is not unusual.

Less experiential learning. Yale is a strong academic institution, and the faculty instructors tend to concentrate heavily on theory. Other MBA programs have put significant resources into "experiential learning," including numerous lab courses in which students serve as consultants to companies on live projects. Schools such as UCLA Anderson, Michigan Ross, and Tuck at Dartmouth incorporate incorporate major, hands-on projects where students work for months with outside companies. Columbia and NYU Stern utilize their New York City location to offer students hands-on experiences outside the classroom. Yale utilizes some experiential learning opportunities in the classroom, but the offerings are more limited.

Cross-registering electives. As we mentioned, SOM seeks to be the business school that is most integrated with its parent institution to leverage the great assets of Yale University. Students may take electives across the university, which is a common practice at most MBA programs. However, at Yale the students actually take advantage of the opportunity, with three-quarters of students taking a class outside of SOM—at least three times more than at most other MBA programs. This is particularly valuable at SOM since the program is fairly small, and it belongs to one of the best universities in the world. Why wouldn't you take advantage?

> **SOM students have the option to take electives across the university. Three-quarters of the class exercise this opportunity.**

YALE AT A GLANCE

APPLICANTS BY SCHOOL

Perhaps due to Yale's increased class size, its percent admitted is quite a bit higher than some other top-tier schools. With the Class of 2016, nearly 24% of all applicants were admitted to Yale.

◀ Percent admitted

Yale 2,756	Stanford 7,355	Harvard 9,543	Wharton 6,111	Duke 3,453
23.7%	7.1%	11%	20.7%	25.1%

AVERAGE GPA

3.56	3.67	3.74	3.60
Yale	Harvard	Stanford	Wharton

GMAT SCORES

720	726	732	728
Yale	Harvard	Stanford	Wharton

NATIONALITY

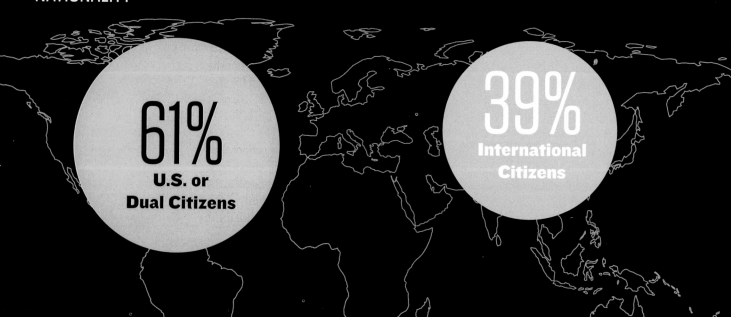

61%
U.S. or Dual Citizens

39%
International Citizens

UNDERGRAD MAJORS

Yale admits the highest percentage of humanities/social science majors (38%) of any top MBA program, although some report higher numbers when they include economics as a social science.

- ▢ STEM
- ▢ Humanities/Social Science
- ▢ Business
- ▢ Economics
- ▢ Other

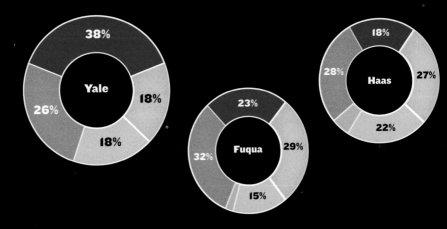

Yale: 38% / 18% / 18% / 26% / 18%

Fuqua: 23% / 29% / 15% / 32%

Haas: 18% / 27% / 22% / 28%

WOMEN

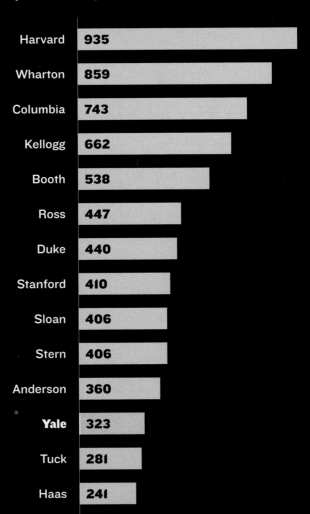

Yale 37%

Tuck 32%

Duke 35%

Haas 41%

U.S. MINORITIES

25%

Yale

24%

Harvard

32%

Columbia

14%

Tuck

CLASS SIZE

Although Yale's class size remains one of the smallest compared to peer schools, its class size has increased by 41% over the past three years.

Harvard	935
Wharton	859
Columbia	743
Kellogg	662
Booth	538
Ross	447
Duke	440
Stanford	410
Sloan	406
Stern	406
Anderson	360
Yale	323
Tuck	281
Haas	241

YALE

A new grading policy. Although SOM is known for its student-led culture and strong collaboration among students, faculty members, and administrators, the faculty unilaterally announced a controversial change in grading policies for fall of 2014, causing an uproar among students. The new policy adds a tier to the former system of Distinction, Proficient, Pass, and Fail, where as many as 85% of students received a Proficient grade. Stricter curves were put into place, and full disclosure of grades is now included on transcripts.

Students were upset that they were excluded from such a major decision, particularly one that may affect the collegial and non-competitive nature of the school's culture. However, at Veritas Prep, we have found that grade non-disclosure policies have little impact on the culture of a school. For example, the Kellogg School of Management at Northwestern University has perhaps the most friendly and collegial atmosphere of any elite MBA program, and it has never had a grade non-disclosure policy. We'll be looking closely to see if Yale's culture is impacted by this decision.

Nuts & Bolts

Yale's curriculum works very differently from any other business school's, so we'll walk you through a few of the details to help you decide if this is the right program for you.

Academic sessions. Each semester is divided into two academic sessions, essentially offering a four-quarter system of seven weeks each. In your first year, Fall 1 is composed exclusively of a series of core courses called *Orientation to Management*. In Fall 2 you'll begin the *Organizational Perspectives* courses, which continue through both spring sessions. You'll also have six to eight units available to take electives in the spring.

> **The core curriculum is broken into nine multidisciplinary areas referred to as Organizational Perspectives.**

Orientation to Management. The first seven weeks of the core curriculum introduce basic language, concepts, tools, and problem-framing methodologies that will be drawn on broadly throughout the curriculum. *Orientation to Management* includes *Basics of Economics, Basics of Accounting, Problem Framing, Careers, Managing Groups and Teams, Probability Modeling and Statistics, Spreadsheet Modeling,* and *Introduction to Negotiation.*

Organizational Perspectives. The next portion of the curriculum is designed to present concepts and content in a manner more representative of the way managers face problems in the world of business. The core curriculum is broken into nine multidisciplinary areas referred to as *Organizational Perspectives,* namely *Competitor, Customer, Investor, Employee, Innovator, The Global Macroeconomy, Sourcing and Managing Funds, State and Society,* and *Operations Engine.* These perspectives focus on issues encountered both inside and outside of the firm in a relevant context. Many core classes are taught by a team of professors from different academic disciplines, bringing a truly integrated experience into the classroom.

Integrated Leadership Perspective. The final course of the core curriculum is the *Integrated Leadership Perspective,* which combines different perspectives in a series of interdisciplinary raw cases focusing on the challenges faced by leaders of organizations of differing size, scope, and sector. The course is organized into four parts: 1) organizations that are just beginning, 2) the leadership challenges associated with organizations in transition, 3) mature organizations, and 4) high-level, modern management challenges bridging the public, private, and nonprofit sectors.

Leadership Development Program. *Leadership Fundamentals* and *Advanced Leadership* coursework is integrated into the first year core, along with sessions with your "development group," made up of fellow students. The first year culminates with a 360-degree assessment. In addition, first-year students must develop their own personalized plan for their leadership practicum that will be executed throughout second year. Students identify leadership areas on which they would like to focus and plan specific actions that will help them build those skills. These actions are integrated with other aspects of the MBA program, such as club leadership, community service, and entrepreneurial ventures. Peer and professional coaching sessions are also added during the second year.

Global coursework. At the end of Fall 1 in October, SOM participates in a Global Network Week, when students may take mini courses taught by faculty specialists at each network school. At Yale, classrooms are wired with cameras, projectors, and microphones so that students may participate together in a class taught by a professor halfway around the globe. Another Global Network Week falls in March, when students may also choose to travel for 10 days to a global location as part of an *International Experience (IE)* course. During the semester, students may also take online *Global Network* courses with classmates scattered around the world from any of the 27 members schools.

Global exchanges. For an even more immersive experience, students may spend fall semester of their second year on exchange at London School of Economics and Political Science (LSE), HEC Paris, IESE Business School in Barcelona, National University of Singapore (NUS), or Tsinghua University in Beijing. This exchange program is fairly limited compared to those of larger MBA programs, but the school has clearly shifted its focus to the Global Network offerings and has put less emphasis on student exchanges.

> At Yale, classrooms are wired with cameras, projectors, and microphones so that students may participate together in a class taught by a professor halfway around the globe.

Popular Professors & Courses

Yale's tight-knit community extends beyond the students; professors are also known for being extremely accessible. Many of the great professors have been teaching at Yale for years, and they don't seem to be losing steam whatsoever. The following were recommended highly by recent and current students:

Strategic Leadership Across Sectors
Senior Associate Dean Jeffrey A. Sonnenfeld

Dean Sonnenfeld is very much the face of SOM; he appears regularly on television news shows and in the most prestigious news publications, and is also an award-winning author. His course *Strategic Leadership Across Sectors* is perhaps the most popular course at SOM, as he brings in CEOs and other executives from all aspects of business in both the public and private sectors. Named one of *Businessweek*'s Ten Most Influential Business School Professors, Dean Sonnenfeld uses a case study approach that is heavy on class discussion and mixes it with insights from a panel of the very CEOs and executives in his cases.

Basics of Economics
Strategic Management of Nonprofit Organizations
Professor Sharon M. Oster

Professor Oster served as the dean of Yale SOM from 2008 until Dean Snyder's arrival in 2011. She has since moved back to her faculty role at the school. Professor Oster was the first woman to receive tenure at SOM and was instrumental in the innovative redesign of the SOM core curriculum. She is also popular for her *Basics of Economics* course in the core curriculum, where she gives students the real-world applicability of the economic theories in a down-to-earth, congenial manner. She also teaches a student-favorite public sector course, *Strategic Management of Nonprofit Organizations*. In 2011, she was rated the #7 most popular professor by students among all top-30 business schools.

Policy Modeling
Professor Edward H. Kaplan

Professor Kaplan is a perennial favorite among SOM students. His research has been reported on the front pages of the *New York Times* and the *Jerusalem Post,* editorialized in the *Wall Street Journal,* recognized by the *New York Times Magazine*'s Year in Ideas, and discussed in many other major media outlets. At SOM, Professor Kaplan teaches electives such as *Policy Modeling,* which applies statistical techniques to analysis of public policy decisions, such as those around HIV funding, drug prevention, and capital punishment.

Probability Modeling & Statistics
Operations Engine
Professor Arthur J. Swersey

Professor Swersey is one of the most well-loved and well-respected professors on campus. A master of both statistics and operations, he teaches both *Probability Modeling & Statistics* and *Operations Engine* in the core curriculum. Professor Swersey is known for making sure every one of his students understands the material, no matter the amount of time it takes. As such, he has won numerous teaching awards from various classes and alumni at SOM.

Behavioral Finance
Professor Nicholas C. Barberis

Professor Barberis researches behavioral finance and uses cognitive psychology in pricing of financial assets. He teaches the first-year core concept *Investor,* which gives students a perspective on how behavioral finance solves real-world problems. He also teaches an elective on the subject. One of Professor Barberis's recent projects involved using prospect theory to explain human behavior at casinos. The subsequent paper was a hit among students who had the chance to discuss it in class.

Marketing Strategy
Professor Ravi Dhar

Professor Dhar is an expert in consumer behavior and branding, marketing management, and marketing strategy. His dynamic teaching style engages students and keeps them involved in each topic. He is a favorite in the core curriculum and is well-known for his second-year elective *Marketing Strategy*. He has written more than 40 articles and serves on the editorial boards of leading marketing journals, such as *Journal of Consumer Research, Journal of Marketing, Journal of Marketing Research,* and *Marketing Science.* He also has an affiliated appointment as professor of psychology in the Yale University Department of Psychology.

Similar Academic Programs

As we've mentioned, the Yale SOM academic program is quite unique, so there are no programs that take an identical approach. However, if Yale's integrated, general management curriculum is appealing to you, then we recommend investigating the following programs.

Dartmouth (Tuck). Tuck and SOM share a number of similarities, including a small class size. Tuck's program, at about 275 students per class, is now a bit smaller than SOM's for the first time. Tuck refers to its required curriculum as "integrated," because the classes are carefully designed to complement and build on one another through the first year. However, they still represent more traditional disciplines of finance, marketing, operations, accounting, etc. Tuck's learning teams, academic calendar, and leadership development program are all remarkably similar to Yale's.

Cornell (Johnson). If you like the idea of Yale's integrated curriculum, but would like it tailored to a particular career path such as investment banking, asset management, marketing, or sustainability, then Johnson's immersion experience may be the right fit for you. The school crams basic courses in accounting, economics, leadership, finance, and strategy into the first semester so that you may choose an immersion for your second semester. Immersions combine elective courses, site visits, professional coaching, and live cases within one professional industry or career interest for an integrated experience.

Berkeley (Haas). Haas is also known for having a strong nonprofit program, although it sends far fewer graduates into the nonprofit and public sectors than does SOM. It has the smallest class size among top-10 MBA programs, with just 250 students per class. Haas's extensive core curriculum requirements fill up much of the first year, as do Yale's, although the curriculum follows a more traditional path similar to Tuck's. The Haas admissions committee also tends to look for applicants with strong academic statistics and friendly social skills; its average GPA is quite high and range of GMAT scores is very narrow.

EMPLOYMENT & CAREERS AT YALE SOM

What SOM Is Known For

Nonprofit and government. As you know by now, Yale is widely known as the #1 MBA program for nonprofit in the world. It sends double the percentage of graduates into the field (8%) than most other MBA programs do. However, the program has been working hard to shed its image as "just a nonprofit school," since nine out of 10 students take a job in the private sector!

Honestly, one of the biggest issues with SOM's brand is that the program isn't currently known for much outside of the nonprofit industry. However, the school has plenty of strengths beyond this sector. In the next section, we discuss career paths and recruiting opportunities at Yale SOM that you oughta know about.

Graduates entering nonprofit/government jobs

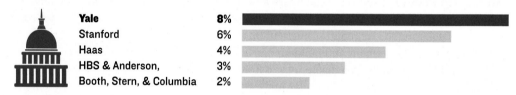

Yale	8%	
Stanford	6%	
Haas	4%	
HBS & Anderson,	3%	
Booth, Stern, & Columbia	2%	

You Oughta Know

Yale sends 26% of its class into the finance industry —nearly as much as Harvard and Stanford, and more than Kellogg, Ross, and MIT Sloan.

Wall Street finance. New Haven, Connecticut, may seem like an unusual destination for those interested in investment banking or other finance jobs, but a surprising number of SOM students head into the field upon graduation. Don't get us wrong: The traditional "finance schools" of Wharton, Columbia, NYU Stern, and Chicago Booth still outpace Yale's numbers, but more than a quarter of the SOM class goes into finance, with 14% of students taking an investment banking job at graduation. At 26%, Yale sends nearly as much of its class into the finance industry as Harvard (33%) and Stanford (30%), and more than UCLA Anderson (21%), Duke (18%), Kellogg (14%), MIT Sloan (14%), and Ross (12%). *Who knew?*

In fact, a contingent of students will choose to live in New York City for their second year, choosing to take the 90-minute train ride to New Haven to attend classes while taking advantage of their Manhattan location to network with Wall Street firms.

Graduates entering the finance industry

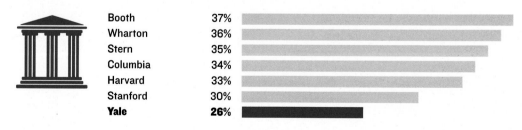

Booth	37%	
Wharton	36%	
Stern	35%	
Columbia	34%	
Harvard	33%	
Stanford	30%	
Yale	26%	

Note, however, that just three years ago the school sent nearly 40% of its class into finance. Some might interpret the recent decline as a sign that the school is slipping in the finance sector, but we believe the decrease is more the result of an increasingly diverse pool of incoming students with interests outside the finance sector.

Consulting. While a relatively low proportion of Yale's graduating class goes into the management consulting industry (just 26%, compared to 35% at Kellogg), a high number of graduates (36%) describe their job function as "consulting"—more than any other top business school. This means that a significant number of SOM grads take jobs as consultants in other industries, such as nonprofit and technology. Given Yale's strong emphasis on general management, this trend is not surprising.

Graduates taking consulting-related positions

Tuck	40%	
Columbia & Sloan	37%	
Yale	**36%**	
Kellogg	35%	
Duke	34%	

General management. SOM sends about 11% of its class into general management roles upon graduation. This may not seem like much, but it's more than schools with "traditional" recruiting profiles, such as Wharton (6%), Columbia (8%), Chicago Booth (8%), and NYU Stern (3%). In general, MBA graduates tend to take more advisory roles such as consulting, finance, or marketing upon graduation

Graduates entering general management positions

Tuck	18%	
HBS & Cornell	13%	
Yale	**11%**	
MIT Sloan & Anderson	10%	
Kellogg, Haas, & Duke	9%	
Stanford	7%	

Energy. Although not traditionally known for its placement in this industry, interestingly, Yale placed one of the highest percentages of graduates from the Class of 2014 into the energy sector after UT Austin (McCombs). Six percent of the Class of 2014 pursued careers in the energy industry after graduation, which is not far behind McCombs's 8% placement in this field. Yale's placement in energy jumped substantially from last year's 2% placement in this industry, so it is not clear if this is an anomaly or a sign of a developing trend.

Graduates entering the energy industry

McCombs	8%	
Yale	**6%**	
Haas, Anderson & Ross	4%	
Booth & Duke	3%	

Entrepreneurship. Despite its focus on the intersection of business and society, Yale has never put a great emphasis on entrepreneurship. That recently changed with the launch of a new, formalized entrepreneurship program, including a new director, courses, scholarships, and student activities. As with all of Dean Snyder's initiatives, the entrepreneurship program is heavily integrated with broader university resources, including the Yale Entrepreneurial Institute (YEI) and Yale Center for Engineering Innovation and Design (CEID). The new program is housed in the Entrepreneurial Studies Suite in Evans Hall, with working space for budding student ventures. Entrepreneurship appears to be taking off at Yale, with 10% of the Class of 2014 starting their own companies (4%) or pursuing roles at startups (6%). The school recently announced a loan-deferral program for students who launch a startup upon graduation, so this figure is likely to continue to grow.

Graduates electing to start their own business

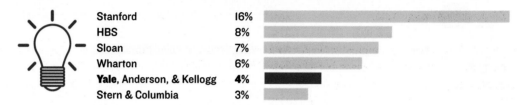

Stanford	16%	
HBS	8%	
Sloan	7%	
Wharton	6%	
Yale, Anderson, & Kellogg	4%	
Stern & Columbia	3%	

Broad range of opportunities. At most schools, two or three industries really dominate their recruiting, whether it's consulting, finance, technology, or all three. Yale has the most balanced recruiting profile of any of the top-tier business schools, even though the consulting and finance industries comprise 52% of jobs after graduation. By comparison, these two industries make up 68% of the accepted jobs at Columbia and 64% at Booth!

Careers in the curriculum. The first-quarter *Orientation to Management* curriculum includes a module about careers, taught by SOM's career development team. This is yet another example of Yale's nontraditional approach to management education. Very few other MBA programs integrate professional development directly into the curriculum.

Northeast dominance. More than half (59%) of the Class of 2014 remained in the Northeast; that's higher than any other top-tier school except NYU Stern (70%).

Even top-rated business schools tend to place the majority of their graduates close to home. While this is often a result of stronger relationships with employers in a school's region, graduates often choose to attend a business school where they ultimately wish to live post-MBA. Most schools have mobility and strong alumni networks across the country and globally, but applicants would be wise to consider placement statistics by location when considering which schools to target.

Similar Programs for Professional Opportunities

Dartmouth (Tuck). Tuck sent 25% of its class into the finance industry last year, almost the same as Yale's placement in this sector. Most people don't think of Yale or Tuck as "finance schools," but they both have strong reputations in the industry. With its strong general management emphasis, Tuck also sends a large percentage (18%) of its class into general management roles.

Harvard and **Stanford.** If you're looking for classmates who go into a wide variety of industries, where recruiting isn't dominated by just one or two of the "traditional" MBA feeder industries, the Yale SOM profile is quite similar to both Harvard's and Stanford's. As a result, SOM often becomes a fallback school for applicants to these extremely competitive programs. Stanford sends a large number of applicants into nonprofits each year (6%), leading all other top-tier MBA programs except Yale.

Virginia (Darden). Academically, Darden is a pretty different beast from SOM, as the former has an extremely traditional, case-based curriculum. But professionally, the two schools share a number of similarities. Darden sends just less than a quarter of its class into the finance industry, with 11% of graduates taking an investment banking job. The major difference is that 9% of Darden grads go into manufacturing, which is double the proportion of most other top-15 MBA programs, with only Kellogg (5%) and HBS (5%) coming close. The school is known for its strong general management curriculum, and this bears fruit in general management recruiting opportunities as well.

UCLA (Anderson). If you're looking for a student body that isn't dominated by just one industry, then Anderson may be the right fit. Consulting and finance comprise just more than a third (37%) of jobs after graduation. This represents the broad range of interests of the students, including consumer goods/retail (12%), media and entertainment (7%), real estate (4%), and technology (28%).

Duke (Fuqua). Duke sends a few more candidates into the consulting industry and fewer into finance, but the two schools have fairly similar recruiting opportunities. Duke also sends more candidates into marketing and healthcare positions than does Yale. Fewer Fuqua grads go into nonprofit, but this is still a fairly strong sector for the school compared to peers. If you're interested in a career outside the private sector, you should take a close look at the Duke MBA.

CULTURE & CAMPUS LIFE AT YALE SOM

What SOM Is Known For

Many applicants initially view SOM as a second-tier school on their short lists, but they are often won over after visiting campus and experiencing the program's unique culture for themselves. While there's no substitute for this firsthand experience, we've highlighted some aspects of campus life here.

> **Everyone from the students to faculty to administrators at Yale is remarkably warm, approachable, and down-to-earth.**

A family atmosphere. With Yale University's Ivy League history and Gothic architecture, you might have the image that it has a very formal, impersonal environment. At SOM, nothing could be further from the truth. Everyone from the students to faculty to administrators is remarkably warm, approachable, and down-to-earth. By the time you complete your Yale SOM experience, you'll likely know every member of your graduating class by name.

Proudly passionate and diverse. The admissions committee seeks to build a class of smart and accomplished, yet caring and passionate individuals. Despite its numerous diversity initiatives including the *Global Pre-MBA Leadership Program* and its membership in *The Consortium for Graduate Study in Management*, the school tends not to attract large numbers of underrepresented minority applicants. Nonetheless, you'll find many different backgrounds, perspectives, career paths, and opinions among your class at Yale SOM, and there's a strong emphasis on embracing one another's differences and learning from them.

New building with a new vibe. SOM's previous building had a common area called the "Hall of Mirrors" along a major hallway to classrooms. Students heading to class would cross paths with those studying or just hanging out, so they had the opportunity to see nearly all of their classmates every day. This helped foster a family-like atmosphere for generations of SOM students. Designers of the new facility attempted to re-create this phenomenon in Evans Hall in an area now referred to as the "Hall of Murals." However, it remains to be seen whether this area will serve as the hub of activity that designers envisioned or whether students will congregate in areas closer to classrooms.

You Oughta Know

The surrounding community. In the 1990s, New Haven, Connecticut, was known primarily for two things: Yale University and violent crime. Traditionally a manufacturing town, New Haven's economy was hit hard by the industrial decline in the Northeast over the past several decades. The city had one of the 10 highest violent crime rates per capita in the nation, and Yale students rarely left campus. However, New Haven's economy has started to rebound over the past 10 years, and its crime rate has dropped dramatically. It is now a great walking town, with many popular restaurants, bars, museums, university sports arenas, and theaters all within a stone's throw of the campus.

Student organizations. Both professional and social clubs are a big part of the SOM experience. Soon after setting foot on campus, first-year students will be bombarded by second-years reaching out and soliciting participation in student clubs to get them involved in major events such as professional conferences. Most students will take an active leadership role in at least one or two clubs during their tenure at Yale, with active participation in a couple more. In addition, professional clubs can act almost as gatekeepers for recruiting opportunities, particularly in finance and consulting.

Popular hangouts. GPSCY (pronounced "gypsy"), the Graduate and Professional Student Club at Yale, has long been the most popular hangout for SOM students on campus, as it is essentially a school-sponsored bar. However, its popularity has declined in recent years, and it remains to be seen if GPSCY will remain a social hot-spot for SOMers. Off campus, there are several restaurants, bars, and clubs in downtown New Haven that SOM students frequent. Toad's Place (known as "Toad's") hosts a number of popular concerts in town. Many students also take the Metro North train to New York City.

Major events and activities. As you research the program and speak with SOM students, be sure to ask them about Halloween at GPSCY, the fall and spring formals, and, of course, the never-to-be-missed Harvard–Yale football game!

Similar Programs Culturally

Dartmouth (Tuck). We've listed Tuck as a similar program to SOM academically, professionally, and culturally, and for good reason! Both programs belong to Ivy League institutions located away from major metropolitan areas, although Tuck's location in Hanover, New Hampshire, is far more remote than New Haven. The programs are roughly the same size, with a familial atmosphere among students and their partners.

Cornell (Johnson). Of all the programs we list here, Johnson may be the most similar culturally. The facilities at Johnson are beautiful, and its two-year MBA class is just slightly smaller, which gives the entire program a family feel. Cornell is located in Ithaca, New York, which is more isolated than New Haven. It is about four and a half hours by shuttle bus from New York City, which is likely a major reason why candidates may leave the school off their short lists. However, it has one of the best career services teams in the country and the S.C. Johnson family has often offered recruiters use of its private jet, so students have plenty of access to top employers.

Berkeley (Haas). Although Haas has a decidedly more "West Coast" vibe than SOM, the two schools share a number of similarities. Haas students are often described as nice, warm, and friendly, and the student body is quite small. It also belongs to a well-respected and prestigious university; UC Berkeley is commonly referred to as a "Public Ivy."

MIT (Sloan). Because of MIT's reputation in engineering and technology, there tend to be more students with engineering backgrounds at MIT Sloan than at Yale SOM. However, Sloan is known for having an extremely friendly student body, which may be unexpected to some applicants. Its intellectual yet friendly vibe is similar to SOM's.

> **Soon after setting foot on campus, first-year students will be bombarded by second-years reaching out and soliciting participation in student clubs to get them involved in major events such as professional conferences.**

YALE

ADMISSIONS AT YALE SCHOOL OF MANAGEMENT

What Yale SOM Is Looking For

In our recent visit to the newly opened Evans Hall, we had the opportunity to sit down with Assistant Dean and Director of Admissions Bruce DelMonico and members of his staff about admission to Yale SOM. They offered some concrete insights about the "perfect applicant" to Yale SOM.

Growth mindset. Recent research on mindset by Stanford University psychologist Carol Dweck has caught fire in business schools today. In short, Yale admissions officers look for evidence of a growth mindset: a belief that intelligence and talents are not simply fixed traits, but areas that can be developed through dedication and effort.

> **Successful candidates will see themselves as the product in development, rather than the customer who desires to make a knowledge transaction.**

Product orientation. In conjunction with a growth mindset, SOM admission officers are looking for candidates who have a "product orientation" as opposed to a "customer orientation." These candidates will see themselves as the product in development, seeking every opportunity to improve, rather than the customer of an institution who desires to make a knowledge transaction. Students with a customer orientation tend to use the argument "I paid X thousands of dollars in tuition. Therefore as your customer I *deserve* to receive Y."

Experience at leading. Admissions officers will be actively looking for experiences that show how you were accountable for something—anything—and how you led others to fulfill that responsibility. Ideally, you'll show this experience in your professional life, but it may be expressed in your undergraduate experience and extracurricular activities as well.

Emotional intelligence. SOM has started using the Mayer-Salovey-Caruso Emotional Intelligence Test (MSCEIT) in its first-year curriculum and is looking into the possibility of incorporating it into the admissions process as well. In the meantime, the committee seeks emotionally intelligent and humble candidates who respect others as they evaluate applicants through essays, video responses, and in-person interviews.

Self-starters. Bruce DelMonico uses the term "aggressive self-starter" to describe the perfect applicant. This isn't to say that SOM students have aggressive personalities, but they don't wait for opportunities to fall in their laps. SOM is a small program, a bit off the beaten path, and so students need to have a clear vision of what they want to do post-graduation, and be willing to dive in and achieve their goals through focused effort.

 If you are looking for tips on 2016–17 admissions essays, you're in luck! Check out our website at **veritasprep.com/YaleSOM** for our latest advice.

Preparing to Apply

Reading this Essential Guide is a great first step in your preparation. Hopefully, this insider's glimpse has been helpful in understanding the most important aspects of the school. However, nothing can replace gaining firsthand knowledge and experience of Yale School of Management yourself.

Reach out to current students. Even if you don't have any personal connections to SOM, you can reach out to current students and get their insight and advice. On the school's Student Clubs & Groups page, you'll find a list of all campus clubs. Find a few clubs that fit your interests and reach out to the officers. Remember: These are very busy MBA students so you don't want to intrude too much on their time, but you could ask for a 10- to 15-minute conversation or elicit some advice via e-mail. If you're planning to visit campus, perhaps you might even arrange a coffee chat or lunch, if they are available.

Visit campus. If you have the means, we highly recommend you visit the Yale campus, along with a handful of others, to understand the significant differences in culture, teaching style, student body, recruiting opportunities, facilities, and so forth. A campus visit does not directly impact your admissions chances in any way, but you will be surprised by just how different each school can be.

We encourage you to take advantage of the formal campus visit program, including a class visit, campus tour, information session, and student lunch, as available. However, we also encourage you to go to the cafe, grab a bite to eat, and talk to a few current students. The formal program gives a good surface-level experience of SOM, but impromptu conversations can be incredibly enlightening. Ask students about items that pique your interest in this Guide and get their unique perspective on the SOM experience.

Other events. We know that many applicants will not be able to travel to New Haven to visit campus, but you should take advantage of other admissions events, such as information sessions, webinars, and specific-audience events. Get to know the school and its culture as well as you can, because your familiarity can shine through your application and essay to help you stand out.

YALE

You Oughta Know

DEADLINES

Round 1
16 Sep 2015
Notification: 7 Dec 2015
Deposit Due: 12 Feb 2016

Round 2
7 Jan 2016
Notification: 25 Mar 2016
Deposit Due: 6 May 2016

Round 3
21 Apr 2016
Notification: 20 May 2016
Deposit Due: 31 May 2016

When should I apply? SOM uses a standard three-round system for applications. This means that you may submit your application in any of its three rounds for consideration. However, 90 percent or more of the class will be filled with the first two rounds of applicants, so we do not encourage you to wait until the final round without compelling circumstances. Round 3 candidates will be considered alongside waitlisted candidates from the first rounds. (Waitlisted candidates from Round 1 will be considered with Round 2 applicants, but we've seen a number of R1 waitlistees who were held on the waitlist again and admitted in Round 3.)

Traditional applicants. If you are a traditional candidate from the management consulting or finance industry, we encourage you to apply in the first round (assuming you have a strong GMAT score), as you'll be competing against many candidates with very similar profiles. In a later round, it's possible that the school may see you as a viable candidate, but may have already admitted several other applicants with similar profiles, so it might pass on you to bring greater professional diversity to the class. (Plus, the school knows you've been planning on an MBA since the day you graduated from undergrad, so there's no reason to delay!)

A stronger app is better than an earlier one. Please note that even though the top schools encourage you to apply in the earliest round possible, this does not mean that you should apply with a rushed application or a mediocre GMAT score. There's no sense in applying early if you're just going to be denied. A GMAT score that's above the school's average will do more for your candidacy than applying in the first round.

Navigating deadlines. Yale's three round deadlines are similar to last year's: September 16, 2015; January 7, 2016; and April 21, 2016. Note that, if you apply to Yale in Round 1, you will receive your decision by December 7. This gives you plenty of time to get your Round 2 applications deadlines together for other MBA programs if you don't get good news from Yale.

College seniors. If you are a college senior who will graduate after December 1, 2015, then you are eligible to apply for the Silver Scholars Program. Just a tiny number of Silver Scholars are admitted each year—usually in the low single digits. The school's website has more information about admission criteria for Silver Scholars, so we won't go into great detail here.

One key criteria, however, is impact. As the website states, each Silver Scholar "has made a difference and distinguished him- or herself in a particular field of interest." Showcasing your impact and leadership potential in your field of interest is challenging, but vital to your successful application. Note that Silver Scholar applicants must also submit two letters of recommendation, but one must be from a professor and another from an employer while you were in college (from a full-time internship or part-time employment).

The Online Application Form

SOM's online application form is pretty straightforward, but we'll offer a few tips to reduce anxiety in certain sections.

Picking a round. When you create your application, you'll be asked to select a round immediately. If you're unsure, simply select the earliest round you plan to apply. You will have the opportunity to change it each time you log in.

Personal. Your primary citizenship is typically the country where you were born or where you feel the greatest cultural connection. Secondary is typically a citizenship that was established later in life. However, the order does not matter here for admission purposes.

Members of the U.S. military do not have an explicit advantage over civilians, although SOM highly values leadership experience that can come from military service. It also provides several benefits to U.S. veterans, including a waived application fee and enrollment deferrals for deployed military personnel.

Application information. If you have applied to Yale SOM previously, be sure to note that here. Your previous application and new application will be viewed side-by-side, assuming you have applied within the past two years. The key for re-applicants is to focus on those areas of your profile that have improved since your previous application.

As we mentioned previously, joint-degree candidates comprise about 15% of the SOM class. All joint-degree applicants must be admitted separately by each school. Candidates who have already started their graduate programs in other Yale schools may apply to SOM, usually during their first year.

Current college seniors should indicate their status in this section to be considered for the Silver Scholars program. We recommend all candidates release their information for consideration for outside scholarships. Yale must ask this question due to privacy considerations.

Academic record. Be sure to include coursework from all academic institutions you have attended, unless exchange courses are included on your primary transcript. This includes coursework that you may have taken recently to prepare for your MBA. If your undergraduate grades are not stellar, taking additional courses in relevant topics such as calculus, microeconomics, statistics, finance, and accounting can help build an "alternate transcript" to show admissions officers that you are capable of thriving in the rigorous academic environment at Yale.

Other academic information. This section includes a short-answer "mini essay" with the following prompt: *If you have a graduate degree, how, if at all, does pursuing an MBA relate to your previous graduate studies? (100 words maximum).* Business schools are practical institutions, and they don't like to admit applicants who are simply "eternal students," collecting as many degrees as they can. Even if your MBA doesn't relate directly to your previous studies, you should show how your current pursuits build upon skills you gained previously to achieve your goals.

> **Be sure to include coursework from all academic institutions you have attended, unless exchange courses are included on your primary transcript.**

YALE

Legal questions. Yale conducts background checks on admitted applicants each year, so if you have been convicted of a crime or received other disciplinary actions listed in this section, be sure to report it. You may use the space provided to explain circumstances. At Veritas Prep, we've consulted with many applicants who were convicted of crimes or suspended from school who were admitted to their target schools. This does not need to be a deal-breaker if it is handled appropriately.

Test scores. Yale is true to its desire to attract growth-minded applicants, so it does not punish applicants who take the GMAT or GRE multiple times to improve their scores and achieve their goals. You will report your two highest scores in this section, which can be from the GMAT or the GRE, or one score from each. The admissions committee will use these scores to evaluate you for admission, although later in the process they will see your past five scores from each exam when they compare self-reported scores to the officially reported ones from the test providers.

At Veritas Prep, we know of an applicant who took the GMAT *11 times* before being admitted to SOM, so don't be afraid to retake the test until you achieve a score that will enable you to accomplish your goals! (Note that GMAC has changed its policies and now allows you to take the GMAT just five times in a 12-month period.)

Work experience. Notice that SOM asks for only post-baccalaureate work experience, so do not include internships or full-time work conducted while in undergrad. If you believe this experience is vital to presenting a full profile to the admissions committee, you may include it on your resume. Also, don't embellish your work experience. For example, many applicants have not managed any other employees at this stage in their career, and that's fine! Do not list any direct or indirect reports if you fall into this category.

Career interests. We like that SOM has reduced your career interests in this section to a set of drop-down menus because it encourages honesty and a straightforward answer. Hearing that successful applicants must differentiate themselves, many will try to dream up more "creative" career goals because they fear that the common goals of finance and management consulting will not help them stand out from the crowd. Don't do it! List your genuine career interests in this section and use the rest of your application to stand out.

Motivation for an MBA. Those sneaky admissions officers at SOM have slipped a 150-word essay into the middle of this application—and a vitally important one at that! It reads: *Please describe how you arrived at these career interests (150 words maximum).* On the plus side, the word count has been slightly reduced this year. This is your opportunity to connect the dots among other elements in this section. Help the admissions officers see through your eyes what you've done to this point, what your goals are in the future, and how an MBA from SOM will help you get from here to there. If you currently have fewer than three years of work experience or more than six, you may want to emphasize why you're pursuing an MBA *at this point in time*, because most other applicants will fall into this range.

Gaps in employment. It's best to address any application shortcomings, such as gaps in employment, in a very brief and straightforward way. The shorter, the better! If you took advantage of that time to travel, pursue your passions, volunteer for an organization, or something similar, be sure to mention that here.

Resume. Many applicants put little thought into their resume, perhaps adding a couple of bullet points for their current job and little more. However, it is often the first element of your application that the admissions officer will read, and thus becomes his or her first impression of you. This section offers sound advice for any MBA resume, which is to focus on accomplishments rather than job duties, and emphasize leadership and team roles that you have held throughout your experience.

SOM asks you to include awards, honors, recognition, and other interests, skills, and accomplishments that may be relevant to the admissions committee, in addition to the standard professional and academic items. Most applicants should still be able to fit the necessary information onto one page, although spilling over onto a second page wouldn't be the end of the world. Note that you also have the opportunity to describe up to five activities in the next section of the application, so don't feel obligated to cram everything onto your resume.

Activities/professional affiliations. For many applicants, their true leadership potential and impact on organizations comes through their extracurricular activities more than through their professional life. This is your opportunity to shine! The admissions committee understands that many applicants come from extremely demanding industries where 100-hour workweeks may not be uncommon. In these cases, they understand when applicants have not been actively involved in activities outside of work. Ideally, you'll still be able to show that you used to be involved in outside organizations back when you had a personal life. Investment bankers, you know what we're talking about!

Statement of honesty. Your business school applications have the power to change the course of your entire life. Of course, you may elicit the help of others when crafting your application, just as you would have trusted friends and colleagues proofread your dissertation before you submit it for review. However, the content should be uniquely yours. Besides, the admissions committee wants to get to know the person who is uniquely *you*, not read some generic, cookie-cutter (albeit well-crafted) essay written by someone else.

Our Veritas Prep admissions consultants will not write your essays on your behalf, but we can help you ensure your application will sparkle! No matter how you choose to approach your application, be sure to do it in a way that you can sign your name to this statement of honesty without any reservations.

Essays

Essay: The Yale School of Management educates individuals who will have deep and lasting impact on the organizations they lead. Describe how you have positively influenced an organization, as an employee, a member, or an outside constituent. (500 words maximum)

Defining a leader. Yale SOM requires just one essay, and for that one essay the School of Management has chosen a topic that focuses on one of the defining attributes of a leader: the ability to have a positive impact on those around you. When you hear the term "leader" it's normal to envision an elected official or a CEO, but leaders exist at every level of an organization, even if they don't have any people reporting directly to them. And one of the best ways to spot a leader in a group is to find the person who is able to positively impact those around him or her.

Professional or personal? The essay question does not specify whether you should cite an example from your professional or personal life. In general, we believe that professional examples will have the most impact, since this essay is one of the few opportunities you have in Yale's slimmed-down application to showcase your professional strengths. However, if you believe you can show through your resume and other sections of the application that you have unquestioned professional credentials—and many applicants will—then it may be valuable to show the impact you've had in your volunteer or other outside activities. This may be particularly valuable if you don't feel that you are able to properly demonstrate your extracurricular involvement in other portions of the application.

From "what" to "how." Note that the Yale admissions team not only wants to know what you accomplished, but also wants to understand exactly what you did to make it happen. Examples in which you went above and beyond the call of duty, or went beyond your standard job description, will be the most powerful here. For this essay you can use the classic SAR (Situation–Action–Result) format: Describe the challenge or opportunity you identified, explain in detail what you did, and then spell out exactly how your actions positively influenced those around you.

Results are more than numbers. Although the question highlights the deep and lasting impact leaders can have on an organization, it does not define how that impact should be measured. Instead, it asks how you *positively influenced* an organization, and this influence may take many forms. Perhaps you observed longstanding practices that you thought could be improved, reached out to a number of stakeholders about the reasons behind those practices, and proposed a better solution. If the company or organization took action on your proposal, this would certainly qualify as a positive influence on an organization.

Or perhaps your influence on an organization is not quite as concrete as a specific proposal for change. Perhaps you have influenced the entire culture of an organization through your efforts, or enabled others to achieve their goals through your mentorship. Remember that Yale is looking for candidates whose actions stand out among their peers, so be careful not to be so generic that you say, "I'm such a happy person that my great attitude has positively influenced my organization!" without offering any specific actions that you've taken and their corresponding results. Take time to think about which anecdote will showcase your leadership skills the best, and be willing to try out different stories among several drafts.

Demonstrating leadership in any role. Finally, note that this question focuses on the impact that your actions had on your organization, not the role you were in. In other words, admissions officers care about what positive impact you truly have on those around you much more than they care about your job title.

Optional Information: If any aspect of your candidacy needs further explanation (unexplained gaps in work experience, choice of recommenders, academic performance, promotions or recognitions, etc.), please provide a brief description here. (200 words maximum)

Yes, it's really optional. As we always tell applicants with these optional essays: Only answer this essay prompt if you need to explain a low undergraduate GPA or other potential blemish in your background. No need to harp on a minor weakness and sound like you're making excuses when you don't need any. If you don't have anything else you need to tell the admissions office, it is entirely okay to skip this essay.

Choice of recommenders. As we discuss in the next section, SOM prefers to have a recommendation from your current supervisor or manager. If you do not include a recommendation from this person, they ask that you briefly explain it here. Many applicants have not yet told their current supervisor there is a chance they will be leaving the company to go to business school. This can be explained with a line as simple as "I have not yet informed my current supervisor that I may leave the company to pursue a business education, as this may affect my project assignments and upcoming bonuses. Therefore, I have selected a professional mentor of three years, John Doe, who serves in a senior-management capacity at our company and can speak to my professional potential from firsthand experience."

Required for Reapplicants Only: Since your last application, please discuss any updates to your candidacy, including changes in your personal or professional life, additional coursework, or extracurricular/volunteer activities. (200 words maximum)

Focus on improvement. Re-applicants are often admitted at higher rates than first-time applicants, so don't be afraid that you'll be "tainted goods" if you choose to apply to Yale SOM a second time. However, you must show some kind of improvement in your profile since your last application, as both applications will be viewed side-by-side. If you had a middling GMAT score, this is a great area to focus on. If your undergraduate performance was less than stellar, you might think about taking a course from a local community college or accredited online program. Perhaps your career goals were not perfectly clear and your "mini essay" in the application revealed a lack of direction. You might speak with people currently working in your desired industry, position, or company about the likelihood that you would be able to make a career switch. Feel free to discuss the process you went through to refine your goals.

Video Essays

As Yale SOM Admissions Director Bruce DelMonico wrote in early 2014, the work that goes into your application overall should prepare you well for the video questions. Following are a few more insights to help you answer them with confidence.

How does it work? Once you submit your written application, a new link will appear on your applicant status page. You'll need a computer with a webcam and microphone. You'll have just one practice question and then the real questions will begin. Once you start the official questions, you'll have just 20 seconds to gather your thoughts for each question and up to one minute to respond. This may not seem like much time to develop a cohesive answer, but think about an in-person interview: You're asked a question and respond immediately, usually within two or three seconds.

What are they looking for? You'll be asked three questions that are meant to elicit some insight on who you are, how you act, and how you think. As DelMonico mentions in his blog post, the school isn't looking for a perfect level of polish. In fact, the more off-the-cuff your remarks seem, the more likely you are to come across as authentic. You shouldn't ramble for 90 seconds, but your answers should be just as they probably would be in an in-person interview: imperfect, yet succinct and convincing. We don't know about the other admissions officers, but Bruce told us that he doesn't even look at the videos when he's reviewing applications; he simply listens to them.

What will I be asked? The questions aren't intended to be difficult. One question will ask for a quick introduction about yourself. If there's something new that you can provide with your answer, it would be nice to offer new value with this questions. Something like "My resume will tell you that I'm X, Y, and Z, but my friends would say that..." will utilize the more personal medium of video to offer additional context not found elsewhere in your application. The second question will ask a behavioral question along the lines of "Tell me a time when...." Consider a number of stories beforehand that address several different situations, such as overcoming an obstacle, leading a challenging team, using creativity to solve a problem, and so forth. Try to utilize stories that you haven't already used in your written essay. In your final question, you'll likely be faced with a statement with which you need to agree or disagree. You'll be asked to take a stand and provide your reasoning. This is a quick exercise to see how well you think on your feet.

What are some tips for success? We recommend that in addition to the practice question offered by Yale, you practice recording yourself with your webcam in the place where you're going to record the real thing. Are there distractions in the background? Will the admissions officer be able to hear you? Do you use lots of filler words (*um, er, ya know*, etc.)? Again, SOM doesn't expect this to be a professional production, but reducing distractions will be helpful. Practice answering questions similar to those we've described. You want to be natural and conversational in the actual recording, so we don't recommend memorizing your answers, or you may come off as stilted. Dress in business attire, as you would in your admissions interview. Lastly, relax! This is meant to be a fun conversation between you and the admissions committee member, so don't be afraid to let your personality come through.

Recommendations

Each applicant must submit two professional recommendations with the application. The school generally discourages academic recommendations from college professors unless you've had significant professional experience working with them. In this section, we list the questions your recommender will be asked so that you can select recommenders who know you best and can answer them thoroughly.

First, your recommenders will be asked to fill out basic contact information (pre-populated with information that you provide). Then they will be asked to fill out a "Leadership Behavior Grid."

Leadership Behavior Grid. Your recommender will be asked to assess you on a multiple-choice scale regarding the following skills/qualities: *Results Orientation, Strategic Orientation, Team Leadership, Influence and Collaboration, Communicating, Information Seeking, Developing Others, Change Leadership, Respect for Others,* and *Trustworthiness.*

Each skill/quality has a different description for its 1–5 rating scale. For example, the scale for Results Orientation is as follows: *1) Fulfills assigned tasks, 2) Overcomes obstacles to achieve goals, 3) Exceeds goals and raises effectiveness of organization, 4) Introduces incremental improvements to enhance business performance using robust analysis, 5) Invents and delivers best in class standards and performance.*

Note from Veritas Prep: It would be highly unlikely for a genuine recommendation to include a perfect 5 rating on all skills or qualities. In fact, if your recommender simply marks 5s down the page, then the recommendation may be viewed skeptically, as it provides little information about your true strengths and weaknesses.

Peer comparison. Based on your professional experience, how do you rate this candidate compared to her/his peer group? Multiple-choice: *Below Average; Average; Very good (well above average); Excellent (top 10%); Outstanding (top 5%); The best encountered in my career.*

Overall recommendation. Multiple-choice: *Recommend enthusiastically; Recommend; Recommend with reservations; Do not recommend.*

Recommendation letter. *Please write an assessment of the applicant that addresses the prompts below. We are looking for your candid and accurate assessment of the applicant's potential to be a successful leader and what specific traits the applicant possesses that evidence this potential. Please be as specific as possible and use concrete examples where applicable. Do not incorporate anything drafted by the candidate in your recommendation or have the candidate submit the recommendation on your behalf.*

- *Please comment briefly on the context of your interaction with the applicant. If applicable, describe the applicant's role in your organization.*

- *How do the candidate's performance, potential, or personal qualities compare to those of other well-qualified individuals in similar roles? Please provide specific examples.*

- *Describe the most important piece of constructive feedback you have given the applicant. Please detail the circumstances and the applicant's response.*

Recommenders are not given any word limits for their letters. Several schools, including Yale, have decided to consolidate their recommendations, asking nearly identical questions to help relieve the burden on supervisors to write several recommendations for each applicant. Some other schools recommend 300 words for the second question and 250 words for the third. These word counts would be perfectly appropriate for Yale's recommendation as well.

If your recommenders don't have time to fill out the entire form in one sitting, they may save changes for later and return to the form.

Find recommenders who know you well and can answer the essay questions with depth and detail.

Selecting your recommenders. Both recommenders should provide professional references, and at least one must be able to offer an evaluation of your current job (ideally, your current supervisor). Even though they will be asked to list their job title, don't reach out to distant contacts simply because they happen to have impressive titles or are alumni of the school. It is far more important to find recommenders who know you well and can answer the essay questions with depth and detail.

Should I draft it myself? Many applicants to business school are asked by their superiors to draft the recommendation themselves and the recommender will tweak and approve it. We strongly recommend that you do not write the recommendation yourself for several reasons. First, your writing style and choice of phrasing are unique, and admissions officers will notice if the recommendations are similar to each other and to your essay. Second, you will tend to be too humble or generic. Your supervisor might use language such as "one of the top analysts I've seen in my entire career" that you would never dare include if writing on his or her behalf. Third, and perhaps most importantly, the admissions officer is looking for a third-party perspective on your candidacy, so writing a recommendation yourself is an unethical breach of trust with the school you are looking to join. Yale expresses very explicitly that you are not to draft any portion of the letter yourself, although having a conversation about the recommendation is perfectly acceptable.

We have a three-part series on the Veritas Prep blog about how to get recommenders to write enthusiastic letters.

Preparing your recommenders. Instead of writing the recommendation yourself, you should sit down and have candid conversations with your recommenders about the reasons you want to go to business school and why you've selected your target schools, your professional goals, and your experience to date. Ask them if they would have the time to write a strong recommendation on your behalf. (This also gives them a nice "out" by telling you that they are too busy rather than saying they don't feel comfortable giving you a positive recommendation.)

Bring a copy of your resume and a bulleted list of projects that you've worked on together and accomplishments they have seen you achieve. Let them know that admissions committees prefer to see specific, detailed examples in recommendations. Then, let them know that you'll serve as a "project manager" to follow up and ensure that they are able to submit your recommendation ahead of the deadline.

The Interview

How many applicants are interviewed? Similar to many elite business schools, SOM grants interviews on an invitation-only basis. However, with just a third or fewer of applicants interviewed, simply receiving an invitation is a strong signal of the admission committee's interest. Of those interviewed, more than half will receive an offer of admission.

Who conducts them? Interviews are offered both on campus (by admissions officers or by current students) and off campus with alumni. In both instances, the interview is "blind," in the sense that the interviewer does not have access to the candidate's application materials. The interviewer is only provided with a copy of the candidate's resume. Interview invitations may go out at any time throughout the round until final decision date.

How does it work? The SOM interview will be fairly conversational, and the interviewer will try to keep you at ease and connect with you throughout. On average, interviews will last 30 to 45 minutes. Interviewers will try to keep it closer to 30 minutes, and they will try to take notes throughout the interview, so do not let those facts distract you. If the interviewer is a bit distracted while feverishly trying to take notes, this is not a sign that you did or said something wrong.

What are they looking for? SOM typically takes a standard approach to its interview questions, and will generally have you walk the interviewer through your resume. This is done either through several specific questions, or by directly asking you to walk him or her through your curriculum vitae. Interviewers are generally seeking the behavioral aspect of your academic and career history—*why* you made the choices you did and if you think you made the correct choices along the way.

They also want to see if there is a clear, unifying theme connecting your past to your present to your future. If the interviewer is an admissions officer, there is a greater chance that a curveball question or two will be thrown in there as well, though that will be interspersed with walking through your resume.

How should I prepare? During the interview, you need to be an expert about yourself and your history. This may sound obvious, but many miss the fact that you have to not only know the rote facts as listed on your resume, but you also have to be prepared to answer what your thought process was along the way—particularly as you switched from one job to another.

What should I ask? At the end of the interview, you will have an opportunity to ask questions of the interviewer. This is a great time to ask questions that you could not gain complete insight into in your previous research. There is not anything curriculum- or community-related that will be out of bounds, so make use of this access wisely. This also helps to show your level of commitment to being an SOM student. However, if you do not have any questions, do not feel the need to craft the perfect, clever question to impress the interviewer, as he or she will see through that. Just keep it simple and honest.

> **With just a third or fewer of applicants interviewed, simply receiving an invitation is a strong signal of the admission committee's interest.**

BERKELEY-HAAS

Nobel Prize–winning professors, a West Coast culture, and a mission to challenge the norm.

BERKELEY, CA

CLASS SIZE
241

PROGRAM FOUNDED
1898

NICKNAME
CAL

CHARACTERISTICS
INNOVATION, CALIFORNIAN, PUBLIC IVY

BERKELEY-HAAS SNAPSHOT

What Berkeley-Haas Is Known For

"Public Ivy" prestige. The Haas School of Business is one of several top-ranked programs at the University of California, Berkeley. UC Berkeley (often referred to as "Cal") is noted for its prestigious engineering, natural science, and social science programs, as well as for its top-10 graduate programs in law and education—and, of course, business. As one of the nation's top public universities, UC Berkeley is a leader in areas of national importance, such as social responsibility, clean energy, and technology. Berkeley-Haas has had five Nobel Prize–winning economists on its faculty, including the 2009 winner Oliver Williamson. (Only Chicago Booth has more Nobel Laureates at a business school, with six.)

> **Haas is more of a regional MBA than most top-10 schools: The vast majority of students settle locally or in the western U.S.**

Innovation and social responsibility. Innovation and social responsibility are core values at Haas. In keeping with the school's position in the Bay Area and just north of Silicon Valley, *Leading Through Innovation* is the school's mission statement, and this concept permeates the program, with even more emphasis today on developing "innovative leaders," as reinforced through recent changes to the curriculum. Haas has a tremendous emphasis on technology management—including new thinking in cleantech and sustainability—though students interested in many other areas, including consulting and finance, are also set up for success after going through its program.

Regional reputation. Partly because of geography, and partly because of the state's resident population mix, Berkeley-Haas (along with its fellow University of California school UCLA Anderson) has somewhat more of an emphasis on Asia and the Pacific Rim than you might find at other top-tier MBA programs. At the same time, Haas is more of a regional MBA than most top-10 schools: The vast majority of students (often 70% or more) settle locally or in the western U.S.

What Makes Berkeley-Haas Different

The Haas culture. The Berkeley-Haas "Defining Principles" were first articulated by the school in 2010. We have found these principles spot-on in describing the type of student Haas accepts and the way Haas develops those students into innovative leaders. The Defining Principles are:

- **Question the Status Quo.** "We lead by championing bold ideas, taking intelligent risks and accepting sensible failures. This means speaking our minds even when it challenges convention. We thrive at the world's epicenter of innovation."

- **Confidence without Attitude.** "We make decisions based on evidence and analysis, giving us the confidence to act without arrogance. We lead through trust and collaboration."

- **Students Always.** "We are a community designed for curiosity and lifelong pursuit of personal and intellectual growth. This is not a place for those who feel they have learned all they need to learn."

- **Beyond Yourself.** "We shape our world by leading ethically and responsibly. As stewards of our enterprises, we take the longer view in our decisions and actions. This often means putting larger interests above our own."

Technology. While "innovation" is not limited just to high tech, a key distinction at Berkeley-Haas is the focus on technology. Haas sent an impressive 43% of the Class of 2014 into the tech sector, which leads all top-tier MBA programs, including Stanford, MIT Sloan, and UCLA Anderson. This result is, of course, enabled by the school's proximity to Silicon Valley as well as the wealth of resources available on the larger Berkeley campus. Haas offers a distinctive Management of Technology certificate (open not just to business and engineering students but to other UC Berkeley grad students as well, such as those in Environmental Design). The Haas Technology Club is one of the largest and most active student groups on campus.

Increasing global reach. Nearly every business school currently espouses a "global perspective," but Haas combines its international focus with its emphasis on experiential learning. The International Business Development program places about 150 students a year in all corners of the globe for three-week consulting projects. While the MBA program itself is sometimes seen as regional—most graduates stay on the West Coast after finishing the program—Haas has an expanding network of connections in the business and academic communities around the world. With the Class of 2016, Haas increased its percentage of international students to 43% of the class (up from 31% the year prior). It has even changed its branding to "Berkeley-Haas" to leverage UC Berkeley's global reputation.

Berkeley-Haas Is a Good Fit for You If...

You're *not* fresh out of undergrad. Haas is pretty strict about requiring extensive work experience in students. The average age of a Haas student is 28—though the gap with some other schools has narrowed.

You're interested in technology (including biotech and nanotech). Whether you want to develop software, or develop a software company, Haas is a great place to expand your expertise in the areas of product development, product management, the management of innovation, and bringing new technology ideas to market. The program offers opportunities unheard of at other schools, especially in the areas of nanotechnology and biotechnology. The campus-wide Nano Club hosts the Berkeley Nanotechnology Forum every year, and electives in biotech are available at Haas.

You may pursue a career in cleantech. Few other business schools offer any curriculum at all in the field of renewable energy or cleantech, and even fewer have demonstrated a commitment to leading these fields forward into the future. Student members of the Berkeley Energy and Resources Collaborative have teamed up with scientists at the Lawrence Berkeley National Lab (LBNL) to create a program called Cleantech to Market (C2M), which sends five student teams out each year to study the commercial opportunities that might arise out of the various clean energy technologies under development at LBNL.

You're looking to go into health care. Haas has great support for educating future leaders in health care. Berkeley is known for its joint MBA/MPH (Master of Public Health) program, and it offers a graduate program in Health Management as well. Haas is a natural fit for someone interested in tackling some of the biggest problems facing the world.

Cleantech to Market (C2M) sends five student teams out each year to study the commercial opportunities that might arise out of clean energy technologies under development.

You want to start a business. Haas is one of the leading schools for graduates launching businesses, anchored by the Lester Center for Entrepreneurship. Students put on two business plan competitions a year, and the school has a significant number of students start businesses upon graduation.

You want to start a nonprofit or social venture. One of the strongest business schools for nonprofit management has traditionally been Yale. Haas has similar strengths, with a somewhat different emphasis on the innovation side. Someone considering an application to Yale for nonprofit might want to also consider Haas for similar reasons. As an example, Haas has a business plan competition (the Global Social Venture Competition) specifically geared toward folks interested in starting businesses with a social purpose. Launched in late 2013 and led by former dean Laura D'Andrea Tyson, the school also houses the Institute for Business and Social Impact, an umbrella designed to house four existing centers: the Center for Social Sector Leadership, the Center for Responsible Business, the Graduate Program in Health Management, and the Global Social Venture Competition.

You want to stay on the West Coast after graduating. A large number of Haas alumni reside up and down the West Coast, from Los Angeles to Seattle. Although it's certainly possible to take the Haas MBA to other parts of the country or the world, Haas has fewer connections to Wall Street, and it can be a little tougher for students to break into East Coast financial firms from Berkeley.

You're a woman or a U.S. underrepresented minority. Haas is a leader among top business schools in initiatives reaching out to women and to underrepresented ethnic groups through programs and organizations such as the Forte Foundation and The Consortium. While Haas does not change its standards for female or minority applicants, the school does seem to be interested in improving the proportions of students in these categories and may give such candidates a closer look. The school has consistently lagged behind its top-tier counterparts in attracting female students—until now, that is. Forty-three percent of the class entering in 2014 was female—the highest percentage of women of any top-tier business school. That's a historic high and the school is justifiably proud. However, keep in mind that with the school's small class size (~250 students), a small increase in the numbers means a big jump in the percentages. The increase from last year's 29% to this year's 43% equates to approximately 35 individuals.

ACADEMICS AT BERKELEY-HAAS

What Berkeley-Haas Is Known For

Teaching philosophy. The Haas School's guiding philosophy for its MBA program is to provide a strong experiential learning environment that will fit the school's "leading through innovation" approach and produce graduates who possess "confidence without attitude." Haas professors are luminaries and world-class researchers and authors, yet the instruction in classrooms tends to be very practical in nature (rather than steeped in theory, as some might expect). Most classes at Berkeley-Haas feature some amount of lecturing, but also include a heavy dose of case studies, project work, computer simulations, behavior modeling, and guest speakers.

Customizable curriculum. The curriculum at Berkeley-Haas is organized around seven areas of general management fundamentals, which, when combined with the school's extensive elective offerings (many available to first-year students), permits a high degree of customization. Areas of Emphasis provide further opportunity for students to focus their studies and prepare for their future careers.

Innovation. While lots of schools talk about innovation, Berkeley-Haas actually requires it. An applied innovation requirement is included in the core curriculum; students may choose from 12 course options, almost all of which include a team-performance component. Berkeley-Haas also offers a number of innovation-related electives. Innovation features prominently in the school's extracurricular opportunities, which include a number of competitions, conferences, student organizations, and speakers.

Experiential learning. As a component of the core curriculum, Haas students also have an experiential learning requirement, with a menu of 13 choices, ranging from *Advertising Strategy* to *Corporate Social Responsibility* to *Hedge Fund Strategies*. Haas provides students with two overlapping skill sets: an ongoing emphasis on leadership, and a toolkit of knowledge and relationships that provide the foundation for effective decision making.

You Oughta Know

Haas@Work. Haas@Work is one option that fulfills the innovation requirement. This experiential learning option gives students access to potential employers—and the opportunity to solve real problems—by working on a business challenge that a client organization faces. First, student teams are required to submit recommendations to address the challenge. Then the solution that is chosen is implemented over the course of a semester by the team. It is a great way to apply many of the theories learned in the classroom and build experience within a certain discipline, organization, and industry.

Launch. The interdisciplinary and entrepreneurial emphasis at UC Berkeley shines through in this entrepreneurship event at Berkeley-Haas (previously known as the Berkeley Business Plan Competition). Students, alumni members, and researchers across the university participate in this premier business plan competition hosted by the Haas School. $25,000 in cash prizes are awarded to winners of this competition based on the reviews of top venture capitalists from the Bay Area, as well as the audience. The business plan competition provides students an opportunity to showcase their innovative ideas and a thoughtful review of the business case through the creation and presentation of a business plan.

Social responsibility and social entrepreneurship. Haas prides itself on being the preeminent institution for research, teaching, experiential learning, and community outreach in areas of Corporate Social Responsibility (CSR). Haas offers more than a dozen different programs and initiatives around social responsibility and business sustainability, woven into the core curriculum. Nonprofit management is also a focus here. With the University's radical history, and the very liberal government and policies in the surrounding city of Berkeley, it is to be expected that many are attracted to Haas because of an interest in changing the world. This is a positive quality that can be nurtured through the ecosystem of the Haas School, including the Center for Social Sector Leadership, a specialized curriculum, and a range of social venture courses.

BERKELEY AT A GLANCE

APPLICANTS BY SCHOOL

Due to its small class size, Berkeley-Haas is one of the most selective MBA programs in the world, bested only by Harvard and Stanford. When the program opens a new building and its class size grows, we anticipate its admission rate to eventually fall in line with other top-10 schools, around 20%.

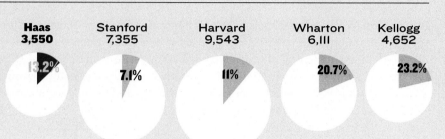

Haas 3,550	Stanford 7,355	Harvard 9,543	Wharton 6,111	Kellogg 4,652
13.2%	7.1%	11%	20.7%	23.2%

◄ Percent admitted

U.S. MINORITIES

Haas	Anderson	Stanford	Harvard
41%	27%	23%	24%

GMAT SCORES

717	730	732	728
Haas	Harvard	Stanford	Wharton

NATIONALITY

Berkeley-Haas has one of largest international student populations of any top-tier program, with 43% of the Class of 2016 coming from abroad. Interestingly, 38 countries were represented in the Class of 2016, which is nearly half the number of countries represented at Harvard (73) and Wharton (71), both of which have much larger class sizes, but have significantly smaller percentages of international students.

57%
U.S.

43%
International Citizens

38 Countries Represented

WOMEN

With women comprising 43% of its class, Berkeley-Haas has the highest percentage of women of any top MBA program. This marks a huge jump from the Class of 2015, which had just 29% women. Clearly, the school is making an attempt to attract more female candidates to its program.

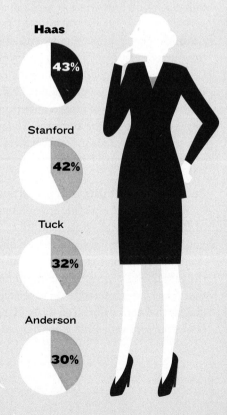

Haas
43%

Stanford
42%

Tuck
32%

Anderson
30%

UNDERGRAD MAJORS

Nearly half the Haas class (49%) studied business or economics as undergraduates. Relatively fewer were humanities or social science majors compared to peer schools.

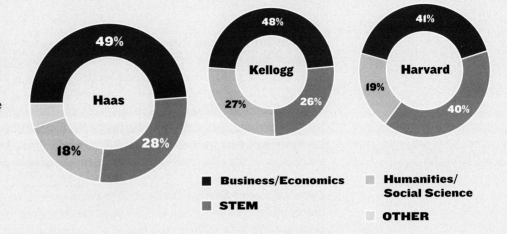

Haas
49%
28%
18%

Kellogg
48%
26%
27%

Harvard
41%
40%
19%

■ **Business/Economics**   ■ **Humanities/ Social Science**

■ **STEM**   ■ **OTHER**

AVERAGE GPA

Haas has far less tolerance for low undergraduate GPAs than most peer schools. Just 10% of the admitted class had a GPA of 3.35 or lower.

3.62
Haas

3.67
Harvard

3.74
Stanford

3.60
Wharton

CLASS SIZE

Harvard	935
Wharton	859
Columbia	743
Kellogg	662
Booth	538
Ross	447
Duke	440
Stanford	410
Sloan	406
Stern	406
Anderson	360
Yale	323
Tuck	281
Haas	**241**

FROM CONSULTING/FINANCE SECTOR PRE-MBA

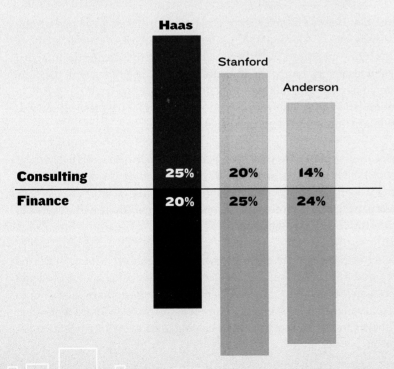

	Haas	Stanford	Anderson
Consulting	25%	20%	14%
Finance	20%	25%	24%

Student-initiated electives. Student-initiated elective courses are a tradition at Haas. Every semester, Haas offers several courses that are initiated and run by students with faculty guidance. Typically, such courses focus on a specific theme or industry.

Global Social Venture Competition (GSVC). The largest and oldest student-led business plan competition for social ventures, the GSVC provides mentoring, exposure, and prizes for leaders of social enterprises from around the world. Since its inception in 1999, the GSVC has awarded more than $250,000 to these emerging social enterprises.

Dean's Speaker Series. The Dean's Speaker Series is one of several programs that bring industry leaders to Berkeley-Haas. This program brings highly distinguished business leaders to Haas to share some of their experiences and lessons. An opportunity to hear some of these individuals speak in person is extremely rare, and the reputation and relationships of the Haas School continue to attract prestigious business minds such as Vinod Khosla (founder and partner of Khosla Ventures) and Paul Otellini (CEO of Intel).

Nuts & Bolts

Class organization. During the first year at Haas, the 240 students who make up the incoming class are divided into four cohorts of 60 to 65 students each. The Gold, Blue, Oski, and Axe cohorts are launched at the pre-term "Cohort Olympics." Each cohort takes all first-semester core classes as a group, allowing the members to easily bond and get to know their classmates. Cohorts are further divided into study groups of four to six members, and these groups stay together through all first-semester classes. This predetermined grouping approach creates diverse cohorts and teams in terms of background and skills. Shuffling of cohorts is done before the second semester, allowing students to get to know more of their classmates intimately throughout the first year.

> **Students at Haas vote each year whether or not to have a grade non-disclosure policy.**

Grading policies. Students at Haas vote each year whether or not to have a grade non-disclosure policy, and most years the vote is in favor of the non-disclosure policy. As a result, students are not required to provide future employers with their grades, a policy that fosters the intended culture of collaboration and teamwork among the students. However, beginning with the 2006 incoming class, an academic honors program was implemented to recognize the top 10% in each graduating class, measured by GPA. This provides an opportunity for the most exceptional group to be recognized while maintaining the culture of collaboration.

The grading system varies from professor to professor. Some professors use a relatively strict curve, while others provide grades based on performance relative to absolute measures. Typically, grades are based on a weighting of projects (including smaller assignments), exams (midterm and final), and class participation. Professors are open and transparent with respect to their grading policies in the introduction to the class.

Course enrollment. One particular element of life at Haas that students get to know well is the course bidding system, in which Haas students bid on elective courses using points. Students receive 1,000 points each semester and must allocate them based on the courses they want to take and the professors from which they most want to learn. If a course can fit 50 students, then the 50 students who bid the highest will all get in, at their bidding price, allowing students to get into their classes of interest.

The bidding system forces students to make choices—and often those choices are based on who is teaching a course. At times, students will have to decide between taking a highly ranked professor (students review professors after each class, and these reviews are public) or taking a less-dynamic professor for a desired class. Of course, many classes are offered several times a year and the popular ones are taught most semesters, so the likelihood of getting into a specific class that is of interest is extremely high. One of the advantages to Haas's small full-time class is that students often have an easier time getting into courses they wish to take than at some of the larger MBA programs.

Core classes. The breadth of Berkeley-Haas's core curriculum reflects the school's general management focus. The 12 required courses run the full gamut of B-school disciplines, ranging from *Data and Decisions* to *Ethics* to *Finance*. Most of the core courses are required during the first year of the program, although some may be waived by taking an exam before classes begin.

Areas of Emphasis. Most Berkeley-Haas students choose to focus their studies using the school's general management fundamentals (similar to majors) or "Areas of Emphasis." Although not formal majors, these areas allow students to create their own specialized education. In addition, Berkeley-Haas students may earn a Certificate in Real Estate as a supplement to the MBA degree after the completion of a designated number of courses and special projects.

Exchange programs. Haas has agreements with top business schools in Europe and Asia to allow its students to study there. Unlike many schools, Berkeley-Haas also opens up its exchange programs to more than just its full-time MBA students. In addition to second-year full-time students, Evening/Weekend MBA students who have completed their core coursework requirements may also participate in the exchange program during Fall Semester.

Popular Professors

The Haas faculty is populated with many prominent business leaders, researchers, and teachers, with a heavy slant toward economists (Nobel Prize, anyone?). Among Haas students, there are a handful of professors who are considered a "must have" for a class, due to their reputation both as educators and as researchers. This list isn't merely a collection of famous names, but rather the instructors that Haas students deem to be essential for the full experience. Faculty evaluations are completed periodically and are available to students for the classes they are considering. The most popular professors include:

David Aaker

E.T. Grether Professor Emeritus of Marketing and Public Policy
Professor Aaker is the creator of the Aaker Model, a four-fold perspective on the idea of building brands. He is also the author of *Building Strong Brands*, which was published in 1996 and remains a key text in this area of study. In fact, many credit Professor Aaker with bringing "brand equity" out of the sole realm of trademark lawyers and to the forefront for marketing professionals. With a laid-back presentation style and an "aw shucks" demeanor that belies his prominence in academia, Professor Aaker is very approachable and a favorite among students at Haas. Now an emeritus member of the faculty, Professor Aaker no longer teaches full courses but still has a strong presence on campus with an ongoing speaker series.

General Management Fundamentals

Accounting

Business & Public Policy

Economic Analysis & Public Policy

Finance

Management of Organizations

Marketing

Operations & Information Technology Management

Areas of Emphasis

Finance

Marketing

Strategy/Consulting

Corporate Social Responsibility

Energy and Clean Technology

Entrepreneurship

Global Management

Health Management

Social Sector Leadership

Real Estate

Technology

BERKELEY (HAAS)

Jerome S. Engel

Senior Fellow at the Lester Center

Founding Executive Director Emeritus of the Lester Center for Entrepreneurship

Professor Engel is the director emeritus of Haas's Entrepreneurship Program as well as the Lester Center for Entrepreneurship and Innovation, which he founded in 1991. He is also a general partner with Monitor Ventures, specializing in high-tech entrepreneurship and venture capital, which consistently puts him front and center in the VC world. His *Venture Capital and Private Equity* course is one of the most popular at Haas, and a bidding war erupts each year over seats for this class. Professor Engel is known for bringing as many perspectives as possible to the classroom, from cutting-edge new cases to high-profile investment professionals.

Professor Ho's Pricing Policy class is arguably the most sought-after course in the entire MBA program.

Teck Ho

William Halford Jr. Family Chair in Marketing

Director of Asia Business Center

Professor Ho has received the Earl F. Cheit Award for Excellence in Teaching several times, and teaches classes for the MBA program as well as for the Center for UC Berkeley Executive Education. His *Pricing Policy* class is arguably the most sought-after class in the entire MBA program. Professor Ho is known for being a dynamic and entertaining teacher, and students appreciate how practical his courses are, as Professor Ho's primary teaching method is all about applying theories to real-life scenarios.

Steven Tadelis

Professor of Economics

Professor Tadelis is a Barbara and Gerson Bakar Faculty Fellow most recognizable for teaching Haas's *Microeconomics* core course. Along with Professor Glazier (marketing), Professor Tadelis is a huge favorite among professors of core classes. Formerly a fan favorite in the econ department at Stanford (where his *Game Theory* class was enormously popular), Professor Tadelis came to Haas in 2005 and immediately became the kind of professor that gets mentioned in every student chat and building tour as a classroom favorite. Part of this is due to his witty and engaging teaching style, but another major factor in his popularity is that he uses very interesting and unique examples to bring theoretical principles to life.

Suneel Udpa

Lecturer, Haas Accounting Group

Professor Udpa teaches both the *Accounting* core course as well as the highly recommended *Managerial Accounting* course. Part of the reason he is such a noteworthy professor is that his classes are loved by students despite the fact that the subject matter is a bit dry. Most "must take" professors—at any business school—teach subjects that tend to be more exciting to students, such as marketing, entrepreneurship, or investments. It is no small achievement that Professor Udpa is able to make accounting such a memorable experience for students. As one student said, "If you can make accounting fun, you can do anything." A recent Haas graduate compared going to Professor Udpa's class to attending a stand-up show at a comedy club. Therefore, it is no surprise that there is actually a "Suneel Udpa Fan Club" on campus (complete with t-shirts).

Cameron Anderson

Lorraine Tyson Mitchell Chair in Leadership & Communication II

Professor Anderson teaches the *Power and Politics* course, which consistently receives the highest number of bid points (along with Teck Ho's *Pricing Policy* course). The points are worth it, though, as students learn the most effective ways to advance their careers post-graduation.

Terry Taylor
Milton W. Terrill Chair of Business Administration and Associate Professor
Professor Taylor teaches the core *Operations Management* class and is consistently ranked one of the top professors at Haas. Teaching operations principles using his distinctive crisp teaching style (and sometimes beer), Professor Taylor has become one of the most-loved professors at Haas.

Similar Academic Programs

Cornell (Johnson). Johnson also requires a broad range of core classes and places a heavy emphasis on experiential learning. Johnson calls this concept Performance Learning, and it includes semester-long immersions into one of seven subject areas. There's a bonus of a highly collaborative, friendly culture. And there's snow!

Virginia (Darden). If the idea of taking a broad array of required courses appeals to you, Darden is also worth a look. It's another strong, general management program that still has an extensive list of required courses. Its tight, cohort-based classroom environment also fosters strong relationships among students. However, Darden follows a near-100% case-based curriculum, which differs from Berkeley-Haas's experiential learning emphasis.

UCLA (Anderson). You'll find a more flexible core curriculum at Anderson than at Berkeley-Haas (it requires nine courses to Haas's 12), but the "learn by doing" philosophy is alive and well at Anderson through the Applied Management Research (AMR) capstone project. (Anderson actually started the concept of field study nearly 50 years ago.)

EMPLOYMENT & CAREERS AT BERKELEY-HAAS

What Berkeley-Haas Is Known For

Technology. Given Haas's location near Silicon Valley, it is not a surprise that technology companies dominate the top recruiter list, ranging from internet marketplaces like Amazon to device luminary Apple. Be aware, however, that Berkeley-Haas graduates tend to gravitate toward product management roles. At Bay Area rival Stanford, there is a stronger pipeline into technology venture capital firms, whereas Haas grads will have to roll up their sleeves and make their own connections in this field.

Haas sent 43% of the Class of 2014 into tech.

Graduates entering the technology industry

School	%
Haas	43%
UW Foster	41%
Sloan, Anderson, & Texas	28%
Stanford	24%
Ross	20%
Kellogg	18%

Digital media. Another focus of interest among many students is entertainment and the convergence to digital forms. Haas students are very active in the Berkeley Center for New Media and the Digital Media and Entertainment Club (DMEC), which puts on the annual Play Digital Media Conference. The DMEC also hosts on-campus speakers and organizes career treks to New York and Los Angeles.

Energy and sustainability. In addition to the top-tier consulting firms BCG and McKinsey and Company, Haas has also seen a significant number of energy companies recruit on campus, ranging from large incumbents like Chevron and PG&E to newer entrants such as Bloom Energy and SunPower.

Graduates entering the energy industry

Texas	8%
Yale	6%
Haas, Anderson, & Ross	4%
Booth & Duke	3%

Entrepreneurship. For students who would rather start their own tech firm than work for one, Berkeley-Haas offers a number of career resources, including the Haas Entrepreneurs' Association, Innovators at Cal (which helps students generate new business ideas), and Skydeck (a UC Berkeley accelerator for student/alumni startups).

You Oughta Know

Less emphasis on finance. Just 13% of Haas students take finance-related roles upon graduation, the lowest proportion of any top-15 MBA program, along with Ross. However, 13% is a long way from zero, so particularly if you're interested in staying on the West Coast, Haas isn't a bad place to land a finance job.

Quality vs. quantity. Given its general management emphasis, Berkeley-Haas attracts employers from almost all industries and functions. Top destinations for graduates of the Class of 2014 reflected the school's strengths; the list includes Bain & Company, Amazon, Genentech, Facebook, and Zynga. However, students sometimes report frustration that, as a smaller program, Berkeley-Haas sometimes lags larger schools in the sheer quantity of recruiters recruiting on campus.

Salaries. Not that all you care about is money, but surely you want to make sure your MBA investment is worthwhile. So it should make you happy to learn that the average base salary for Berkeley-Haas's Class of 2014 was $121,816, with consulting hires landing the highest base of approximately $132,770. (Just remember to be a bit careful when looking at overall average salary numbers because they can be skewed by high salaries in particular industries. Schools that send fewer students to those industries can be at a disadvantage.) But wait—that's not all! The average signing bonus was just under $26,865; just more than 70% of students reported receiving them.

Career development resources. Berkeley-Haas's Career Management Group runs on-campus recruiting, advises students on career choices, and connects with prospective employers to encourage them to hire Haas students and graduates. Not surprisingly given the intimate nature of the program, career advisors get high marks for individual coaching, which can sometimes suffer at large institutions. Alumni may also utilize career management resources, including networking opportunities, webinars, and job boards.

Similar Programs for Professional Opportunities

MIT (Sloan). If you're attracted to Haas's emphases on technology and entrepreneurship, you should also consider MIT Sloan, as both programs boast strengths in these areas. Both schools are particularly well known for opportunities in biotech.

Stanford. Haas's Bay Area neighbor also has strong ties to the tech powerhouses of Silicon Valley, and many graduates from both programs find jobs with some of the leading firms in this area. If you're interested working for a technology firm or pursuing your own tech startup after graduation, you should consider applying to Stanford as well.

Texas (McCombs). Given McCombs's Texas location, it's not surprising that the school is strong in the energy sector; it sends about 8% of graduates into the field. Austin's burgeoning technology sector is also a huge magnet. More than a quarter (28%) of McCombs grads went into the field last year.

UCLA (Anderson). In part due to the growth of technology companies and startups in West Los Angeles known as Silicon Beach, Anderson has had a recent surge in students interested in technology jobs after graduation. In response, the school has added significant resources in this area. Anderson and Haas share many of the same recruiters, as both schools tend to keep a very high percentage of their class in California after graduation.

Michigan (Ross). Similar to Berkeley-Haas, the Ross School of Business at the University of Michigan places a large emphasis on sustainability, clean technology, and the environment.

Northwestern (Kellogg). In absolute numbers, Kellogg sent more graduates to Silicon Valley firms in 2014 than either Berkeley-Haas or even Stanford, thanks to its large class size. Like Haas, Kellogg sends relatively few graduates into the finance industry; however, Kellogg is a management-consulting powerhouse. Other strong sectors include consumer goods and retail firms (largely due to its strength in marketing), manufacturing, and health care.

CULTURE & CAMPUS LIFE AT BERKELEY-HAAS

What Berkeley-Haas Is Known For

Down-to-earth students. As we mentioned earlier, one of the four pillars of Berkeley-Haas is "Confidence without Attitude." Other MBA programs encourage similar environments, such as Kellogg, Ross, and Tuck, but no other business school has formally ensconced this principle as a pillar of its program like Haas. Admissions officers specifically look for applicants who have confidence without attitude, so this characteristic has become a vital part of the school's culture.

Beautiful learning environment. Haas students are often envied by the rest of the UC Berkeley community, as Haas is widely known to have the nicest facilities of any school on campus. The Haas building opened in 1995, making it one of the newest at the university. Haas has its own library, career center, auditorium, cafeteria, study area, and extremely large courtyard that has just undergone renovations (see below). Most of the classrooms are built to accommodate the intimate 60- to 65-person class sizes that Haas seeks to maintain. Seats in every classroom are organized in a circular fashion to facilitate discussion and interaction among students.

New building for fall 2016. Haas broke ground in late 2014 on a new North Academic Building, which will contain classrooms, study rooms, a cafe, and a 300-seat event space that overlooks the San Francisco Bay. With the building expected to open in time for classes to start in fall 2016, the cohort size is expected to expand to 70 students. Even with this 15% growth, Haas's full-time class will remain the smallest of top U.S. MBA programs. We would be surprised if the class size didn't continue to grow in future years, perhaps increasing chances for acceptance.

Several programs under one roof. The campus is shared by the undergraduate program, as well as the Evening/Weekend and Executive programs. However, the schedules are structured such that it very seldom feels crowded. Haas's location at the east end of campus, right next to the football stadium, makes the school easily accessible. The faculty center is also located very close to the Haas School, and students often spend time eating, meeting, or attending company presentations there. The convenience and availability of resources on campus create the best of both worlds for Haas students, as there is rarely a reason that students must go beyond campus, yet the proximity of Berkeley, San Francisco, and the greater Bay Area affords them a tremendous amount of culture and an endless supply of things to do.

While Haas students utilize a number of resources from their parent institution, the business school doesn't exhibit the same activist culture as other schools on campus.

A storied Berkeley history. Founded in 1868 (just 18 years after California became a state), UC Berkeley is the crown jewel in the state of California's highly regarded University of California system. Berkeley has a long history of activism dating from the early 20th century, peaking during the Free Speech Movement of the 1960s, and continuing to the present with the "Occupy Cal" demonstrations. While Haas students utilize a number of resources from its parent institution, the business school doesn't exhibit the same activist culture as other schools on campus.

You Oughta Know

Where to live. Berkeley-Haas students live both on campus and off campus, in Berkeley and nearby Oakland, with a few commuting from San Francisco. Most MBA students end up living in North Berkeley, as South Berkeley tends to draw more undergrads. In the Bay Area, any housing option will make a serious dent in your monthly finances. And the on-campus housing options aren't exclusive to Haas, so you might find yourself living next door to a law or computer science student. To keep expenses lower, many students elect to live with roommates.

Getting to campus. The Berkeley campus is accessible via public transportation, but getting to Haas requires a walk up a fairly steep hill. (There's another way to save money: Cancel your gym membership!) Although some students do have cars, it's not necessary and campus parking is at a premium. Bikes, scooters, and shared car services are other popular ways to get around.

Popular hangouts. Haas MBAs tend to congregate at Kip's Bar, located just a block from the UC Berkeley Campus, for drinks and after-hours entertainment. Another popular spot was the Bear's Lair, an on-campus bar at the Berkeley Student Union complex. However, the Bear's Lair has been closed down to make way for a $223 million overhaul of Lower Sproul Plaza. Dean Rich Lyons was known to play his guitar there! It remains to be seen where the dean will crown his new crooning hot spot.

Student organizations. As an important complement to coursework, students get involved in clubs and community service. Haas hosts more than 50 clubs on campus, sponsored by the MBA Association (MBAA), which serves as a liaison between the student body of the business school and the school's administration. Involvement is a big element of the Haas culture and is something that the admissions committee looks for in a candidate. Haas students can expect to dive right in and contribute, as the smorgasbord of available activities at times seems to dwarf the corresponding student population.

> **Involvement is a big element of the Haas culture and is something that the admissions committee looks for in a candidate.**

Similar Programs Culturally

Yale. Yale and Haas have two of the smallest class sizes of any of the top programs, and as a result both programs foster very tight-knit communities and collaborative cultures. Yale is also well known for its strength in nonprofit leadership, as is Berkeley-Haas.

Dartmouth (Tuck). Tuck is now the only other U.S. top-tier MBA program with a class size of less than 300 students. It also offers an intimate, collaborative learning environment with a loyal alumni network. However, the climate in Hanover, New Hampshire, is decidedly colder than the Bay Area, and the Dartmouth campus is quite remote.

UCLA (Anderson). Although the class at Anderson is a bit larger than you'll find at Haas, UCLA shares its Northern California counterpart's welcoming, collaborative culture. However, given its location, there are many more beach-related activities at Anderson!

Northwestern (Kellogg). Kellogg and Haas are often mentioned together because their students tend to be friendly, welcoming, and humble. Kellogg's class is more than double the size of Haas's, so students have to be willing to jump in with both feet or risk being lost in the shuffle.

ADMISSIONS AT BERKELEY-HAAS

What Berkeley-Haas Is Looking For

Cultural fit. Haas stresses its "leading through innovation" mantra in students and looks for key characteristics in applicants to show cultural fit. With such a small class, Haas often has one of the lowest acceptance rates of any business school worldwide so it can select candidates who strongly fit with its tight-knit program. Showcasing this fit requires extra care and thought in an application (see the extensive slate of essay questions below), but also creates a unique opportunity to express meaningful ways in which Berkeley-Haas matches your own philosophy and style. For instance, part of the "innovation" element is that Haas prides itself—much in the way that NYU Stern does—on being a place where careers can be furthered, but also launched or reset. Not all top business schools in the recent economic climate have been as openly encouraging to career changers, yet Berkeley-Haas stresses this openness.

Commitment to deep involvement. Extracurricular involvement and leadership are two other key elements of the Haas admission criteria. Similar to Wharton, Haas fosters a high level of involvement in its students and expects applicants to have been previously involved in their communities. This applies to on-campus leadership in college as well as a desire to "make the world a better place."

Traditional criteria. Beyond these elements, Berkeley-Haas looks for a lot of the usual angles in the admissions process, including academic ability (particularly analytical and quantitative skills), strong letters of recommendation, and an interview indicative of fit. On top of the "on-paper" evaluation, some weight is given to applicants who demonstrate determination and resilience. Not only that, but persuading the admissions committee that Berkeley-Haas is indeed a top pick for the applicant can be a deciding factor and should be conveyed convincingly.

 If you are looking for tips on 2016–17 admissions essays, you're in luck! Check out our website at **veritasprep.com/haas** for our latest advice.

You Oughta Know

When should I apply? Haas's Round 1 and Round 2 deadlines are exactly the same as they were last year. The one bit of news here is that while the school used to wait until mid-January to notify Round 1 applicants, now applying in Round 1 means that you will get your decision by December 17, giving you at least a couple of weeks before most schools' Round 2 deadlines, should you need to scramble and apply to some backup schools. Looking at Round 3, Haas pushed back this deadline by nearly three weeks versus last year, matching similar moves at some other top schools to hopefully catch a few more great candidates who may have missed the earlier rounds. Our standard advice still applies: Earlier is usually better than later, but you shouldn't rush a mediocre application just to make Round 1. As Berkeley-Haas says in its FAQs, "Applicants are encouraged to apply as early as possible, provided that you do not sacrifice the quality of your application to do so."

GMAT or GRE. Berkeley-Haas now accepts either a GMAT or a GRE score for its full-time program.

Haas now accepts either a GMAT or GRE score for its full-time program.

TOEFL. A frequent source of consternation among international candidates interested in Haas is that the school has stricter requirements for the TOEFL than any other top business school. Haas requires applicants to take the TOEFL if the country where they earned their undergraduate degree is non–English speaking. Other business schools only require the TOEFL when the course of instruction at their university was not done in English. The Berkeley-Haas policy means that candidates whose last degree was conferred at a university in India must take the TOEFL. However, if you are an international candidate school and completed at least one year of education from a school in the U.S., Canada, Australia, or the UK with grades of B or better, then the TOEFL is waived.

Undergraduate education. Another potential glitch for some applicants is that Berkeley-Haas does not accept the three-year degree from many international universities (particularly Indian) as meeting its educational prerequisite. Many other business schools are willing to evaluate an application from a candidate with only a three-year undergraduate education. At Haas, it must be a four-year bachelor's, or a bachelor's plus a master's degree. The good news here is that if you are an Indian candidate with a master's degree earned in the U.S. or another English–speaking country, then you not only meet the educational requirements, you also do not need to take the TOEFL.

ADMISSIONS DEADLINES:

Round 1
1 Oct 2015
Notification: 17 Dec 2015
Deposit Due: 8 Mar 2016

Round 2
7 Jan 2016
Notification: 24 Mar 2016
Deposit Due: 3 May 2016

Round 3
31 Mar 2016
Notification: 12 May 2016
Deposit Due: 26 May 2016

Preparing to Apply

Reading this Essential Guide is a great first step in your preparation. Hopefully, this insider's glimpse has been helpful in understanding the most important aspects of the school. However, nothing can replace gaining firsthand knowledge and experience yourself.

Reach out to current students. Even if you don't have any personal connections to Berkeley-Haas, you can reach out to current students and get their insight and advice. On the school's Campus Groups page, you'll find a list of all campus clubs. Find a few clubs that fit your personal and professional interests, and reach out to the officers. Remember: These are very busy MBA students so you don't want to intrude too much on their time, but you could ask for a 10- to 15-minute conversation or elicit some advice via e-mail. Come prepared with specific questions (preferably those that aren't already answered online). If you're planning to visit campus, perhaps you might even arrange a coffee chat or lunch, if they are available.

Visit campus. The school's website can only tell you so much; by far, a personal visit is the best possible research in the application process. If you have the means, we highly recommend you visit Berkeley-Haas in person along with the campuses of your other top choices to understand the significant differences in culture, teaching style, student body, recruiting opportunities, facilities, and so forth. You may be surprised at just how different each school can be and and how the reality can differ from the perception. We encourage you to take advantage of opportunities to visit campus; because informal and impromptu encounters can be the most informative, don't be afraid to approach students in less-formal settings.

Other events. We know that many applicants will not be able to travel to Berkeley to visit campus, but you should take advantage of other worldwide admissions events, such as information sessions, virtual sessions, and specific-audience events. In fact, these off-campus events can offer great opportunities for quality time with admissions officers and even other applicants, who can be a great resource and support through the admissions process. Get to know the school and its culture as well as you can, because your familiarity can shine through your application and essays to help you stand out.

The Essays

After chopping away at its essay count in the recent past, Berkeley-Haas has held steady this year, keeping the required essay count at three. But, interestingly, the school has made some changes that make this year's application look more like the application that Berkeley-Haas used two years ago.

Essay One: If you could choose one song that expresses who you are, what is it and why? (250 words)

Reveal the real you. This question is new this year, although Haas actually used it before dropping it last year. Now it's back, and it's clear that the Haas admissions team wants to get past the normal jargon and stuffy language, and get a real sense of your personality here. That means you shouldn't be afraid to have a little fun or reveal the real you here. If an admissions officer reads this essay and then still has no sense of what it would be like to meet you in person, then you haven't made good use of this essay. That doesn't mean your choice of a song needs to be wacky or so deep that it will make the reader cry, but avoid the temptation to choose a song that merely echoes one of the more straightforward themes you will cover below. And, we're willing to take bets on the number of applicants who say their favorite song is John Lennon's "Imagine." Save the high-minded "I want to save the world" stuff for another essay! This one is more for just helping admissions officers feel like they know you at least a little bit.

Essay Two: Please respond to one of the following prompts: (250 words)
- ***Describe an experience that has fundamentally changed the way you see the world and how it transformed you.***
- ***Describe a significant accomplishment and why it makes you proud.***
- ***Describe a difficult decision you have made and why it was challenging.***

Identify an experience. All three of these essay prompts try to get at the same thing: identifying an experience in your life that led to growth and transformation. The first one is essentially carried over from last year's application, and the second one is quite similar to a prompt from last year, although it's a little broader this time around (it can be any accomplishment, not just a professional one). The third question is new this year. And, most notably, you're picking just one, while the first two questions were actually two separate required prompts on last year's application. We like that Haas gives applicants three different ways to go about this one; your best story may come from an accomplishment, or from overcoming a setback, or from making a tough choice in life. Why not let you choose which story to tell here?

Use SAR method. No matter which essay prompt you choose, think about the SAR (Situation–Action–Result) essay framework here: Describe what happened, what you did, and then what happened as a result. Sounds obvious, right? You would be surprised how often applicants get lost in the details and end up using most of their words merely to describe to the situation. Then, the result gets tacked on in two sentences at the very end! That's too bad because the result—not just what happened in that situation, but also how you changed as a result—is what Haas really wants to know here! Even seemingly smaller accomplishments or life events, such as the first time you spoke in front of a large group, can make for a really impactful essay here.

Significance to *you*. Many people have difficulty deciding which of their accomplishments is most significant. Even the selection of the accomplishment tells the admissions committee something about yourself; it shows them what's significant to you. If there's a story that you would like to share with the admissions officer that is significant to you but may not seem as quantifiably impressive, you may choose to include a line in your essays that reads something like "I have included a number of achievements in my resume of which I am particularly proud, but the accomplishment that has meant the most to me is...." This way, you can explain how the accomplishment made an impact on your organization in a less-quantifiable way and provided you opportunities to learn and grow. However, don't feel like you must include an example that's touchy-feely, either. If you have a deal, sales goal, financial target, or other more traditional professional accomplishment that you would like to showcase, go for it! Just be sure to include elements of what you learned from the experience and how you grew—professionally or personally.

Question the Status Quo. We haven't spent much space in this Guide elaborating on Berkeley-Haas's first pillar: *Question the Status Quo*. This essay is a great opportunity to show how you fit with the Haas approach: "We lead by championing bold ideas, taking intelligent risks and accepting sensible failures. This means speaking our minds even when it challenges convention. We thrive at the world's epicenter of innovation." Your goal with this essay will be to show how you stand out from your peers. Questioning the status quo and challenging convention are great ways to show how you shine.

> **Questioning the status quo and challenging convention are great ways to show how you shine.**

Essay Three: Tell us about your path to business school and your future plans. How will the Berkeley-Haas experience help you along this journey? (500 words)

Answer the question directly. This is the more conventional "Why an MBA? Why this school?" question that MBA programs often ask. Ask yourself these questions: Where do you see yourself in a few years (and beyond that), and why do you need an MBA to get there? Specifically, why do you need a Haas MBA to get there? Why not another top-10 MBA program? Really force yourself to answer that question, even if not all of your answer makes its way into your final essay response!

Do your homework. The Haas admissions team gave you a big hint here: On the Haas website, check out the paragraph that introduces the essays. It describes the four key principles that define the Haas culture: Question the Status Quo, Confidence without Attitude, Students Always, and Beyond Yourself. Your goal here is not to see how many of these you can cram into your essay (this is not merely an exercise to see if you bothered to read the website), but if none of that appeals to you, and you can't even articulate why Haas is the right way for you to invest in yourself, then you need to take a step back before drafting this essay. You obviously are an unfinished product, which is why you're considering business school. Help the admissions committee believe that Haas is the right place for you to grow for the next two years, invoking those four key principles where you can.

Optional Essay: Is there any other information you would like to share that is not presented elsewhere in the application? You may also use this essay to provide further explanation of employment gaps or your quantitative abilities. (500 words maximum)

It really is optional. As we always advise our clients when it comes to optional essays, only use this essay if you need to explain a low undergraduate GPA or other potential blemish in your background. No need to harp on a minor weakness and sound like you are simply making excuses when you don't need any. If you don't have anything else you need to tell the admissions office, it is entirely okay to skip this!

Supplemental questions. Haas also has a series of supplemental questions. These are not essays per se, but instead are answers filled out in the online application. Be concise in these. The school is not looking for pages and pages of detail here. Short lists in many cases are absolutely fine. The focus on strong academics and quant skills should not be overlooked. Haas has one of the highest average undergraduate GPAs of any school., and with the incredible strength of the economics faculty (all those Nobel winners), it's not a place for lightweights. Haas doesn't expect applicants to be perfect across the board, but it does look for evidence of intellectual capacity and academic achievement. These supplemental questions are an opportunity to present the admissions committee with evidence of those abilities that come from perhaps less-traditional aspects of your life, so feel free to explore any areas that are noteworthy in this section in order to provide a big-picture view of your profile.

Recommendations

Two professional recommendations are required with your application to Berkeley-Haas. As with most schools, Berkeley-Haas strongly prefers professional recommendations over academic recommendations. If you cannot obtain a recommendation from your current supervisor (you have a new job, you have a new boss, etc.), you must provide an explanation in the optional essay. Berkeley-Haas does not permit additional recommendations.

Written assessment. Your recommender will receive the following questions with these instructions: *Please write an assessment of the applicant that addresses the prompts below. We are looking for your candid and accurate assessment of the applicant's potential to be a successful leader and what specific traits the applicant possesses that evidence this potential. Please be as specific as possible and use concrete examples where applicable. Do not incorporate anything drafted by the candidate in your recommendation or have the candidate submit the recommendation on your behalf.*

- *How does the candidate's performance compare to those of other well-qualified individuals in similar roles? Please provide specific examples.*
- *Describe the most important piece of constructive feedback you have given the applicant. Please detail the circumstances and the applicant's response.*
- *In the Berkeley MBA program, we develop leaders who embody our distinctive culture's four key principles [www.haas.berkeley.edu/strategicplan/culture] one of which is "confidence without attitude" or "confidence with humility". Please comment on how the applicant reflects this Berkeley-Haas value.*
- *(Optional) Is there anything else we should know?*

Scaled assessment. Your recommender will be asked to rate you on the following traits in relation to your peers: self-confidence, communication skills, self-awareness, maturity, open to different viewpoints, empathy, ability to influence without authority, ability to accept constructive feedback, intellectual curiosity, analytical ability, quantitative ability, ability to question the status quo, initiative, adaptability, resilience, personal integrity/ethics, relationship-building skills. Each trait is rated on the following scale: *Truly Exceptional (top 1%), Superior (Top 5%), Very Good (top 10%), Good (top 25%), Average (top 50%), Below Average (below 50%), No Opportunity to Observe.* As noted in the form, it should be "extremely rare" for any candidate to receive "truly exceptional" for every attribute. Recommenders should genuinely rate your strengths and weaknesses to make the most impact on your admission.

Overall recommendation. Finally, your recommender will be asked to make an overall recommendation regarding your admission to Haas:

- *To what degree do you recommend this applicant to be admitted to the Berkeley Full-time MBA Program?: [Enthusiastically recommend, Recommend, Recommend with reservations, Do not recommend.]*

Selecting your recommenders. The best recommenders are people who can provide very detailed examples of your actions and behavior. In general, the admissions committee will be far more impressed by a genuine and passionate letter from a middle manager who is your supervisor than a polite letter from a well-known CEO that lacks depth and detailed anecdotes about you. Look for people who can speak very clearly about your performance in relation to peers. In other words, don't ask your company's CEO, whom you might or might not have met once in the cafeteria. Berkeley-Haas is clear that recommendations from "co-workers, someone you have supervised, relatives, or personal and family friends" are inappropriate.

Should I draft it myself? Many applicants to business school are asked by their superiors to draft the recommendation themselves and the recommender will approve it. We strongly recommend that you do not write the recommendation yourself for several reasons outlined earlier in this Guide. Check out the Veritas Prep blog for a three-part series on how to elicit letters of recommendation with a "Pound the Table!"–level of enthusiasm from your superiors.

Preparing your recommenders. Instead of writing the recommendation yourself, you should sit down and have a candid conversation with your recommenders about the reasons you want to go to business school and why you've selected your target schools, your professional goals, and your experience together. Ask them if they would have the time to write a strong recommendation on your behalf. (This also gives them a nice "out" by telling you that they are too busy rather than saying they don't feel comfortable giving you a positive recommendation.) Bring a copy of your resume and a bulleted list of projects that you've worked on together and accomplishments they have seen you achieve. Let them know that admissions committees prefer to see specific, detailed examples in recommendations. Then, let them know that you'll serve as a "project manager" to follow up and ensure that they are able to submit your recommendation ahead of the deadline.

The Interview

Who will interview me? Berkeley-Haas conducts interviews both on campus (mostly by second-year students) and off campus (usually by an alumni). In both instances, the interview is "blind" in the sense that the interviewer does not have access to the candidate's application materials except for the resume. The school claims no advantage to interviewing on campus. The interview is almost always required as part of the application process, and interviews are by invitation only.

What should I expect? Relative to other schools, a lower percentage of candidates is interviewed, so it is generally a great sign if a student receives an invitation to interview. Each interviewer has his or her own style, but you should be prepared to answer the standard questions (e.g., Why an MBA?; Why now?; Why here?). Be prepared to walk the interviewer through your resume, and be able to provide a little more detail on each of your roles, if prompted. In particular, discuss the elements of your professional life that have been fulfilling and a thing or two you've learned from experiences along the way. You should prepare for a number of behavioral questions, which typically start with "Tell me a time when you...." In addition, you should anticipate at least one question inquiring about how you have demonstrated Haas's core values in your personal and/or professional life, so be prepared to have an answer for each core value.

Use specific, personal stories to make your points. Anyone can tell an admissions officer that they think "leaders need to communicate a clear vision to their team and then empower them to succeed," but the most impressive interviewers will then follow up broad statements like this with personal stories that exemplify you actually doing it. Don't wait for the interviewer to prompt you to provide examples; be proactive. Use the Situation–Action–Result model to structure your stories so the interviewer can understand a little bit about the background, the specific actions you took (and why), how things turned out, and what you learned.

How should I prepare? We recommend that you get introspective and prepare several stories from your personal and professional life that could serve as an answer to any number of different questions, particularly the core values. For example, you might have an experience which you led a team to success beyond the stated expectations of management. This could showcase your leadership skills, teamwork abilities, questioning the status quo, and innovative problem-solving skills. Other examples could include: a time when you needed to think creatively to solve a problem, worked in a challenging team environment, made an impact on an organization (both professionally and in extracurricular activities), and so forth. As much as possible, use stories that are not included in your essays so that the interviewees adds greater value to your overall application.

What happens next? To be honest, the interview is primarily a vehicle to evaluate whether you think well on your feet, can present yourself well to recruiters, and would be a good cultural fit with the school. It's just a small slice of your overall application. We've seen candidates get admitted who felt they performed terribly and others be denied despite a great connection with their interviewer. Ultimately, the admissions committee will evaluate all parts of your application and make a holistic decision.

VERITAS PREP
AND YOUR BUSINESS
SCHOOL APPLICATIONS

The top business schools receive thousands of applications every year, so making an impression with each admissions committee is a real process. To guide you through this challenge, Veritas Prep has developed the most qualified and diverse team of admissions consultants ever assembled. Don't just take our word for it; check out our team yourself on our website! If you are interested in maximizing your chances for admission, our team will help you every step of the way.

Your Personalized Consulting Team

MBA admissions decisions are quite subjective, and no two members of the admissions committee will view a candidate in exactly the same way. As a result, Veritas Prep uses a unique team-based approach in our consulting to offer multiple expert perspectives.

In your Comprehensive School Package, you'll work with a **Head Consultant™** who has admissions experience at a top-tier MBA program to guide you through the process from start to finish. Head Consultants have evaluated MBA candidates themselves, so they can provide an invaluable insider's perspective to answer every question and help you avoid common application pitfalls.

You'll also work with a **School Specialist** for each top-tier school in your comprehensive package. School Specialists were personally immersed in your target schools' cultures for two years and will ensure your applications are perfectly tailored based on the strengths, programs, and culture of each school.

The Ultimate Admissions Committee™

In addition to your personalized consulting team, if you have all of your application materials ready at least two weeks before the school's application deadline, you may submit them to the Veritas Prep Ultimate Admissions Committee™. This committee is composed of former directors and associate directors of MBA admissions—those who have made thousands of admissions decisions on candidates just like you. The committee will review your application and provide final feedback before you submit.

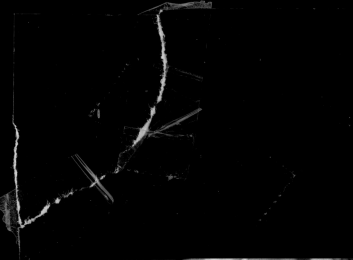

How it Works

First, we'll talk with you about your profile and understand exactly what you're looking for in a Head Consultant. Based on your personal and professional background, goals, target schools, working style, and personal preferences, we'll match you with the best Head Consultant for your needs. If you have a particular consultant in mind, you may request to work directly with him or her. Your Head Consultant will assist in every step as you examine your strengths and weaknesses, map out your ideal application strategy, select the best MBA programs for your unique background and goals, craft your resume, brainstorm and outline essays, exchange several essay drafts, and complete your online application form.

Your School Specialist will discuss the classes, majors, clubs, conferences, activities, and other resources available at your target school that are most relevant to your goals and interests. In addition, if you're invited to interview, your Specialist will conduct a mock interview, often with the same questions you'll face in your actual interview, and provide feedback for improvement. If you get waitlisted, we'll provide tips and advice to move into the "admit" column. Your success is our success!

About Veritas Prep

Founded in 2002, Veritas Prep has emerged as the global leader in GMAT(R) and GRE(R) education, and MBA admissions consulting. The company's business school team includes more than 300 graduates of the world's elite MBA programs, managed from its headquarters in Malibu, California.

The Veritas Prep consulting model is built on adding value to a candidate's application process by providing both mentorship and expertise. The business school admissions process has become increasingly competitive and applicants must do everything possible to showcase their value. Our consultants assist applicants in presenting their unique stories in the most professional and meaningful way possible. In a sense, our consultants are translators—helping an applicant discover raw materials and information and then helping that candidate articulate a unique story in a language that admissions committees understand. More than anything, Veritas Prep gives candidates a sense of ownership and control over the process. Quality of work, attention to detail, care for the client, and integrity are the lynchpins of a successful consultation.

In addition to elite MBA admissions consulting services, Veritas Prep also offers the finest SAT, ACT, GMAT, and GRE preparation available in the industry, as well as admissions consulting for undergraduate programs, law school, medical school, and other graduate programs.

For comprehensive information on Veritas Prep's many services, please visit our website.